# CIVIC LONGING

★

# CIVIC LONGING

*The Speculative Origins of U.S. Citizenship*

CARRIE HYDE

★

HARVARD UNIVERSITY PRESS

*Cambridge, Massachusetts & London, England / 2018*

*Frontispiece:* Washington Peale, *The three days of May 1844. Columbia mourns her citizens slain* (Philadelphia: Colon & Adriance, 1844). Library of Congress Prints and Photographs Division, Washington, DC. LC-USZ62-46533.

*Library of Congress Cataloging-in-Publication Data*
Names: Hyde, Carrie, 1982– author.
Title: Civic longing : the speculative origins of U.S. citizenship / Carrie Hyde.
Description: Cambridge, Massachusetts : Harvard University Press, 2018. |
Includes bibliographical references and index.
Identifiers: LCCN 2017017585 | ISBN 9780674976153 (alk. paper)
Subjects: LCSH: Citizenship—United States—History—18th century. |
Citizenship—United States—History—19th century. | Citizenship—United
States—Philosophy—History.
Classification: LCC JK1759 .H94 2018 | DDC 323.60973—dc23
LC record available at https://lccn.loc.gov/2017017585

It is a singular fact that, unlike all other nations, this nation has yet a question as to what makes or constitutes a citizen. The great basis of our civil architecture is yet unsettled.

—Wendell Phillips, antislavery speech at Cooper Institute (1865)

# Contents

I. READING "CITIZENSHIP"

Introduction
*Citizenship before the Fourteenth Amendment*                                        3

1. The Retroactive Invention of Citizenship
*A Textual History*                                                                 18

II. THE HIGHER LAWS OF CITIZENSHIP

2. "Citizenship in Heaven"
*Biblical Exegesis and the Afterlife of Politics*                                   43

3. Citizens of Nature
*Oceanic Revolutions and the Geopolitics of Personhood*                             85

III. THE LETTERED CITIZEN

4. The Elsewhere of Citizenship
*Literary Autonomy and the Fabrication of Allegiance*                              117

5. Stateless Fictions
*Negative Instruction and the Nationalization of Citizenship*                      153

Coda
*Wong Kim Ark and "The Man Without a Country"*                                     181

*Appendix: Bible Translations*                                                     187
*Notes*                                                                            191
*Bibliography*                                                                     269
*Acknowledgments*                                                                  295
*Index*                                                                            299

CIVIC LONGING

# ★ I ★

## READING "CITIZENSHIP"

# Introduction

## *Citizenship before the Fourteenth Amendment*

> It were to be wished, that we had some law adduced more pre-
> cisely defining the qualities of a citizen or an alien.
>
> —James Madison, *Speeches in the First Congress* (1789)

> Who is a citizen? What constitutes a citizen of the United States?
> [ . . . ] For aught I see to the contrary, the subject is now as little
> understood in its details and elements, and the question as open to
> argument and to speculative criticism, as it was in the beginning
> of the government. Eighty years of practical enjoyment of citizen-
> ship, under the Constitution, have not sufficed to teach us either
> the exact meaning of the word, or the constituent elements of the
> thing we prize so highly.
>
> —U.S. Attorney General Edward Bates, *Opinion on Citizenship* (1862)

THE TERM "CITIZEN" enjoys a privileged status in modern political thought. It is an exalted and almost sacralized word that conjures some of the most powerful and persistent fantasies of U.S. politics: the promise of inalienable rights, the sovereignty of self-governance, and the dream of democratic equality. In the U.S. political tradition, citizenship's inaugural lore is rooted in culturally charged origin stories that alternately celebrate and mourn citizenship as the newly empowered form of political member-ship borne of the American Revolution—and defined by the rights it selec-tively conferred on a privileged few. Over the last few decades, scholars have done much to recover the plural meanings of "America" and the "United States," and to decouple both terms from teleological narratives of nation formation that project the U.S. nation-state backward in time and across heterogeneous spaces and communities.[1] However, "the citizen," the child and protagonist of these nationalist plots, is still routinely treated as if it were a relatively coherent concept and category from the moment the United States collectively declared independence from Britain. This book tells a different story. It recovers the formative role that fiction and a number of other imaginative traditions played in shaping emergent conceptions of citizenship within and across the several states in the tumultuous era before the Civil War—when the legal category of U.S. citizenship, as we now know it, did not yet exist.

The several revolutions that swept across the Americas and Europe in the late eighteenth and early nineteenth centuries helped create a powerful colloquial association between the rights-bearing subject and "the citizen," but the formal legal category of political membership that citizenship now names in the United States is a much more recent invention—established almost a full century after the American Revolution, with the ratification of the Fourteenth Amendment on July 9, 1868. Citizenship defines the U.S. political experiment, but for eighty years after the ratification of the Constitution, the term "citizen" remained undefined in U.S. law. The designation "citizen(s)" appears eleven times in the Constitution, as originally ratified, but these initial uses were unaccompanied by an expository formulation of citizenship's juridical heft.[2] There was no statutory definition of citizenship until the Civil Rights Act of 1866, which laid the groundwork for the Fourteenth Amendment.[3]

The Fourteenth Amendment provided the first substantive legal definition of U.S. citizenship, and it remains today—roughly 150 years after its ratification—the preeminent juridical formulation of U.S. citizenship. According to its Citizenship Clause, the first sentence of Section I, "All persons born or naturalized in the United States, and subject to the jurisdiction thereof, are citizens of the United States and of the State wherein they reside."[4] Economically expressed in these twenty-eight words is the now familiar concept of birthright citizenship—the notion that citizenship is a direct and automatic effect of being born within the territorial limits of the United States.

The practical meaning of the Citizenship Clause and the scope of birthright citizenship remain hotly contested today, as immigration fuels a new era of debates about citizenship in the twenty-first century. There is still little agreement about who belongs in the United States and is entitled to full rights within it. However, political commentators now know what document to read, invoke, and interpret in order to make compelling claims about who should be counted as a citizen. Whatever our partisan affiliations might be, the Citizenship Clause offers us a textual common ground for today's debates about citizenship. As a result, we now readily recognize what "citizenship" names, as an official legal status that describes a person's inclusion in a community that is defined in national terms. This definition is so rudimentary that it hardly feels like much of a definition at all.[5] Yet it encapsulates a number of basic assumptions about citizenship that had remarkably little traction in the period before the Fourteenth Amendment, when the cultural and juridical meaning of "citizenship"—as well as its scope—was under-articulated and open to debate.

In the early United States, the doctrine of *jus soli* (right of the soil), which underwrites the modern concept of birthright citizenship, did not guarantee political membership. Nativity was an exceptionally unreliable predictor of the borders of citizenship, which were subject to the genealogical bonds of *jus sanguinis* (right of the blood), as well as the changeable internal landscape of loyalty. For this reason, this book takes political allegiance—rather than geopolitical borders—as the principal unit of politics. It draws on the insights of transnational criticism to address a political climate in which distinctions between the foreign and the domestic, traitors and patriots, aliens and citizens were constantly being redrawn. The transnational turn has helped theorize the routes of culture, commerce, and power outside the static and univocal conceit of nationalism. However, in privileging the disruptive effects of transnational crossings, this paradigm sometimes reinforces the assumption that nations, taken in themselves, are coherent ideological formations. This is manifestly not the case in the early United States. Before the Civil War, the United States was a federation of states but not yet a unified nation. In keeping with this, this book uses the "United States" as the term was itself used in the period between the Revolution and the Civil War: as a collective but plural designation for a loosely knit federation of states, which were essentially heterogeneous and yet complexly interrelated—both institutionally and imaginatively.[6]

In the early United States, the language of citizenship was pervasive—and the idea of consent colloquially associated with it was idealized—but neither the Constitution nor the slew of laws that followed it clearly designate *which* protections and obligations define citizenship, *whether* the primary unit of political membership is state or federal, or *if*/how it departs from the model of natural and perpetual allegiance associated with British subjecthood. Citizenship's terminological prolixity and legal under-conceptualization in the early republic was, understandably, a source of confusion. As James Madison lamented in a congressional speech in May 1789, "It were to be wished, that we had some law adduced more precisely defining the qualities of a citizen or an alien." The difficulty of answering questions related to citizenship, as Madison explained, was that "particular laws" on citizenship "have obtained in some of the states," but many states lacked relevant legislation on the subject and there was no centralized federal definition of citizenship to which politicians could refer for guidance.[7] As such, Congress and the courts regularly were called on to offer case-specific rulings on citizenship in the absence of relevant legislation. Madison's interpretative solution to this legislative challenge was relatively simple. "[W]here the laws do not expressly guide us," Madison concluded, "we must be guided by principles of a general nature so far as they are applicable to the present case."[8] With no official definition of citizenship upon which to rely, Madison and other early political commentators redirected their interpretative energies away from the letter of the law and became authorial participants in the cultural fabrication of "citizenship."

Madison was not the only politician to remark on the early definitional perplexities of citizenship, but his frustration is especially striking, if not surprising. As the proverbial "father of the Constitution," Madison had been uniquely well positioned to offer the very definition of citizenship for which he soon pined, less than one year after the ratification of the Constitution. How did Madison find himself in this situation? Was he simply late in recognizing the expedient value of defining citizenship? If not, why were the framers reluctant to define "citizenship" in the Constitution? I revisit these questions in Chapter 1, but this book does not attempt to recover the "original intent" of Madison or of any of the other officials who contributed to the fractured legal conceptualization of citizenship. The interpretative theory of Originalism presumes that the ideas and terms that we turn to the Constitution to understand were fully conceived by the founders and that the words they committed to law were readily understood by contemporaries. Originalism seeks a pure knowledge of the founding era that is unachievable under even the best circumstances, and this interpretative paradigm presents special challenges when it comes to "citizenship," whose early usages only partially resemble the modern legal category it now names. Moreover, as Madison's frustration makes clear, the challenge of understanding the early usages of "citizenship" is not merely a problem of historical distance and translation. Twenty-first-century readers have inherited a long-standing problem. At its origins, citizenship was juridically unregulated, politically inconsistent, and indelibly shaped by the assumptions, fears, and aspirations of the individuals who presumed to merely describe it.[9]

Instead of searching for a categorical understanding of citizenship, which the founders themselves lacked, this book takes up a set of questions implicit in Madison's concluding solution to the definitional poverty of citizenship within the law: Where did Madison expect legislators and denizens to look to discover the "general" principles of citizenship? And if such principles were presumed to be the stuff of "common sense," which traditions helped establish their broad cultural currency? In an era in which the law provided a partial and often contradictory framework for ongoing debates about citizenship, to what other traditions did Americans turn to develop and contest nascent models of political membership? To answer these questions, this book examines the speculative making of citizenship in the early United States: its definitional fluidity, its fungible entitlements, and its extralegal origins.[10] By approaching the political and cultural history of citizenship textually, through the language and arguments of individual texts, *Civic Longing* seeks to return "citizenship" to the acts of reading and writing whose generalizing tendencies strategically, and sometimes unwittingly, have eclipsed the uneasy, speculative birth of a term-turned-concept whose meaning has never been a self-evident truth.[11]

Citizenship is now a codified juridical concept, but it continues to be an elastic site of political fantasy and debate. The language of "citizenship" pervades politics and popular culture today, and it is also one of the most written about and widely used keywords in U.S. historiography, literary criticism, cultural studies, and political philosophy.[12] Scholars regularly use the term and concept of citizenship to explain the political importance of individual texts, and of humanistic study more broadly. In the humanities, citizenship has played a key role in twentieth- and twenty-first-century defenses of liberal education, which identify cultural analysis and literary study, in particular, as didactic tools that provide the training ground for preparing students to be active, discerning, citizens.[13] Citizenship, in short, has offered a powerful paradigm for communicating the present and future stakes of our ongoing study of the cultural history of the United States. Yet perhaps for this very reason, we rarely emphasize the unique definitional questions and paradigms that distinguish the early uses of "citizenship."[14]

Over the last thirty years, a wealth of new scholarship on race, gender, class, indigeneity, and disability has done much to demythologize traditional, emancipatory narratives of American Independence, which selectively celebrate the liberty the Revolution brought to a small subset of the population.[15] However, by approaching citizenship negatively as the absent possibility of political belonging and fulfillment, scholars sometimes reinforce an idealized conception of citizenship itself—making the category of citizenship seem more coherent and empowering than it actually was in the early United States. This book offers a new prehistory of U.S. citizenship.[16] By excavating the many unanswered questions that animated early legal debates about citizenship, *Civic Longing* offers a historically grounded account of the formative political power of the imaginative traditions that played an instrumental role in shaping the early history of citizenship—and that have long allowed Americans to retell the many failures of citizenship as the tragic story of its as-yet-unrealized promise.

Laws traditionally enjoy a privileged status in rhetoric-centered accounts of political history, because they express the normative desires and fears of state actors, and because the mandates they issue are backed by the institutional authority of the state.[17] However, the law is only one aspect of the cultural imagination of citizenship, and in the period before the Fourteenth Amendment, the law was not yet the default tradition for asking and answering questions about citizenship. In the absence of a centralized legal definition of citizenship, as we will see, politicians and writers regularly turned to several highly speculative traditions—political philosophy, Christian theology, natural law, literature, and didactic writing—to author and defend visions of what citizenship was and/or ought to be. The growing investment in the language of citizenship—at a moment in which its juridical meaning was not yet codified—added definitional urgency to representations of political membership developed outside the official discourse of the law.[18] It also allowed writers and politicians to authorize heterogeneous models of citizenship that shared little with the racialized and gendered ideology of the still emergent juridical "citizen." In the early United States, the legislative and judiciary interpretation of citizenship predated its statutory elaboration, so politicians and judges—as much as authors and reformers—had to look beyond the imperatives of the law to develop and authorize emergent definitions of citizenship. The speculative making of citizenship, however, was not always politically progressive or empowering. As I emphasize in Chapter 1's reexamination of the Supreme Court's infamous ruling against black citizenship in *Dred Scott vs. Sandford* (1857), the under-articulation of the "citizen" in early U.S. law may have been enabling for political reformers, but it also left citizenship vulnerable to the exclusionary constructions of ideologues in the courts.

This book seeks to move beyond the binary paradigm of inclusion/exclusion, which preserves the incorporative telos of the American Dream by equating citizenship with political self-realization. Building on scholarship on citizenship's exclusionary history and its complex entanglement with the violence of settler colonialism, *Civic Longing* tracks the disappointments of early U.S. citizenship back into the innermost ranks of political privilege.[19] It extends the work of recent scholarship on citizenship by asking not only "Who made claims to citizenship in the early United States?" but also "What meanings did 'citizenship' hold in the formative period of its conceptualization?"[20] These questions have very different answers, because the cultural meaning of citizenship was not (and is not) reducible to a specific set of legal privileges or the lives of actual citizens.[21] "Citizen" is an official designation for belonging, but the generalized concept of citizenship is, by necessity, an imagined category. And the individuals excluded from full political membership have been, for that very reason, all the more attuned to citizenship's distinctly reparative promise.[22] The most ardent fantasies about citizenship have long come from outside the sphere of the law's protections—built out of narratives by and about the political outsiders whose trials have brought urgent meaning to the potentially abstract (and, in the early United States, still remarkably underspecified) privileges of political membership. To address this negative definitional impulse, which persists in modern scholarship and popular culture, *Civic Longing* explores the politics of identification, which cross and unsettle the ontological divisions of identity politics.[23] Civic longing—the longing to belong—is a basic desire that often has united people who, demographically speaking, shared little else. This is a book about citizenship rather than citizens, longing rather than belonging.

The following chapters traverse the fields of literary criticism, history, cultural studies, political theory, and law in order to deepen our understanding of a word-turned-concept that was (and continues to be) invested with a range of meanings that make it both politically dynamic and terminologically vexed. Citizenship is an exceptionally capacious topic, but I have purposely not attempted to treat citizenship's meanings across all of U.S. history and the many, many ways that Americans have written about, experienced, and critiqued those different meanings. Instead, this book focuses on the uniquely fraught period of citizenship's emergence, the period between 1776 and 1868, what I refer to in shorthand as the "early United States."[24]

The historical problem of citizenship's meaning before the Fourteenth Amendment guides the three interlocking arguments of this book: (1) The history of citizenship cannot be told solely from the perspective of the law. In the early United States, citizenship was less a legal category than an emergent extralegal concept that accumulated its meaning flexibly in rhetorical experiments that traversed several genres.[25] Throughout this book, I use the term "extralegal" in two ways: both in a simple sense, to collectively describe a number of nonlegal traditions of political authorization, and in a more specialized sense, to highlight the negative definitional impulse that has sustained and fueled the almost melancholic idealization of citizenship from its changeable outer limits. (2) To fully understand the prehistory of citizenship, we need to undo a relatively modern interpretative bias that treats fiction and other imaginative traditions as secondary and subordinate expressions of political practice. In a period in which there was no single, authoritative legal definition of citizenship, imaginative formulations of citizenship did not engage predetermined norms about political membership. They actively theorized something that was still essentially up for grabs. In this spirit, I read the imaginative traditions of citizenship as historically activated genres of political theory. (3) Although citizenship lacked substantive content in early U.S. law, Americans sustained an idealized image of citizenship by imagining it from the outside. Amid turbulent contests over political membership, an unruly assemblage that I term "negative civic exemplars"—expatriates, slaves, traitors, and alienated subjects—offered uniquely potent figures for the anxieties and allures of republican affiliation. Within this negative paradigm, the ever-present (and pathetic) prospect of political exclusion and exile offered a comparative lens for investing citizenship with a cultural significance that it had not yet achieved within the law. As a result of this tragic mode of political fantasy, even the most idealized portraits of citizenship in the early United States were shot through with anxieties about political disenfranchisement, disunion, and statelessness.

## Overview

The best historiographical work on citizenship—by James Kettner, Judith Shklar, Linda Kerber, Eric Foner, Nancy Isenberg, Rogers Smith, Douglas Bradburn, and others—has helped illuminate the contradictions and silences that structured official, state-based formulations of citizenship.[26] However, the juridical under-conceptualization of citizenship also begs another set of questions, which drive the following chapters: How did the term "citizen" come to carry so much cultural currency in a period in which its legal meaning was still remarkably under-specified? What other traditions shaped the imagination of citizenship in the era before its late legal codification? These questions are both historically and methodologically instructive. They recall us to the inevitable limits of legal statutes, which offer only one rather specialized form of information about the way a people imagines itself at different moments in history. These questions also prompt a renewed attention to the imaginative genres that shape what kinds of political membership are *thinkable* at any given point in time.

The early history of citizenship asks us to think expansively about the kind of documents that are integral to politics. This point bears special emphasis, because many of the textual subdivisions and hierarchies we now take for granted—and which form the generic basis of disciplinary divisions between fields like English, philosophy, history, and political science—had not yet fully solidified in the early United States. Republican and antebellum primers, for example, brought together a wide range of speeches, fiction, poetry, and philosophy—and did so without expressing anxieties about the political relevance of these varied forms. Indeed, in *The North American Reader: Containing a Great Variety of Pieces in Prose and Poetry from Highly Esteemed American and English Readers* (1835)— which sought to remedy the still-heavy reliance on the *English Reader* in the American schoolroom—the editor explains his inclusion of literature authored by American citizens by observing that we cannot reasonably expect students to learn and uphold the "political and civil institutions" of the United States "unless the children and youth of our country are made to understand them, by books, and other means of instruction."[27] In a country still anxious about the "greatness" of its native literary productions, the political importance of U.S. literature was actually more obvious than its formal or aesthetic merits. And as we will see in Chapters 4 and 5, the very aspects of fiction that elicited anxiety within the censorious framework of Enlightenment empiricism—fiction's artifice, virtuality, and possibilistic episteme—ultimately helped position literature as an ideal medium for developing and refashioning the cultural meaning of citizenship in the classroom and beyond.

So what exactly does it mean to understand fiction and other imaginative traditions as instrumental to the conceptualization of citizenship? The five following chapters all offer somewhat different answers to this question. However, they are united in their attention to the role that tropes and other habituated forms of literary and cultural expression play in establishing and shaping political customs that are so pervasive as to be almost omnipresent. The law may be the official language of governance, but individuals are also governed by a number of informal, extralegal traditions. And as James Fenimore Cooper reflects in *The American Democrat* (1838), the unlegislated imperatives of custom hold special sway in a representative democracy—which idealizes "public opinion" as the legitimate foundation of governance. Although the "political liberty of this country is greater than that of nearly every other civilized nation," Cooper explains, Americans "defer more to those around them" and are thus "more under the control of extra-legal authority . . . than in almost every other country."[28] Cooper, who had just returned to the United States after several years abroad, was not inclined to valorize any of the national traits he identifies in *The American Democrat*. His Anglophilic disdain for U.S. provinciality in *The American Democrat* prevents him from considering the power that this model of "extra-legal" governance holds for him in his capacity as a novelist and a political theorist.[29] Yet were Cooper to get his "wish"—if the law were, in fact, the only legitimate source of political authority—his decision to write *The American Democrat* would have indicated a certain superfluousness of purpose. Why write a long political polemic if not to convince other people to "defer" to an opinion that is neither official nor original to the readers Cooper clearly hopes to persuade? I underline this tension, because—despite Cooper's evident nostalgia for a more monolithic form of centralized political authority—he was attuned to custom's power as an extralegal mechanism of governance. Public opinion, as Cooper recognized, is an incredibly effectual—and by necessity, unlegislated—mechanism of social regulation and political coercion.

The decentralized, extralegal development of citizenship offers an instructive opportunity for reexamining what it means to think of the imaginative arts as properly political—rather than normatively social or descriptively historical.[30] In the spirit of John Dewey's *The Public and Its Problems* (1927), I argue that the political character of the extralegal traditions of citizenship derives from the affiliatory possibilities they conjure, not their indexical capacity to present already established historical practices. For Dewey, the solution to the often-lamented antisocial proclivities of liberal individualism is "communication," which "insures participation in a common understanding" by "securing similar emotional dispositions and intellectual dispositions."[31] The form best suited to this purpose, Dewey argues, is not the standardized calendrical commons of the newspaper, but art—because the thing to be conveyed is not information, but ways of seeing in common. "Poetry, the drama, the novel, are proofs that the problem of presentation is not insoluble. Artists have always been the real purveyor of news, for it is not the outward happening in itself which is new, but the kindling by it of emotion, perception and appreciation."[32] In identifying art as a means of "presentation," rather than a secondary medium of representation, Dewey isolates the performative dimension of communication, its ability to transform by persuasion.[33] Understood as a creative form of social brokering, political fantasies are not the individualizing excesses of private persons; they are the affiliatory aspirations that draw disparate individuals into relation—the voluntary bonds that pull us out of the orbit of self-interest and into the political realm of relation.[34]

*Civic Longing* attends to the everyday power of language as a medium of political persuasion and world-making. The following chapters draw on a wide range of documents—novels, tales, poems, sermons, Bible translations, philosophy, political ephemera, legislative debates, and unpassed bills—to identify the political tropes that shaped the unlegislated customs of citizenship in the early United States. Chapter 1, "The Retroactive Invention of Citizenship," is a terminological case study. It examines the nascent meanings of "citizenship" in early state and federal law and offers an overview of the interpretative strategies that lawyers and judges developed to manage the juridical under-conceptualization of citizenship. Building on Chapter 1's examination of the nominal status of the "citizen" in early U.S. law, the subsequent chapters examine the extralegal traditions of citizenship in two interlocking parts. Part II, "The Higher Laws of Citizenship," addresses the two primary discourses of "higher law": divine law and natural law. Part III, "The Lettered Citizen," examines two different ways of thinking about the political effects of the literary imagination: the romantic conceit of an autonomous literary realm, which transcends everyday life and politics, and the scholastic ideal of the lettered citizen, which values literature's instructional utility as a medium of civic education. Together, Parts II and III trace a shift from a fixed natural order to the changeable constructed human world of law—a world held together not by necessity but by choice.

Chapter 2, "Citizenship in Heaven," excavates one of the most pervasive but under-examined usages of "citizenship" in the early United States: the surge of revised post-Revolutionary translations of a key passage in Paul's Third Letter to the Philippians, which recast the traditional ideal of Christian estrangement and heavenly fellowship (*"conversation* in heaven") in the politicized idiom of *"citizenship* in heaven." The chapter tracks the Bible's idiomatic and conceptual impact on the imagination of citizenship across a range of materials, including sermonic treatments of citizenship, the manuscript of Charles Thomson's first American translation of the Bible in 1808, David Walker's fiery *Appeal to the Coloured Citizens of the World* (1829), and Harriet Beecher Stowe's second antislavery novel, *Dred: A Tale of the Great Dismal Swamp* (1856). The extraordinary political power of disaffiliation in the early United States (the power to *choose* to not belong), the chapter shows, had as much to do with Christian theology's idealization of worldly estrangement as with the secular history of liberal individualism.

The notion "that there is a higher law than the Constitution," as New York Senator William Henry Seward famously argued in the halls of Congress in March 1851, was crucial to constructing the aspirational meaning of citizenship in the early United States.[35] The comparative concept of a "higher law" provided a powerful and flexible political framework for developing notions of citizenship.[36] Chapter 3, "Citizens of Nature," shifts its focus from the expressly theological tropology of "citizenship in heaven" to examine the interrelated higher law tradition of natural law, which drew on the universalist ideal of unlimited rights in the state of nature. The chapter reassesses the relationship between natural and national rights by analyzing the legal and fictional narratives surrounding the 1841 maritime slave revolt aboard the *Creole*, in which 135 slaves obtained freedom by redirecting a U.S. ship to the British territory of Nassau, Bahamas. Reading Frederick Douglass's fictional reconstruction of the revolt on the *Creole* in

"The Heroic Slave" (1853) in conjunction with Daniel Webster's diplomatic response to the international dispute it set in motion, the chapter shows that the conceit of natural law allowed writers to portray the state-based laws of chattel slavery as mere "local fictions." Douglass's novella never forfeits the idea that rights ought to be inalienable by nature, but by recognizing that rights are alienable (transferable) in practice—not simply that they are often divested and withheld, but that they *can be transferred* to those who do not already possess them—he narrates the extralegal drama of political legitimation.

Chapter 4, "The Elsewhere of Citizenship," treats the civic importance of fiction more broadly by showing how the gradual differentiation of the "literary" as a discursive category in this period contributed to higher law critiques of the artificial and imposed conventions of positive law. The romantic conception of the "literary" as an autonomous realm apart from everyday experience, I argue, made it an ideal tradition for the continued development of the higher law tradition of citizenship. Taking cues from Nathaniel Hawthorne's influential theorizations of "romance," I argue that politicized anxieties about the dangers of reading fiction help illuminate the unfinished cultural work that the romantic revaluation of the speculative dimension of fiction facilitated: namely, the belated and contentious idealization of an artificial form of allegiance that was subject to dissolution and revision.

Chapter 5, "Stateless Fictions," places Edward Everett Hale's popular patriotic allegory of Confederate secession, "The Man Without a Country" (1863), at the center of a broader discussion of literature's didactic role in civic education. Despite its peripheral status in literary criticism, "The Man Without a Country" was a touchstone in secondary education from its initial publication until the 1970s. The well-documented reception history of "The Man Without a Country" helps illuminate two shifts that are key to this book: the late nationalization of citizenship, and the related emergence of a new way of understanding the relationship between literature and citizenship: the now almost reflexive belief in literature's utility in preparing students to be engaged national citizens. Finally, drawing on an allusion to "The Man Without a Country" in the Supreme Court's ruling in *Wong Kim Ark* (1898), one of the most important early interpretations of the Fourteenth Amendment's Citizenship Clause, the book concludes by showing how the extralegal traditions of citizenship that *Civic Longing* traces were domesticated in the wake of the Civil War to solidify a newly secularized form of Christian nationalism, in which national belonging was itself envisioned as a transcendent sacral ideal.

## Citizenship as Method

To orient readers in the extralegal approach to citizenship taken up in this book, Chapter 1 outlines the fractured legal conceptualization of citizenship at length so that it can more convincingly leave behind a way of thinking about the relationship between literature, law, and political history that might otherwise haunt this study: the notion that the law (and official history writ large) is a relatively coherent realm of order and normativity and that fiction and other imaginative traditions are resistant genres that disrupt the political status quo.[37] This oppositional theory of the politics of literature is an outgrowth of romanticism's own aspirational association of the imagination with dissent.[38] And in theory, it celebrates literature, insofar as it associates the literary with protest, critique, and progress. Yet in practice, it flattens history and literature alike by figuring each as phenomenologically discrete realms, structured by reality and description, on the one hand, and *poiesis* and creation, on the other. By focusing on the political tropes that are common to a number of different genres, this book seeks to offer a dynamic understanding of fiction's political power without reinforcing the medium-specific triumphalism that haunts comparative formulations of the politics of fiction, wherein "history" is tacitly rigidified to emphasize the radical, revisionary nature of fiction.

Part of the methodological gambit of this study writ large is to illuminate the formative political power of aesthetics—a power that has been difficult to address in literary criticism, which has, for several decades, turned to historicism in search of something more solid and "real" than the complexities of "literary ambiguity."[39] As several literary critics have observed, in the wake of deconstruction, which enjoyed its heyday in the 1970s and 1980s, literary criticism began to move away from the formalist interpretative practices associated with "close reading"—which increasingly was spurned as outmoded, historically myopic, and dangerously apolitical. In the decades that followed, formalist practices did not disappear altogether, but the confluence of a number of factors—including the rise of the cultural studies paradigm and the methodological dominance of "new historicism"—helped situate the practice of historical contextualization as a disciplinary "virtue."[40] The problem with this is that, for literary critics, this "disciplinary virtue" is not obviously "our" disciplinary virtue; it is one that historians monopolize, by training. As a result, the rise of historical contextualization in literary criticism helped solidify what Eric

Slauter, Elizabeth Dillon, and others have aptly described as the "trade deficit" between English and history, in which literary critics perennially import the work of historians with little to no citational reciprocity.[41]

Literary criticism's one-way disciplinary love affair with history is a natural extension of the methodological assumptions that underwrite the text/context model of history and the related "revisionist" model of the politics of literature.[42] When we talk about how a particular work of fiction expresses or disrupts the cultural norms that governed politics in the period in which it was written, we presume that the happenings of "history" have enough internal consistency that they can be treated as a unified historical context—which, in turn, becomes the interpretative "ground zero" for analyzing the political and historical stakes of specific works of literature. In theory, historical contextualization need not privilege some kinds of texts over others. In etymological terms, contextualization (from *con-* "together" + *texere* "to weave") simply describes reading a text together—and, in the case of historical contextualization, with "history." However, the very notion of reading "with" history implies that texts are not part of the textual fabric of history from the very beginning.[43] And in practice, fiction and other imaginative traditions tend to be marginalized in this interpretative regime, because they do not presume to describe things as they already are (as history does) and because they cannot channel the state's institutional authority to compel compliance (as the law does).[44]

This book uses the prehistory of citizenship to see anew the historical and political importance of literature, broadly understood, as well as the text-based interpretative methods that have developed and evolved in relationship to changing assumptions about the cultural power of letters. The extralegal traditions of citizenship traced in the following chapters are all openly speculative. They do not aspire to the descriptive neutrality of the indicative, and they do not carry the imperative force to command obedience. Yet they enjoy a different kind of power. Their political efficacy resides in *subjunctive* formulations—where the possible (what might or could be) and the prescriptive (what should or ought to be) collide in language that seeks to compel by persuasion. The "political subjunctive," as I designate this aspirational mode of politicking, concretizes different ways of envisioning political membership that have clear implications for how it *might* or *should* be defined, but nonetheless lack the law's coercive power.[45] The subjunctive offers a uniquely instructive paradigm for understanding the political power of rhetoric writ large, because—in keeping with the methodological ambitions of the chapters that follow—its modal (rather than generic) framework isolates the speculative mode that fiction exemplifies but that also structures a number of other cultural forms.

The grammatical mood of the subjunctive has gradually fallen out of common usage in English, but the aspirational impulse to which it lends formal idiomatic support has never lost its insistent hold on the political imaginaries of the United States, which, as with Walt Whitman's hopeful vision of the future of democracy in *Democratic Vistas* (1871), has been almost painfully oriented toward the fantastic promise of political perfectibility.[46] Sometimes this aspirational "civic longing" took the inverted form of nostalgia, which projects political futures backward through idealized pasts. Yet whether they looked to an imagined past or to a possible future, the subjunctive orientation of the extralegal discourses of citizenship made them uniquely responsive to the definitional problem that shaped debates about citizenship in the early United States. As many early U.S. political commentators recognized, citizenship was "open to argument and to speculative criticism" well into the 1860s, and the very things that might make these traditions seem a little less impactful or serious today proved to be the source of their unique power.[47] Their tendency toward conjecture, supposition, and even fantasy—freed them from the burden of trying to account for citizenship as it already *was,* allowing them to invent its meaning anew, again and again.

# CHAPTER ONE

# The Retroactive Invention of Citizenship

## A Textual History

> As the Constitution of the United States does not define the word *citizen,* the definition must be sought in the exact meaning of the word itself, altogether independently of the Constitution. Herein, after all, lies the great and only safeguard against the corruption or centralization which grow out of a written constitution. Language, and words with their distinct meaning at the time of its adoption are the only record to which we can safely go back as a barrier against new and forced or false interpretations.
>
> —James McCune Smith, "Citizenship" (1859)

> I am aware that some of our most learned lawyers and able writers have allowed themselves to speak upon this subject [citizenship] in loose and indeterminate language. They speak of "all rights and immunities guaranteed by the Constitution to the citizen" without telling us what they are. They speak of a man's citizenship as defective and imperfect, because he is supposed not to have "all the civil rights," (all the *jura civitatis,* as expressed by one of my predecessors,) without telling what particular rights they are nor what relation they have, if any, with citizenship.
>
> —U.S. Attorney General Edward Bates, *Opinion on Citizenship* (1862)

THIS BOOK BEGAN with a relatively straightforward question, raised by Nathaniel Hawthorne's use of "citizen" in the preface to *The Scarlet Letter* (1850). When the narrator declares, "I am a citizen of somewhere else"—in a passage that is full of the classic tropes of Hawthornian fiction (a "village in cloud-land" seen through the "haze of memory" and peopled by "imaginary inhabitants")—what sort of political membership, rights, and duties did readers understand him to be giving up?[1] And insofar as the narrator's identification as "a citizen of somewhere else" can be understood as a kind of "literary citizenship"—a symbolic allegiance to the imaginative realm of the "republic of letters"—how might this formulation help illuminate the political power and possibilities of literature? What is the relationship between the imagined communities forged in fiction and the everyday institutional and imaginative life of citizenship? I return to these last two questions in the following chapters. This chapter sets the foundation for the arguments that follow by outlining the broader interpretative challenges and methodological opportunities that this initial inquiry raised. When I turned to the law in the hope of gaining a better sense of how Hawthorne and other writers were representing and/or revising the dominant legal sense of the term "citizen," I was surprised (if not initially a little disappointed) to find that there was no single "ready-made" legal definition of citizenship in this period, which might offer a self-contained gloss of this keyword. To ventriloquize an instructive and extraordinary disclosure in U.S. Attorney General Edward Bates's 1862 *Opinion on Citizenship* (to which I soon will be turning), "I have been often pained by the fruitless search in our law books and the records of our courts, for a satisfactory definition of the phrase *citizen of the United States*. I find no such definition, no authoritative establishment of the meaning of the phrase."[2]

So what did Americans understand themselves to mean when they spoke of "citizenship" in the period between the Revolution and the Fourteenth Amendment? And when they did not use this term, what assumptions, convictions, and aspirations shaped the way they thought and wrote about political membership? To begin to answer these questions, this chapter carefully distinguishes the *term* "citizen" from the legal *category* of citizenship (codified with the Fourteenth Amendment) and also from the philosophical *ideal* of consensual allegiance (prospectively envisioned in the Age of Revolutions). The definitional poverty of "citizenship" in early U.S. law, I argue, did not inhibit its cultural idealization; it actually facilitated it. The terminological pliancy of citizenship in early U.S. law helped establish the citizen as the preferred cultural palimpsest for theories of political membership and rights, which could, initially, have coalesced around a number of different titular personages (whether subject, human, person, etc.). With few clearly specified boundaries, "citizenship" was a uniquely powerful terminological cipher for a range of political ideals and agendas.

After discussing the role the French Revolution played in establishing the terminological association between the term "citizen" and a newly empowered rights-bearing subject, the chapter moves backward from Attorney General Bates's "fruitless search" for a definition of citizenship in the 1860s to the foundational legal texts and debates to which he and other political commentators turned in the hope of answering questions that, as many acknowledged, had no officially recognized answers. Finally, the chapter concludes with a reexamination of Chief Justice Roger B. Taney's selective reconstruction of the legal history of citizenship in his infamous ruling against black citizenship in the *Dred Scott* case (1857). I use Taney's influential opinion as an object lesson in the interpretative dangers—and also ethical responsibilities—that twenty-first-century readers of "citizenship" share in as inheritors of the speculative prehistory of citizenship.

## The Terminological Origins of the Subject/Citizen Revolution

The word "citizen" evokes a constellation of meanings, both practical and emotive. It is a designation that often has seemed to be a privilege in and of itself. To be a citizen—and perhaps more importantly to not be a "subject"— is presumably to enjoy some form of political self-authorization.[3] Understood through the liberatory paradigm of American independence, the practical political achievement of the Revolution was not only the collective sovereignty of the United States as a country, but the newly empowered form of consensual political membership to which it ostensibly gave rise.[4] This oppositional conception of "citizenship," as an emancipation from "subjecthood," provides the narrative hinge for one of the first authoritative accounts of U.S. citizenship, David Ramsay's *Dissertation on the Manner of Acquiring the Character and Privileges of a Citizen of the United States* (1789). "The principle of the government being radically changed by the revolution, the political character of the people was also changed from subjects to citizens," Ramsay writes. "The difference is immense," he continues. "Subject is derived from the latin words, *sub* and *jacio*, and means one who is under the power of another; but a citizen is an unit of a mass of free people, who, collectively, possess sovereignty."[5] For Ramsay, the difference between subjecthood and citizenship is immanent to the words themselves. To be a subject is to be marked by one's subjection to another, while a citizen is the sovereign unit of a form of territorially delimited collectivity, which exercises a mediated kind of self-rule through the election of kindred representatives.

Ramsay's recourse to etymology allows him to sidestep the juridical perplexities of "citizenship." He presents the fabular transformation of British subjects to U.S. citizens as an artifact of linguistic transformation rather than legal process. "A nation was born in a day. Nearly three millions of people who had become subjects, became citizens."[6] Ramsay enumerates the modes of acquiring citizenship, but they take the form of philosophical principles rather than legal procedure. Access to citizenship, for example, is open to "parties to the original compact, the declaration of independence," and by oaths of fidelity, "tacit consent and acquiescence."[7] Ramsay's theorization of political membership as the outgrowth of compact and consent echoes the voluntary form of allegiance set out in John Locke's influential *Second Treatise on Government* (1690), which identifies society as an outgrowth of an artificial (and so dissolvable) contract that supersedes the turbulent state of nature. According to Locke, since men enter society for the protection of their property, "whenever the legislators endeavor to take away, and destroy the property of the people, or to reduce them to slavery under arbitrary power, they put themselves into a state of war with the people, who are thereupon absolved from any further obedience."[8] For Locke, government is an institution of convenience that loses its value (and legitimacy) as soon as it infringes on the natural rights of its constituents. It is this notion of the voluntary and so amendable nature of allegiance that defines Locke's often-remarked philosophical importance for the American Revolutionary ethos—as it is encapsulated in the Declaration of Independence, which directly parallels select arguments from Locke's *Second Treatise* in several places.[9]

As one of the first major historians of the American Revolution, Ramsay has, both directly and indirectly, shaped the way many Americans came to understand the meaning of Independence.[10] Yet Ramsay's recognizably Lockean narrative is as misleading as it is iconic. The conceptual importance of Locke for U.S. intellectual history is undeniable, but as we will see when we turn to the legal history of expatriation, the voluntary, contractual theory of allegiance that Locke theorizes had almost no juridical traction in U.S. law.[11] Moreover, we risk anachronism when we speak about Locke's philosophical contribution to the debates surrounding the Revolution in the language of "citizen" or "citizenship"—terminology that Locke does not use at any point in either of his influential treatises on government.[12] Locke provides the conceptual framework for something that Jean-Jacques Rousseau and others later identified as "citizenship," but which few writers spoke of in this language prior to the French Revolution. When Rousseau published his own take on contract theory seventy years after Locke, in *Social Contract* (1762), he retroactively fixed on "citizen" as a specialized designation for the sovereign political agent whose entrance into society was voluntary and self-willed. As Rousseau recognized, this specialized usage of "citizen" had little precedent in previous political philosophy. "The true meaning of this word ['citizen']," Rousseau mused in a footnote, is almost entirely lost on modern man. . . . I have not found in my reading that the title of *citizen* has ever been given to the subjects of a prince, not even in ancient times to the Macedonians or in our own time the English, although they are closer to liberty than all the others."[13]

Ramsay's strong differentiation of "subject" and "citizen" does not track back to Locke. It registered a terminological shift that was just beginning to take root when he published his dissertation in 1789, the same year as the French Declaration.[14] The idealized association of the term "citizen" with an all-empowered rights-bearing subject was, by and large, a transatlantic aftershock of the "citoyen" of the French Revolution. During the American Revolution, "citizen" and "subject" were used as roughly synonymous terms.[15] It was only after the American Revolution—and in dialogue with the revolutions that followed—that this familiar terminological distinction gradually gained traction in colloquial speech. Documents like the French Declaration of the Rights of the Man and of the Citizen (1789) helped position "citizen" as a differential term for the rights-bearing subject. However, the initial, more generic sense of "citizen" as a designation of membership (synonymous with "subject") persisted well into the nineteenth century.[16]

In the early United States, "citizenship" was an exceptionally malleable word. It offered a flexible conceptual rubric for a range of political ideals and disappointments. The language of citizenship was sometimes employed in ways that sound familiar in retrospect (as, for example, in the phrase the "American citizen"), but these invocations tend to mislead the contemporary reader because they make the early rhetorical experiments in citizenship seem more familiar (and nationalistic) than they really are.[17] This sense of continuity, to some extent, is endemic to term-based analysis. Terminological continuities easily obscure conceptual dissimilarities. In the early United States, citizenship was not yet a fully articulated ideological concept. It was, to borrow Raymond Williams's formulation, an emergent "structure of feeling . . . at the very edge of semantic availability."[18] The uneven development of citizenship in the eighteenth and nineteenth centuries is the history of a term made concept. This erratic transformation has often been neglected, because it is difficult not to read the modern concept of citizenship back into its nascent iterations.[19]

## "Citizenship" as Term and Concept

Citizenship's terminological prominence and juridical impoverishment in the early United States did not go unnoticed. It prompted confusion, disappointment, and also fantasy. "Who is a citizen? What constitutes a citizen of the United States?" Attorney General Edward Bates queries in his 1862 *Opinion on Citizenship*.[20] Prompted by a letter from Secretary of the Treasury Salmon Chase that inquired "whether or not colored men can be citizens of the United States," Bates grapples with the definitional ambiguities that attended the early conceptualization of citizenship well into the

1860s. Bates's answer to the question of black citizenship is thus another set of questions:

> Who is a citizen? What constitutes a citizen of the United States? I have been often pained by the fruitless search in our law books and the records of our courts, for a satisfactory definition of the phrase *citizen of the United States*. I find no such definition, no authoritative establishment of the meaning of the phrase, neither by a course of judicial decisions in our courts, nor by the continued and consentaneous action of the different branches of our political government. For aught I see to the contrary, the subject is now as little understood in its details and elements, and the question as open to argument and to speculative criticism, as it was in the beginning of the government. Eighty years of practical enjoyment of citizenship, under the Constitution, have not sufficed to teach us either the exact meaning of the word, or the constituent elements of the thing we prize so highly.[21]

Coming from the attorney general, seventy-five years after the ratification of the Constitution in 1787, this reflection on the residual ambiguity of the central term for political membership is astonishing. Bates dramatizes the difficulties endemic to any comprehensive account of citizenship in the early United States: the "fruitless search" for its definition in law books, the inconstant course of judicial decisions, its conceptual pliancy to "speculative criticism." And yet, as the final line of the passage makes clear, the uncertain meaning of citizenship in early U.S. law did not diminish its significance; it only made its benefits more inestimable.

Bates acknowledges the many unanswered questions about citizenship in early U.S. law, but this does not stop him from answering Chase's initial question about "whether or not colored men can be citizens of the United States." Bates concludes that "free m[e]n of color" who are "born in the United States" are "citizens" of it.[22] Bates's conclusion that free men of color were automatically citizens by virtue of their birth within the United States breaks with the precedent-setting U.S. Supreme Court ruling in *Dred Scott vs. Sandford* (1857), in which the majority found that individuals of African American descent were not eligible for citizenship. Interestingly, Bates does not discuss Judge Taney's ruling in his own inquiry into black citizenship. Bates does not focus on how others have interpreted the law. Unlike Taney, whose opinion hinged on his extratextual invocation of "original intent," Bates is not interested in what the founders may have intended or how the founding documents have been read at different moments in time. Bates is an insistent textualist. "Our nationality," Bates emphasizes, was created and our political government exists by written law, and inasmuch as that laws does not exclude persons of that [African] descent, it follows inevitability that such persons, born in the country, must be citizens."[23] Adopting a literalist reading practice that was popular among abolitionists, Bates invokes the letter of the law—in this case, its definitional reticence about citizenship—to counteract prejudicial inferences about the racial limits of citizenship.[24] For Bates, and for many others in the early United States, the under-definition of citizenship was not a political liability, but an opportunity.

Bates's *Opinion* never fully resolves the larger questions about citizenship that it so elegantly poses. However, it offers a useful definition of the affiliatory problems that "citizenship" constellates. In a clarification of the most basic connotations of the term in the period, Bates explains that "the Constitution uses the word citizen only to express the political quality of the individual in his relations to the nation; to declare that he is a member of the body politic, and bound to it by the reciprocal obligation of allegiance on the one side and protection on the other."[25] Allegiance did not always guarantee protection, as Frederick Douglass and others pointed out.[26] Yet the expectation that the relationship between allegiance and protection was (or ought to be) "reciprocal" was a promise that "citizenship" regularly demarcated in this period.[27] Throughout this book, I use the term "citizenship" in the structural sense of the term identified by Bates, in order to designate the affiliatory concerns that revolve around the interlocking problems of protection (privileges, immunities, rights) and allegiance (loyalty and duties). With Bates's basic structural definition in place, we can better appreciate the partial and plural meanings that "citizenship" took on in early U.S. law and in the "speculative criticism" that Bates mentions in passing—and which this book identifies as formative imaginative and political resources in the cultural development of citizenship in the era of its legal nascence.

Needless to say, "citizenship" continues to elicit intense passions and debate in the twenty-first century—and it will carry somewhat different meanings for each reader of this book. So before turning to the specific legal texts that Bates would himself have consulted in his search for a definition of citizenship, I want to offer a brief overview of the four basic innovations of the form of political membership that came into being with the two-part juridical reconstitution of "citizenship," which I collectively identify as the "twin legal reformations of 1868": the Fourteenth Amendment and the 1868 Expatriation Act, passed the day before the ratification of the Fourteenth Amendment. I will begin with the two most familiar of these changes, ushered in by the Fourteenth Amendment. First, the amendment's Citizenship Clause made citizenship available to all African-American men, regardless of their previous condition or ancestry (*jus sanguinis*, right of the blood), by establishing the territory of one's birth (*jus soli*, right of the soil) as the natural foundation of political membership. Second, the Citizenship Clause established the primacy of federal citizenship over state citizenship. In so doing, it resolved long-standing debates about the primary unit of political membership, as well as the scope of the obligations and protections it structured. Third, in line with the federalization of citizenship, the Fourteenth Amendment's Privileges and Immunities Clause declared that "No state shall make or enforce any law which shall abridge the privileges or immunities of citizens of the United States; nor shall any state deprive any person of life, liberty, or property, without due process of law; nor deny to any person within its jurisdiction the equal protection of the laws."[28] This clause is crucial from the perspective of the terminological inconsistencies discussed in the next section, because it retroactively identified the rights enumerated in the Bill of Rights—not as generic rights of "the people"—but as constitutive rights of a newly substantive and federal juridical personage, the "citizen."

Finally—and of key significance for Chapter 4's reassessment of the politics of literary autonomy—the 1868 Expatriation Act belatedly formalized a model of "citizenship" that Ramsay prematurely lauded (and which scholars often still mistakenly take for granted): the notion that "citizenship," for those who enjoyed it, designated a newly voluntary form of political membership from the beginning. The iconic mythology of political consent is rooted in an overreliance on the Declaration of Independence, taken as an aspirational textual blueprint for the new government it helped authorize. The Declaration celebrates the collective right to "dissolve the political bands which have connected [one people] with another," but—as with many of its other universal claims, including the equality of "all men"—the right of individuals to voluntarily refuse allegiance was deeply contested in the decades that followed the Revolution.[29]

The British common law doctrine of *indefeasible* (natural and perpetual) allegiance did not, in fact, end with British imperial rule. In the early United States, those who met the narrow qualifications for naturalization could *become* citizens, but the parallel and interconnected right to expatriate—and thereby voluntary *relinquish* the reciprocal rights and duties that automatically extended to most native-born white men by virtue of their nativity—was a source of active debate. Virginia and its sister-state, Kentucky, were the only two states to explicitly recognize the right to expatriate in the early United States.[30] The Supreme Court tended to disfavor expatriation, but it was variously affirmed and denied in the lower courts.[31]

British common law provided the default framework for political allegiance in the early United States—and for the many questions that had not yet been addressed in U.S. legislation. In this respect, some continuity between the models of political membership developed in each legal tradition was all but inevitable in a still burgeoning republic. However, the late recognition of the right to expatriate in 1868 was not an oversight of early legislators. In 1817, Congress considered the question of expatriation at length. After appointing a committee "to inquire into . . . the right of expatriation," the House of Representatives reviewed a bill in December 1817 "by which the right of citizenship may be relinquished."[32] There were numerous objections to the bill: that allegiance to the state is natural and perpetual,[33] that federal legislation on the issue would infringe on state sovereignty,[34] and even that allowing expatriation would create a class of licentious outlaws "without home and destitute of country."[35] After much debate, the bill was rejected by a narrow margin (75 to 64).[36] Congress did not recognize the right to expatriate for another fifty years, when the 1868 Expatriation Act recognized "the inherent and inalienable right of man to change his home and allegiance."[37] Juridically speaking, the shift from the model of perpetual allegiance associated with British "subjecthood" to the defeasible (artificial and so dissolvable) model of voluntary political membership associated with Lockean social contract theory was—like the legal category of citizenship—a late development in U.S. legal history.

The 1868 Expatriation Act marked a shift away from the perpetual model of allegiance born of British common law. Yet the Fourteenth Amendment's solidification of the doctrine of *jus soli* did not itself mark a departure from the British model of political membership. It actually marked a *return* to a principle established in British law in 1608 with Sir Edmund Coke's influential ruling in Calvin's Case—the same case that established the doctrine of perpetual allegiance. Calvin's Case identified the territory in which one was born as the foundation of political membership, but it also understood this allegiance to be natural and perpetual—the main doctrine challenged by the 1868 Expatriation Act.[38] In this respect, the form of citizenship codified in the twin legal reformations of 1868 was both more and less like the form of political membership the American colonists had ceded in the Revolutionary War: from thence forward, the bonds of allegiance and the protections that extend from it were an automatic outgrowth of the territory of one's birth, but these reciprocal ties were now voluntary (and so relinquishable).

The precedential innovation of the Fourteenth Amendment was not in relation to British common law, but America's own feudal history. In formalizing a territorial conception of native allegiance—based on *jus soli*—the Fourteenth Amendment departed from the United States' historical investment in *jus sanguinis,* a model of citizenship by descent, which was integral to the genealogical structure of chattel slavery. The condition of enslavement was passed matrilineally from enslaved mother to child—regardless of the race of the father.[39] The gendered transmission of slavery was mirrored by another, lesser-known, aspect of *jus sanguinis:* when children were born abroad to two white parents, the hereditary transmission of citizenship was effectively confined to patrilineal descent. Beyond the jurisprudential limits of the United States, citizenship only could be transmitted through white fathers who were U.S. citizens, and who had also been "residents" of the United States at one point. The 1790 Naturalization Act specified that "the right of citizenship shall not descend to persons whose *fathers* have never been resident in the United States."[40] The enslavement of the mother may have trumped the legal personhood of the father within the institution of slavery, but when children were born outside of the territorial limits of the United States, the citizenship status of white women did little to secure the citizenship of their children. Children born abroad were not eligible for naturalization by virtue of their mother's nativity.

The patrilineal transmission of citizenship abroad was one of the many effects of the legal doctrine of coverture, wherein the legal entitlements and obligations of married women were subsumed under their husband's legal status. Coverture began to lose some of its force with the enactment of married women's property acts beginning in 1839. Yet it persisted in different forms until 1992, when the Supreme Court finally abolished it in a ruling related to Planned Parenthood.[41] The patrilineal transmission of citizenship abroad lost traction somewhat sooner. It was overturned in a 1934 statute, which recognized the equal civic capacity of women to transmit their citizenship to children born abroad.[42] As even these few staggered developments remind us, the evolution of citizenship has never been free of ambiguities, nor have its developments been unqualified.

## Citizenship's Legal Nascence

Naturalization law is a useful starting place for retracing the juridical usages of "citizenship," because the path to becoming a citizen through naturalization was more clearly and consistently defined than its formal features. Unlike most aspects of citizenship, which were presumed to fall within the scope of state regulatory power, naturalization was fully federalized from the beginning. By virtue of article I, section 8 of the Constitution, Congress enjoyed an unambiguous "power to establish a uniform rule of naturalization."[43] In the early United States, Congress made quick and frequent use of its power to regulate which (and when) foreign-born persons

were eligible to naturalize as U.S. citizens. According to the first naturalization act, adopted in 1790, "any Alien being a free white person . . . of
good character" who had resided in "the jurisdiction of the United States"
for two years "shall be considered as a Citizen of the United States."[44]
The 1790 act provided the template for subsequent naturalization acts,
but residency requirements changed quickly and dramatically in the years
that followed in response to shifting perceptions of the dangers of foreign
influence. Indeed, the two-year residency requirement was almost immediately supplanted. The 1795 Naturalization Act extended the residency period to five years. Then, at the height of anxieties about the unruly and
potentially seditious effects of francophone culture, Congress passed the
Alien and Sedition Acts in 1798, extending the residency period to four-
teen years. As the reactionary climate of these cascading revisions attest,
Congress's power to change naturalization law, as and when it sees fit, has
made it a uniquely volatile and responsive barometer of changing legislative assumptions and anxieties about access to citizenship.

Naturalization law witnessed some of the most explicit and also inegalitarian formulations of citizenship in early U.S. law. The openly exclusionary
terms of early naturalization laws—which restricted the transmission of
citizenship abroad to patrilineal descent and limited naturalization to "free
white persons"—made explicit the inegalitarian assumptions that often
lurked, unstated, in the background of debates about citizenship. Still, as
Peter Coviello observes in a nuanced discussion of naturalization law, even
the 1790 Naturalization Act does not offer an unequivocal formulation of
white citizenship: "The Act does nothing to validate the civic status of
white subjects [many of the propertied did not have the right to vote]; nor
does it preclude the citizenship of non-white subjects already in the nation."[45] Naturalization laws zealously policed the line between aliens and
citizens, but, as with many other negative formulations of citizenship, the
juridical constitution of citizens as *not* aliens did not help to answer questions like Bates's, which sought to identify the internal meaning of citizenship. The specification of which non-natives could become citizens did
not clarify the basis of political membership, whether by virtue *jus soli* or *jus
sanguinis,* the perpetuity of political allegiance, or the specific protections
and obligations that structured the reciprocal bonds of citizenship.

The under-definition of citizenship is fundamental to the Constitution, as
originally ratified. As Bates and other commentators were uncomfortably
aware, the Constitution "does not declare who are and who are not a citizen,
nor does it attempt to describe the constituent elements of citizenship."[46]
The eleven original references to "citizen(s)" in the Constitution are nominal
rather than substantive. Traditionally, the Comity Clause (in article IV, sec-

tion 2) is understood as the most definitive of the original constitutional references to citizenship.[47] The Comity Clause extends "all Privileges and Immunities of Citizens in the several States" to the "Citizens of each state," but it does not specify what these privileges and immunities are.[48] This omission was not an oversight. The reticence about citizenship's meaning was integral to the delicate and fraught making of the Constitution. The Comity Clause's vague allusion to "*all* Privileges and Immunities of Citizens in the several States" addressed an anxiety that was brought to a head in the context of debates about the Bill of Rights: the enumeration of rights, the founders recognized, had the potential to cut both ways—it solidified the rights specifically named, but it also, implicitly, delimited rights that might otherwise be presumed. In this spirit, James Wilson, Pennsylvania delegate in the Continental Congress, famously warned that the adoption of the Bill of Rights was not only "unnecessary" but also potentially "dangerous," because the very existence of a list of rights implies that only explicitly enumerated rights are reserved for the people. Since very few people understand the "whole rights of the people, as men and as citizens," Wilson stressed, it was best not to confine these rights to writing.[49] Wilson's objections to adopting the Bill of Rights came to naught. However, in a broader sense, the desire for ambiguity he voiced prevailed. "Citizen," appropriately, does not appear anywhere in the Bill of Rights. It uses the more generic designations of "the people" and "person." The proliferation of nonequivalent designations in the U.S. Constitution and in the constitutions of the several states left more than ample interpretative leeway for the speculative constitution of citizenship in the years to come.

The Constitution's definitional reticence, it should be said, was not limited to citizenship. Many of the beliefs and doctrines that shaped early debates about the state and federal government (and that continue to shape both today) do not appear in the Constitution proper. These principles appear instead in legislative enactments, judicial opinions, and a number of other extra-constitutional legal documents.[50] Part of what made the Constitution's reticence about citizenship uniquely problematic was that ancillary legal precedents were in relatively short supply when it came to citizenship—and those that existed often were in direct tension with one another because of unresolved questions about the relationship between federal and state governments. In theory, state and federal citizenship—as presented in the Comity Clause—were interlocking and complementary forms of political membership, whose privileges and immunities were transferable across state lines. Yet in practice, this dual model of allegiance created deep schisms between what were, in fact, several distinct legal traditions.[51]

The definitional problem of citizenship in early U.S. law was not merely the absence of a clear statutory definition of citizenship, but also the varied, partial meanings that were assigned to it within a nascent and exceptionally heterogeneous legal tradition. Of the eight state constitutions adopted in 1776—in New Hampshire, South Carolina, Virginia, New Jersey, Delaware, Pennsylvania, Maryland, and North Carolina—only Pennsylvania and North Carolina even use the term "citizen." And they only use the term once each in passing: the Constitution of North Carolina states that "any foreigner" who settles in the state and takes an oath of allegiance to it will be "deemed a free citizen" after a year of residence;[52] and the Pennsylvania Constitution stipulates that no man can "be justly deprived or abridged of any civil right as a citizen, on account of his religious sentiments or peculiar mode of religious worship."[53] The language of citizen appears more regularly in subsequent state constitutions, but as with the U.S. Constitution, the use of "citizen" in these documents was usually nominal rather than substantive. Even if we were to assume (rather reductively) that all references to "free inhabitants," "freeman," property-holding "inhabitants," and so on, are roughly interchangeable ways of characterizing the citizens of each state, these kinds of terminological equivalencies do not yield a unified model of citizenship.

The legal requirements for being a citizen, and the protections it guaranteed, were ill-defined and varied from state to state and from year to year. There is thus no simple answer to the question of whether women were deemed citizens in this period.[54] As scholars often note, from 1776 to 1807 women briefly enjoyed the right to vote in New Jersey. The 1776 Constitution of New Jersey granted suffrage to "all inhabitants . . . worth fifty pounds." The gender-neutral use of the term "inhabitants" made it possible for women to vote, but the property requirement further limited suffrage in practice. Under the common law doctrine of coverture, married women could not hold property, so even during the brief period of female suffrage in New Jersey, only *unmarried* women could vote.[55]

Common law was the default precedential framework for adjudicating questions not treated explicitly in U.S. law, so in the absence of provisions that explicitly empowered women, the British common law doctrine of coverture was persistent and difficult to dislodge. Still, as recent historians of women's rights have begun to discuss, coverture found countervailing precedents in some rather unlikely places. Under civil law, the Roman-inspired system of law practiced in the Spanish and French empires, women enjoyed a host of rights foreclosed in British common law—including the right to hold property, make contracts, and sue.[56] As a result, in some cases,

U.S. imperial expansion and incorporation of Spanish and French colonies resulted in internally fractured amalgamations of Anglo/Continental law that partially undercut the doctrine of coverture. Historian Laurel Clark captures these tensions with nuance in her paradigm-shifting reexamination of women's property rights in early Florida. As Clark observes, "American expansion into Florida yielded an unintended consequence for marital property law: civil law marital property rights were upheld, and therefore common law coverture (the common law rule that married women cannot own separate property) was partially overturned."[57] In Florida between 1820 and 1860, women's right to hold property initially was rooted in treaties, but after Florida became a U.S. state in 1845, this right was explicitly confirmed in statutes. Early precedents for women's right to hold property in Florida were limited to white women—and, as Clark emphasizes, these seemingly progressive formulations of property rights were rooted in imperial expansion, and they also actively facilitated imperial racial regimes by protecting and reinforcing the property-based system of chattel slavery in a southern borderland territory-turned-state. Thus, one of the earliest and under-discussed precedents for women's right to hold property was not only racially delimited, it actively worked to reinforce a broader system of racial inequality. As is so often the case, when we delve into the intricacies of early U.S. law, we leave with more qualifications than categorical claims—and a related recognition that often what looks like a political victory and an expansion of political rights, from one perspective, was, from another, a complicated renegotiation of abiding political divisions and inequalities.

From the beginning, white, propertied men loomed large in the U.S. legal imaginary. However, as with gender, unqualified characterizations of the whiteness of citizenship only partially capture the insistently gradated and changeable demarcations of legal personhood in the early United States. In several cases, racial constraints for suffrage were only introduced to state constitutions in their later amendments. In Tennessee, for example, the 1796 constitution declared, "Every free man of the age of twenty-one years and upwards, possessing a freehold in the county . . . shall be entitled to vote," but in 1835 the language was changed to "every free white man."[58] Similarly, in 1821 New York passed property qualifications for blacks but abolished them for whites, thus limiting black suffrage in practice.[59] By 1855 only five states admitted black suffrage.[60] Overall, the trend was not toward increasingly inclusive definitions of political membership but toward further restriction; and in this sense, the conceit that the historical practice of rights gradually caught up to the founding rhetoric of liberty is particularly misleading.[61] Legally speaking, the meaning of citizenship was actually more capacious in the early post-Revolutionary period, precisely because its limits had not yet been clearly established.

The belated introduction of racial formulations of suffrage bears emphasis on a number of levels. It belies the Whiggish narrative of citizenship—with its conceit of the progressive move toward increasingly inclusive political practices. It also offers a useful reminder of the incompleteness of the law as an index of political opinion. The comparatively inclusive scope of suffrage in these earlier state constitutions was consequential both practically and imaginatively, but the legal narrowing of suffrage cannot be neatly equated with a narrowing of public opinion. Rather, as abolitionist and women's rights movements gained momentum in the nineteenth century, some of the exclusions that had gone unspoken in the immediate aftermath of the Revolution were quickly losing self-evidence as both women and blacks availed themselves of privileges that they had not been denied, but had also not been positively granted. In this respect, what the law leaves unsaid is itself a valuable indication of broader assumptions at various moments in history.


## Thinking Sovereignty beyond Citizenship

In a limited sense, the Constitution's reticence about citizenship actually helped preserve and fuel the colloquial association of "citizen" with a nebulously idealized rights-bearing subject. With few clearly specified boundaries, "citizenship" was a uniquely capacious terminological cipher for the "whole rights of the people." However, as we have seen, Wilson's apparent faith in a shared understanding of citizenship was not particularly well founded. Being able to presume the designation "citizen" was certainly a good starting place, but in the era before the Fourteenth Amendment, citizenship was not yoked to a relatively unified set of juridical practices and privileges.

The residual continuities between citizenship and subjecthood were both structural and terminological. In the early United States, "citizen" was an essentially contested designation understood in an uneasy continuum with a range of divergent subject positions. Even if/when one was acknowledged as a citizen, it could mean different things—not only because of rapidly changing state policies, but because many commentators did not imagine citizenship as a *singular* category, but as a sliding scale with several "intermediary" forms. As one politician observed in a discussion of "colored suffrage" at an 1846 convention for revising the New York state constitution, there is "a strange disposition to overlook the existence of the conditions of extraneous alienage and the various stages of *quasi* citizenship intermediate between the condition of chattel slavery, and that of complete citizenship."[62] The very notion of "quasi citizenship" cuts against the ambiguously idealized "whole rights of the people" that Wilson had hoped to preserve. However, in some ways, the definitional reticence about citizenship created the conditions for the fractionalization of citizenship. In practice, the decentralized, presumptive usages of "citizen" in the law positioned citizenship as a sliding scale of legal personhood, unequally associated with fractional rights. As such, no rights safely could be taken for granted. Indeed, as Bates emphasized in 1862, even suffrage, the right that we now most closely associate with citizenship, was not consistently recognized as a right of *all* citizens.[63]

Ultimately, the problem with Wilson's idealized defense of the nonenumeration of rights was that it presumed a vernacular, commonsense understanding of citizenship, which as the subsequent years showed simply did not exist.[64] To be called a citizen was not in itself a meaningful admission of political agency. Nominal as its meaning was in the law, "citizen" named political obligations as well as privileges, duties as well as rights, and governmental coercion as well as protection. William Apess's *Indian Nullification of the Unconstitutional Laws of Massachusetts Relative of the Mashpee Tribe; or, The Pretended Riot Explained* (1835) is particularly instructive in this respect. In Apess's incisive account of the Massachusetts government's narrative strategies for quelling the Mashpee Revolt, he notes that when officials sought to "explain" the laws, they told the Mashpees "that merely declaring a law to be oppressive could not abrogate it; and that it would become us, as good citizens whom the government was disposed to treat well, to wait for the session of the Legislature and then apply for relief. (Surely it was either insult or wrong to call the Marshpees citizens, for such they never were, from the Declaration of Independence up to the session of the Legislature in 1834)."[65] Massachusetts officials incentivized obedience by presenting the spectacle of the government's benign disposition toward the would-be "good citizens," who just happened to be amid revolt. "Citizens" as used in response to the Mashpee Revolt indicates an unqualified expectation of compliance divested of the rights associated with political obligation in the reciprocal model of allegiance and protection described by Bates.

The nominal characterization of the Mashpee as "citizens," as Apess recognized, was a strategy of delegitimation that reframed the violent subjection of settler colonialism as a contingent promise of protection.[66] Apess's response to this imperial strategy was to advance a claim to a kind of dual citizenship, in which—as with the dual structure of the Comity Clause—the Mashpees would be "entitled to all Privileges and Immunities of Citizens in the several States" but would still preserve their political autonomy as a sovereign people. Apess's strategic comparison of the Mashpee Revolt to the Nullification Crisis of 1832—in which South Carolina invoked state sovereignty to justify its refusal of new federal tariffs—is crucial in this respect, because it allowed him to recast the Mashpee Revolt not as the breach of Massachusetts's law but as the fulfillment of the culturally resonant regional ideal of state sovereignty.[67] Revolt, as Apess knew, may be extralegal, but it was also a culturally idealized expression of political entitlement, which established rights through a refusal of unjust obligations. This claim to rights *without* obligation was no more reciprocal as a structure of allegiance than the model of top-down subjection it was used to counter. Yet reciprocity was not itself the goal within the tradition of rights by dissent that Apess invoked. Apess's primary gambit was to authorize the sovereignty of the Mashpee. Sovereignty, not citizenship, was the paradigmatic symbol of Native autonomy and political empowerment in the early United States. So although Apess and other Native writers occasionally drew upon the extralegal traditions of political authorization that Walker and other reformers regularly invoked, this book does not try to explain or assimilate indigenous arguments within the interpretative rubric of citizenship.

In the context of Native Americans' uniquely fraught skirmishes with the federal government in the early United States, citizenship was a uniquely problematic conceptual and legal rubric for political autonomy. In ways that differed markedly from its currency in abolitionist discourse, in struggles for Native sovereignty in the early United States, "citizen" was a structure of colonial subjection as well as a symbolic remedy to it. This double relation to citizenship began to shift over the course of the nineteenth century, both because citizenship gained new meaning in post–Civil War law and because the prospect of achieving a meaningful form of political sovereignty apart from the United States seemed increasingly unlikely as the nineteenth century advanced.

Seen from the perspective of early contests over indigenous sovereignty, it is little surprise that the doctrine of *jus soli* did not enjoy the same primacy in the early United States as it does today. As the Fourteenth Amendment's explicit exclusionary provision—"excluding Indians not taxed"—itself later registered, the notion of soil-based rights conjured a logic that lent itself to indigenous claims to sovereignty and later citizenship. The Fourteenth Amendment also delimited indigenous claims to citizenship through another more subtly phrased but consequential clause: by restricting citizenship to "persons . . . subject to the jurisdiction" of the United States, the Citizenship Clause formalized citizenship as a specialized form of subjection, in which U.S. governmental protection is purchased by ceding any claims to sovereignty *before* (or in the case of the higher law traditions discussed in the next two chapters, *above*, the United States).[68]

Native Americans had no clear statutory path to citizenship until the Indian Citizenship Act in 1924, more than half a century after the Fourteenth Amendment. And the Indian Citizenship Act was itself an ambivalent development. Considered from the perspective of the landmark 1831 Supreme Court case *Cherokee Nation vs. Georgia*—which subjected indigenous tribes to allegiance without protection by theorizing them as "domestic dependent nation[s]"—the legal recognition of Native Americans as "citizens" in 1924 was unquestionably a historic victory.[69] However, from the perspective of earlier defenses of tribal sovereignty, it also marked the foreclosure of a different form of political sovereignty.[70] This point bears emphasis because when we presume the monolithic desirability of citizenship in the early United States, we impose our own political fantasies on a period that was populated by many ways of envisioning political membership—not all of which measured the success of their political projects through the incorporative dream of citizenship.

## *Dred Scott* and the Retroactive Making of Citizenship

In the early United States, the cultural constitution of citizenship was a speculative artifact of narrative fabulation, not an interpretative hermeneutic of statutory law. Some of these fables were produced in courts and some in novels, tales, sermons, and instructional literature. Yet despite their generic range, these narratives of citizenship share with Bates's opinion an occasionally uncomfortable awareness of the invented character of the "citizen" they describe. To underline the far-reaching questions about citizenship that inspired Bates and others officials to look beyond the law to theorize citizenship, I close this chapter with a brief reexamination of Taney's decision in *Dred Scott vs. Sandford*. Taney's decision operates in a very different ideological register than Bates's opinion, but it too bears the pronounced traces of his own speculative reading practice.

The lynchpin of Taney's argument rests on his interpretation of the Declaration of Independence, a document that has a complex, antagonistic relation to legal tradition: both in relation to the British laws that it seeks to nullify by force of its invocation of higher law, and also in relation to the American political tradition it helped bring into being. For all of its political significance, the Declaration, as legal historians point out, "lacks the legal force of the law."[71] The extralegal status of the Declaration of Independence bears remark, but it is the way Taney reads the Declaration that I want to underline in closing. With no clear definition in the Declaration on which to ground his narrow definition of citizenship, Taney turns his interpretative focus from the text of the Declaration to the men who authored it. Taney's evidence for his claim that "it is too clear to dispute, that the enslaved African race were not intended to be included, and formed no part of the people" has little to do with the language of the Declaration. It comes instead from a twofold interpretative assumption: first, that the meaning of the Declaration lies in the intentions of its authors; second, that these intentions can be reliably determined on the basis of their actions.[72] Taney belabors this second gambit, explaining that the Declaration's framers "were great men—high in literary acquirements—high in their sense of honor," who were, as such, "incapable of asserting principles inconsistent with those on which they were acting."[73] As "literary" men, Taney suggests, the framers could be trusted to understand the meaning of their words, and as honorable men they could be trusted to act in ways that accorded with their convictions. Thus, Taney infers, they could not have intended "the people" to include "the negro race."[74] I underline the inferential, extratextual character of Taney's interpretation of the Declaration, because scholars regularly cite the opinion as the legal benchmark of citizenship without recognizing its vexed relationship to the legal history it purports to rehearse.[75]

Treating Taney's decision as speculative may seem deflationary, since we tend to associate the speculative power of fiction with its potential to disrupt and overthrow rigid systems of thought. Yet this recognition also levels the discursive playing field in a different way, because it identifies Taney's decision as one of many competing formulations of citizenship, none of which were self-evidently definitive in the early United States. Not all formulations of citizenship enjoy equal authority, of course. However, the disproportionate historiographical reliance on Taney's decision runs the risk of oversimplifying the history that it so concertedly retells. Impact and representativeness are two very different things. Taney's opinion was impactful, but it offers a very partial and somewhat skewed view of citizenship's erratic cultural and legal history in the preceding decades. Indeed, if we treat the racially inclusive scope of many of the early state constitutions as the definitional benchmark for citizenship, it is Taney's explicitly racialized decision that appears revisionary.

The absence of a clear constitutional definition of citizenship made it possible for abolitionists like Ohio representative Philemon Bliss to caricature Taney's decision as not only unjust but also "illegal"—as seen through the prescriptive lens of higher law. "This court is itself a democratic anomaly—a solecism," Bliss observed of Taney's opinion, because it "has overthrown the law of citizenship, and published pages of gross and illegal *dicta* upon the law of Slavery."[76] Bliss, though firmly entrenched within the legal system himself, adopts the extralegal paradigm of "higher law" to delegitimize Taney's decision. "I ordinarily feel bound to treat judicial opinions with respect, though they disagree with mine," Bliss remarks in a pointed re-writing of Taney, but "I can have no reverence for men merely as judges; and if they descend from their high calling as protectors of liberty and law, to become their betrayers."[77] Taney's decision incited outrage among abolitionists, who saw in it a failure of the law itself, as measured through the unwritten principles of a "higher law."

The two dissenting opinions in the *Dred Scott* case, delivered by Justices Benjamin Curtis and John McLean, are themselves instructive reminders of the Supreme Court's own fractured interpretation of the legal history of citizenship. In historian Christopher Tomlins's discussion of the dissenting opinions in *Freedom Bound* (2010), he draws a useful contrast that I would like to echo here but with significantly different emphasis. "Whereas Taney embraced a substantive citizenship filled with content protected by racial exclusivity," Tomlins writes, "McLean and Curtis were ready to distribute citizenship more widely while simultaneously depriving it of content." Tomlins identifies the *Dred Scott* case "as the convulsive climax and endpoint" of the racialized concepts of civic identity he discusses in the context of the colonization of the Americas, so for his purposes, what sets the dissenting opinions apart is less interesting than the different ways in which they too participate in the racialized logic that Taney openly embraces. Tomlins's emphasis on the flat, contentless meaning of "citizenship" in the dissenting opinions is insightful and illuminating, but it is also misleading to suggest that these opinions "*emptied* the concept of citizenship of virtually all substantive content."[78] As we have seen, "citizenship" did not yet have the legal content with which it is now associated, so to characterize these flat formulations of citizenship as a diminishment of its meaning is to retroactively give it a substantive juridical meaning it did not have. Understood in relationship to the nominal "citizen" examined in this chapter, we are left with another (equally disconcerting) realization: Taney played an active role in retroactively giving "citizenship" the substantive juridical meaning it holds today, and he did so by generalizing and reinforcing a racialized logic that was integral to chattel slavery and early naturalization laws but that had not yet been established as part of a broader centralized definition of citizenship.

To a degree, Taney was simply making explicit a racial logic that was there from the beginning. However, Taney's explication of the racial logic that haunted the formation of the juridical citizen marked a significant and consequential departure from the insistent vagaries of citizenship's early legal conceptualization—ambiguities that, once foreclosed, made it increasingly difficult for politicians and writers in the late 1850s and early 1860s to authorize racially inclusive interpretations of "citizenship" within the idiom of the law. Understood in relation to the broader arguments of this book, Taney's decision was doubly significant. It facilitated the law's increasing control over the meaning of "citizenship," and it marginalized abolitionist theorizations of citizenship by pushing them to the periphery of cultural practice. Yet because the case helped bind the legal meaning of "citizenship" to the precepts of chattel slavery, Taney's decision also added new political urgency to the alternate conceptions of "citizenship" developed in the "higher-law" traditions of citizenship examined in Chapters 2 and 3.

The historical and juridical intricacies of citizenship, as we have seen, do not lend themselves to sweeping generalizations. At various moments in time, simplified characterizations of inclusion and exclusion—such as the common abolitionist trope that analogized the bonds of marriage to the chains of slavery—have proven politically enabling and even necessary, catalyzing denizens to act collectively and with a sense of urgency.[79] However, as with Taney's opinion, similarly broad generalizations about the exclusionary history of citizenship also have foreclosed more inclusive models of political membership, for which there were and are coexisting juridical precedents. The loopholes in the juridical history of U.S. citizenship were not always intentional, and—as with women's suffrage in New Jersey—these political openings were often quickly closed in the years that followed. Still, as Attorney General Bates emphasized, in a legal culture beholden to the written law, these ambiguities and omissions were and are consequential. For this very reason, generalizations about the racial and gender makeup of the "citizen" function differently when they are framed in terms of our juridical past rather than our political present. U.S. law functions by way of historical precedent, so characterizations of the juridical past are never merely descriptive nor ideologically reparative. Positive law gains its authority from the legal past, which is grounded in a written Constitution in the United States. So even as we consider the most inegalitarian aspects of U.S. political history, it is worth being circumspect about how we characterize the legal history of citizenship, lest these generalized characterizations become naturalized futures.

There is, admittedly, no single panacea to the interpretative quandaries that surround the early usages of "citizenship." However, by grappling with its uneasy evolution from term to concept, we can bring a redoubled self-awareness to our own interpretative involvement in the retroactive making of citizenship. For, as with Bates, Taney, and Bliss, where we place our interpretative emphasis determines the broader field in which we "discover" citizenship's meaning. The speculative prehistory of citizenship thus has far-ranging methodological consequences that extend beyond the period covered in this book. Among other things, it dramatizes the fundamental limitations of originalist readings of the Constitution and of early U.S. political literature broadly understood. When we recognize that "citizenship" as we use it today and "citizenship" at is was used in the early United States do not name identical—and so interchangeable—models of political membership, the idea that we can recover its original meaning starts to look not only optimistic but also specious.[80]

The two dominant modes of originalism—original intent and original meaning—may locate the source of the Constitution's meaning in different expressive "agents" (the authors' intentions and the culturally recognized meanings of their words), but both share a common fantasy of interpretative neutrality in which the interpreter is, at least in theory, squarely outside the authorial sphere of meaning making.[81] The terminological and conceptual stability Originalism retroactively confers on early U.S. political thought is especially misleading when it comes to the prehistory of citizenship. Indeed, as we will see most dramatically in Chapter 2's examination of the expressly theological usages of "citizenship," when we look closely at the term's usages at various moments in time, we see something more profound than change over time—we realize we are looking at fundamentally different concepts.

# ⋆ II ⋆

## THE HIGHER LAWS OF CITIZENSHIP

# "Citizenship in Heaven"

## Biblical Exegesis and the Afterlife of Politics

> No man with a genius for legislation has appeared in America. . . .
> For eighteen hundred years, though perchance I have no right to
> say it, the New Testament has been written; yet where is the legis-
> lator who has wisdom and practical talent enough to avail himself
> of the light which it sheds on the science of legislation?
>
> —Henry David Thoreau, "Resistance to Civil Government" (1849)

THE U.S. CONSTITUTION is "Godless," as Isaac Kramnick and Laurence Moore memorably observe in their influential defense of the separation between church and state.[1] However, as this chapter shows, Christian theology and Protestantism, in particular, played an important role in the development of U.S. governance and citizenship both within the law and beyond it. Christian theology's importance for the cultural history of citizenship is evident as soon as we look beyond the textual limits of the Constitution. Unlike the federal Constitution, the early state constitutions are littered with references to an expressly Christian God.[2] Take the New Jersey Constitution of 1776. It prohibited the establishment "of any one religious sect," but it also restricted protection against religious discrimination to "Protestant inhabitant[s]," who could not be "denied enjoyment of any civil right, merely on account of his religious principles"—a caveat that effectively established Protestantism, in its varied forms, as the faith of the state and a precondition for full civil rights.[3] In similar fashion, Article XXXII of the 1776 Constitution of North Carolina stated that "no person, who shall deny the being of God or the truth of the Protestant religion, or the divine authority either of the Old or New Testaments . . . shall be capable of holding any office or place of trust or profit in the civil department within this State."[4] In the 1835 North Carolina constitutional convention, "Protestant" was replaced with "Christian," but religious faith in this slightly broadened form remained a requirement for holding public office.[5] Like North Carolina, the early Vermont and New Jersey constitutions both identified Protestantism as a requirement for holding public office.[6] These and a range of other religious provisos gave anti-Catholic, anti-Semitic, and anti-Islamic sentiments an explicit foothold in early laws governing state citizenship. The latter two groups were especially marginalized in the early state constitutions, in which "Christian" appeared far more frequently than "Protestant." Faith-based criteria for civil rights are relatively well-known. Yet as we will see they are simply the most visible, formal signs of Christian theology's broader role in shaping the early history of citizenship in the United States. To appreciate some of Christian theology's most profound and occasionally perplexing effects on the cultural evolution of citizenship, we need to look beyond the law to that Book of books: the Bible.

In an era in which the most substantive legal formulations of citizenship were confined to the local constitutions of individual states, the Bible offered a uniquely authoritative (and broadly applicable) textual touchstone for debates about citizenship. The Bible's role in shaping the heterogeneous meanings of citizenship in the early United States was both conceptual and idiomatic. In its modern usage, "citizen" is an official designation for political membership in the nation; its meaning is circumscribed by legal precedent and territorial borders.[7] However, in the period treated in this book, "citizenship" was regularly used to name forms of affiliation that were only tangentially related to the technical question of a person's status under the law. Indeed, one of the most pervasive uses of the word "citizen" in the late eighteenth and early nineteenth centuries concerned the spiritual membership of Christians in the kingdom of God, not the secular relation between individuals and the government. In addition to its varied significance as a term for membership in different governmental polities (the city, state, and nation), "citizen" routinely was used to describe religious fellowship in the heavenly city: *citizenship in heaven.*

The use of "citizen" to designate spiritual belonging in the heavenly kingdom dates back to the 1420s, which places the first theological usage of "citizen" less than a century after the word's earliest use as a designation for residence in a city.[8] However, the idiom of heavenly citizenship gained new prominence in the late eighteenth century through its printed circulation in modernized translations of the New Testament, which began to render a popular passage from Paul's Third Letter to the Philippians in the language of citizenship.[9] In an emblematic warning against a life enthralled in the appetites of the flesh, Paul exhorts the Philippians to lift their "minds" from "earthly things" to make themselves "conformable to his glorious body," because "we are *citizens* of heaven, from which we earnestly expect a savior, the Lord Jesus Christ."[10] Long rendered as "for our *conversation* is in heaven" in the standard King James Version, from roughly the 1790s onward modernized translations of the New Testament regularly turned to the language of "citizenship" to convey the otherworldly orientation of devout Christians.[11]

Paul's remarks epitomize the tradition of "Christian estrangement," the notion that true Christians are pilgrims and strangers in this world who must renounce worldly desires and attainments to ensure their spiritual passage to a heavenly home.[12] Christian estrangement, as crystallized in one of its proverbial formulations, takes as its central edict the notion that Christians "are to be in the world, but not of it."[13] For those who saw politics as quintessentially worldly (in the pejorative Christian sense of the word), Paul's call to heavenly citizenship was, by necessity, a call away from the distracting and ultimately fleeting concerns of the political life. Yet because "citizenship" was beginning to assume new significance through its transatlantic association with rights discourse in this period, the idiomatic turn to citizenship in post-Revolutionary recensions of Philippians 3:20—"But we are *citizens* of heaven" and "For our *citizenship* is in heaven"—made the theological promise of heavenly fellowship sound like a model for political membership rather than an alternative to it.[14]

In a period that witnessed the institutional separation of the church and the state, the circulation of the idiom of "citizenship in heaven" in revised Bibles, exegetical guides, sermons, and fiction suggestively fused Christian and republican thought at the level of terminology, even as it expressed an earlier sense of the incompatibility of these two realms. Although the precise legal significance of citizenship was exceptionally open-ended before the Civil War, the growing rhetorical identification of "citizen" with the rights tradition brought political resonance to even the most insistently theological uses of "citizenship." It was increasingly hard to speak of "heavenly citizenship" without evoking the question of political membership. As a result, the metaphor of heavenly citizenship no longer offered a relatively neutral (spatial) metaphor for spiritual comportment and ascension. It also carried freighted implications for contemporaneous debates about the political rights enjoyed by virtue of one's residence in the state and the nation. For these reasons, Philippians 3:20 provided a uniquely charged but also ambivalent textual touchstone for formulating the political implications that Christian theology held for "citizenship," terminologically, and also for the concept of political membership with which it is now all but synonymous. That the term "citizen" regularly was used in contradistinction to the concept of political membership offers an instructive reminder of the extraordinarily uneven fusion of these two discrete but interlocking aspects of the historical development of citizenship—aspects that were as yet erratically coupled in the early United States.

The theological usages of "citizen"—and the related doctrinal wariness of political pursuits—have never have been examined as an integral component of the cultural history of citizenship in the United States.[15] Nor is this oversight especially surprising given the secular bent of the legalistic framework within which citizenship is typically examined. Yet political membership does not encompass the full import of "citizenship." Politics is only one of the several arenas within which the language and concept of citizenship took on meaning. This chapter addresses this gap in the cultural history of citizenship. It uses its treatment of the theological usages of "citizenship" to reexamine the broader role that Christian theology played in shaping nascent formulations of political membership in the early United States.[16] After discussing the political and otherworldly forms of fellowship that the trope of heavenly citizenship conjured for readers in the early United States, the second half of this chapter explores the power and limitations of theological uses of "citizen" for abolitionist critique, and for two very different Christian abolitionists in particular: David Walker and Harriet Beecher Stowe.

The notion of citizenship that developed in and around modernized recensions of Philippians 3:20—and the broader discourse of Christian estrangement of which it is a part—offers important insight into some of the oft-noted peculiarities of citizenship. Among other things, it helps explain the ease with which "citizen"—which was primarily a designation of political belonging—became so closely associated with postures of political renunciation, most notably the right to refuse allegiance.[17] The extraordinary political power of disaffiliation in the early United States (the power of *choosing* to not belong), I argue, was fueled by Christian theology's idealization of worldly estrangement, as much as the more frequently discussed tropology of liberal individualism. By identifying heaven rather than the nation as the supreme home to which one owed allegiance, the tradition of Christian estrangement lent a distinctly oppositional framework to already ambivalent notions of political membership. Seen through the renunciatory ideal of religious devotion that Paul's passage articulates, politics is a fallen sphere of shortsighted contests whose losses and victories seem vain and trivial when viewed through the long *durée* of one's spiritual immortality. Compared to Christian theology's traditional *existential* wariness of worldly attachments, the modern institutional separation of church and state under the First Amendment appears relatively superficial.

As long as Christian theology remained one of the key textual and conceptual precedents for understanding "citizenship," it helped structure a deep-seated skepticism about the value of political membership. The tradi-

tion of Christian estrangement (and its complex exegetical link to citizenship) also helps illuminate the unique political currency of a common trope
in Christian abolitionism: the close tropological association between the
heavenly state and political egalitarianism—which finds one of its best-
known and most troubling expressions in the conclusion to Stowe's *Uncle
Tom's Cabin* (1852). When at the close of the novel the now-grown young
master George laments that he has come too late to "buy" Tom and "take
[him] home," Tom's often-quoted reply identifies heaven as a fatalistic alternative to political life in Kentucky. "The Lord's bought me, and is going to
take me home,—and I long to go. Heaven is better than Kintuck."[18] Heaven
in this passage does not provide a theological model for a more inclusive
form of political citizenship; it functions, instead, as a reparative substitute
for freedom in the here and now.[19] Passages that model this dangerous,
substitutionary logic have understandably made it difficult to appreciate
the political stakes of formulations of citizenship that hinge on narratives
about who "May be refin'd and join th'angelic train" (as enslaved poetess
Phillis Wheatley rendered the concept of heavenly fellowship).[20] To fully
understand the political efficacy and drawbacks of abolitionist invocations
of the trope of "citizenship in heaven," I argue, requires a careful attention
to the meaning it assumed within two distinct doctrinal traditions in the
early United States: Christian estrangement and Christian nationalism—a
domesticated and nationalized form of Christianity that identified the progress and development of the government with the realization of God's
kingdom on earth. As we already have begun to see, the world-wary episteme
of Christian estrangement has an ambivalent relation to political practice—
both because it idealizes tribulation as an occasion for faith and because it
understands these experiences as essentially temporary inconveniences.
However, the rise of Christian nationalism brought new political currency to
theological formulations of citizenship by reimagining the state as an exalted
corollary and *precursor* to "th'angelic train." As we will see, political commentators who successfully fused these two competing strains of Christian
thought were able to repurpose the otherwise merely fatalistic metaphor
of heavenly citizenship as a theological call to arms and reform.[21] Recast in
the materialist episteme of Christian nationalism, claims to citizenship
in heaven doubled as claims to political membership.

## Christian Estrangement

In a deeply religious culture with a still-nascent legal tradition and terminology, writers and political commentators were just as wont to invoke the

Bible as the Constitution to articulate and answer questions related to political membership and conduct.[22] In New York minister John Mason's *The Voice of Warning, to Christians* (1800), he marvels at the notion that politics and religion could be separated. "*Yet religion has nothing to do with politics!* Where did you learn this maxim? The bible is full of directions for your behavior as citizens."[23] Like many in the period, Mason saw the Bible as the definitive handbook on citizenship, but he also acknowledged the abiding temporal tension between political and theological fellowship. "[I]f our religion had had *more* to do with politics, if, in the pride of our *citizenship,* we had not forgotten our *Christianity:* if we had prayed more and wrangled less about the affairs of our country, it would have been infinitely better for us at this day."[24] Mason attributes the troubles of the young republic to an overinvestment "in the pride of our *citizenship,*" but his solution is not a categorical renunciation of the world of politics. Instead, he seeks to reprioritize these two realms, so that political citizenship is seen as a subordinate worldly precursor to a higher fellowship to come.

Mason's subtle subordination of the worldly realm that takes "pride" in political citizenship to a higher theological membership is crucial to his broader insistence that "[t]he bible is full of directions for your behavior as citizens." Mason retains a traditional apprehensiveness about the vanities of the worldly, but he is not calling for citizens to renounce their political interests altogether (as some interpreters of Philippians 3:20 did). Mason's insistence on the translatability of theological and political principles evinces his sympathies with the basic fantasy of Christian nationalism: the notion that the nation could (and should) reflect and realize God's kingdom on earth. However, unlike some of the better-known formulations of Christian nationalism, which invoked God's will to shore up state authority and imperial expansion, Mason's attachment to a godly state leads him to be more critical of it. The moderated form of Christian nationalism modeled in Mason's pamphlet reflects its refracted debt to the world-wary episteme of Christian estrangement, whose residual influence in the early United States remains underappreciated.

Mason's insistence on the religious foundation of citizenship came with an agenda: the delegitimation of Thomas Jefferson's campaign for the presidency.[25] For Mason, the election of an "unbeliever in the scripture," as he described Jefferson, was a troubling symptom of a broader "war upon revelation" and "against the miraculous *facts* of the scripture."[26] Mason's pamphlet did not prevent Jefferson's election, of course, but unlike most campaign pamphlets it continued to hold interest for readers well after its targeted objective had failed. *Voice of Warning* was reprinted and anthologized late into the nineteenth century, under a revised title that announced its engagement with a topic that gained new layers of relevance in the years to follow: "Politics and Religion."[27] In these later editions, the cultural currency of Mason's polemic had less to do with Jefferson, the man, than with its disputation of one of the broader tenets associated with Jeffersonian republicanism: the so-called "wall of separation between church and state," as Jefferson most famously construed the import of the First Amendment's Establishment Clause.[28]

Neither Jefferson's election nor disestablishment marked the diminishment of theology's cultural power in the early United States. Instead, as religious historians have stressed, Jefferson's election coincided with a revival in religiosity and a new wave of reflections about the relationship between religion and politics.[29] This resurgence is not itself surprising. In some sense, disestablishment's structural separation of church and state actually facilitated newly integrated forms of religiosity. By separating the mandates of Christian theology and political governance, disestablishment arguably made it easier for Americans to see themselves as both Christians and citizens. Disestablishment did not itself resolve the long-standing tensions between heavenly and political affiliation. Instead, it enabled new varieties of religiosity and secularism alike.[30]

The entangled fate of politics and Christian theology took many forms in the early republic: from millenarian visions and world-wary Christians, to the doctrine of manifest destiny and the persistence of forms such as the "American Jeremiad" that linked "social criticism to spiritual renewal."[31] The Bible proved pivotal to ongoing sectional debates, but there was remarkably little agreement about its implications for the institution of slavery.[32] Both the North and the South, as Abraham Lincoln famously reflected in his Second Inaugural Address (1865), "read the same Bible and pray to the same God, and each invokes His aid against the other."[33] For Christian nationalists like Lincoln, the problem of interpreting the Bible was *how* it applied to ongoing political debates—not *if* its doctrines were political in nature. Yet for others who retained an Augustinian skepticism of any apparent correlation between worldly prosperity and spiritual salvation, the latter question was crucial since theology's purchase was supposed to be heavenly, not temporal.[34]

For the most politically wary, it remained unclear if one could be both a good Christian and a good citizen, since true religious piety seemed to require the renunciation of politics as a worldly and materialistic enterprise. Thus in an 1840 sermon on "American Politics," Connecticut Reverend Horace Bushnell took the "history of Christ's trial and crucifixion" as an exemplary scene of politics.[35] Not surprisingly, given his subject matter, Bushnell's conclusions were far from encouraging. "The public mind," he observes, "is so deeply absorbed in the politics of the country, that we can hardly get a hearing for the more spiritual truths of the Gospel" ("AP," 189). Bushnell emphatically rejects the presumption that "democracy is holy," recalling that it was a "high majority" that swayed Pilate to crucify Christ ("AP," 200). Bushnell expresses a common anxiety about majoritarian rule, shared by Alexis de Tocqueville and Henry David Thoreau: that it privileges force over right. However, for Bushnell the problem is fundamental to politics as such, whatever form it takes. In a dramatic conclusion, Bushnell exclaims, "Under any and all forms of government you will have unholy work; for man is unholy, your king is unholy, your democracy is unholy, full of mischiefs, treacheries, cruelties and lies" ("AP," 200). Bushnell's conviction that politics leads "our moral habits . . . into an abyss of irreligion" was relatively extreme ("AP," 190). However, his characterization of the fallen nature of politics highlights vestigial tensions between religious and political affiliation that persisted alongside the rise of Christian nationalism.

The idea of the United States as a "Christian nation" is so familiar that it is easy to miss the conceptual problematic that the discourse of Christian nationalism sought to resolve: the basic tension between the traditionally post-worldly purview of theology and the temporal ends of governance. This tension is elided in the nationalistic emplotment of secularization. As a principal of periodization, the American Revolution often serves a double function in scholarship: it is seen not only as a decisive turning point in American political history, but one that marks the emergence of a newly secular understanding of time. With the political founding of the United States, it is often assumed, came a new investment in the temporal domain of everyday, civic life—and a gradual rejection of the eschatological strain of early American theology (its obsession with final things, the time *after* time). Yet this eschatological zeal had much more residual force in the early United States than critics have acknowledged, and it underwrote a range of ambivalent ways of envisioning the relationship between the individual and the state.[36]

Depictions of the conjoined fate of Christianity and America were prevalent in the early United States, but they were neither unchallenged nor unequivocal. As Pennsylvania theologian John Nevin warned in an 1853 baccalaureate address, "The spirit of the age is always at war in reality with the actual truth of things, as we find this exhibited in the Gospel and in the Church; there is a necessary contradiction between this world (the present *seculum*) and the Kingdom of God."[37] This Augustinian presumption of a discordance between religious and civic experience presented Christians with a predicament. As an article reprinted in *The Millennial Harbinger* the same year put it, inasmuch "as a heavenly mind can find no rest short of God, to it there is no external world. . . . The child of God has ascertained that all is enchantment. He is divorced from earth. His *citizenship is in heaven*. He is a stranger and pilgrim here. He is in the world, but not of it."[38] Within these terms, any sense of civic or worldly affiliation appears at best delusory and at worse bespeaks an excessive, unchristian materialism. This either/or logic—engaged citizen *or* expectant Christian—was precisely what Christian nationalism tried to overcome by proclaiming a special convergence between being Christian and being American.[39]

Despite the growing appeal of Christian nationalism, scriptural devaluations of worldly affiliation persisted in the early United States—providing a uniquely decisive language for critiquing extant political and legal conventions. The Bible offered plentiful narrative figures for the antislavery cause—the exodus of the Israelites, the blessedness of the poor, the redemptive character of worldly suffering, and emancipation during the year of jubilee, to name only a few. Indeed, the gospel itself, according to an 1843 book on Christian citizenship, "comes to enrich the poor, to strengthen the feeble, to comfort the afflicted, to relieve the oppressed, to let the captive go free." The gospel, it continues, "would impart all the elements of the best regulated self-government; forming *that* constitution where men may say we are 'free indeed.' Here it would equalize all mankind in the hopes and sympathies of Christ; raise the entire family of our race to the citizenship of heaven."[40]

Christian estrangement offered moral vindication to oppressed groups, above and beyond the exclusionary practices of the state. In this capacity, Christianity offered both personal solace and a culturally entrenched rationale for abolitionism. As Vermont-born missionary Hollis Read remarked in 1856, "There seems to have been among the slave population of our country a singular susceptibility to religious impression."

> Or, to speak more correctly, the Blessed Comforter seems to have compassioned their lowly and oppressed condition, and especially to have favored them with his merciful visitations.
>
> Probably so large a proportion of no other class of our people have, within the same time, been made partakers of the consolation of religion and *gained a title to a free citizenship in heaven*.[41]

According to this compensatory model of salvation, the oppressed condition of slaves in the world is precisely what ensures their "title" to heavenly citizenship.

Not surprisingly, the trope of the theological benefits of political estrangement is prominent in early black Atlantic literature, whose distinctly

Christian formulation of the project of emancipation was deeply inflected by the competing values that Christian "citizenship" so often named. Within the compensatory model of salvation, worldly tribulation is a harbinger of fortune in the life to come. It is thus that James Gronniosaw, the enslaved African prince, embraces his reversal of fortune with such strange zeal in his 1772 slave narrative. "I who, at home, was surrounded and guarded by slaves . . . have been inhumanely threatened with death . . . yet I never murmured, nor was I discontent. I am willing, and even desirous to be counted as nothing, a stranger in the world, and a pilgrim here; for 'I know that my Redeemer liveth,' and I am thankful for every trial and tribulation that I've met with, as I am not without hope that they will all be sanctified to me."[42] The rhetoric of religious pilgrimage returns at the end of Gronniosaw's narrative, where he explicitly links the predicament of worldly estrangement to the promise of heavenly belonging. "As Pilgrims, and very poor Pilgrims, we are travelling through many difficulties towards our Heavenly Home, and waiting patiently for this gracious call."[43] The politically inflected formulation of the compensatory model of theological redemption that Gronniosaw invokes works on two different levels. It offers consolation in the here and now for those who are "counted as nothing" in the political systems in which they live. Yet it also serves as a moral rebuke to those who were responsible for this suffering. For, even if suffering could be counted as a virtue for those who endure it, it certainly did not follow that it is virtuous to occasion the suffering of others.

Christian estrangement's insistent disarticulation of material and spiritual gains invites a peculiar assumption: that worldly estrangement is requisite for religious devotion. Political and theological forms of affiliation, in these terms, appear not only divergent but also potentially incompatible. This tension was by turns generative and fatalistic for abolitionist formulations of citizenship. The exalted rhetoric of Christian estrangement promised the imminent salvation of the enslaved, even as it often identified theology and death—rather than political action—as the means of ensuring liberty. Within this negative paradigm, heavenly citizenship made one's actual political status (whether citizen, slave, or alien) relatively inconsequential, but it also made the feeling of estrangement a privileged expression of theological fellowship. As a result, those who were actively excluded from the body politic could appear better situated for salvation than those in more eminent positions.

The renunciative ethos of Christian estrangement shaped basic assumptions about the ends and meaning of political membership. It had profound ramifications within and beyond abolitionism. As discussed in Chapter 1, the "right to refuse allegiance" (to borrow Thoreau's famous phraseology) did not have a solid foundation in early U.S. law prior to the 1868 Expatriation Act.[44] However, it did resonate deeply with many tenets in Christian theology and with the culture of Protestantism in particular. As once transcendentalist Orestes Brownson observed in an insightful 1846 review published shortly after his conversion to Catholicism, "the essential mark or characteristic of Protestantism is, unquestionably, *dissent.*"[45] Transcendentalism's investment in private judgment and its skepticism of external authority, Brownson argued, was not an idiosyncratic "'Yankee notion,' confined to a few isolated individuals in a little corner of New England"; it was "as rife in one section of our country as another," because "at bottom, it is nothing but the fundamental principle of the Protestant Reformation itself."[46] Brownson's conversion to Catholicism made him increasingly less sympathetic to the culture of dissent that Protestantism helped normalize. However, Brownson's early involvement in transcendentalism left him well attuned to romantic philosophy's deep-seated and complex debt to the tradition of Protestant dissent.

Christian estrangement and liberal political philosophy share a common renunciative impulse. Whereas the dream of liberty forged in liberal political philosophy places the individual in an antagonistic relation to the government, Christian estrangement fosters a more unqualified antipathy toward the worldly. Liberal political philosophy channeled the renunciative imperatives of Christian theology in order to present disaffiliation as a political good, but as we will see in Chapter 4, the virtue associated with Christian estrangement did not translate very well into the other extralegal traditions of citizenship. Rejecting the world to embrace God was one thing, but it was harder to defend renunciation when it seemed to serve individual self-interest or the autotelic pleasures of the literary imagination.

Christian estrangement was not always formulated in explicitly political terms, but when it was, it took on many of the characteristics typically associated with liberal individualism. To note one especially illustrative motif in the exegetical literature of Philippians 3:20, commentators often narrated heavenly citizenship in the politicized framework of expatriation and emigration. Unlike defenses of the right expatriate, the imperative of Christian estrangement was not to exchange one political allegiance for another, but rather to renounce all politics as such. For example, in "May Christians Be Politicians?"—a British editorial piece published in 1868, a few months after the U.S. Congress officially recognized the right to expatriate—the writer explains that one can "only become a French citizen by renouncing his English citizenship. So, if we have citizenship in heaven, we are to give up citizenship on earth." The author valorizes this global expatriation from the earthly by invoking the classic tropology of Christian estrangement, explaining that since Christians "are to be 'strangers and pilgrims,'" "[a]ll entanglement in politics is unnecessary, and so hinders spiritual life."[47]

In another politically deflationary twist on the metaphor of heavenly expatriation, *The Better Land; or, The Christian Emigrant's Guide to Heaven* (1853), the author presents "emigration" to heaven as an alternative to political emigration in the here and now. Written by a Yorkshire Evangelical reverend in response to the "popular excitement of the age on the subject of EMIGRATION," *The Better Land* identifies heavenly citizenship as the virtuous remedy for "the restless millions" who are "affected with a kind of a mania for the "gold regions of California."[48] Even if the United States had come to be seen as a New Jerusalem, *The Better Land* cautions, its allegorical and economic appeal should not distract Christians from their ultimate pilgrimage to the Celestial City.[49] According to the fatalistic logic of *The Better Land,* because "we have no continuing city here," we should "emigrate at once from the Spiritual Egypt to the Celestial Canaan."[50] The political lesson of Christian estrangement was not always as fatalistic as this compensatory guide to heavenly emigration would have it. However, the very notion of a "better land" expressed otherworldly aspirations that haunted even the most insistently reform-oriented formulations of heavenly citizenship.

As we have seen, commentators who invoked the trope of heavenly citizenship often explored its political connotations, but the conclusions they reached varied considerably. The trope was invoked to support more inclusive definitions of citizenship and, on the other extreme, to suggest that heavenly citizenship could only be obtained by relinquishing political membership. As with any form of textually mediated form of political interpretation, the ideological tenor of exegetical arguments has as much to do with the frustrations and ambitions of the interpreter as with the text. As a result, exegesis and biblical translation are sensitive registers of the individual and collective histories of which they are part. With this attention to the barometrical quality of exegesis as a process of cultural transcription in mind, the next section tracks the phraseological evolution of "citizenship in heaven."

## Idiomatic Revolutions

In the page adjacent to Philippians 3:20 in Unitarian minister and writer Edward Everett Hale's personal copy of the Bible, he wrote "v.20 'conversation'" and then scrawled "πολίτευμα" [*politeuma*]—the Greek word long rendered as "conversation" and, eventually, as "citizenship."[51] The scare quotes around 'conversation,' coupled with Hale's recourse to the original Greek, suggest his puzzlement at the translation. Hale was not alone in his confusion. For nineteenth-century readers, "conversation" increasingly seemed to be "an unhappy translation" of Paul's passage, in part because the meaning of conversation had itself changed.[52] As Alexander Campbell remarked in the preface to his 1826 edition of the New Testament, during the reign of King James "[t]he term conversation . . . signified what a person *did*; it now denotes what a person says. Then it was equivalent to our word *behavior,* but now it is confined to what proceeds from the lips."[53]

While "conversation" had lost its tie to conduct, the term "citizenship" encompassed the dual activities of the "political realm," which as Hannah Arendt would later argue "rises out of acting together, 'the sharing of words and deeds.' "[54] But whereas for Arendt, citizenship "denoted all kinds of active engagement in the things of *this world,* " the literalist tendencies of nineteenth-century exegesis tended to naturalize Paul's metaphor of theological affiliation such that citizenship inhered in one's comportment toward the *otherworldly* kingdom, rather than one's current standing in the body politic.[55] Within this framework, the Bible, rather than legislation, appeared as the principal textual authority for good citizenship. According to an 1848 treatise on the duties of Christian citizens, as "citizens of the heavenly world," "we are governed by its laws in contradistinction from those of any earthly community."[56] To take the newly politicized translation of Paul's remarks seriously required at least entertaining the possibility that religion and politics were not twinned enterprises but antithetical commitments.

The major translations of the Bible that preceded the King James Version—the unauthorized Wycliffe's Bible (1382), the Tyndale Bible (1534), and the Catholic Douay–Rheims (1582)—had either used "conversation" or, in the case of Wycliffe, "living" in the stead of "citizenship" (see the Appendix). However, the association of citizenship with Paul's letter was not itself unprecedented. Indeed, for the select individuals familiar with the Greek word that conversation/citizenship each translates, *politeuma* (the origin for the term "politics"), the political resonance of the passage was apparent from the beginning. "Citizenship" was closer to the original Greek word, *politeuma,* but it had also taken on new significance when these translations of the Bible appeared in the late eighteenth century. The debates surrounding the revolutions in America, France, and Haiti recast the "citizen," as not merely a *resident,* but a fictive personage of rights. To speak of "citizenship in heaven," in this context, did more than evince the elasticity and pervasiveness of republican concepts. It organized the political significance of citizenship—the "reciprocal obligation" of allegiance and protection[57]—in the extended extra-political *durée* of eschatology: death, judgment, heaven, and hell.[58] In this sense, modernized recensions of Philippians 3:20 located "citizenship" within a traditional theological framework, even as they reinvented theological concepts in an increasingly politicized idiom.

The surge of biblical and exegetical uses of "citizenship" in the 1790s made Christian theology's ambivalent implications for political member-ship newly visible at a moment in which the meaning of "citizenship" was itself rapidly evolving. The first Bible in which the modernized recension of Philippians 3:20 appeared, Gilbert Wakefield's 1791 translation of the New Testament, was published in London just two years after the French Declaration of the Rights of Man and of the Citizen (1789), which argu-ably did more than any other document in this period to yoke the term "citizen" to the growing discourse about the liberal rights-bearing sub-ject.[59] In and of itself, the cultural impact of Wakefield's translation was not as definitive as the French declaration. However, each marked an important turning point in the terminological development of "citizenship" that played out in a much wider body of political and religious writing in the following decades. One identified political empowerment and rights as core principles of citizenship, while the other turned its gaze away from the sphere of political action to the prospect of religious belonging in the immaterial and necessarily speculative sphere of the heavenly kingdom.

Wakefield's translation was highly lauded. At least two charitable London organizations sought to reprint his "new and accurate Translation of the New Testament" at their own expense.[60] Wakefield agreed, but a previous arrangement he made with his bookseller on publishing the second edition combined with other obstacles to frustrate subsequent efforts to obtain an even larger audience for Wakefield's translation.[61] The circulation of Wakefield's edition was relatively limited. However, the second London edition was reprinted in the United States in 1820, and it also was widely cited in the modernized recensions of the Bible that began to proliferate in the nineteenth century.[62] "For our citizenship is in heaven" ultimately be-came the new phraseological standard. It was incorporated into the English Revised Version (1881), which served as the basis of the American Standard Version Bible (1901).[63]

The complex entanglement of theological and political models of affili-ation that the modernized recension of Paul's passage increasingly seemed to name in the tumultuous era of citizenship's modern birth was not merely idiomatic. At least two of the translators who first used this phraseology in historic new translations of the Bible did so with a keen appreciation of the political connotations of "citizenship."[64] Wakefield's 1791 New Testament is not the only written record of his engagement with Philippians 3:20. He uses "citizenship" to gloss *politeuma* in a 1781 letter that uses this phraseology to frame his interpretation of Paul's characterization of Hagar, Sarah's Egyptian "bondwoman," in Galatians. "Hagar corresponds to the present earthly Jerusalem, which is in bondage with her children, the Jews. . . . But Jerusalem, which is above (i.e. the heavenly Jerusalem) is the free woman. . . . [Paul] says elsewhere, our πολιτευμα, our citizenship, is in heaven; and on the one side you have the bond-woman, and the earthly Jerusalem; on the other the free woman, and the heavenly Jerusalem."[65] As applied to Galatians by Wakefield, the "our" of Philippians 3:20 is not an inclusive category but a differential one. Heavenly citizenship, according to Wakefield, is a privilege enjoyed by "free women" but denied to the "bond-woman." Wakefield clearly understood heavenly citizenship in relation to worldly forms of freedom, but unlike abolitionist applications of this trope, for Wakefield, heavenly citizenship is not idealized as an inclusive alternative to political hierarchies in the here and now. Instead, in this letter, heavenly citizenship is a realm of spiritual belonging that is accessible only to those who already enjoy the material privileges of worldly freedom.

This passage in Galatians was not always interpreted through the phraseology of Philippians 3:20, but it encapsulates a way of envisioning freedom that assumed special definitional salience in the United States, where the cultural value of citizenship was consistently envisioned negatively against the backdrop of numerous forms of disenfranchisement and marginalization: indigeneity, alienage, slavery, and coverture (to name just a few). Seen through the lens of Wakefield's epistolary reflections, it is little surprise that Galatians became a touchstone for proslavery apologists, who interpreted Hagar's bondage—as well as her son Ishmael's disinheritance—as biblical corollaries to the institution of chattel slavery in the United States. As proslavery apologists were keen to emphasize, Sarah and Hagar's respective conditions as freewoman and bondswoman were passed down to their sons conceived with Abraham: when Sarah gives birth to Isaac, Hagar and her son, Ishmael (who is Abraham's firstborn), are cast into the wilderness. In the hands of proslavery apologists, Hagar and Ishmael were proofs of a divinely sanctioned and uncrossable divide that separated citizens and slaves on the basis of matrilineal descent. Unlike the abolitionist invocations of heavenly "citizenship" to which we will soon turn, for proslavery advocates slavery and citizenship were divine destinies, not worldly circumstances.[66]

Modernized recensions of Philippians 3:20 flourished on both sides of the Atlantic. And the concept it names is not only extra-national, but also

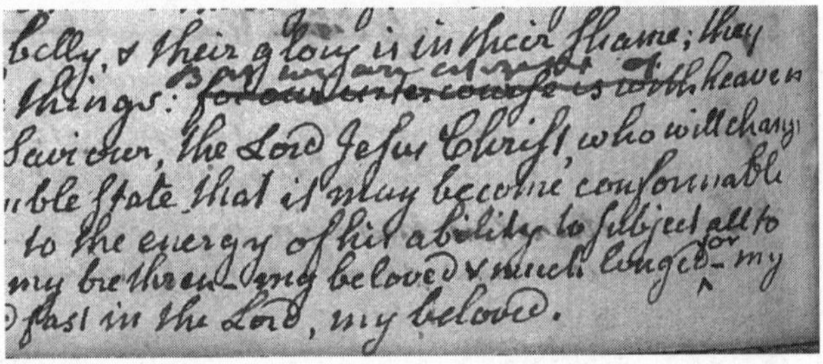
belly, & their glory is in their shame; they
things: But we are citizens of for our intercourse is with heaven
Saviour, the Lord Jesus Christ, who will chang
uble state that it may become conformable
to the energy of his ability to subject all to
my brethren my beloved & much longed for my
fast in the Lord, my beloved.

FIGURE 1. Philippians 3:20 from Charles Thomson's 1808 New Testament translation, Charles Thomson Papers, Coll. 658. Historical Society of Pennsylvania, Philadelphia.

post-worldly. Yet the language of "citizenship in heaven" took on ambivalently localized connotations in the early United States, where the word "citizen" enjoyed a quasi-sacral political status. The modernized recension of Philippians appeared in the first version of the Bible translated and published in the United States, *The Holy Bible, Containing the Old and New Covenant* (1808). Translated by former secretary of the Continental Congress Charles Thomson, and doubly notable as the first English translation of the Greek *Septuagint, The Holy Bible* is an important transitional translation that is uniquely illustrative of the political conditions that informed revised translations of Paul's letter in this period. Thomson's rendition of Philippians 3:20–21 echoes the wording of Wakefield's 1791 translation, but its phraseology was not a foregone conclusion.[67] In the manuscript of Thomson's Bible, he initially translated the passage as "for our intercourse is with heaven . . ." and then crossed it out and wrote, "But we are citizens of" above the line in lighter ink (see Figure 1).[68] Considering Thomson's involvement in the Continental Congress, the final phrasing seems all the more deliberate. As a recent hyperspectral study of the Declaration of Independence confirms, "citizens" was not the presumed designation of the colonists but one self-consciously assumed in the stead of "subjects."[69] If Jefferson's substitution of "citizens" for "subjects" had accented an exigent claim for political autonomy, Thomson's revision alternately presented "citizenship" as the *timeless* condition of all Christians. Thomson's fusion of republican and Christian thought changed each in the process, evincing the conceptual muddiness engendered by the "incarnation of the church into popular culture" that Nathan Hatch terms the "democratization of American Christianity."[70]

What makes Thomson's Bible political is not only that it chooses the term "citizens" over the more generic words "conversation" and "intercourse," but also the underlying commitment, which it bespeaks, to making the Bible accessible to a new generation of readers. Thomson's *The Holy Bible* literalized the democratizing potential of new biblical translations in its very form, by proffering mass availability over the physical and economic markers of prestige. For although Thomson initially intended to publish his translation in the relatively expensive and cumbersome form of a quarto, Thomas Jefferson persuaded him to dispense with English bookselling conventions and release it as an octavo since "the *bulk of readers* generally wait" for this format anyway.[71] The distribution of the Bible, as Jefferson's comment suggests, was a democratic value in itself. Thomson may not have been the first to render Philippians 3:20 as "we are citizens of heaven," but this language assumed a newly reflexive relevance in a Bible self-consciously conceived for a culture that sacralized both the rhetoric and the precepts of democracy.

Thomson's revised translation of the New Testament was part of a much larger scriptural revolution in the United States that was directly enabled by the American Revolution. Before the Revolution, the Colonies were subject to the British Crown's royal copyright, which granted the Crown exclusive right to publish the King James Version—and in so doing restricted the publication of the Scriptures in the British colonies. In this respect, as Paul Gutjahr argues in a groundbreaking account of the production history of the Bible in America, the political independence of the United Colonies turned United States also affected a new degree of religious independence, at least when it came to the translation and printing of the Word.[72] Translators and printers took full advantage of this new exegetical liberty. A staggering 1,238 new editions of the Bible were introduced in the United States between 1777 and 1880—including thirty-five new translations of the Bible.[73]

The printed diversification of the Bible did not immediately dislodge the cultural authority of the King James Version. Amid this seismic scriptural shift, the KJV continued to enjoy a disproportionate reign over the phraseological authority of the printed Word. Indeed, as religious historian Mark Noll has noted, "fully 90% of the separate 1,784 separate editions of Scripture published in America from 1776 to 1865 were of the King James Version."[74] The impressive staying power of the KJV has made it easy for scholars to underestimate the cultural impact of these new editions.[75] One result of this monolithic flattening of the Bible into one coherent text is that the variant phraseologies of passages like Philippians 3:20 remain largely unexplored avenues for understanding the impact of the Bible on early United States politics and on citizenship in particular.

Scholars are used to treating the Bible as a site of cultural and political conflict, but we tend to frame this heterogeneity in terms exogenous to the text itself—as if readers were invariably the "authors" of these divergent meanings. Yet as the surge of new editions and translations of the Bible in the early United States instructively reminds us, the interpretative selectivity that shapes individual moments of biblical exegesis was further conditioned by phraseological and textual variations endogenous to the printing and transmission of the Bible. Non-KJV editions did not dominate the marketplace numerically, but the endogenous heterogeneity they introduced had much broader ripple effects. "In attempting to woo buyers and readers to their bible editions," Gutjahr argues, "American publishers helped erode the timeless, changeless aura surrounding 'the Book,' by making it 'the books.'"[76] New translations, I would stress, effected a similar but more local displacement—replacing "the Word" with "words." The proliferation of competing translations of the Bible decentered the King James Version on a phraseological level, and the idiomatic variations between them dramatized, in the most material way, the Book's mediated relationship to the Word of God. In this way, the onslaught of new editions and translations of the Bible fundamentally changed the theological and cultural status of the Word.

The phraseological heterogeneity of the Bible bears redoubled emphasis in any discussion of Christian theology's role in shaping debates about citizenship and slavery in the early United States, because it complicates a familiar understanding of the difference between abolitionist and proslavery readings of the Bible. In a concise formulation of a relatively common way of understanding the Bible's role in debates about slavery, religious historian Mark Noll observes, "Proslavery advocates had largely succeeded in winning the Bible, when taken in its traditional sense," but abolitionists who did not "abandon the Bible" altogether appealed to its "spirit" to challenge proslavery arguments that relied on literalistic readings of specific passages.[77] Noll's characterization is apt, in many respects. The Bible's several references to slavery certainly made it a challenging political resource for exegetically minded abolitionists. However, these interpretative tendencies also highlight the unique political currency of Philippians 3:20 for abolitionism: "citizenship in heaven" provided reformers with a quasi-literalistic formulation of the political rewards of being Christian.

While there was little consensus about what "citizenship in heaven" meant, the debate over its meaning helps illuminate why Christian nationalism was more appealing to some individuals than others. By understanding the nation as a material incarnation of God's kingdom, Christian nationalism tended to affirm the established order, tacitly equating an individual's social and spiritual standing. Christian nationalism's circular logic lent legitimacy to those satisfied with both the state of the nation and their standing within it. In contrast, the Augustinian distrust of any apparent correlation between the earthly and heavenly city was uniquely suited to the exoneration of exiled and persecuted Christians—the group for whom *The City of God* was itself originally intended.[78] For Christian nationalists, who were invested in the dream of realizing heaven on earth, formulations of the heavenly city and its citizenry had immediate and pressing political implications. It was this fantastic promise of a heaven on earth that continued to bring Christian abolitionists back to the vexed trope of heavenly citizenship.

## Theological Common Sense

"Citizenship in heaven" was only one phraseological thread of a broader scriptural revolution. However, it was uniquely politically charged, and it also helps to bring into focus Christian theology's complex and often ambivalent role in shaping the early cultural imagination of "citizenship." To get at theology's peculiar relation to the aspirational formulations of citizenship that this book collectively discusses in terms of the "political subjunctive," I want to momentarily shift our focus from the word "citizen" to a grammatical peculiarity evident in some (but not all) of the theological uses of "citizen." According to an 1851 London article entitled "The Bible, Our True Magna Charta," "If ever the slaves there [in the United States] are free, it will be the Son who makes them free, even socially and politically." For "[w]hilst formerly men said, *I am a citizen*—a defense from which slaves and others were excluded—now we are to say, *I am a man,* even though a slave, and ought to be a citizen, for God has provided me a citizenship in heaven."[79] Part of the value of theological models of citizenship, as this passage suggests, is that they provided a clear alternative to the convention-bound structure of positive law. Positive law is circumscribed by history and convention, so its reparative scope is rather narrow: it provides a system for redressing political grievances that involve incursions against persons whose legal rights have been recognized in the past, but it does little for those who cannot readily claim "citizenship" in the simple indicative: "I *am.*" The "ought" of political reform seeks to override the perpetuity of such descriptors—which project political conditions forward based on historical conventions. To give these aspirations the rhetorical force of necessity, higher law critics presented the "oughts" of reform not as change, but as the fulfillment of transcendent (post-empirical) indicatives: the higher truths of Christian theology and nature. The grammatical peculiarity of higher law formulations of citizenship, in this respect, is that their ostensibly reparative claims of what "ought" to be depend on aspirational reconstructions of what already "is."[80]

Heavenly citizenship's powerful fusion of the *is* and the *ought* bespeaks the unique status of theological imaginaries within the broader category of the political subjunctive. The oddly literalistic figure of heavenly citizenship created a rhetorical bridge between subjunctive and indicative states of belonging—a grammatical achievement whose political enactment is the basic ambition of reform-directed politics. While all genres of the political subjunctive seek to move beyond speculation and toward the material realization of the possibilities they envision, theology—which addresses itself to the unseen and the unseeable—is a special case, because the higher truths it envision are post-empirical, but they are not (strictly speaking) fictive. Heaven may be counterfactual in an empirical sense, but for believers it is no less real for its nonmateriality. These grammatical distinctions might seem abstract, but they get at the heart of the special possibilities Christian theology presented for political critique in the early United States: Christian theology's epistemic skepticism toward the worldly carried within it the potential to fundamentally interrogate and critique the basic fabric of reality, upon which all political conventions depend.

Few writers were able to channel Christian theology's skepticism toward the worldly without seeming to undercut the temporal priorities of political reform in the process. Freeborn black abolitionist David Walker's *Appeal to the Coloured Citizens of the World* (1829) stands as a notable exception. Walker's *Appeal* is known for its polemical militancy and for the extraordinary panic that it inspired among officials, who feared that its emancipatory pronouncements would spread dissent and insurrection. The militancy of Walker's *Appeal* sets it apart from the more familiar conventions of Christian abolitionism, discussed in subsequent sections, but its very exceptionality is useful for my purposes here because it brings into focus ways of understanding citizenship that Christian abolitionism helped to advance, but which it did not always realize so successfully. The rhetorical power of Walker's *Appeal,* I will argue, lies in its critique of historical practice and its interrelated lionization of what we might think of as a "theological common sense," a set of habits for understanding the world, politics, and language that are anchored in the transcendent, immaterial truths of Christian theology.[81]

"Do you understand your own language?" Walker rebukes after quoting the Declaration of Independence at length in *Appeal.*[82] In case we do not—and have failed to understand the significance that the Declaration

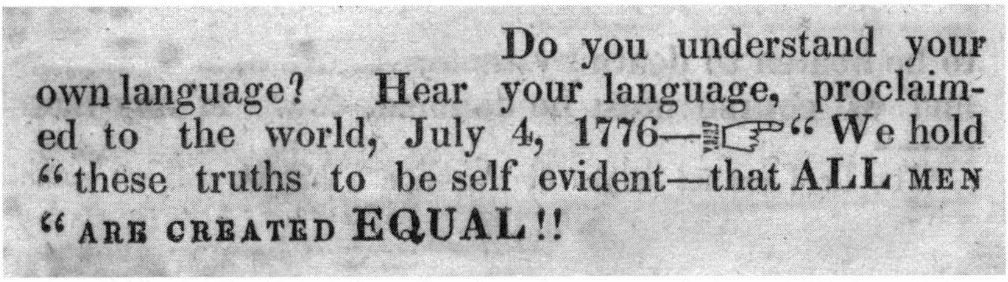

Do you understand your own language? Hear your language, proclaimed to the world, July 4, 1776—☞ " We hold " these truths to be self evident—that ALL MEN " ARE CREATED EQUAL!!

FIGURE 2. Sample of typography from David Walker, *Walker's Appeal, in Four Articles, Together with a Preamble to the Coloured Citizens of the World, but in Particular and Very Expressly Addressed to Those of the United States* (Boston: Printed for the Author, 1829), 73–74.

holds for slavery—Walker repeats the salient lines from the preamble once more, using typographical cues and uneven fonts to defamiliarize and lay bare the meaning of the words "ALL MEN ARE CREATED EQUAL" (see Figure 2).

Walker does not decode the preamble. He does not need to. Or that, in any case, is the gambit. We need only "see" the Declaration and "hear [its] language," to "understand" it.[83] Walker's *Appeal* channels the Declaration's own claim to "self evidence," but it does so in an expressly theological register. Walker dedicates *Appeal* "to the Lord, for your inspection, in language so very simple that the most ignorant, who can read at all, may easily understand."[84] For Walker, the self-evidence of equality is underwritten not by the facts of secular history, but by the higher proofs of religious revelation. As such, Walker can treat the global community his text seeks to produce, "coloured citizens," as a fact rather than an argument.

Walker's appeal to a theological common sense allows him to separate the language of the Declaration—and the egalitarian promise it holds out—from the way it was intended (by Jefferson) and the way it was routinely understood (by contemporaries). Walker exhorts the reader, "Compare your own language above, extracted from your Declaration of Independence, with the cruelties and murders inflicted by your cruel and unmerciful fathers and yourselves on our fathers and on us,"[85] but—and this bears emphasis—he does not interpret the Declaration through the empirical fact of chattel slavery; he views the historical inequities of slavery through the transcendent "truth" of equality. "As true as the sun ever shone in its meridian splendor," Walker prophesies, "my colour will root some of them out of the very face of the earth. . . . I say if these things do not occur in their proper time, it is because the world in which we live does not exist and we are deceived with regard to its existence."[86] Walker's *Appeal* harnesses a theological skepticism of the worldly to portray egalitarianism as a higher truth that transcends mere opinion and belies the legal fiction of chattel slavery, which treats people as things.

Walker's invocation of an expressly theological conception of common sense opens up ways of understanding universalist and global idioms rarely considered in scholarship. For scholars reading Walker's *Appeal* today, the subtitle's reference to "citizens of the world" readily evokes the kind of cosmopolitan ideal that transnational scholarship has recuperated in recent years.[87] However, unlike most recent transnational scholarship, the globality of Walker's *Appeal* does not celebrate a secular vision of Enlightenment cosmopolitanism; it channels and reimagines an older transnational imaginary that found its moral imperatives in the ideal of God's heavenly city. Heaven provides the paradigm for the global community that Walker both greets and seeks to create in the opening pages of *Appeal*. "It is expected that all coloured men, women and children of *every nation, language and tongue under heaven,* will try to procure a copy of this Appeal and read it."[88] Walker presents his own expectations about his audience impersonally ("it is expected"), as if channeling the same divine authority that underwrites his vision of global citizenship.

Walker's use of the passive voice to construct a global audience ("under heaven") provides the syntactical foundation for the kind of "positive collective incorporation" that literary critic Joanna Brooks has identified as key to the formation of a "black print counterpublic."[89] As Brooks observes, the black church was a one of the "key institutional venues for black entry into the public sphere of print," and this is certainly true of Walker, who attended the same Methodist church in Charleston, South Carolina, as the famed Denmark Vesey, the alleged leader of an 1822 insurrectionary conspiracy that created widespread panic in the plantation South.[90] The possible impact of Vesey or the subsequent trials on Walker's text has been a source of generative speculation, but it has also proven difficult to document—as has the Vesey conspiracy more broadly. Yet setting these historiographical questions aside, which I have treated at greater length elsewhere, I want to emphasize a rather simple but consequential point that is never directly addressed in Brooks's important article: religion was more than an institutional venue for developing black counterpublics; it also intimately shaped the kinds of imaginaries that emerged from these venues. The revolutionary black collectivities (summoned in Walker's *Appeal* and worried over in the official records of the Vesey conspiracy) draw their sublime force and their cultural weight from the expressly theological imaginaries they each channel.[91]

The fact that theology, as distinguished from the institutional space of the church, is not discussed in Brooks's account bears remark, because it speaks to a broader scholarly hesitation and reluctance to theorize emancipatory politics through Christian theology, which, in a number of different ways, was linked historically and culturally to structures of subordination and inequality. To what extent can we understand Christian theology—which played a decisive role in the colonizing logic of manifest destiny and was also regularly invoked by proslavery apologists—as a viable discourse for political critique?[92] What makes this question additionally difficult is that the historical practice of religion cannot be separated from the timeless precept of Christian theology—and, as the cultural reception of Philippians 3:20 itself reminds us, these timeless precepts have been understood very differently at different moments in history. As with the other extralegal discourses traced in *Civic Longing*, Christian theology provided a way of authorizing visions of citizenship that exceeded the racialized, gendered logic of the still-emergent juridical citizen. However, its extralegal imaginary was itself inevitably shaped by ongoing debates in the law and beyond it. So any unqualified answer to the question posed above is bound to be historically inadequate. The very terms of political critique, at any given moment, are themselves deeply shaped by the conventions they seek to expose and unsettle, but that does not necessarily make them politically unviable or insufficiently radical.

Part of what makes Walker's *Appeal* so instructive in this broader sense is that it illuminates the uniquely disruptive "counterpublic" uses to which Christian theology could be put *because* of its broader public currency. As with Denmark Vesey and Nat Turner, Walker's exegetical authority is part of what made *Appeal* politically dangerous. Because Christian theology was so often invoked to reinforce the racialized inequalities of the South, Walker's invocation of a theological common sense represented an epistemic assault on the popular conventions on which chattel slavery depended. In this respect, the transgressive character of *Appeal* was more fundamental than its break from Southern law. As Harrison Gray Otis, mayor of Boston, acknowledged in an 1830 letter about Walker's *Appeal* written in response to the mayor of Savannah, "Notwithstanding the extremely bad and inflammatory tendency of the publication, [Walker] does not seem to have violated any of these laws [of the city of Boston]."[93] Southern officials did not share Otis's assessment of the legality of Walker's *Appeal;* they treated Walker's text as "sedition" and jailed the agents who distributed it.[94] However, Otis's account points to something that goes beyond the jurisprudential question of the distinct sets of laws that governed the various cities within which Walker's pamphlet circulated: Walker's polemic does not assault the law within its own terms; it challenges the authority of positive law by summoning a higher heavenly law, "in the courts of heaven." The court of heavenly appeals is a familiar trope, but for Walker, "heaven" serves a retributive function, not a reparative one. In Walker's *Appeal,* heaven is itself militant and militarized: "the armies of heaven" augur the imminent overthrow of chattel slavery.[95]

The countercultural threat posed by Walker's *Appeal* was theological as well as legal. Walker's claim to exegetical authority was itself indelibly politically charged, and it disrupted the norms of emergent abolitionist discourse. Indeed, it was in part Walker's claim to a theological common sense that Quaker abolitionist Benjamin Lundy seems to have found so unnerving. When Lundy reviewed Walker's *Appeal* in 1830 in the antislavery paper he edited, *Genius of Universal Emancipation,* he denounced Walker's theological gambit as false religion. According to Lundy, Walker "indulges himself in the wildest strain of reckless fanaticism. He makes a great parade of technical phraseology, purporting to be religious, but religion has nothing to do with it."[96] Religion, I am suggesting, had everything to do with Walker's arguments and with the panic they elicited. To be sure, no militant form of abolitionism was likely to be widely popular at this time. Yet as Lundy's hyperbolic denunciation of Walker's *Appeal* attests, even white readers who were relatively sympathetic to *Appeal*'s basic abolitionist argument were unnerved by Walker's radical reinterpretation of the scripture. Walker's exegetical authority positioned him as something more than a strategic adaptor of an implicitly white Christianity; it placed him as an unpredictable leader and prophet of a global vision of black citizenship that was both united and authorized by the Word.

## From Dread to Dred

At a moment at which the juridical meaning of "citizenship" was more open to interpretation than proslavery commentators were willing to acknowledge, Christian theology offered radical abolitionists like Walker something more powerful than a language of counter-critique. It provided a normative framework for refiguring political critique not as resistance, per se, but as the destined fulfillment of an egalitarian truth that precedes (and so trumps) human-made law. However, as we all know, not all formulations of Christian abolitionism were as recognizably radical as Walker's— either politically or theologically. Bearing this qualification in mind, this section turns to Stowe's iconic forays into Christian abolitionism, using the little-known theological usages of "citizen" to defamiliarize a body of work that in many respects has suffered from the aura of familiarity that surrounds sentimental literature.

Stowe's iconic brand of Christian abolitionism crystalizes both the power and limitations of political invocations of theological conceptions of "citizenship." As Jane Tompkins observes in her influential reassessment of *Uncle Tom's Cabin,* since "most modern readers regard . . . political and economic facts as final, it is difficult for them to take seriously a novel that insists on religious conversion as the necessary precondition for sweeping social change."[97] Tompkins's point that "political and economic facts" were not deemed "final" in a culture entrenched in eschatological narratives is instructive, but she underplays the problem theology poses for reform—presuming that for Stowe's contemporaries theology offered an unproblematic model for politics.[98] In fact, the assumed tension between religion and politics is a traditional one that held residual power well into the nineteenth century—and it was only in light of the secular presumptions of Christian nationalism that the distinction between the two came to seem increasingly negligible.[99]

As the daughter of the influential Calvinist preacher Lyman Beecher, Stowe was alive to the nuances of Christian theology from a young age. And from all appearances, Stowe's sensitivity to mid-nineteenth-century theological debates served her well both as an author and reformer.[100] *Uncle Tom's Cabin* was an explosive bestseller, whose popularity in the nineteenth century was exceeded only by the Bible. And Stowe's own importance for abolitionism was made mythical by Abraham Lincoln's rumored greeting of Stowe in 1862 as "the little woman who started this great war."[101] Despite these remarkable facts, Stowe has a notably vexed standing in twentieth- and twenty-first-century criticism. As Susan Ryan observes in "Charity Begins at Home" (2000), "It continues to matter how 'good' Stowe's politics were, and not only because her most famous novel is so explicitly and passionately activist. Stowe has come to represent—perhaps most pointedly for Euro-American women in the academy—earnest, middle-class, white activism. In the process, she has proven to be a vexing icon—both an honored foremother and a specter of good intentions gone awry."[102] Stowe's race, gender, and class certainly have played a key role in her critical reception, but it is Stowe's relationship to theology that has given these traits the unappealing, somewhat pernicious character to which Ryan alludes. Were it not for Stowe's relentlessly Christian stratagems, we would be much more likely to see her—in the company of other white and non-white female authors—as pioneers of the historical alliance between early feminism and abolitionism.

To understand the way Christian theology has been racialized as "white" in Stowe scholarship, we need only revisit James Baldwin's influential indictment of *Uncle Tom's Cabin* in "Everybody's Protest Novel" (1955), which has been a touchstone in criticism on Stowe for more than half a century. In one of the most widely cited lines from Baldwin's piece, he argues that *Uncle Tom's Cabin* is "activated by what might be called a theological terror, the terror of damnation."[103] Baldwin's remarks raise a way of thinking about the politics of Christianity that is not addressed explicitly in the preceding pages. In Baldwin's formulation, Christian abolitionism is only incidentally invested in recognizing the humanity of the enslaved. Its primary focus, he suggests, is less altruistic: the spiritual salvation of slaveholders and the broader public complicit in slavery's sins. Stowe's occasional novelistic addresses to an imagined audience in the South lend some support to this view. Stowe seems to have been less invested in absolute judgment—of sinners and the saved—than in the transitive work of political conversion, which involves the salvation of the sinner.

Without reinforcing Baldwin's secular judgment of Stowe, which already has played such a decisive role in her critical reception, I would like to take seriously and also historicize the political power of "damnation" and its spatialized alter ego, heaven. To do that, in the remaining pages of this chapter, I turn away from the well-trodden arenas of Stowe's celebrity (and infamy) to her second abolitionist novel, *Dred* (1856), which offers her most philosophically and typographically diverse exploration of the divergent ways that Christian theology shaped early debates about slavery and citizenship.[104] *Dred* channels the militant form of Christian abolitionism associated with the Denmark Vesey conspiracy, but it also dramatizes the anticipatory structure of Christian estrangement, which made it an unlikely but powerful model for theorizing alternate forms of citizenship that rejected the worldly property-logic of Lockean individualism. Drawing on a passage in *Dred* that uses Philippians 3:20 to envision a transracial community of estranged Christians, I reassess Stowe's iconic commitment to domesticity and national reform by attending to the "unhomely" calculations of heavenly citizenship. Stowe's dual claim to fame as an abolitionist and a writer of domesticity, I argue, has led us to overemphasize the familiar domestic tropes that shaped her writing without fully grappling with the uncanny, theological weirdness of Stowe—which is unevenly realized, but nonetheless crucial to her abolitionist fiction and the forms of citizenship she theorized within it.

*Dred*'s eponymous protagonist is a fugitive who inhabits the Great Dismal Swamp, the marshlands at the edges of North Carolina and Virginia, which famously became the home to several maroon settlements in the early United States because its difficult terrain sheltered it from the egress of the law. During Dred's occasional forays into the neighboring plantation of Canema, the focus of the novel's domestic developments, he wields the Old Testament to prophesize the imminent overthrow of slavery. Stowe literalizes Dred's insurgent roots by presenting him as the fictive son of the historic Denmark Vesey, who allegedly used the African Methodist Episcopal (AME) Church in Charleston as the organizational forum for hatching a wide-scale conspiratorial plot.[105] Dred's actual inheritance from his father, quite appropriately, is Vesey's personal copy of the Bible, which Stowe identifies throughout *Dred* not only as an abolitionist urtext but a revolutionary one. The Bible and the Declaration of Independence, Stowe emphasizes, set Vesey "on his course," and the former also inspired the slave rebellion led by Nat Turner in Virginia in 1831.[106]

The plot of *Dred* unfolds episodically, moving between the divergent Christian teachings of two white preachers—Father Bonnie's proslavery preaching and Father Dickson's self-sacrificing abolitionist humanism—and between two different models of Christian's meaning for the enslaved, the Christian sufferance of a female slave, Milly, and the militant, prophetic Christianity of Dred. As even this brief gloss suggests, it is easy to see the main characters in *Dred* as allegorical personifications of a number of theological-political worldviews. Critics, in this vein, have tended to treat Dred and Milly as a study in contrast between Old Testament wrath and New Testament forbearance—with Milly cast as a female version of Uncle Tom.[107] However, neither of these typologies ultimately holds up. Although Dred's prophecies find partial confirmation in a cholera epidemic that strikes the community, he is killed while still awaiting a divine signal for the revolt, for which "the token is not yet come!"[108] Dred, then, is a forbearing insurrectionary despite his rhetorical vehemence. Milly, moreover, is far from a prototype of patient Christian sufferance; she enters a "trance of wrath" when she recounts the trials that led to her conversion.[109] Dred and Milly do not personify antithetical responses to enslavement—resistance and acquiescence—instead they bring into focus two interlocking aspects of the fraught tradition of Christian estrangement.

*Dred* is a novelistic meditation on the anxieties of theological expectation. The novel's original title, *Dread: A Tale of the Great Swamp,* made this even more explicit. Stowe decided to change the title to evoke the ongoing *Dred Scott vs. Sandford* case, but characterizations of the "dreadful" fill the pages of the novel.[110] In a letter from Calvin Stowe to his wife's publisher, he reflects on the original title's cautionary relevance for the antebellum United States, remarking that the name was "startling, suggestive, perfectly appropriate, full of meaning, and in the present aspect of our country's affairs, has a fearfully symbolic, prophetic sound."[111] *Dred's* original title announced its decisive shift away from Uncle Tom's enervated ethos of Christian patience and forgiveness and toward a kind of political gothic that mobilizes the specter of imminent insurrectionary violence, on the one hand, and the anticipatory anxieties of Christian estrangement, on the other.[112]

Drawing on Baldwin's famous claim that *Uncle Tom's Cabin* is "activated by what might be called a theological terror, the terror of damnation," several critics have observed that in Stowe's second novel this "terror" centers on the threat of black revolutionary agency that Dred's insurrectionary prophesies foretell.[113] Because Dred offers the most recognizably militant form of resistance in the novel, his untimely death before its close has seemed to register all the more starkly Stowe's failure to pursue the revolutionary implications of the model of militant theological critique she flirts with in *Dred*. However, it is perhaps misleading to say that Stowe recoils from Dred's revolutionary potential, midcourse. As Jacob Stratman observes in an insightful modification of this narrative of revolutionary failure, "Dred's insurrection ultimately fails (actually, it never really begins)."[114] From the very beginning of the novel, Stowe divests Dred's prophecies of their immediacy by presuming the nonoccurrence of divinity in the world. Dred's death, in this respect, does not actually signal a conceptual shift in the novel. It is, instead, disappointingly faithful to the delayed insurrectionary temporality that structures prophesy as a future-oriented, predictive grammar of transformation. God's coming may be imminent in *Dred,* but imminence is an imperfect substitute for presence.

Prophecy blurs the lines between what *is* and what *will* be, making it difficult to distinguish the delay of God's will from its failure to manifest. As Dred cryptically enjoins, "[T]he vision is sealed up for an appointed time. If it tarry, wait for it. It shall surely come, and shall not tarry!" (*D,* 279). Theologically speaking, to experience expectation as delay is to doubt God's rightful selection of the "appointed time." Yet when is change coming? How will it come about? And at what point does an unfulfilled prophecy lose its predictive promise and begin to look like a false promise or lie? Readers of *Dred* continue to struggle with variations of these questions: Is the absence of a successful revolution in *Dred* evidence of a lack of revolutionary intention (on Stowe's part)? And how would Stowe's contemporaries have processed the looming threat the novel fails to resolve? Would they have greeted this outcome with resolute relief or with anticipatory dread?

The interpretive problems posed by theological expectation return us, somewhat unexpectedly, to another aspect of *Dred*'s cultural commentary: the plot that inspired *Dred* and birthed its protagonist—the Denmark Vesey conspiracy. Although it might sound strange, *Dred*'s foreclosure of its hero's insurrectionary prophecies actually deepens its premised connection to the Vesey conspiracy, in which the alleged conspirators were charged with plotting an insurrection that they never brought to fruition in the form of open violence. The speculative nature of the charges white officials brought against Vesey and other alleged ringleaders has led some historians to suggest that the insurrectionary plot was a white fiction, invented by officials to strengthen their control over free and enslaved blacks in South

Carolina.[115] The problem with this historiographical claim, as I have argued elsewhere, is that conspiracy itself is a prospective crime, one that, legally speaking, is formalized in the agreement to commit an act in the future. To presume that open violence offers the only unequivocal "evidence" of insurrectionary intention is to fail to grapple with the legal peculiarity of conspiracy as an "inchoate crime," which is considered an actionable crime the moment the intention to commit a crime is formalized in a linguistic compact.[116] Enslaved resistance is certainly easier to locate when it took the form of open insurrectionary violence, but physical resistance is only one form of resistance—and this basic point bears redoubled emphasis because our own methodological preference for quantifiable forms of resistance threatens to naturalize one of the most pernicious claims of slavery's apologists: that outward compliance is evidence of a deeper, complacent acceptance of the hierarchical structure of chattel slavery.[117]

As with the Vesey affair, the fact that Dred's insurrectionary prophecies are never fulfilled did little to allay the dread he inspired in readers. For Stowe's contemporaries, Dred's conspiratorial words were themselves deeply unsettling. A contemporary review of *Dred* in *The Christian Examiner* was shocked by "the rant of 'Dred'" and warmly rejected his character: "This nightmare monstrosity is an offence to us, a humbug, a most unnatural, impossible, unnecessary, and unavailable being, or what not?"[118] As the reviewer's startlingly casual refusal of Dred's very "being" ("being, or what not") suggests, this particular reader was unlikely to be a ready convert to any meaningful form of abolitionism. Abolitionist-minded readers were not as likely to denounce Dred's revolutionary words, but they were even less likely to idealize the insurrectionary agency they foretell. After all, William Lloyd Garrison's pacifist brand of resistance was still the mainstay of abolitionism. In effect, the novelistic fulfillment of Dred's insurrectionary plot—the thing for which we now wish—almost certainly would have diminished its political efficacy in the 1850s. Stowe's recourse to the prospective plots of Christian expectation and legal conspiracy was doubly strategic, in this respect. Dred's unrealized insurrectionary prophecies stage revolution negatively, through anticipatory longing—allowing readers to mourn for the loss of a prospect that for Stowe's contemporaries would likely have seemed only ominous if it had been fulfilled on the page.[119] From this perspective, the novel's negative relation to insurgency arguably tells us more about Stowe's sense of her contemporary readership than it does about her own political convictions. Indeed, as we will see in Frederick Douglass's novelistic retelling of a contemporary slave revolt in the next chapter, even abolitionists who were far more strident than Stowe were often reluctant to depict black insurrectionary agency directly because spectacular violence troubled characterological attempts to present and reclaim the humanity of the enslaved.

The political implications of what we count as resistance bears emphasis in relation to Stowe's novel as well as the Vesey conspiracy proper, because it calls attention to the limits of any plot-based analysis of the politics of *Dred* (or any other novel, for that matter). As we will see most dramatically in Chapter 5's treatment of political tales of "negative instruction," which inspired readerly patriotism by presenting the tragic plight of characters doomed to statelessness, plot is an extraordinarily limited barometer of the political ambitions and impact of any given piece of fiction. This point is relatively straightforward when put so baldly, but it can be difficult to acknowledge it in practice because of the kinds of expectations and hopes we invariably bring to our interpretative engagement with extreme political problems like slavery. Simply put, it is hard to recognize texts as properly political when they fail to meet our own political standards. Christian abolitionism poses this difficulty even more profoundly, because, as with the material discussed in the foregoing sections of this chapter, it brings into view the epistemic chasm between our own, implicitly secular conceptions of agency and texts produced in a period in which this shift was still very much in progress.

So does *Dred's* death constitute the failure of Stowe's revolutionary imagination in *Dred,* as a whole? From one angle, it undoubtedly does. Even if it brings the novel closer to the specter of unrealized but imminent insurrection circulated in legal accounts of the Vesey affair, it also brings *Dred* much further from the slave rebellion led by Nat Turner, in which Turner's own insurrectionary exegesis did, in fact, culminate in open revolt. Theological critique was not always prospective. So Stowe certainly might have pursued a more recognizable revolutionary course within the pages of *Dred.* However, the abortive character of Dred's insurrectionary energies does a different kind of work. Precisely because Dred's insurrectionary prophecies remain unrealized and yet imminent, their imaginative trajectory is not contained within the fictive time of the novel; they continue to loom for readers in historical time. Stowe, in this way, extends the arena of divine judgment from the fictive world of *Dred* to the historical moment of its readership.

*Dred's* words, as much as the speech of its protagonist, were meant to be read as a kind of prophecy. For Stowe, who famously claimed that God wrote *Uncle Tom's Cabin* and that she "merely did his dictation," the written word on the page doubled for the Word.[120] For Stowe's readers, prophecy was political, and the recognition that theological critique could (and did) inspire open insurrection brought a sort of spectral agency to even prospective formulations of insurgency. This, arguably, is the lesson of "Dread" and the

Vesey conspiracy that inspired it. Plotting on and off the page projects new political futures that have the potential to transform the political present—even if these plots are never fully realized by their authors.

## Stowe's Theological Uncanny

In *Dred,* as in its precursor, conversion takes the place of emancipation as the definitive trope of liberation. In the opening scene of *Dred,* Nina Gordon, the mistress of Canema, announces that she is engaged "to three gentlemen, and am going to stay so till I find which I like the best" (*D,* 8). Despite her avowed coquetry, it is evident from the beginning that one of the three, an idealist named Edward Clayton, will play the minister to Nina's yet "wholly unawakened nature" (*D,* 20).[121] The fulfillment of their romance, however, is not marriage—Nina's untimely death forecloses this possibility. Instead, their courtship finds its resolution in their respective reformations: Nina's spiritual ascension and Edward's development from an excessive idealist to a practical abolitionist. Edward's concluding role in assisting the slaves from Canema in their escape to the North, and in subsequently removing his own plantation to Canada, offers a proximate resolution of the novel's thwarted romantic and revolutionary plots, even as it dramatizes the novel's struggle to imagine an *ending* for slavery, apart from the negative terms of flight and death.[122]

The law, as critics have emphasized, is central to the plot and arguments of *Dred.*[123] From the scenes of Milly's trial, interpolated passages from the official report of Vesey's trial, and its prominent allusion to the ongoing trial of Dred Scott—the legal history of U.S. slavery provides both the grammar and urgency for the novel's abolitionist aspirations. And yet, precisely because the novel insistently identifies early U.S. law with the iniquitous practice of chattel slavery, *Dred* ultimately leaves the law behind. Like Edward Clayton, who dramatically renounces the legal "profession" to "retire forever from the bar of my native state," *Dred* pursues theological models of resistance and critique in its stead (*D,* 355). Christian theology, nonetheless, poses its own set of problems for the novel's abolitionist argument. Stowe's insistence on the Christian disposition of slaves may have established their spiritual equality with white Christians, but as George Eliot observed, it also suggested "that the negro race was vastly superior to the mass of whites . . . a state of the case which would singularly defeat Mrs. Stowe's sarcasms on the cant of those who call Slavery a 'Christianizing Institution.' "[124] Stowe addresses this tension in *Dred* by emphasizing the improbability of Milly's conversion as a slave. However, Stowe's persistent identification of suffering with Christianity (especially

its New Testament form) threatens to make enslavement itself seem redemptive. The narrator acknowledges that "where one soul is thus raised
[through slavery] to higher piety, thousands are crushed in hopeless imbe-
cility," but she also suggests that the very extremity of Milly's affliction
strengthens her conversion (*D,* 51). "At first she had met this doom with
almost the ferocity of a lioness; but the blow, oftentimes repeated, had
brought with it a dull endurance, and Christianity had entered, as it often
does with the slave, through the rents and fissures of a broken heart" (*D,* 51).
Piety, according to the narrator, may be rare among slaves, but when it
does occur, it outstrips the development of even "the best instructed,"
because the desolation of slavery facilitates the disavowal of worldly experience implicit in the structure of Christian estrangement (*D,* 51).

At times, *Dred* romanticizes the stark religious potential of slavery—
even describing Milly's conversion in the language of violent subordination,
an effect of "the blow, oftentimes repeated." However, unlike *Uncle Tom's
Cabin, Dred* extends this model of despairing faith beyond the historically
and racially inscribed subject positions of master and slave to encompass the
proselytizing effects of worldly affliction more generally. Father Dickson,
who is one of the only white abolitionist preachers in the novel, is absolutely
crucial to Stowe's reimagination of Christian estrangement in *Dred*—which
provides the novel with an affiliatory alternative to the hierarchical logic of
sympathy. While, as Jeannine DeLombard observes, Clayton's advocacy for
Milly and his own slaves reinforces the hierarchy of "white paternalism,"[125]
Father Dickson's identification with the slaves takes the comparative form
of commiseration. Dickson is himself portrayed as destitute and vulnerable to the whims of the slaveholding parishioners, in whose service he offers his spiritual labors.

> Every one in the state knew and respected father Dickson; and, like the gener-
> ality of the world, people were very well pleased, and thought it extremely
> proper and meritorious for *him to bear weariness and painfulness, hunger and
> cold, in their spiritual service.* . . . Father Dickson was one of those who had
> never yielded to the common customs and habits of the country in regard to
> the holding of slaves. A few, who had been left him by a relation, *he had at
> great trouble and expense transported to a free state,* and settled there com-
> fortably. The world need not trouble itself with seeking to know or reward
> such men; for the world cannot know and has no power to reward them.
> *Their citizenship is in heaven,* and all that can be given them in this life is like
> a morsel which a peasant gives in his cottage to him who to-morrow will reign
> over a kingdom. (*D,* 247, emphasis added)

Father Dickson is exemplary in *Dred,* less because of his advocacy for
slaves (which remains relatively ineffectual), than because, as his subse-

quent attempted lynching makes explicit, he is a deracialized figure for the slave, through which the novel idealizes Christian estrangement. The emphasis on Father Dickson's uncompensated "service" establishes an analogy between his suffering and the trials of slavery. The passage, however, suggests more than a figurative *equality* between Dickson and the slaves. Dickson places the needs of the slaves he inherits above his own, sacrificing the economic means of his own worldly comfort in order to ensure their freedom. The attendant reversal of fortunes, wherein the slaves settle "comfortably" while he "bear[s] weariness and painfulness, hunger and cold," grounds the abstract analogy between Father Dickson's "service" and slavery in a material economy. The exchange of money, however, is an ambivalent figure for the transferability of symbolic positions. For while the slaves gain immediate freedom, Father Dickson's economic sacrifice, the reader is assured, will be repaid in spiritual capital, "citizenship . . . in heaven."

Dickson seems to symbolize everything other than his own white masculinity. Stowe's rhetorical presentation of Dickson's subjection comes to a dramatic climax when he is nearly lynched by a mob of angry whites led by Tom Gordon, Nina's tyrannical brother. As Dickson rides toward a nearby church, singing "'Jesus Christ has lived and died—/What is all the world besides?'" an armed throng confronts him, declaring, "We an't going to have any of your d—d abolitionist meetings here" (*D*, 476, 479). When Dickson refuses to stop preaching against slavery, Tom tells the gang, "[W]e had better bring matters to a point! Here, tie him up to his tree, and give him six-and-thirty! *He is so dreadful fond of the niggers, let him fare with them*" (*D*, 484, emphasis added). One of the gang then takes out a "slave-whip" and beats Dickson, until Clayton and a group of "gentlemen," who happen to be passing by, intervene (*D*, 484).[126] Dickson's timely deliverance, however, proves ambivalent. The magistrate admonishes the lynch mob, but he also reiterates their sentiments by treating Dickson as the transgressor. As an abolitionist, the magistrate explains, Dickson seeds dissent with the "kind of preaching" that "excites brawls and confusion, and inflames the public mind" (*D*, 487).

The magistrate counsels Dickson "to leave the state," but he also calls for a broader separation between church and state. "Now, I wish, for my part, that ministers would confine themselves to their appropriate duties. 'Christ's kingdom is not of this world'" (*D*, 487). As the incarnation of the law's administrative enforcement, the magistrate's function is to preserve the law, not to change it. In consequence, he perceives Christian theology as an anarchic discourse that needs to be controlled. The magistrate affirms the very thing the novel laments: the division between theological and political law. The idea that abolitionism is beyond the "appropriate" and limited theological sphere of ministerial concerns is antithetical to Stowe's express project. *Dred* lampoons the Church's "moral apathy" about slavery, portraying religious sects as opportunistic political parties, driven by interdenominational struggles for "public favor" (*D*, 359, 395).[127] *Dred's* moral, in this respect, is that politics should take Christianity as its model, and not the other way around.

When heavenly citizenship is presented as a substitute for political citizenship, rather than a model for citizenship in the state and/or nation, it ceases to be a catalyst to reform and, instead, reinforces existing hierarchies by eviscerating the rationale for change. The compensatory model of heavenly citizenship, as we have seen, assumed a distinctly fatalistic teleology for the gendered and raced subjects denied political agency.[128] This tendency is what makes Stowe's depiction of Father Dickson's heavenly citizenship so noteworthy. Stowe's depiction of Father Dickson's lynching and heavenly recompense transcends the popular nineteenth-century analogy between the bonds of marriage and enslavement, in order to make disaffiliation appear as a *representative* predicament, inherent to Christian experience. Father Dickson is not particularly distinctive or inspiring in himself, but his very commonality is instrumental to the political ambitions of *Dred*. For, it is in Stowe's belabored portrait of Dickson's spiritual comparability with the slaves that the novel approaches a model of Christian egalitarianism. In *Dred*, Stowe casts estrangement as a predicament common to all Christians. This theological reformulation of citizenship and subjection places all Christians in the same position relative to each other. Unlike the individualist vision of egalitarianism held out in liberal philosophy, this relative equality under God is rooted in a notion of a more fundamental, theological subjection.

What distinguishes Stowe's invocation of Philippians 3:20 in *Dred* from the thematic invocations of heavenly citizenship in early black Atlantic literature and also from *Uncle Tom's Cabin* is that it is embraced by a white man, who is portrayed as the exemplar of a form of suffering that in the other cases is an unchosen and imposed circumstance. This racial reversal is crucial because it disrupts the exceptionalist logic that makes it possible for the Christian idealization of suffering to slip so seamlessly into a reification of extant inequalities. *Dred* develops the idea of heavenly citizenship promised in Philippians 3:20 as a template for a form of theological expectation that structures the present *seculum* as well as the world to come. Stowe preserves the present-tense translation of Philippians 3:20 ("Their citizenship *is* in heaven"), but as with Dred's prophecies, the novel also empties this "is" of its immediacy, substituting imminence for presence. The novel, in this respect, operates within a distinctly theological understanding of the indicative, in which factuality is not confined to the present but also encompasses the theological truths (that *should be* expressed in the world) but that will, in either case, become manifest in the kingdom to come.

Stowe's emphasis on the prospective orientation of Christianity was not atypical. However, as we have already seen, some antebellum commentators, frustrated by the "misconception" that "we are called on by religion to concern ourselves seriously only about what will happen when this life is over," tried to reappropriate the relevance of Philippians 3:20 for worldly experience.[129] In this spirit, Stowe's brother, Henry Ward Beecher, insisted on the immediacy of heavenly citizenship. "Can you say with the apostle, 'Our conversation'—that is, our citizenship, our life—'our conversation is,' not shall be, '*is* in heaven.'"[130] Similarly, an 1862 British sermon by Robert Graves remarks, "It may be noted in the first place that the text is not 'our citizenship *will be* in heaven,' but, 'our citizenship is in heaven;' from which we might fairly infer that the enjoyment by Christians of their privileges as *citizens of heaven* is not altogether a future enjoyment, to be entered upon for the first time when this life terminates, but, in some degree at all events, a present enjoyment."[131] The sermon's printed subtitle, "The Heavenly Elements of Earthly Occupations," underscores its refusal of both the temporal and spatial separation of heaven. Graves does not localize citizenship to heaven, but instead identifies it as a generalizable attribute (heavenliness). The difference between location and essence, in fact, is already implicit in the two predominant translations of the passage that the sermon alternately uses: "'citizenship *in* heaven'" and "citizens *of* heaven." The three successive formulations—"will be," "is in," and "of"—progressively refine the relation to heaven, moving first from futurity to spatial presence, and culminating in genitive affiliation. In its genitive version, heaven is both the provenance of Christians and the ideal to which they aspire.

While the "heavenly," extracted as an attribute, allows Graves to present the harmony between heaven and earth, Stowe's insistence on the discord between the two serves as both lamentation and protest. *Dred* recovers "higher law" as a justification for reform, even as it casts worldly immersion as a form of theological estrangement.[132] Nina's conversion makes this explicit. When the novel opens, Edward remarks that Nina, his "pretty little sinner," "has lived only in the world of sensation" (*D*, 20). Nina is reluctant to convert, as the narrator later explains, because she fears that becoming a Christian means ceding the pleasures of life. "Nina had often *dreaded* the idea of becoming a Christian, as one shrinks from the idea of a cold, dreary *passage, which must be passed to gain a quiet home*" (*D*, 345, emphasis added). Christianity, Nina suspects, reduces the world to a dreadful "passage," a mere obstacle to be surpassed.[133] To reach the true "home," one must renounce the world and life itself. Nina's death (which occurs a mere thirty pages after her conversion) is the ultimate expression of her Christianity. *Dred*, in this respect, is not particularly concerned with disproving Nina's initial concern that Christians are strangers in this world. Indeed, the description of her eventual conversion provides inadvertent confirmation of her earlier qualm with Christianity—as she finds a "strange *unearthly* happiness" in "God's love" (*D*, 376, 375, emphasis added).

*Dred* disaggregates "home" from its worldly, and properly domestic, identification with the house. The novel withdraws the home into a theological realm that is inaccessible to those who survive Nina. "'I think I am called!' she said. 'O, I'm so sorry for you all! Don't grieve so; my Father loves me so well,—he cannot spare me any longer. He wants me to come to him. That's all—don't grieve so. It's *home* I'm going to—*home!*" (*D*, 380, emphasis in original). Nina does not console her friends for the friendship they will lose by her death, but for what they themselves miss out on in not dying as well. In contrast, in the analogous deathbed scene in *Uncle Tom's Cabin*, Little Eva's "essentially decorative" death, as Ann Douglas refers to it, domesticates death, divesting it of its foreignness.[134] "The bed was draped in white; and there, beneath the dropping angel-figure, lay a little sleeping form—sleeping never to waken!"[135] The analogy of death to sleep makes it appear innocuous and familiar, while the "angel-figure" attests to the domestic presence of heaven. Whereas *Uncle Tom's Cabin* domesticates the divine (bringing it into Eva's bedchamber), Nina's death estranges domesticity by bringing into focus the chasm between the domestic sphere and the final home to come.

As with Christian nationalism, which has dominated developmental narratives about the political meaning of Christian theology, discussions of Christian domesticity have tended to focus on the common analogy between the familial home and the national community—without registering theology's traditional ambivalence toward the worldly home and the nation alike. This ambivalence is evident in even Stowe's most expressly domestic works. According to *The American Woman's Home; or, The Principles of Domestic Science* (1869), which Stowe wrote with her sister, Catherine Beecher, "[T]he end designed by the family state which Jesus Christ came into the world to secure" is "to provide for the training of our race . . . with chief reference to a future immortal existence."[136] Women, in this insistently Christianized version of domesticity, are not supposed to instruct the family to treasure the material household, but to view it in its proper subordination to the divine home in heaven. As the "chief minister" to the family, Stowe and Beecher argue, woman "is to rear all under her care to lay up treasures, not on earth, but in heaven."[137] Stowe and Beecher do not advance any radical feminist claims in *American Woman's Home*. However, as with the resolutions adopted in the historic women's rights convention in Seneca Falls, New York, in 1848, they clearly understood the "moral superiority" that was readily granted to women in the middle of the nineteenth century as the foundation of their cultural power in the present and in the future. As Stowe and Beecher similarly saw it, women's theological authority placed them as instructors and "ministers" in the realm that connected the worldly state with the heavenly home.[138]

In Stowe's unhomely domesticity, the true "home" is not the house but heaven. The fact that *Dred* is set on a plantation amplifies the sense of the failure of domesticity, since it places tyrannical slave owners in the position that ought to be reserved for the "Heavenly Master" (*D,* 189). Yet as Stowe and Beecher acknowledge in *The American Woman's Home,* the mere house always falls short of the ideals it attempts to embody, when judged by the standards of heaven.

In *Dred,* the perceived misfit between the material artifacts of domesticity—house and family—and the heavenly home finds it narrative denouement in the thwarted engagement of the romantic plot between two of *Dred's* younger Dickson-like white abolitionists, Nina and Edward.[139] In the passage that stands as the novel's most direct confirmation of Dred's theological omniscience, Dred foretells the personal losses the cholera epidemic augurs for the couple. When Edward hears that a cholera epidemic has broken out on Canema, he rushes back to the plantation, encountering Dred, who forewarns, "I know who you seek, but it shall not be given you. . . . The time of the dead has come, that they shall be judged" (*D,* 373). Despite Edward's skepticism about the accuracy of Dred's prediction, the encounter terrifies him, leaving him with a "weight of fearful foreboding" (*D,* 374).[140] Edward's dread, as the narrator casts it, is existential. "This life may be truly called a *haunted house,* built as it is on the very confines of the land of darkness and the shadow of death. A thousand living fibres connect us with the unknown and unseen state" (*D,* 374, emphasis added). Dred, as this passage makes clear, is a living medium of "the unknown and unseen state." His prophecies provisionally connect the material world with the theological unknown, but, in so doing, they engender terror, not the harmony Stowe seeks. In Stowe, the "unseen" Kingdom renders the entire world a "haunted house." And in this respect, theology extends the more local disappointments with politics into a *universal* predicament—making characterizations of political dispossession seem the inevitable effects of worldly experience, more generally.

As with the beloved Eva from *Uncle Tom's Cabin,* the sympathies of antebellum readers of *Dred* centered disproportionately on the novel's fatalistic white female protagonist, the "incomparable Nina," who, according to a reader in *The Methodist Quarterly Review,* "both Mrs. Stowe and Clayton seem hardly to care enough to bury."[141] Likely in response to readers' frustration with Stowe's fatalistic emplotment of her protagonist, Nina survives in the play version of *Dred,* which John Broughman Esq. dramatized with Stowe's "special permission" in 1856.[142] In Broughman's revision of the novel, the plot comes to a close with Nina's hopeful prophesy of a better future to come that is implicitly located in the temporal sphere. Rejoicing the passing of the cholera epidemic—which serves as an emplotted symbol of God's wrath in *Dred*—Nina exclaims, "The clouds have broken away; the valley of the shadow of death passed; and now the blessed light of hope and joy illumines our onward path. May we profit by the teachings of the time gone by, as to make beautiful the records of our future lives!"[143] The play's peaceful and optimistic resolution undercuts the urgency of Stowe's reformist mission. However, the play also lends new power to *Dred*'s prophecies by providing external evidence of his prophetic authority. When Dred calls on God directly in the play, his call for wrath is met with lightning. "Wake O arm of the Lord—awake, put on thy strength, rend the heavens and come down, to avenge the innocent blood. Cast forth thine arrows, and slay them; shoot out thy lightnings, and destroy them utterly." When a "flash of lightning" immediately appears, striking a nearby tree, Harry "hail[s] it as a sign."[144] In the play, the lightning offers unqualified confirmation of the righteousness of Dred, which is something the novel never unequivocally confirms beyond the cholera outbreak.

The cholera outbreak, it should be said, is itself a peculiar figure for divine restitution, because its biological virulence strikes all within the community with equal force—without moral discrimination. Cholera's contagious transmission moves us away from a model of individual sin and salvation and toward a model of communal crime and restitution. This communal logic is registered in the review in *The Methodist Quarterly,* which later refigures its lamentation of Nina's death in terms of the stricken community of which she is a part. "Mrs. Stowe spreads her cholera so summarily, that it reminds us of the *total massacre of all the characters* in the Titus Andronicus of the pseudo-Shakespeare."[145] Stowe might not depict open revolutionary violence in *Dred,* but she uses the cholera epidemic to kill off the novel's most fully developed vision of domestic union and worldly belonging.

Stowe's abolitionist rehabilitation of the tradition of Christian estrangement in *Dred* moves away from the sentimental terrain of interracial sympathy and Christian domesticity and toward an estranged, theological commons. If *Dred* succeeds at moments in suggesting the rightful equality of blacks and whites, it does so foremost by comparing the despair of unchosen political exclusion to the universal ontological predicament of Christian estrangement. What joins slaves and Christians in *Dred* is not the charitable sympathy of white abolitionists, but the sense that, theologically speaking, estrangement is endemic to life.[146] The insight of Stowe's second abolitionist novel is to bring the defamiliarizing power of Christian estrangement to bear on the entrenched hierarchical logic of chattel slavery, while using an egalitarian image of heavenly citizenship as a counterfactual imperative for a racially inclusive model of political citizenship in the United States. It is this uneasy fusion of Christian estrangement and Christian nationalism that lends political purposiveness to a set of convictions that would otherwise be *merely* fatalistic. Understood through the lens of Christian estrangement, the political power of heavenly citizenship shares little with the tacitly hierarchical structure of sympathy. Its political force resides in the supposition that estrangement is not an exceptional predicament but one that is common to Christian experience.[147]

Within the renunciative framework of Christian estrangement, Christians must disavow the house to get to the heavenly home. This renunciative impulse sets *Dred* apart from the narrative strategies of the domestic consolation literature that Stowe is often seen to epitomize. Elizabeth Stuart Phelps's wildly popular *The Gates Ajar* (1868) offers a uniquely illustrative counterexample because it too invokes Philippians 3:20—but it does so only to unequivocally reject the form of Christian estrangement associated with Paul's lines. Early in *Gates Ajar,* the allegorically named Reverend Bland gives a sermon on Philippians 3:20 that leaves the protagonist "empty uncomforted, groping. . . . I wanted something actual, something pleasant, about this place into which Roy has gone. He gave me glittering generalities, cold commonplace, vagueness, unreality, *a God and a future at which I sat and shivered.*"[148] Faced with the grief of her brother, Roy's recent death in the Civil War, the protagonist is impatient with the distinctly consoling heaven that emerges from Bland's reading of the passage. Its abstract and distant heaven fails to offer the kind of worldly consolation that came to seem increasingly urgent and necessary in the wake of the mass grief of the Civil War.

Instead of the estranged heaven proffered in Philippians 3:20, *Gates Ajar* imagines a hedonistically well-furnished heaven fitted with all the comforts of home, including a piano. Phelps might easily have envisioned this materialist heaven without any reference to Philippians 3:20, but like many before her, she uses it as a touchstone for Christian estrangement and the renunciative imperatives it represents. The novel's rejection of this ethos is the epistemic pivot of the novel. And in keeping with its materialist ethos,

*Gates Ajar* destroys the physical extension of Christian estrangement: Bland's sermon. Bland himself destroys his sermon following his own conversion to the comforts of a materialist heaven. When Bland's wife dies, he is confronted "with the *blank heaven* of his belief."[149] "No Greek and Hebrew 'original,' no polished dogma, no link in his stereotyped logic, not one of his eloquent sermons on the future state, came to his relief."[150] After a parishioner tries, unsuccessfully, to comfort Bland, he calls her back "with a saddened smile. 'At least I will never preach *this again*. . . . He held up before her a mass of blue manuscript, and threw it, as he spoke, upon the embers left in his grate. It smoked and blazed up and burned out. It was that sermon on heaven."[151] With Bland's exegetical treatment of Philippians 3:20 consigned to the flames, *Gates Ajar* theatricalizes its generic departure from the renunciative epistemology of Christian estrangement.

The denouement of *Gates Ajar* encapsulates two epistemic shifts that began to coalesce on the heels of the Civil War: the ambivalent shift away from Christian estrangement and toward Christian nationalism, and a further shift away from the clerical model of biblical exegesis and toward populist practice. As Edward Everett Hale urged a decade later, in one of three addresses given two years before the publication of the highly anticipated 1881 English Revised Version, "We must look on this whole enterprise of revision as a final death-blow to that idolatry of the Bible. . . . The whole idolatry of the letter is of course tumbling to its fall. From this time forth, as I believe, we may look for another advance—slow but sure—of the religion of life."[152] Understood in relation to the tradition of Christian estrangement it casts aside, the cultural achievement of the kind of consolation literature exemplified by *Gates Ajar* is that it makes heaven—traditionally the locale of death—into an untroubled extension of the arena of life.[153]

Unlike Phelps, Stowe values the house and family as means for preparing Christians for heaven, not as ends in and of themselves. The renunciative demands of this insistently Christianized conception of domesticity belie one of the central binaries within Americanist criticism, between the antisocial tradition of high canon masculine fiction (associated with Irving, Hawthorne, and Melville) and the socializing commitments of popular domestic fiction. In "Home as Heaven, Home as Hell: *Uncle Tom*'s Canon," Leslie Fiedler reflects on his seminal arguments in *Love and Death in the American Novel* (1960) from the perspective, more than thirty years later, of a substantially expanded canon. Fiedler charges himself with "accepting as eternally valid a canon of American novels which had, in fact, been established only a few decades before" and proceeds to broaden his more monolithic narrative about the flight from civilization in American fiction to account for domestic literature.[154] In addition to the "myth of interethnic male bonding," he argues, there is a "second myth of equal importance . . .

with which it exists in dialectical tension. What I am talking about is the myth classically formulated in *Uncle Tom's Cabin* (let us call it the myth of Home as Heaven)."[155] Masculinist literature that "celebrated the flight from civilization," he explains, "reinforc[es] the myth of Home as Hell."[156] Fiedler revises the scope of his earlier argument, but he preserves a stark opposition between the flight from civilization (home as hell) and domestic idealization (home as heaven).

The distinction is attractive, by virtue of its very clarity. Yet part of what this narrative misses is the extent to which insistently theological versions of domesticity cultivate ambivalence toward the worldly home. Within the renunciative terms of Christian estrangement, Christians are strangers in the world, who, in the words of Tiff in *Dred,* need "to find out de shortest way . . . to be got to heaven!" (*D,* 336).[157] In *Dred,* the problem is precisely that home is *not* heaven, but that heaven is the true home. Thus if characters in Melville's, Twain's, and Hawthorne's fiction might be said to seek different routes of escape (whether by sea, river, or the obscure recesses of history), Christian theology in Stowe structures parallel forms of estrangement in its very epistemology. Within these two traditions, the house (as figure and counterpoint) is a touchstone for the articulation of transcendent ideals, but it is located differently within the symbolic landscape of each: the flight from civilization abandons the house to seek transcendence in nature, while Christian domesticity positions the house as the training ground (the "cold, dreary passage") to the transcendent home. In the eschatological purview of Christian estrangement, the world is an uncanny realm where even citizens are aliens and where freedom and rights are prospective rewards at the end of time.

In the eschatological *durée* of heavenly citizenship, Christians must choose either the world *or* God, that is, choose either estrangement from God or estrangement from the world. Life, not death, marks a separation from the true community of God. According to an 1859 sermon, delivered in New Hampshire following the death of a pastor's wife, the "paramount interest in the heavenly society" derives from its promise to reunite families that death has divided: 'These relations—which, year by year, death seems to divide, though it ought only to have lengthened, not broken, the chain of sympathy—gives us all, whether we own it or not, a deep and paramount interest in the heavenly society; thus making us, by the allotment of the Divine Providence, citizens of heaven, whether we are living as citizens or as aliens."[158] The promise of citizenship in heaven trumps political differences between those "living as citizens or as aliens," offering a qualified grammar for the common entitlements of Christians.

As we have seen in this chapter, theological uses of "citizenship" offered an infinitely adaptable landscape for sculpting the theological precepts of higher law critique, but their exegetical link to heaven also tended to limit their efficacy as catalysts for reform in the here and now. As one of the characters in Martin Delany's *Blake; or, The Huts of America* (1859) declares in a moment clearly meant as a rebuttal of the Christian martyr paradigm of *Uncle Tom's Cabin,* "What is religion to me? . . . I'm tired of looking at the other side; I want hope on this side of the vale. I want something on this earth as well as a promise of things in another world."[159] Frederick Douglass shared this insistent focus on realizing political change "on this side of the vale," but—as his public disagreement with Delany's dismissal of Stowe's *Uncle Tom's Cabin* makes clear—he was reluctant to critique Stowe's abolitionist efforts, even though they differed from his own more secular tactics. "Is not the field open?" Douglass asked. "Why, then, should any man object to the efforts of Mrs. Stowe, or any one else, who is moved to do anything on our behalf."[160]

Douglass's very pragmatism made him reluctant to dismiss the potential political efficacy of an approach to abolitionism that, from today's standpoint, might seem "like an imaginary 'solution' to a real" historical problem, to borrow Fredric Jameson's famous critique of romance.[161] Christian theology remained a vital albeit variegated part of U.S. culture and politics, and for believers, the unseen world of God's kingdom was the only real truth. As with David Walker, this skepticism toward the worldly had the potential to authorize a fundamental and far-reaching critique of political practice and custom. Still, as all of these writers were keenly aware, advocates of slavery, as much as its critics, turned to the Bible to support a range of political interests. And as Eliot and Douglass both recognized, Christian theology's renunciative ethos was easy to recast as a rationale for the continuance of the so-called Christianizing institution. In a particularly pointed critique of the proslavery uses of heavenly fellowship, Douglass closes *Narrative* (1845) with a polemical parody of "Heavenly Union," a hymn popular in the South. "'Love not the world,' the preacher said,/And winked his eye, and shook his head; He seized on Tom, and Dick, and Ned,/Cut short their meat, and clothes, and bread,/Yet still loved heavenly union." The efficacy of a theological critique of political injustice, as Douglass was keenly aware, required a genuine investment in Christian theology. Christian abolitionism, in this respect, failed to take into account what Douglass characterized as the "partial and hypocritical Christianity of this land."[162] For these reasons, as we will see in Chapter 3, Douglass set aside the expressly theological model of higher law critique—utilized by Gronniosaw, Wheatley, Walker, and later Stowe—to develop a universalist vision of egalitarian citizenship that drew its extralegal authority from the worldly tropes of natural law discourse.

CHAPTER THREE

# Citizens of Nature

## Oceanic Revolutions and the Geopolitics of Personhood

> It has often given me pleasure to observe that independent America was not composed of detached and distant territories, but that one connected, fertile, widespreading country was the portion of our western sons of liberty. . . . A succession of navigable waters forms a kind of chain round its borders, as if to bind it together. . . . This country and this people seem to have been made for each other, and it appears as if it was the design of Providence that an inheritance so proper and convenient for a band of brethren, united to each other by the strongest ties, should never be split.
>
> —John Jay, *The Federalist Papers,* No. 2 (October 1787)

> The only law which the alleged slave has a right to know anything about, is the law of nature. This is his only law. The enactments of this government do not recognize him as a citizen, but as a thing.
>
> —Frederick Douglass, "Freedom's Battle at Christiana" (September 1851)

IN FEDERALIST NO. 2, published on October 31, 1787, John Jay takes evident satisfaction in the "succession of navigable waters" that encloses the United States, because it forms a "chain" that makes the political federation of states seem immanent to nature itself.[1] For Jay, the waters that encircle the states bind them together, and symbolize their collective autonomy from foreign interference. The United States and its citizenry, Jay argues, were "made for each other," and their harmony with their natural environs is but further proof of "the design of Providence." Jay's zeal for a native government, indivisible from "this country and this people," helped catalyze one of the first territorial formulations of citizenship. In July 1787, a few months before Jay's first contribution to *The Federalist Papers,* he wrote to George Washington—then the presiding officer of the Constitutional Convention—urging the wisdom of "a strong check to the admission of Foreigners into the administration of our national Government" by "declar[ing] expressly that the Commander in chief of the American army shall not be given to, nor devolve on, any but a natural born Citizen."[2] Jay's anxious insistence on the need for a commander in chief whose dispositions and sympathies were a "natural" outgrowth of the land that he sought to present as a "natural nation" has had enduring effects well beyond the 1780s.[3] The proviso Jay outlines in his letter was formalized in one of the eleven nominal uses of the term "citizen" in the Constitution as originally ratified: the Natural-Born Citizen Clause, which states that "[N]o person except a natural born Citizen, or a Citizen of the United States, at the time of the Adoption of this Constitution, shall be eligible to the Office of President."[4]

What assumptions about the structure of political membership in the early United States can we glean from the Constitution's passing reference to "natural born citizen[s]"? In its inception, the Natural-Born Citizen Clause depended on a territorially defined conception of foreignness and nativity. And in this respect, it anticipated the modern theory of "birthright citizenship" that the Fourteenth Amendment codified almost ninety years after the Constitution came into force in 1789. Both the Natural-Born Citizen Clause and birthright citizenship identify the territory of one's birth (*jus soli,* right of the soil) as the "natural" foundation of political allegiance.[5] However, in the early United States, the ambiguously invoked "naturalness" of citizenship continued to be inflected by the biological bonds of *jus sanguinis* (right of the blood).

Within the blood logic of chattel slavery, "foreignness" was not a geopolitical descriptor, determined by the place of birth. It extended metaphorically to the biopolitical divisions that shaped the internal boundaries of political membership within the United States. Nativity availed little for enslaved people. As legal historian James Kettner and others have emphasized, "Slaves were neither aliens nor citizens"; they had neither foreign allegiance nor comprehensive domestic protections.[6] Those born into slavery in the United States were in the peculiar position of being native aliens, stripped of rights, and without any path to naturalization.[7] Slavery, as a condition of "natal alienation," instituted a formal separation between nativity and citizenship.[8]

The Natural-Born Citizen Clause did nothing to guarantee political membership to all native residents of the United States. The juridical applications of this clause were and remain extraordinarily narrow: this nativist delimitation of presidential eligibility is only relevant for the fraction of the populace that is inclined to campaign for this high office. However, in an era in which all constitutional references to citizenship were nominal, the Natural-Born Citizen Clause offered an evocative constitutional touchstone for understanding and reimagining eligibility for citizenship. In the hands of abolitionists and feminists, the constitution's preferential delimitation of the presidency seemed to encapsulate a broader nativist theory of political membership in which all native-born denizens (regardless of race or gender) enjoyed a presumptive claim to citizenship. As the New York abolitionist William Goodell emphasized in 1863, "Nothing is said here [in the Natural-Born Citizen Clause] of color or condition in life." "Should Frederick Douglass receive a majority of electoral votes, he would be constitutional President. Had Madison Washington the victorious hero of the brig 'Creole,' been elected President, while he was held in slavery, the result would have been the same."[9] As Goodell's identification of Frederick Douglass and Madison Washington as would-be "constitutional President[s]" attests, the Constitution's idealization of the "natural" citizen provided a suggestive statutory framework for higher law formulations of citizenship that invoked the proverbial "law of nature." And as we will see, the two men Goodell identifies as would-be presidents both contributed, albeit in very different ways, to the cultural refinement of natural law–based arguments for the abolition of slavery.

This chapter moves from the otherworldly formulations of "citizenship in heaven," discussed in Chapter 2, to divine law's unabashedly "worldly" cousin, natural law.[10] Since the geopolitical landscape of slavery and citizenship was in continual flux in the period of this study, this chapter avoids generalizations about the tradition of natural law writ large. Instead, it unfolds its claim in the form of a case study, taking its cues from a territorial dispute that straddles the transformative decades of the 1840s and 1850s—the event that informs Goodell's abolitionist interpretation of the Natural-Born Citizen Clause and that also links the two men he identifies as would-be presidents: the 1841 slave revolt onboard the *Creole,* in which 135 slaves obtained freedom on arriving in the British territory of the Bahamas.

The revolt on the *Creole* provided a limit case for mid-nineteenth-century debates about the relationship between civil rights within the state and the "natural rights" that regularly were identified as its foundation. Because the revolt occurred at sea, in international waters, and because it led to the emancipation of over one hundred enslaved people, when the *Creole* subsequently docked outside of Nassau, within the juridical reach of British law, the revolt set into motion a charged debate over the geopolitical boundaries of enslavement and personhood. Although the limits of U.S. jurisdiction were deeply debated in the international dispute that followed the revolt—with critics of Britain's "interference" arguing that the ship was still technically within the legal "territory" of the United States—the implicit assumption shared by both sides was that slavery could exist only by force of statutory law. Outside the United States, commentators argued, the local fictions of the state give way to the laws of nature. These arguments did more than simply point to the discontinuity between natural and political rights; they made the fact of this separation the basis for political critique. The objective, of course, was to reform existing laws so that they reflected the rights of nature, and in this respect, the imagination of the ocean as a space of natural liberty more generally was not an end in itself, but an instructive myth that epitomized the unfulfilled ideals of the United States.

Given the politically charged interplay between the conceptualization of nature and the nation, this chapter does not read the *Creole* case within the unified conceptual framework of the "Black Atlantic."[11] Instead, it attends to the divided symbolic character of maritime law—which conceptualizes the ocean as "international waters," but also insists on the national character of the vessels that traverse it (as ships of state). I pay special attention to the rhetorical strategies of the two orators who arguably did the most to shape the cultural reception of this successful but under-discussed revolt: U.S. Secretary of State Daniel Webster and Frederick Douglass.[12] Webster, as we will see, invokes the rhetoric of natural disaster to deny the agency of the insurrectionists, while Douglass uses climatological tropes to develop a notion of natural rights that controverts the geopolitical partitioning of freedom. Their politics could not be more dissimilar. However, both arguments hinge on ideologically charged characterizations of nature and the natural. Nature, for each, provides the epistemological foundation, or conceptual ground zero, for visions of citizenship that they present as incontrovertible and destined.

## Geographies of Agency

On October 30, 1841, the *Creole* ship left Hampton Roads, Virginia, with 135 slaves bound for New Orleans—but it never arrived. Following a slave revolt at sea, the leaders of the insurrection directed the ship to Nassau, Bahamas, a British colony where slavery had been abolished since 1833. The details of both the revolt and its aftermath remain hazy; what is known comes primarily from the accounts of the white crew in two widely reprinted "protests," as well as the diplomatic correspondence between U.S. and British authorities after the ship's arrival in Nassau.[13] According to the second and most comprehensive of the protests, Elijah Morris (a slave of Thomas McCargo) informed shipmaster Gifford that "one of the men had gone down aft among the women" (Doc. 51, 37). Upon further investigation, a passenger, Mr. Merritt, found "Madison Washington, a very large and strong slave belonging to Thomas McCargo," who was "the last man on board of the brig [he] expected to find [t]here." Madison ran forward, and Elijah Morris fired a pistol, the ball of which grazed the back part of Gifford's head. Madison then shouted, "We have commenced, and must go through; rush, boys, rush aft; we have got them now" (Doc. 51, 38). During the skirmish, John Hewell, a white passenger and slaveholder who had "the particular charge of the slaves of Thomas McCargo," fired a musket and was subsequently stabbed to death by the slaves (Doc. 51, 37, 38–39). Madison then intervened to spare Merritt's life, "on his promising to navigate the vessel to any port they required" (Doc. 51, 39). "Madison said that they wanted to go to Liberia," but, on learning that they did not have sufficient provisions, several slaves "said they wanted to go to the British islands . . . where Mr. Lumpkin's negroes went last year," alluding to a group of slaves who had obtained their freedom when a U.S. schooner was shipwrecked in the British islands the previous year (Doc. 51, 40).[14]

When the *Creole* arrived in Nassau on November 9, two days after the revolt, U.S. Consul John Bacon sent a letter to Governor Francis Cockburn to "request that your excellency will be pleased not to suffer any of the slaves on board to land until further investigations can be made" (Doc. 51, 5). On the fourth day after the ship's arrival, British magistrates boarded the ship to identify the nineteen slaves actively involved in the mutiny.[15] After taking depositions and securing the mutineers as prisoners, George Anderson, the British colonial attorney general for the Bahamas, announced that the other slaves were free to go to shore. He then signaled to several ships of black soldiers—who had surrounded the *Creole* in increasing numbers since its arrival—to help the slaves to shore.[16] In the absence of an outstanding extradition treaty, Britain refused to surrender the accused mutineers for trial in the United States. Four months later, British authorities released the nineteen incarcerated fugitives, satisfied that, in the words of Parliament, "there was no authority to bring the persons who had escaped in the Creole to trial for mutiny or murder, or even to detain them in custody."[17]

The *Creole* revolt was compared to several other international disputes over slavery—including the *Amistad* (1839) and the *Hermosa* (1840)—but the rhetorical strategies popularized by the Somerset case (1772) proved particularly decisive. The case involved a petition for habeas corpus on behalf of Somerset, who had been brought to England from the American colonies as a slave but who had escaped, only to be subsequently recaptured and detained on a ship bound for Jamaica. In Lord Mansfield's famous decision in favor of Somerset, he held, "The state of slavery is of such a nature, that it is incapable of being introduced on any reasons, moral or political; but only positive law, which preserves its force long after the reasons, occasion, and time itself from whence it was created, is erased from memory: It's so odious, that nothing can be suffered to support it, but positive law."[18] Implicit in Mansfield's argument is the idea that slavery and the laws that enable it are abhorrent to nature. Still, Mansfield refrains from such a categorical position, concluding more modestly, "I cannot say this case is allowed or approved by the law of *England;* and therefore the black must be discharged."[19] As historian William Wiecek observes, "Technically considered, the judgment in *Somerset* settled only two narrow points of English law: a master could not seize a slave and remove him from the realm against the slave's will, and a slave could secure a writ of habeas corpus to prevent that removal."[20] Despite Mansfield's attempt to delimit the legal ramifications of the decision, it had a sweeping rhetorical legacy.[21] U.S. abolitionists elaborated the precepts into a "neo-*Somerset*" doctrine that presumed the fundamental "tension between slavery and natural law."[22]

The rhetorical afterlife of the Somerset case was much more encompassing than Mansfield's actual decision, in part because it also drew on the memorable arguments of Francis Hargrave, one of Somerset's most eloquent lawyers. According to Capel Loftt's report of the trial, Hargrave declared that England is "a soil whose air is deemed too pure for slaves to breathe in it"—a territory in which positive (statutory) law and natural law are in essential harmony.[23] A similar argument is attributed to Mansfield in Lord Campbell's *Lives of the Chief Justice of England,* but Campbell's idiosyncratic version is typically deemed "spurious" by historians. It reads, "The air of England has long been too pure for a slave, and every man is free who breathes it."[24] Whether Mansfield echoed this sentiment, the claim itself was not unprecedented. As Steven Wise notes, the conceit of the liberatory properties of England in *Somerset* drew on a common law tradition that may have dated as far back as an obliquely documented case involving a Russian slave in 1569, "in which the court freed [the slave] with the pronouncement that 'England was too pure an air for slaves to breathe in.' "[25]

These invocations of a natural order relativize the authority of positive law, but neither Hargrave's reanimation of this tradition nor the earlier 1569 pronouncement fully relinquishes the territorial distinctions that positive law propagates. Indeed, Hargrave's imagination of rights is decisively localized to natural elements that are yoked to England: "the air of England," its "soil."[26] In this nationalist fantasy, natural rights may be grounded equally in all locales (in theory), but their self-evidence is confined to England. As William Cowper's versification of the conceit dramatizes ("Slaves cannot breathe in England. . . . They touch our country and their shackles fall"), the neo-Somerset doctrine tacitly reinforced the nationalistic logic of jurisprudence: imagining natural rights as a special property of England.[27] Although the implications of the *Somerset* decision were initially restricted to England proper, by the time of the *Creole* revolt—eight years after the abolition of slavery throughout the British Empire—its language had been invested anachronistically with the teleology of British emancipation more generally. Thus, in Barrister Robert Phillimore's consideration of the *Creole*, he seamlessly invokes Mansfield's decision to defend Britain's response to the revolt, arguing that since the *Somerset* case, the "maxim . . . to refuse a recognition of the personal disability of slavery" has "never been impugned with success."[28]

U.S. officials did not dispute the liberatory prerogatives of British law, but Secretary of State Daniel Webster attempted to circumvent its implications for the *Creole* case by arguing that, legally speaking, the ship had remained outside of British jurisdiction.[29] The *Creole* affair, as Lord Ashburton remarked, hung like a "great plague" over ongoing negotiations for the Webster-Ashburton Treaty (signed August 9, 1842),[30] intended to resolve the "boundaries" between U.S. and British territories in North America, support "the final suppression of the African Slave Trade," and provide for the mutual extradition of criminals.[31] Just eight days before signing the treaty—which expressly committed the United States, as well as Britain, to maintain vessels for the suppression of the African slave trade—Webster pressed Ashburton for noninterference with even the international expressions of the presumptively regional institution of plantation slavery. Alluding to the *Somerset* precedent, Webster writes, "The usual mode of stating the English law is, that no sooner does a slave reach the shore of England than he is free. This is true; but it means no more than that when a slave comes within the exclusive jurisdiction of England he ceases to be a slave, because the law of England positively and notoriously prohibits and forbids the existence of such a relation between man and man" (Doc. 1, 119). Whereas in the *Somerset* case, Lord Mansfield concludes that slavery can only be upheld where positive law explicitly supports it, here Webster reverses this characterization to depict the emancipatory laws of England as themselves exceptional, and essentially local.

Webster attempted to undermine the forceful rhetorical correspondence between the natural and political properties of England by belaboring the distinction between the jurisdiction of the nation and its geographic boundaries. Interrogating the seemingly most straightforward facts of the case, he maintains that even though the *Creole* ship entered British waters, the circumstances of its "unlawful" arrival override its physical presence.

> If, therefore, vessels of the United States, pursuing lawful voyages, from port to port, along their own shore, are driven by *stresses of weather,* or caused by unlawful force, into English ports, the Government of the United States can not consent that the local authorities in those ports shall take advantage of such misfortunes. . . . Such vessels, so driven and so detained by *necessity* in a friendly port, *ought to be regarded as still pursuing their original voyage,* and turned out of their direct course only by disaster, or by wrongful violence. (Doc. 1, 121, emphasis added)

Webster subordinates the geographical location of the ship (in the Bahamas) to a speculative narrative of how it "ought to be regarded" (in keeping with U.S. jurisdiction).

Prefiguring his ambivalent role brokering the 1850 Compromise as a Massachusetts senator, Webster evades the question of whether the slaves *should* be free, and reduces the question to a territorial disagreement in which the prospect of freedom is contingent both on geographical borders and contentious narratives of the agency of arrival. Webster argues that the cause of the ship's redirection—rather than the geographical fact of its arrival—determines whether it is subject to foreign authority. Alluding to the concept of *force majeure,* "that great and practical rule, which declares that that which is the clear result of necessity ought to draw after it no penalty and no hazard," Webster suggests that "unlawful force" should be regarded in the same manner as any act of "superior power" (Doc. 1, 117).[32] "If *against the will of her master,* or owner, she ["a vessel"] be driven or carried . . . into port," Webster asks, "what reason or justice is there in creating a distinction between her rights and immunities, in a position, thus the result of *absolute necessity,* and the same rights and immunities *before superior power had forced her out of her voluntary course?*" (Doc. 1, 117, emphasis added). In other words, for Webster, the ship did not technically enter foreign territory because its redirection was not part of its original itinerary. To argue that the *Creole* preserves its original national character (as it would on the high seas), Webster has to fabricate an alternative narrative, set "before" the revolt and in the hypothetical space of the "original voyage."

Webster displaces the fraught power dynamic between the insurrectionary slaves and the owners/traders onto the inert and yet unmanageable figure of the ship (which is "carried," passively, "against the will of her master"). This doubling between the slaves and the ship is made conspicuous by the unwieldiness of the analogy. The "owner" of a ship and its "master" (a designation most proximate to the station of the captain) are not equivalent, nor do they exert the same degree or even type of control over its movements. The displacement of the embodied power struggle between the insurrectionists and crew onto the image of the ship's navigation enables Webster to construct jurisdiction as an artifact of consent. Jurisdiction is not an extension of decisive spatial boundaries[33]—movement across which carries unavoidable political consequences—it is contingent, here, on the "voluntary" character of the ship's course (or more strictly speaking on the volition of the captain). By making the legitimacy of jurisdictional authority contingent on the intention and volition of the crew, Webster imagines that even foreign dominion operates by virtue of a form of compact, but a racially restricted one.

Webster obscures the agency of the insurrectionists by at once prioritizing the rhetoric of voluntarism and restricting it to the white crew. The labyrinthine rhetorical paradigm he develops admits to only two possibilities: the positive volition of the white crew or the complete capitulation of all agency to "absolute necessity." For Webster, the slave revolt is comparable to the ungovernable effects of the "weather"; it is a "result of necessity," and so, it would seem, carries no proper agency. Webster's comparison of "unlawful force" to "stresses of weather" deemphasizes the individual agency of the insurrectionists. However, in elaborating the revolt as a "*force majeure*," he also implicitly elevates it to the status of a superior, irresistible event. The comparison, that is, may disembody the force of the revolt, but it also likens the revolt to an act of nature or, as the doctrine of *force majeure* is suggestively styled, an act of God.[34]

Webster characterizes the revolt on the *Creole* as an act of nature, but he stops short of suggesting the unnatural character of slavery. Webster's comparison of the revolt to "stresses of weather" allows him to deemphasize the intent and agency of the insurrectionists. However, as we will see, this same supposition took on very different political meaning in the hands of abolitionists, for whom the natural character of the revolt became a decisive trope for establishing the essential legitimacy of the insurrectionists' bid for freedom. Within the moral framework of natural law, acts of nature are not incidental circumstances; they express a higher will that is not reducible to the resistance of one man or even nineteen men. Needless to say, the suggestion that the slave revolt accords with some higher law could hardly have been further from Webster's purposes. Nor, for that matter, was this the principal effect of his arguments. Thirteen years after the initial dispute, the Anglo-American Commission awarded the slave holders $110,330 in remuneration for the slave "property" lost in the insurrection—but the insurrectionists themselves remained free.[35]

## Fitful Natures

Webster's insistence on the exceptional character (and restricted dominion) of British emancipatory laws highlights the basic paradox of the ideology

of freedom in the antebellum United States. While its self-styled designation as the "land of the free" evinces the same conceit as Hargrave's depiction of England in the Somerset case—namely, that the national ideal of
freedom is so organic as to be immanent in the land itself—Webster's position on the *Creole* case emphasized the palpable rift between America's
liberatory principles and its oppressive laws. As Douglass ironically stresses
in one of his several remarks on the *Creole* revolt during his British tour in
the mid-1840s, "Now Maddison [sic] Washington and his compeers are
treading upon British soil, they had fled from a republican government and
have chosen a monarchical, and are basking under the free sun amid the
free hills and valleys of a free monarchal country."[36] Abolitionist allusions
to the comparative political exemplarity of England were both common
and pointed.[37] The Anglophilic tradition of abolitionism drew its power
from the exceptionalist mythos of American founding. It troubled and rad-
icalized patriotism by presenting the uncomfortable image of the United
States as a harsher tyrant than the government against which it had re-
belled. Douglass's Fourth of July speech plays on these tensions, but its
rhetorical gambit does not ultimately rest in London, nor with the distinctly
Anglophilic strain of abolitionism associated with it. Douglass ultimately
turns to "the far off and almost fabulous Pacific" to offer a global vision of
natural rights. "The iron shoe, and crippled foot of China must be seen, in
contrast with nature," Douglass declares in the closing lines.[38]

    The notion of Britain's oppressive tyranny over the American colonies
remained integral to the oppositional self-conception of the United States
as a democratic country, but this conceit lost much of its self-evidence in
light of the abolition of slavery throughout the British Empire in 1833. This
tension was even more dramatic after the passage of the Fugitive Slave Act
in 1850, which pushed the practical boundary for attaining freedom to the
British province of Canada. The answer to the shifting landscape of the
geopolitics of freedom, as Douglass and many natural law reformers understood it, had less to do with the physical traversal of actual borders than
with the reconceptualization of the binding effects of human law. "The only
law that the slave has a right to know anything about is the law of nature,"
Douglass declares in an 1851 speech on the violent skirmish between a group
of abolitionists in Christiana, Pennsylvania, and a posse of fugitive slave
hunters who entered the state under the authorization of the Fugitive
Slave Act. Because the "government has virtually made every colored man
in the land an outlaw," Douglass argues, it had forfeited its right to compel
their obedience. "The basis of allegiance is protection. We owe allegiance
to the government that protects us, but to the government that destroys us,
we owe no allegiance. The only law which the alleged slave has a right to

know anything about, is the law of nature. This is his only law. The enactments of this government do not recognize him as a citizen, but as a thing."[39] Douglass's claim that natural law is the "only law that the slave has a right to know anything about" is strange for its restrictive formulation of the rights of the enslaved. Yet this negative formulation of the rights of enslaved people is meant to dramatize a recognition that underwrites Douglass's abolitionist arguments in the early 1850s: that U.S. law, as restructured by the Fugitive Slave Act of 1850, works to ensure the unattainability of "rights" for even those fugitives fortunate enough to escape the more immediate infrastructure of chattel slavery.

Douglass's remarks in "Freedom's Battle at Christiana" set the stage for the arguments he pursues in *The Heroic Slave*. Douglass does not mention Madison Washington in "Freedom's Battle," but by this point in time Washington was a frequent touchstone in Douglass's public defenses of the right to violent resistance—a stance that was at the heart of his famed break from William Lloyd Garrison's pacifist school of abolitionism. Douglass discusses the revolt on the *Creole* in multiple speeches he gave in Britain in the 1840s. He also refers to Webster's letters explicitly in two of several speeches in which he reclaims Madison Washington as an abolitionist hero.[40] However, Douglass offers his most substantive repudiation of the logic that underpins Webster's response in his sole venture into fiction, "The Heroic Slave," which was published in a gift book in 1853 and then serialized in Douglass's newspaper.[41] Douglass, as we will see, turns Webster's arguments on their head by using climatological tropes to develop a notion of natural rights that is universalist in its territorial scope. "The Heroic Slave" uses natural imagery to present natural law (and the notion of human rights it sanctions) as an empirical reality, apparent throughout the natural world. In "The Heroic Slave," Douglass legitimizes the insurrection by recalling the "principles of 1776," even while, as with his famous Fourth of July address the year previous, he ironizes the mythic yoking of liberty to the United States.[42] The fulfillment of the United States' promise in Douglass's allegory resides neither in its territory nor in its citizens. Instead, international waters and the British terra are the symbols of freedom, while Madison Washington, a disenfranchised slave, comes to embody the unfulfilled ideals of U.S. citizenship. "The Heroic Slave" restages the drama of the American Revolution on an international scale, but it does not exchange nationalism for the unilateral yearnings of Anglophilia. Douglass turns British emancipation into a nostalgic occasion for reinventing the limits of U.S. citizenship.

When Douglass returned to the *Creole* case twelve years after the height of the controversy to offer his most extensive (albeit highly fictionalized) representation of the revolt in "The Heroic Slave," the Fugitive Slave Act had given new domestic urgency to a question that Webster had treated in terms of international borders: does the legal fiction of chattel slavery translate across geopolitical boundaries?[43] Douglass echoes Hargrave in his depiction of Madison Washington's initial attainment of freedom in Canada (before he is recaptured in Virginia and placed on the *Creole*)—"I AM FREE, and breathe an atmosphere too pure for *slaves*" ("HS," 205)—but the novella also insistently counters the nationalist conceit that natural rights are more or less inherent in any one country. Douglass relinquishes an investment in locality and contained spaces to pursue the episodic and fitful character of natural phenomenon. This dispersion intimately shapes the peculiar form of the novella in two ways. First, Douglass's novella re-configures the heroic genre, replacing the story of an individual agent with the more sporadic agency of nature. Second, by taking the "restless bil-lows" of the ocean as not only the setting of the revolt but a model for both rebellion and reform ("HS," 237), Douglass proffers natural law—and the rights it confers—as a corrective to the structural fallibilities of statu-tory law.

On first glance, the opening of "The Heroic Slave" appears insistent on restoring Madison Washington to a place of conventional eminence within the pantheon of Virginia's "multitudinous array" of "statesmen and heroes" ("HS," 175, 174). Douglass thus remarks, "Let those account it who can, but there stands the fact, that a man who loved liberty as well as did Patrick Henry,—who deserved it as much as Thomas Jefferson,—and who fought for it with a valor as high . . . as he who led all the armies of the American colonies through the great war for freedom and independence, lives now only in the chattel records of his native State" ("HS," 175). Considering the mode of the introduction and the fact that the novella culminates with a representation of the revolt on the *Creole* (albeit a remarkably indirect one), we expect that the novella will offer something of a prehistory of the revolt, through the personal history of its leader. We expect, that is, that the novella will provide practical illustrations of the essentially heroic char-acter of Madison, in terms not dissimilar to those outlined in an earlier piece in *The Liberator,* entitled "From the Friend of Man. Madison Wash-ington. Another Chapter in His History" (June 10, 1842): "The scene on the Creole deck was but one chapter in the history of Madison Washington. Nothing could be more absurd than to suppose that this occasion made Madison, and not Madison made the occasion."[44] What is so striking about the novella as a whole, however, is just how little it confirms an inflated sense of Madison's control over his circumstances.[45] With seemingly reso-lute insistence, Douglass grants rhetorical priority to the natural events that punctuate the course of the novella, over and against Madison's individual agency.

For a work whose emancipatory argument hinges on linking the slave revolt on the *Creole* to the American Revolution, it is striking how cursorily and circuitously Douglass's novella depicts the actual insurrection. As several scholars have argued, Douglass represents the insurrection indirectly in order to avoid the difficulty of making explicit violence appear "heroic."[46] This indirection, however, is characteristic of the novella as a whole. Even its protagonist and hero, Madison Washington, is, as Douglass writes in the preface, "brought to view only by a few transient incidents." "Glimpses of this great character are all that can now be presented. He is brought to view only by a few transient incidents, and these afford but partial satisfaction. Like a guiding star on a stormy night, he is seen through the parted clouds and the howling tempests; or, like the gray peak of a menacing rock on a perilous coast, he is seen by the quivering flash of angry lightning, and he again disappears covered with mystery" ("HS," 175). If, missing the parodic tone of Douglass's hyperbolic homage to the "statesman and heroes" of Virginia, the reader expects a conventional, if fictional, character biography, this climatic prefatory passage comes as both an apology and a warning.[47] As Cynthia Hamilton points out, "the title of the novella declares Washington to be the main protagonist and hero, but without substantial internal support for such a position."[48] Hamilton's subsequent suggestion that the title, in this respect, "could be seen as demeaningly ironic" is somewhat less convincing. However, her more general point, that the "rather overblown and highly conventional" language in the text ironizes rather than simply reproduces the exceptionalist logic of the white revolutionary tradition, identifies a structuring opacity that is often missed in critiques of Douglass's sole foray into fiction.[49] Madison Washington, after all, is not a conventional hero, or even a coherent and defined personage in the novella. From the very beginning, Douglass's elliptical and metaphorical characterizations of his protagonist bypass interiority in lieu of an impersonal and symbolic landscape. Less a character than a cipher, Madison is introduced as a figure for the inevitability of emancipation as a force of nature: "a guiding star on a stormy night"; "the gray peak of a menacing rock"; "the quivering flash of angry lightning."

On a formal level, the narrative deemphasizes Madison's agency by presenting the events of his life as a series of episodic coincidences. The first three sections of "The Heroic Slave" loosely follow the movements of the (future) leader of the revolt, Madison Washington: from an overheard soliloquy on the trials of his enslavement in the forests of Virginia, to Madison's happenstance reunion with the sympathetic auditor of this speech

(Listwell) on his Northward flight, and, finally, Listwell's discovery, while on business in Virginia, that Madison has been recaptured and is being shipped with a chain gang for sale in New Orleans. The revolt itself appears in the fourth section, but, like the actual "Protests," it is narrated retrospectively by the white crew (in this case, by a fictional sailor named Tom Grant).

When the story proper opens, our perspectival distance from Madison takes the generic form of an overheard soliloquy. On a "Sabbath morning, within hearing of the solemn peals of the church," a "Northern traveler" pauses for water "near the edge of a dark pine forest" in Virginia and "caught the sound of a human voice" ("HS," 176). When the traveler (whose name we soon learn is Mr. Listwell) wonders, "To whom can he be speaking? . . . He seems to be alone," his question evinces a textual self-consciousness about the artificiality of the presentation of Madison's character ("HS," 176). While this section offers the most comprehensive portrait of Madison's thoughts and feelings, it also keeps him insistently, and at first literally, just out of full view. The soliloquy—which begins 'What, then, is life to me? it is aimless and worthless, and worse than worthless. . . . That accursed and crawling snake, that miserable reptile, that has just glided into its slimy home, is freer and better off than I" ("HS," 176–177)—apostrophizes on the inhumanity of slavery in general, with little mention of Madison's specific situation. Our knowledge of Madison, as a result, appears too generic to bespeak his personal character.

The fact that the aptly named Listwell (who listens well, as several critics note)[50] forms his initial impression of Madison on the basis of voice alone— "that unfailing index of the soul"—suggests just how much their interracial friendship depends on disembodiment and spectatorship ("HS," 179).[51] When Listwell finally catches "a full view of the unsuspecting speaker," his now increased perception remains one-sided ("HS," 178). "As our traveler gazed upon him, he almost trembled at the thought of his dangerous intrusion. Still he could not quit the place. He had long *desired to sound the mysterious depths of the thoughts and feeling of a slave.* He was not, therefore, disposed to allow so providential an opportunity to pass unimproved" ("HS," 179, emphasis added). Here, what might otherwise have been an assumed good—an opportunity to communicate the feelings and humanity of a slave to white abolitionist readers—is given a notably sinister connotation in the depiction of Listwell's overeager and almost eroticized surveillance of the "unsuspecting speaker."[52]

However, as if in defiance of Listwell's desire for further disclosure, the narrative adds yet another level of formal remove from the type of intimacy that could have been provided with first-person narration.

With the exception of a few embedded quotes, the rest of Madison's soliloquy is not presented in his own words but in the form of a summaric
gloss.

> He resolved to hear more; so he listened again for those mellow and mournful
> accents which, he says, made such an impression upon him as can never be
> erased. He did not have to wait long. There came another gush from the same
> full fountain; now bitter, and now sweet. Scathing denunciations of the cru-
> elty and injustice of slavery; heart-touching narrations of his own personal
> suffering, intermingled with prayers to the God of the oppressed for help and
> deliverance, were followed by presentations of the dangers and difficulties of
> escape, and formed the burden of his eloquent utterances; but his high resolu-
> tion clung to him,—for he ended each speech by an emphatic declaration of
> his purpose to be free. ("HS," 179–80)

The narrative, in fact, represents both Listwell and Madison Washington
indirectly. But the type and quality of knowledge conveyed is different in
each case. Strangely, we know more about Listwell's thoughts and desires
than about Madison's; the closest we come to an understanding of Madison's interior life is through the already externalized—and performative—
expression it assumes in his speech.

The narrative's structural remove from Madison is further compounded
by the fact that his speech is not only generic but oscillates between "his
own personal suffering" and that of "the oppressed" more generally. As in
Douglass's *Narrative,* the balance between the slave as individual and
type is critical to the efficacy of the text's abolitionist argument. This
"intermingl[ing]" of the personal and typical assumes additional importance here given the exceptionalist tendencies of the rhetoric of heroism—
which, as in the case of the text's title, the heroic *slave,* emphasizes the
singularity of agency. The point, in this respect, is ultimately one of effects
rather than intention. For if, as some critics have suggested, Douglass's
fragmentary depiction of his protagonist is conditioned by the limited
historical sources on Madison Washington,[53] this indirection also eschews
the type of ostensibly benevolent spectatorship (exemplified by Listwell)
that permeates abolitionism.[54] By making, as William Andrews remarks,
"the lack of knowledge about Washington, as opposed to the dearth of
historical information about other champions of liberty from Virginia, the
gambit of his text,"[55] Douglass turns the fact of historiographical obscurity
into an occasion for questioning the model of agency that underwrites
biographical narratives of history and, just as importantly, the individualist
mythos of the liberal subject. Of course, this is not to suggest that Madison
Washington's evocative name did not help abolitionists situate the *Creole*
insurrection firmly within the tradition of the American Revolution; for, it

did. As the *New York Evangelist* commented, Madison "wore a name unfit for a slave but finely expressive for a hero."[56] Still, without relinquishing either the heroic stature of Madison's actions or the rhetorically powerful link to the Revolution, the novella insistently displaces biographical (or at least character-bound) expectations with unstable natural metaphors that unsettle the jurisdictional borders of citizenship.

Douglass forswears the possibility of fathoming Madison's character before the novella proper has even begun. "Curiously, earnestly, anxiously we peer into the dark, and wish even for the blinding flash, or the light of northern skies to reveal him. But alas! he is still enveloped in darkness, and we return from the pursuit like a wearied and disheartened mother, (after a tedious and unsuccessful search for a lost child,) who returns weighed down with disappointment and sorrow. Speaking of marks, traces, possibles, and probabilities, we come before our readers" ("HS," 175–176). Douglass introduces his own historiographical method firmly within the possibilistic register of the political subjunctive. With Madison's interior motivations insistently undisclosed, the narrative uses metaphors of natural phenomena to contextualize actions that (without the causal explanation of intentions) appear not only inscrutable but also erratic. Though glimpsed only in fits and starts—"through the parted clouds and howling tempests . . . the quivering flash of angry lightning" ("HS," 175)—what we know most emphatically about Madison derives from the fact of the organizing correspondences between the fitfulness of his character and that of nature. "The Heroic Slave," in this way, refrains from the type of exceptionalist individualism that its title leads us to expect—establishing instead Madison's universalist political authority by elaborating his moral harmony with the natural world.

The proliferation of natural imagery in "The Heroic Slave" shapes more than the presentation and conceptualization of Madison's underlying character. Natural phenomena (clouds, conflagrations, and storms) also provide the logic and impetus for the novella's highly episodic structure. Following the opening soliloquy, the narrative jumps ahead five years to a winter evening at the Listwell's residence in 1840. Listwell and his wife sit before their fire, but the "spirit of the restless night" presses in insistently from without ("HS," 183). "All was still and comfortable within; but the night was cold and dark; a heavy wind sighed and moaned sorrowfully around the house and barn, occasionally bringing against the clattering windows a stray leaf from the large oak trees that embowered their dwelling" ("HS," 182–183). Their "*reverie*" is interrupted when their dog alerts them to the approach of a stranger, who turns out, to Listwell's amazement and delight, to be none other than Madison Washington ("HS," 183, emphasis in original). Madison, who is initially "disquieted" by Listwell's familiarity—since he had been unconscious of Listwell's previous intrusion—explains that "the piercing cold, and the frowning darkness compelled [him] to seek shelter" ("HS," 185, 186). The weather, in this way, becomes an alibi for the narrative's improbable coincidences.

Douglass's continual use of natural phenomena to explain Madison's circuitous path to gaining liberty on the *Creole* establishes the natural world as both a symbol and an agent in the battle for natural rights—even as its erratic cycles suggest the contingency of attaining freedom. Although Madison first attempts to escape just weeks after his forest soliloquy, "a season of clouds and rain set in, wholly preventing me from seeing the North Star, which I had trusted as my guide, not dreaming that clouds might *intervene* between us" ("HS," 189, emphasis added). This "circumstance," Madison explains, "was fatal to my project, for in losing my star, I lost my way; so when I supposed I was far towards the North, and had almost gained my freedom, I discovered myself at the very point from which I had started" ("HS," 189–190). Nature, in this particular moment, is a practical obstacle to freedom rather than a metaphor for its inevitability. The passage, however, does not belie the novella's use of natural imagery as a figure for natural rights. Instead, it underscores, as Peter Meyers argues in another context, that Douglass's imagination of natural law as "self-executing" "did not betray a naive or willful idealism. . . . More painfully than most, he was mindful that the dynamism of nature and history brought reversals for ill as for good."[57] Douglass's attention to the erratic character of natural phenomena in "The Heroic Slave" has a similar effect—suggesting that despite its rhetorical and political force, the extralegal tradition of natural rights does not have the same empirical self-evidence as the physical laws that govern nature.

## Restless Liberties

"The Heroic Slave" recuperates the interpretative contingency of natural law by identifying the erratic events of the natural world as a model for liberty and reform. Although a "season of clouds" frustrates Madison's initial attempt to reach the North, he is later forced back on his journey by a wildfire that drives him out of his hiding place in the neighboring swamps.

The whole world seemed on fire, and it appeared to me that the day of judgment had come; that the burning bowels of the earth had burst forth, and the

end of all things was at hand. Bears and wolves, scorched from their mysterious hiding-places in the earth, and all the wild inhabitants of the un-
trodden forest, filled with a common dismay, ran forth, yelling, howling,
bewildered amidst the smoke and flame. *The very heavens* seemed to rain
down fire through the towering trees; it was by the merest chance that I escaped
the devouring element. Running before it, and stopping occasionally to take
breath, I looked back to behold its frightful ravages, and to drink in its
savage magnificence. It was awful, thrilling, solemn, beyond compare. When
aided by the fitful wind, the merciless tempest of fire swept on, sparkling,
creaking, cracking, curling, roaring, out-doing in its dreadful splendor a thousand thunderstorms at once. . . . It was this grand conflagration that drove
me hither; *I ran alike from fire and from slavery.* ("HS," 193–194, emphasis
added)

Employing the rhetoric of millennialism, Douglass presents the fire as a divine "judgment" against slavery, which returns Madison on his journey for
freedom. Douglass's skepticism about Christianity's efficacy for abolitionist
reform notwithstanding, as with Stowe's *Dred* (1856), the prospect of divine judgment carried unmistakable political currency.

As Douglass's characterization of the sky as "the very heavens" makes
clear, divine law and natural law are difficult to fully separate, because
many in this period understood nature as a material extension of divinity.[58]
Transcendentalism, as I suggested in Chapter 2, owes a debt to the renunciative imperatives of Christian theology. However, despite the movement's
suggestive name (which was initially used as a pejorative by critics), transcendentalists were much less world-wary than Augustinian-style theolo-
gians, who saw the world around them as a fallen realm that they needed
to overcome to reach the heavenly city.[59] According to Ralph Waldo Emerson, the city of God was ever present in the natural world. Viewed in solitude, Emerson wagers in *Nature,* the stars "give man, in the heavenly
bodies, the perpetual presence of the sublime"; they are a perceptible "re-
membrance of the city of God."[60] In the natural law tradition, nature (not
the nation) is the material realm that most closely approximates the heavenly city. Romanticism's spiritualization of the worldly is crucial for understanding the collectivist payoff of Douglass's strategic depiction of
Madison as all but bereft of individual agency. In John Stauffer's analysis
of the sublime character of Madison and Listwell's interracial friendship,
he identifies an aspect of Douglass's romanticism that I would like to echo
here in somewhat different terms. Stauffer argues that Douglass and Melville both "depart strikingly from Burke and Kant (and most other roman-
tics) by transposing sublimity from the natural world, or landscape, to
heroic individuals and human connections specifically through their representations of interracial friendship."[61] Although my emphasis in this chapter

is on the natural world rather than the individual, part of what I am arguing is that "The Heroic Slave" makes it extraordinarily difficult to make this distinction because it forces us to read the individual as continuous with the natural world. Understood in these terms, Douglass's seemingly passive hero emerges as a paragon of the paradoxically impersonal, universalist "self-reliance" that Emerson theorizes in "Self-Reliance" (1841).[62]

By depicting nature as the principal abolitionist agent in "The Heroic Slave," Douglass is able to suggest that the opposition to slavery is natural and, thus, more fundamental than the actions of any one individual or group. Douglass's insistent downplaying of human agency is most dramatic in the representation of the revolt onboard the *Creole*. The force of the insurrectionists is diminished, on a formal level, by the fact that the revolt is narrated only retrospectively—and narrated, moreover, by a sailor who was unconscious during the event in question. The details of the revolt emerge in the course of a dialogue between two white sailors in a Richmond coffeehouse. Jack Williams, "a regular old salt," "tauntingly" addresses the "first mate" of the Creole: "I say, shipmate, you had rather rough weather on your late passage to Orleans?" ("HS," 226). The fictional mate, named Tom Grant, replies, "Foul play, as well as foul weather" ("HS," 226). Williams speaks of bad weather during the insurrection, but it is worth noting that the premise of the squall is one of the fictional elements of Douglass's portrayal. The weather during the revolt was, in fact, unremarkable—there was, to quote the congressional report, "a fresh breeze, and the sky [was] a little hazy, with trade-clouds flying" (Doc. 51, 37). Douglass invented the squall, but this fictionalization also responded to the diplomatic history of the revolt—and to Webster's imagined "stresses of weather," in particular. Given Douglass's familiarity with Webster's letters, the squall can be seen as a rewriting of Webster that strategically reappropriates natural metaphors as a figure for natural rights.

In Webster's letters, "nature" is an unfortunate accident—not a portentous moral force, as it is in "The Heroic Slave." In an argument reminiscent of Webster's, the "old salt" Williams insists that the real cause of that "whole affair" could not possibly rest solely with the slaves. The "whole affair on board of the Creole," Williams declares, "was miserably and disgracefully managed" ("HS," 226). The "whole disaster was the result of ignorance of the real character of *darkies* in general. . . . All that is needed in dealing with a set of rebellious *darkies,* is to show that yer not afraid of 'em" ("HS," 226–227). Had the sailors lost control of the ship as a result of the weather alone, Williams continues to suggest, that at least would have "relieve[d] the affair of its present discreditable features" ("HS," 231). Acts of nature, as Grant reflects, are seen as unavoidable, and so legitimate. "For a ship to go down under a calm sky is, upon the first flush of it, disgraceful either to sailors or caulkers. But when we learn, that by some mysterious disturbance in nature, the waters parted beneath, and swallowed the ship up, we lose our indignation and disgust in lamentation of the disaster, and in awe of the Power which controls the elements" ("HS," 231). By establishing a parallel between "foul play" and "foul weather," the premise of the squall allows Douglass to maintain the agency of the slaves while also suggesting that the revolt (and the resulting emancipation of the slaves) was prompted by an underlying "disturbance in nature."[63]

The retrospective narration of the revolt distances the reader from its drama and urgency, but this remove facilitates Douglass's effort to present Madison's heroism in the more authoritative terms of relative disinterestedness. Tom Grant—who discerns Madison to be "a superior man" but is unwilling to concede that the "principles of 1776" apply to men he deems "inferior" on the basis of "color" ("HS," 238)—is pivotal to the ideological authority of "The Heroic Slave" for this very reason. Offering an intermediary between Listwell's avowed (if still fairly anemic)[64] abolitionism and Williams's blatant bigotry, Grant models a form of conciliatory identification with Madison.[65] The fact that the presentation of Madison's heroism is never free from white mediation in the novella—whether in Grant's reluctant admission of respect, or in the (fabricated) fact that Listwell provides Madison with the files that he uses to free himself and the other slaves ("HS," 223, 235)[66]—has often been regarded as the novella's failure fully to imagine black self-determination.[67] However, the decision to narrate the revolt not only retrospectively, but also dialogically, does not thereby reproduce the ideologically compromised assumptions of the novella's white characters. Instead, the narrative's reliance on figures of mediation and friendship tacitly identifies public *perception* (not the natural capacity of slaves) as the principal obstacle to emancipation.[68] Douglass's suggestive naming of Grant, which has gone unremarked in scholarship, echoes this emphasis—suggesting that rights (even when conceptualized as natural) still require social and legal recognition.[69]

Both of the venues in which "The Heroic Slave" initially appeared—an antislavery gift book and Douglass's newspaper—were likely to attract readers who already self-identified as abolitionists. However, the text self-consciously addresses itself to the unconverted reader. The conversation between Grant and Williams provides a formal mechanism for defamiliarizing commonplace stereotypes about the innate servility of slaves. Grant responds to Williams's imputation that the sailors could have prevented the revolt through better management by arguing that outward submission is strategic and conditioned by context.

> I deny that the negro is, naturally, a coward, or that your theory of managing slaves will stand the test of *salt* water. . . . It is one thing to manage a company of slaves on a Virginia plantation, and quite another thing to quell an insurrection on the lonely billows of the Atlantic, where every breeze speaks of courage and liberty. For the negro to act cowardly on shore, may be to act wisely; and I've some doubts whether *you,* Mr. Williams, would find it very convenient were you a slave in Algiers, to raise your hand against the bayonets of a whole government. ("HS," 228)

By contrasting the open ocean with the Virginia plantation, Grant intimates that slavery, far from natural, can be maintained only in the artificial environs of a plantation. For this reason, as Grant's alternate scenario of Algerian enslavement dramatizes, slavery can as easily claim white auditors as it does the subjects of their curiosity.

The more general perspectival distance from the insurrectionists helps enforce the objective tone of these pointed remarks, but it becomes more fraught in the representation of the revolt itself. As if to take its formal aesthetic of mediation and opacity to a comic extreme, at the beginning of the revolt, Grant, our only eyewitness, is "knocked senseless to the deck" ("HS," 234). When he regains consciousness after an uncertain interval, the violent struggle and subsequent reversal of power have already occurred. "When I came to myself, (which I did in a few minutes, I *suppose,* for it was yet quite light,) there was not a white man on deck. The sailors were all aloft in the rigging, and dared not come down. Captain Clarke and Mr. Jameson lay stretched on the quarter-deck,—both dying,—while Madison himself stood at the helm unhurt" ("HS," 234, emphasis added). Critics tend to suggest that Douglass uses the premise of Grant's unconsciousness to minimize the scene of violence and so facilitate the idealization of Madison as a hero, but violence, it is worth stressing, is not absent so much as displaced onto the portentous figure of the squall.[70]

> By this time the apprehended squall had burst upon us. The wind howled furiously,—the ocean was white with foam, which, on account of the darkness, we could see only by the quick flashes of lightning that darted occasionally from the angry sky. All was alarm and confusion. Hideous cries came up from the slave women. Above the roaring billows a succession of heavy thunder rolled along, swelling the terrific din. Owing to the great darkness, and a sudden shift of the wind, we found ourselves in the trough of the sea. When shipping a heavy sea over the starboard bow, the bodies of the captain and Mr. Jameson were washed overboard. . . . A more savage thunder-gust never swept the ocean. Our brig rolled and creaked as if every bolt would be started, and every thread of oakum would be pressed out of the seams. ("HS," 236–237)

Recalling the constellation of natural metaphors that organizes the elliptical presentation of Madison in the preface—"howling tempests," "the menacing rock on a perilous coast," and "angry lightning" ("HS," 175)—Douglass uses the squall to both express and contain the uncomfortable violence of the revolt. With their precise physical condition undisclosed, and with causality eclipsed in the passive voice, we are thus told that "the bodies of the captain and Mr. Jameson *were washed overboard*." Admittedly less gory than the official account of the insurrection (which includes a knife fight and a shooting), the squall, nonetheless, is not only sublime, but "furious," "terrific," and "hideous." "The Heroic Slave," in this respect, does not repress the violence of the insurrection so much as reconfigure its underlying cause. Douglass presents the revolt as an effect of nature—more fundamental, if also more erratic, than the actions of an individual agent.

Evoking a long tradition of representing national turmoil through the figure of the ship of state tossed to and fro at sea, Douglass uses the ocean as a symbolic counterpoint to extant national law. This is particularly emphatic in the passage that appears to have served as the prototype for Madison Washington's often-quoted proclamation in "The Heroic Slave" that "you cannot write the bloody laws of slavery on those restless billows. The ocean, if not the land, is free" ("HS," 237). In his 1849 speech—whose title, "Slavery, the Slumbering Volcano," itself imagines emancipation as an imminent natural force—Douglass uses the "restless waves" of the ocean as a rhetorical directive for national reform.

> Sir, I thank God that there is some part of his footstool upon which the bloody statutes of Slavery cannot be written. They cannot be written on the proud, towering billows of the Atlantic. The restless waves will not permit those bloody statutes to be recorded there; those foaming billows forbid it; old ocean gnawing with its hungry surges upon our rockbound coast preaches a lesson to American soil: "You may bind chains upon the limbs of your people if you will; you may place the yoke upon them if you will; you may brand them with irons; you may write out your statutes and preserve them in the archives of the nation if you will; but the moment they mount the surface of our unsteady waves, those statutes are obliterated, and the slave stands redeemed, disenthralled." This part of God's domain then is free, and I hope that ere long our own soil will also be free.[71]

This passage, which follows immediately on one of Douglass's several oratory depictions of the revolt on the *Creole*, envisions the ocean as an explicitly denationalizing force. The Atlantic, as Douglass casts it, is not only outside the nation proper; it erodes the coasts that give it form. The analogy between the soil and the laws is significant in this respect. For in underscoring the link between territoriality and positive law, he presents the ocean as a model for an essentially anarchic freedom. Freedom here, as is so often the case, is an expressly negative concept, imagined alternately as baptism and destruction.

The Atlantic—as the personification of natural law—didactically "preaches a lesson to American soil," but it remains an episodic force, unsteady and transient.[72] Drawing together the archetypal liberal tropes of the state of nature and the founding scene of revolution, Douglass represents the ocean as a counterfactual (and changeable) tabula rasa that is both a precondition for constructing political ideals and, if they are not fulfilled, a figure for dissolving and reforming individual communities. Thus, as much as Douglass might idealize the ocean as an extranational utopian space (which if not nowhere is still foremost *not* the nation), his ultimate objective in "The Heroic Slave" is not properly transnational or cosmopolitan, as several recent critics have suggested.[73] Instead, Douglass prescriptively uses the universalizing rhetoric of natural law as a model for freedom on "our own soil."

Douglass continued to come back to the powerful image of nature in revolt. In the appropriately titled "Fighting Rebels with Only One Hand" (1861), Douglass uses the image of a ship floundering at sea to suggest that sectional conflict derives from nature (not mere political agents) and that unjust states will invariably be overturned by the imminent moral force of nature. "The cause of this rebellion is deeper down than either Southern politicians or Northern Abolitionists. They are but the hands of the clock. The machinery moves not because of the hands, but the hands because of the machinery. The ship may be great, but the ocean that bears it is greater. The Southern politicians and the Northern Abolitionists are the fruits, not the trees. They indicate, but are not original causes. The trouble is deeper down, and is fundamental; there is nothing strange about it. The conflict is in every way natural."[74] Douglass's ongoing recourse to natural law, I want to suggest, illuminates his substantive reconceptualization of Lockean liberalism. "The Heroic Slave" reimagines liberalism's negative conceptualization of community (through pre- and extra-social figures like the state of nature and the founding scene of revolution) as an extralegal model for citizenship, in which those who have been systematically *excluded* from the body politic are exemplars of a "natural" nation that had yet to be.

Liberalism's model of rights by dissent, needless to say, was not without its own complex set of problems. As Jeannine DeLombard has argued, liberalism's association of rights with revolt had the troubling effect of establishing criminality as the only recognizable expression of political autonomy for enslaved people. Because "the criminous slave was assigned a degree of legal personhood routinely denied to even free blacks," DeLombard observes, "to commit a crime was to enact one's personhood as never before."[75] Douglass flirts with the kind of criminalized personhood DeLombard discusses, but he refuses the criminality of abolitionist resistance by stressing the illegitimacy of the law and by idealizing revolt as an expression of the higher "law of nature."

Douglass used the broader cultural tendency to idealize citizenship from its outer limits (a paradigm to which we will return in Part III). Douglass's negative conceptualization of citizenship allows him to strategically analogize two otherwise very dissimilar forms of outsiderness: systematic exclusion on the basis of ascribed traits, and the voluntary self-exile associated with the heroic agent of liberal revolt. In "The Heroic Slave," these two categories are re-envisioned as one: the enslaved people on the *Creole,* who are denied rights in their native land, overthrow the artificial legal system of chattel slavery, metonymically through the white crew who stand in for the plantation South on the ship of state. "The Heroic Slave" appropriates the recognizable plot of the liberal subject in revolt for abolitionist ends, but it also breaks from this tradition in two interlocking ways: "The Heroic Slave" rejects landed rights and the form of liberal individualism it underwrites. Douglass's maritime reimagining of the "natural citizen" leaves behind the land—and the property-based conception of rights that it reinforces in the Lockean tradition. In place of a land-based theory of rights, Douglass envisions a property-less conception of rights in the wilds of the sea.

Douglass's landless vision of rights in "The Heroic Slave" echoes one of the most compelling passages in William Ellery Channing's book-length consideration of the implications of the *Creole* revolt. "The sea is the exclusive property of no nation. It is subject to none. It is the common and equal property of all. No state has jurisdiction over it. No state can write its laws on that restless surface."[76] The problem with a property-based theory of rights, as Douglass and Channing recognized, was not only that it breeds an inequality in capital, but that, through the legal fiction of chattel slavery, enslaved people were not only denied equality; they were actively counted as part of the property that unequally empowered the few.

Douglass's novelistic response to the *Creole* revolt literalizes the Constitution's tropic yoking of nature and citizen in order to offer an inclusive formulation of the "natural citizen" that takes its inspiration from the unbounded freedoms mythologized in the philosophical conceit of the "state of nature." Douglass's gambit in "The Heroic Slave" is to reclaim a place of textual and political eminence for Madison Washington and for the many other enslaved people whose life stories were reduced to the monetized transactions of the "chattel records of [their] native State" ("HS," 175). Like Goodell, Douglass plays upon nativist arguments against chattel slavery—particularly in the opening pages of "The Heroic Slave." However, by the time the reader is on the other side of Grant's retelling of the maritime revolt, the novella's political strategies have themselves undergone a sea change. Rather than naturalize a nativist conception of citizenship, which the Know-Nothing Party and other antebellum anti-immigration leagues wielded to exclude foreigners, Douglass relinquishes the nativist trappings of the Natural-Born Citizen Clause to theorize a "citizen of nature"—a citizen whose rights are *granted* by nature and are also legible to the "Grants" of Madison's "native State."

## Local Fictions

Taking the ocean as a model, Douglass denaturalizes the ideological "borders" of the nation in "The Heroic Slave," even as he attempts to salvage the revolutionary potential of U.S. democracy. Douglass's novella, in this way, thematizes something that all of the commentators on the *Creole* case implicitly recognize: namely, that in the indeterminate space of the ocean, any claim to jurisdiction is necessarily contingent on acts of characterization, representation, and construal. Whether these representations invoke the ship of state or arguments about the domestic character of harbors, they have to confront the manifest virtuality of the construction of the nation at sea.[77] Douglass extends this sense of the virtual character of nationalism, in the context of the sea, to a reflection on the contingent authority of national law more generally.

In abolitionist portrayals of the *Creole* revolt, the idealization of the ocean as a figure of natural freedom was not a way of transcending the nation as such, but was instead, and very explicitly, a model for reform within the United States. The unstable interplay between the presentation of the ocean as a distinctly extra-national space and the articulation of ostensibly national values shaped the equivocal legal conceptualization of the *Creole* revolt. In the year following the insurrection on the *Creole,* districts across the North submitted petitions to Congress declaring that slaves "become constitutionally entitled to their freedom by going to sea."[78] Implicit in this wording, which appeared in petitions submitted to Congress on at least eleven separate occasions, is the peculiar supposition that the Constitution only protects slaves outside the proper jurisdiction of the United States. Part of the rationale for this admittedly counterintuitive argument had to do with the dominant understanding of slavery as a local rather than a federal institution. For even if, as Webster maintained, the *Creole* ship was still legally within U.S. jurisdiction (while in the Bahamas) that did not mean that it was still within the jurisdiction of the slave states. In fact, since the revolt on the *Creole* occurred before the passage of the 1850 Fugitive Slave Act, the ship's redirection to a Northern state potentially could have had the same effect as its arrival in Nassau. Using a speculative counterfactual similar to Webster's claim that the *Creole* "*ought to be regarded as still pursuing their original voyage*" (Doc. 1, 121), an 1842 article in the *New York Evangelist* explores what this might have meant in its opening lines: "The Creole Heroes in New-York. They are not here—but suppose they were. Suppose that instead of directing the Creole to Nassau, New-Providence, they had brought her to this city. By what law could they have been reclaimed or punished? If we rightly understand the case, they would have been legally as safe here as in New-Providence."[79]

By emphasizing the international dimensions of the contested jurisdiction over the *Creole,* Webster's diplomatic letters bypass the equally debatable question of the United States' collective stance on slavery. As one New York newspaper inveighs in 1842, Webster's arguments make it impossible to maintain that slavery "is a mere municipal institution—a local interest." "Here we have the Federal Government, putting forth and pledging all its power to protect slavery—not within the United States—not even within the marine league of our own shores, where, by the usage of nations, the jurisdiction of a State applies—but, on the high seas, and even in the harbor of a nation, that does not acknowledge slavery!"[80] Precisely because the revolt occurred outside the highly sectionalized geopolitical landscape of the United States, but yet within its symbolic extension in the ship of state, the dispute over the *Creole* offered a uniquely decisive test case for determining the United States' official stance on slavery.

Northern and Southern newspapers both used the ostensibly common ideological tropes of the American Revolution to convey the significance of the *Creole* affair, but the starkly divergent narratives they developed underscore the essential malleability of the rhetoric of liberty. Abolitionists drew parallels between the principles of the slave revolt and the American Revolution to suggest, in the words of one Christian paper, that "if we as Americans were justified in resisting the oppressions of Great Britain, these slaves had the same rights which we claimed for ourselves." The tacit irony, as the same article hints, is, of course, that from this perspective Britain is no longer the oppressor but the liberator: "It may be remarked that the principle on which our American Revolution was founded, is fully recognized in this [Britain's] decision."[81]

The very fact of Britain's involvement in the case, not surprisingly, was seen very differently by Southerners, who decried Britain's interference as an affront to the liberty of U.S. citizens. A month after the revolt, a Louisiana newspaper proclaimed, "The great lever by which England hopes one day to overturn this government—abolitionism—has been again sit [sic] in motion." "The question now remains to be decided, how much further this government will submit to be trodden on in every way—insulted at every point—by the insolence of our old and bitter foe."[82] As if to refute the power of abolitionism within the United States, the paper depicts it as an essentially foreign doctrine that, if admitted, will "overturn this government," reinstating the subordinate, if not expressly colonial, position of the United States.[83]

Quite evidently, as Edmund Morgan and others have emphasized, slavery was not necessarily seen as incompatible with the principle of liberty.[84] To make this incongruity apparent, it might be said, required extralegal traditions capable of denaturalizing extant power relations. As the *American Jurist and Law Magazine* argues in its 1842 assessment of the *Creole* case, natural law places fundamental limits on the authority of existing legislation:

> Man has a twofold nature. . . .
> Not all the legislation in the world can change the decrees of Providence or reconcile the material nature of property, with the spiritual nature of man. The law of nature and of nations, dealing solely in actual truths, does not recognize *this local fiction.* . . .
> When, therefore, a man, either by force or art, escapes *beyond the limits of that local law,* that fastens slavery upon him, he falls under the benign protection of the *law of nature, which steps in and sets bounds to the local fiction,* and declares that it shall only be respected within the jurisdiction of the community that promulgated it. The law of nature did not make man a slave, and therefore that law shall not keep him one.[85]

The principal claim of the article, alluded to in the inconsistency of the dual nature of man, is that Webster fails to consider that chattel slavery is essentially distinct from other forms of property. Because "the spiritual nature of man" can never be reconciled with the merely physical "nature of property," a slave's status as chattel is a legal fiction—and as such has no authority beyond the local jurisdiction that enforces it. As Deak Nabers suggests in his discussion of the *Somerset* decision, "Insofar as slavery was alien to natural right, it was possible to imagine that the laws occasioning it involved fiction, if not an out-and-out effacement of reality."[86] The conceit of natural law, in this respect, allowed reformers to make the more general ontological point that all positive law is essentially fictive.

As a figure of contested jurisdiction, free of the stable boundaries that enable the demarcation and internal subdivision of land, the ocean offered an ideal site in which the United States tested its own legal fictions. In this respect, the symbolic function of the ocean in the commentary on the *Creole* parallels abolitionist invocations of the heavenly city (discussed in Chapter 2): each served as an imaginative touchstone for an extralegal moral order, untethered from institutional forms of governance. The higher law traditions of citizenship helped dislodge the politically static fictions of a "natural" nation and citizenry that Jay and others used to shore up the authority of the state. This refusal of the naturalness of the nation was absolutely critical to the efficacy of higher law formulations of citizenship, because if "[man's] natural rights are the foundation of all his civil rights," as Thomas Paine argued, and rights are inalienable (inherent and untransferable), this meant not only that the rights of citizens were naturally derived, but also implied that those denied full political membership lacked the character necessary to its possession.[87] The rhetorical link between civil and natural rights initiates a circular logic, in which what already *is* presumably coincides with what *ought to be*. In this respect, it is hardly surprising that Douglass and many other reformers were reluctant to dispense with the nation as a meaningful unit of politics. As we saw in Chapter 2, the higher law traditions of citizenship were only properly political when and insofar as they recognized cities, states, and nations as worthy of reform.

The *Creole* case does not attest to the self-enacting power of natural law outside the coast-bound borders of the nation. Yet it does help illuminate the cultural power and even instrumentality of the higher law discourse—which made it possible to recast political transgression (revolt) as the historical realization of a patriotic ideal that was, in fact, an artifact of a distinctly counterfactual political hermeneutic. Higher law, in both its theological and secularized forms, offered a way out of the self-reinforcing regime of positive law. The densely imagined counterfactuals of higher law provided the subjunctive framework within which it appeared not only possible but also necessary to grant the political character of individuals who were denied rights within their native country. However, the higher law traditions of citizenship were not always politically progressive. From the beginning, natural law and divine law were used to authorize ideologically divergent visions of citizenship. As with Webster's insidious characterization of the revolt on the *Creole* as a natural disaster, the higher law traditions of citizenship were used to justify enslavement and nativist policies—as well as to critique them. As a relativist tradition, higher law was not always necessarily a better law, but its negative relation to the law of the land was crucial to constructing the aspirational meaning of citizenship in the early United States. And in a collective sense, these traditions worked to decenter and delegitimize the racialized model of citizenship that gained new prominence in the 1850s.[88] The proliferation of different understandings of "citizenship"—anchored in Christian theology and natural law philosophy—called attention to the still remarkably porous boundaries of personhood within the law.

Natural law's power to fundamentally shift the categories of "law" and "crime" made it a powerful resource for abolitionists who sought to reclaim the revolt on the *Creole* as a paradigm for citizenship moving forward. And seen from the long *durée* of citizenship's historical development, the fantastic harmony between nature and the nation—which the natural law tradition of citizenship helped cement—was arguably quite successful. The Fourteenth Amendment's formalization of *jus soli,* and its shift away from *jus sanguinis,* gave even broader range to the fantasy of the "natural" character of citizenship that the Natural-Born Citizen Clause registers. Today, this conceit remains as fantastical as it was when Jay leveraged it in 1789. However, of all the extralegal discourses traced in this book, natural law formulations of citizenship are the most recognizable to us today, because as scholars have noted, the Fourteenth Amendment owes a significant debt to abolitionism as a movement—and also because, as I have argued in this chapter, it owes an especially profound debt to the natural law tradition of abolitionism to which the 1850 Compromise Act lent new urgency.[89]

Amid the receding landscape of freedom in the 1850s, it was no longer enough to bypass the physical borders of the slave states. A broader rhetorical assault on the legitimacy of the human laws that policed these borders offered the only viable solution to a newly virtualized model of the flexible jurisdictional reach of the slave South. It was in this context that the conceit of the universality of natural law took on new political significance. Seen through the universalist idiom of nature, national laws were themselves fictions—and in the case of chattel slavery, these legal fictions were dangerous. They obscured the natural rights that enslaved and freed people alike rightfully enjoyed across the continuous and undifferentiated landscape of nature.

## ★ III ★

# THE LETTERED CITIZEN

# The Elsewhere of Citizenship

## *Literary Autonomy and the Fabrication of Allegiance*

Politics is a serious study,—serious as our lives and liberties. . . .
But, strange as it may seem, some of the best thinkers whom the
world has ever seen, have encircled political abstractions with the
zone of beauty, and clothed sober experience with the many-
colored robings of romance. Every age has been enriched by some
figment of a commonwealth.

—J. Sullivan Cox, "Imaginary Commonwealths" (1846)

I am a citizen of somewhere else.

—Nathaniel Hawthorne, "The Custom-House" (1850)

IN THE "HIGHER LAW" traditions of political critique examined in Part II,
the cultural authority for citizenship is not located in the law, but in
the transcendent sources of political legitimation that ostensibly underwrite it: divine law and natural law, or, to recall Jefferson's phraseology,
"the Laws of Nature and of Nature's God."[1] As we have seen, abolitionists
used the otherworldly kingdom of heaven and the unadulterated wilds of
nature to theorize extralegal models of citizenship that placed enslaved
people, fugitives, and freeborn blacks firmly within the narrative limits of
a *morally* constituted civic order. To the "ought" of the moral discourses
that governed citizenship, this chapter adds an examination of another, less
prescriptive dimension of the political subjunctive: its *possibilistic* scope,
which concerns the thinkable as much as the true. Since the authors discussed
in the foregoing chapters frame their arguments and plots in relationship to a
set of transcendent truths, fictionality—the epistemic mode and problem of
the fictive—has not itself been a primary object of consideration. This chapter
examines the civic importance of fiction as a differential mode of expression by
showing how the romantic reconceptualization of the "literary" as a separate,
autonomous realm facilitated the emergence of a secular form of political

critique—one that was structured by the comparative logic of the possible, rather than the moral imperatives of righteousness. Extending scholarship by M. H. Abrams and others who identify the detached contemplations of Christian theology as an important precursor to the disinterested ethos of aesthetic autonomy, I argue that the romantic conceit of literature's separation from everyday politics made the newly differentiated literary realm an ideal arena for the continued development of the higher law traditions of citizenship.[2]

In a limited sense, we already are accustomed to thinking about literature as a resource for citizenship. One of the central tenets of liberal education philosophy is the notion that studying literature helps prepare students to be active and discerning citizens. The position, as political philosopher Martha Nussbaum polemically articulates it in *Cultivating Humanity: A Classical Defense of Reform in Liberal Education* (1997), is that "it is essential to put the study of literature at the heart of a curriculum for citizenship, because it develops arts of interpretation that are essential for civic participation and awareness." Drawing on Ralph Ellison and Walt Whitman, Nussbaum argues that "narrative art has the power to make us see the lives of the different with more than a casual tourist's interest—with involvement and sympathetic understanding, with anger at our society's refusals of visibility."[3] Literature, in this model, serves a substitutionary function; it is a textual prosthesis for the people and problems otherwise unseen and unknown. Within this optimistic but also commonplace view, literature does not simply prepare readers for civic participation, it is an essentially participatory medium; it involves us in the lives of others, from whom we are otherwise divided both socioeconomically and cognitively.

The political significance of literature in the humanistic paradigm resides in the power of fiction to develop and deepen the social consciousness of its readers. As a result, the efficacy of the "narrative imagination" depends on recognizable parallels between the worlds of fiction and the empirical world we occupy—and, in particular, between the characters of fiction and the actual personages who make up the various subsets of society. Without the premise of this proximate substitutability, characters remain merely fantastical, without any obvious applicability to the world in which we live. The referential analogies that underwrite this literalistic approach to the politics of literature place a premium on the sociological accuracy of literature and the basic verisimilitude that makes this social typology legible to discerning readers.

That the notion of literature as means of "social understanding" implicitly privileges realist fiction—which lends itself to direct social analogies and political extrapolations—should hardly come as a surprise. Realism has long been a dividing line in debates about the political power and limitations of literature. At the heart of Georg Lukács's influential critique of surrealism, as "an openly anti-realist or pseudo-realist literature" that "provide[s] an apologia for, and a defense of, the existing system," is the conviction that the only way "to achieve a critical distance from [dominant] prejudices" is "by a deeper probing of the *real* world."[4] Aesthetic distance does not translate into "critical distance," for Lukács. The political efficacy of art depends on its transparency—on its exposure of the real, not its difference from it. This loosely referential approach to fiction privileges the mimetic capacity of literature as both the precondition and the measure of its political significance. Lukács's heir, Fredric Jameson, turned this realist drive into a method, by understanding interpretation as the work of "restoring to the surface of the text the repressed and buried reality of [its] fundamental history."[5] For Lukács and Jameson, as for Nussbaum, the political force of a literary text depends on a moment of recognition, when we see through it (and back into) the social and historical struggles of our own world—the moment, in other words, when we cease to perceive it in the *non*-referential terms of fiction.[6] These influential accounts have given us powerful ways of understanding the politics of individual works of literature, but their abiding epistemic investment in realism and the real also preserves a longstanding ambivalence toward the "fictionality" of fiction—a term that I use in a restricted sense to specify the elements of literature that highlight and occasionally flaunt the otherwise merely descriptive fact of fiction.[7]

The assumption that the political force of literature depends on a degree of realism—and the interpretative investment in restoring this lost "reality" through referential interpretative paradigms like historical contextualization—can be understood as a methodological extension of the classic Enlightenment anxiety about the deleterious effects of the imagination. The entanglement of empiricism (as ontology), realism (as genre), and historicism (as method) is profound and persistent. Yet my concern here is not the genealogy of their interrelationship, but the alternative ways of understanding fiction's importance for citizenship that we can glean from another epistemic trio that gained prominence during the era of citizenship's formative conceptualization in the nineteenth century: Idealism, romance, and "romantic fictionality"—a defensive theory of fiction that reclaimed the non-referential prerogatives of fictional license as a "right." I will return to the relatively familiar, humanist model of civic education in Chapter 5, which traces the emergence of a specifically nationalist political imaginary. This chapter offers a new account of the interrelated development of fiction and citizenship in the nineteenth century by rethinking the political stakes of a term and concept that long has provided realism's symbolic counterpoint in Americanist literary criticism: "romance."[8] Whereas the humanist model of the lettered citizen hinges on literalistic analogies between text and world that allow us to understand character identification as a precedent for social empathy and a more capacious category of the human, this chapter considers the importance of fiction as a differential episteme by showing how the romantic trope of literary autonomy contributed to higher law critiques of the artificial and imposed character of political allegiance.

The trope of literary autonomy might seem like a distinctly unpromising point of reference for discussing literature's historical role in shaping citizenship. After all, writers and critics alike alternately have celebrated and censured the doctrine of literary autonomy as quintessentially apolitical. However, it was (and is) a politically charged doctrine—and it has carried a host of different meanings over time. What meanings did the trope of literary autonomy hold in an era in which the nature and perpetuity of political allegiance was still deeply contested in U.S. law? And how might the little-known debates about the right to expatriate discussed in Chapter 1 help us better understand the ambivalently localized political currency that formulations of literary autonomy took on in the early United States? The trope of literature's separation from everyday politics, needless to say, is not a distinctively U.S. aesthetic doctrine—nor can it be fully periodized. It is a cosmopolitan ideal, born of German and English Romanticism and infused by Christian thought.[9] However, as we will see, the trope of literary autonomy assumed deeply political and often regional import in a country still polarized by debates about the defeasible (voluntary and so relinquishable) nature of political allegiance. I argue that mistaken assumptions about the consensual character of citizenship in the early United States—and an overreliance on the American Revolution as the master trope of U.S. literature and politics—have led critics to take for granted and misconstrue the cultural meaning of romantic formulations of literary autonomy: theories of the liberty of the imagination and the trope of fictional license, what Edward Everett Hale aptly termed the "rights of the writer of fiction."[10] As we saw in Chapter 1, the organic model of natural and perpetual allegiance typically associated with British subjecthood held significant staying power in early U.S. law. And as the fraught history of nullification and secession should remind us, those who invoked this right were often seen as traitors—not as the inheritors of an untroubled principle of voluntary allegiance. As such, the politicized terms in which the literary imagination was censured tells us as much (if not more) about fiction's historical power as a medium of political critique, as do the most celebratory defenses of fictional license.

Fiction's epistemic distance from (and figurative denaturalization of) everyday historical and political realities is central to the romantic theory of fiction, and the civic importance of this particular theory of fiction can only be appreciated if we recognize fiction's difference from institutionally delimited communities as an integral aspect of its distinctive political power. Critics sometimes discuss the overblown unreality of the romantic aesthetic as a kind of "aesthetic dissent," wherein the imagination's departure from history is itself a form of radical protest or revolt.[11] The theory of literature's importance for early U.S. citizenship that I explore here overlaps with this model, insofar as it emphasizes forms of political subjectivity defined apart from (and often in opposition to) the terra firma. However, I do not read romantic fictionality within the redemptive, revolutionary teleology of utopian critique. Fiction may hold out the promise of perfectibility somewhere else, but it is arguably fiction's *failure* to provide an inhabitable alternative to the political present that redirects an impulse that might otherwise be merely escapist into a dynamic episteme for political refashioning.

Each theory of fiction entails a different set of cultural and aesthetic assumptions. In an effort to take these differences seriously, this chapter grounds its reassessment of the politics of literary autonomy in an extended reexamination of an author who played an exceptionally prominent role in cultivating the romantic conception of fiction in the early United States and in the scholarship on it: Nathaniel Hawthorne, who, as Jonathan Arac observes, "was the writer of prose narrative most important in establishing the kind of writing recognized as 'literary.' "[12] Hawthorne, to the fascination and occasional frustration of critics, insisted on the basic incompatibility of political and artistic enterprises, even though his own rise to prominence in antebellum letters was structured by the political appointments he held in the Boston and Salem Custom Houses in the 1840s and as U.S. consul in England in the 1850s. It is easy to turn career narratives into allegories, but Hawthorne's influential and much debated definitions of "romance" offer us something more conceptually substantive. Taking Hawthorne's formulation of romance as the site of unexpected political discernment, and paying special attention to his changing characterizations of the political character of the hermitic retreats of romance—as "neutral," a chosen "right," and, finally, in his essay on the Civil War, "a kind of treason"—I argue that the romantic idealization of fiction's separation from everyday politics allowed U.S. writers to engage and reconfigure contemporaneous arguments about the right to *choose* not to belong, which sought to denaturalize nativity (*jus soli*, right of the soil) as the basis of citizenship.[13]

Far from evincing literature's separation from politics, antebellum theorizations of literary autonomy invited politicized defenses and critiques of
fiction that were both metaphorically and conceptually entangled in contemporaneous debates about the right to refuse allegiance—which came to
a head in debates about the right to expatriate, struggles over state sovereignty, and finally Confederate secession.[14] The analogies between literary
autonomy and political defection were not always as direct as Hawthorne's
figurative characterization of romance as "a kind of treason," but the more
explicitly politicized condemnations of literary autonomy help illuminate
the unfinished cultural work of which it was a part: namely, the belated
and contentious idealization of the voluntary form of political allegiance
that eventually came to be seen as a distinguishing feature of citizenship.[15]
By attending to the fraught political contests that informed the way writers
understood the political stakes of their writing, we can also better understand why—as with Ralph Waldo Emerson's characterization of the transcendentalists as "bad citizens"—they often ended up condemning the very
form of imaginative license that they sought to reclaim.[16] The charged (and
often denigrated) analogy between literary and political autonomy, I argue,
threatened to undercut the moral authority of the literary, but it also situated the realm of letters as a cultural precedent and epistemic resource for
developing the newly voluntary (and so defeasible) form of allegiance that
was colloquially associated with the language of "citizenship," long before
the 1868 Expatriation Act belatedly recognized the "natural and inherent
rights of all people" to dissolve the formal connection that tied citizens to
the state.[17]

## Rights of Romance

The era of citizenship's formative emergence in the United States was an
era in which literature was itself undergoing a dramatic reconceptualization. Over the course of the nineteenth century, an older use of the term
"literature," which broadly designated an "acquaintance with letters or
books," gave way to the specialized romantic conception of "the literary"
as an elevated, aesthetic mode set apart from the norms of everyday expression.[18] This terminological shift went hand in hand with the romantic
idealization of the artist's separation from (and transcendence of) the age
in which she lived.[19] As M. H. Abrams and others have shown, the rise of
the theory of "art-as-such" over the course of the eighteenth century drew
on Christian theology's long-established concern with "disinterested" con-
templation.[20] By idealizing fiction's distance from the everyday world, the

romantic conception of literature reframed the existential problem of Christian estrangement—worldly citizenship or heavenly belonging—as an aesthetic predicament. Fiction, within this view, posed an affiliatory dilemma: engaged political membership *or* literary citizenship—the fanciful "belong[ing] to another sphere" that the narrator of Hawthorne's "The Custom-House" (1850) famously claimed in declaring to be "a citizen of somewhere else."[21]

The gradual reclamation of the imagination and fiction from the anxious strictures of Enlightenment empiricism is one of the oft-told tales of the nineteenth century. According to this narrative, the liberty of the imagination and the virtuality of fiction—once seen as unruly and dangerous—were transformed over the course of the nineteenth century into the defining characteristics of "literary virtue."[22] The absorption of German Idealism into a number of aesthetic and philosophical movements was crucial in this respect. By identifying consciousness as the primary arena of experience, Idealism inverted the epistemic hierarchy of British empiricism—its subordination of the imagination to the senses, idea to matter, word to thing. The emergence of several strains of Idealist thought that championed the instructive character of the imagination helped address early critiques that identified fancy as an epistemic threat to right understanding. However, the Idealist revaluation of the imagination left it newly vulnerable to persistent anxieties about the type of isolation the imaginative life seemed to invite.[23]

The romantic revaluation of fiction in the long nineteenth century helped to rehabilitate the speculative. Romanticism recast fiction's departure from the descriptive regime of the indicative—the "is" of physical facts and moral truths—as an ideal, rather than a deficit. However, critics and writers continued to struggle with parallel anxieties about the political effects of Idealism's life of the mind. Politicized anxieties about the imagination were particularly pronounced in discussions of novels, whose captivating and often fantastic imaginings were viewed warily as a potentially dangerous counterweight to the everyday affiliatory bonds that connect citizens to the people and institutions around them. Take, for example, Thomas Jefferson's remarks in an 1818 letter, where he identifies "the inordinate passion prevalent for novels" as "a great obstacle to good education." "When this poison infects the mind," Jefferson explains, "it destroys its tone and revolts it against wholesome reading. Reason and fact, plain and unadorned, are rejected. . . . The result is a bloated imagination, sickly judgment, and disgust towards all the real business of life."[24] Insofar as fiction involves a kind of epistemic seduction, a drawing of the mind away from the empirical world, many writers and critics have viewed the invention (and readerly occupation) of manifestly fictive worlds as a form of alienation. Within this framework, to turn to novels was to turn away from the "real" world.

Many of the most hyperbolic defenses and critiques of fiction used the language of "romance," a term that broadly designated fiction (as distinguished from fact), but which also was used more narrowly to describe works that highlighted their status as fiction by embracing the unlikely and "fabulous."[25] According to "Romance and Reality," an 1855 essay in *The Gentleman's Magazine,* romance is a threat to good citizenship, because it infatuates the imagination with the "phantoms of ideal life" and becomes a substitute for an active public life.[26] The rise of historical romance, the author avers, aggravates this problem by "antedat[ing]" readers to their own time as they imagine themselves "contemporary with past ages."[27] As such, the critic concludes in a formulation reminiscent of Hawthorne, "The true *romance reader was not a citizen of this world;* he belonged to another sphere."[28] Framed in terms of citizenship, the problem posed by fiction was not the traditional Enlightenment anxiety about the imagination's potentially corrosive effects on the faculty of reason, but the affiliatory pull of fiction—which redirected readers' imaginative life away from the more immediate concerns of the social and political present.[29]

Since few terms in Americanist literary criticism are as meta-critically encumbered as "romance," further terminological clarification will be useful before further elaborating its political dimensions. "Romance" was used widely—and often loosely—in the nineteenth century, but its conceptual importance in shaping Americanist literary criticism is intimately tied to Hawthorne's prominent theorization of this term in the 1850s.[30] Much has been made, in particular, of Hawthorne's attempt to distinguish "romance" from the "novel" in *The House of the Seven Gables* (1851):

> When a writer calls his work a Romance, it need hardly be observed that he wishes to claim a certain latitude, both as to its fashion and material, which he would not have felt himself entitled to assume had he professed to be writing a Novel. The latter form of composition is presumed to aim at a very minute fidelity, not merely to the possible, but to the probable and ordinary course of man's experience. The former—while, as a work of art, it must rigidly subject itself to laws, and while it sins unpardonably so far as it may swerve aside from the truth of the human heart—has fairly a right to present that truth under circumstances, to a great extent, of the writer's own choosing or creation.[31]

Hawthorne defines "romance" negatively in relation to the extremes of credulity: it is not constrained by the exacting calculations of probability, nor does it overindulge in the manifestly wondrous. It is possibilistic rather than referential; its take on the possible is capacious.

At stake in the varying degrees of creative license that Hawthorne uses "romance" and the "novel" to describe are two distinct conceptions of the symbolic reach and limits of state power.[32] Romance and the novel are governed by different expectations about representational fidelity (possibility versus probability), but they also encode two distinct orders of governance. Romance is liberated from the constraints of referentiality, subject only to the intrinsic laws that pertain to "work[s] of art." Romance, for Hawthorne, names the fantastic promise of literary autonomy, while the "novel" connotes the burden of realism as an autocratic form beholden to representational fidelity.

The romance/novel distinction in *The House of the Seven Gables* echoes Walter Scott's "Essay on Romance," first published as a supplement to the *Encyclopedia Britannica* (1824), where he argues that "*Romance*" is a "fictitious narrative in prose or verse; the interest of which turns upon marvelous and uncommon incidents," whereas "the kindred term *Novel*" is a "fictitious narrative" whose "events are accommodated to the ordinary train of human events, and the modern state of society."[33] Despite Hawthorne's known debt to Scott, in the hands of field-forming Cold War–era Americanist literary critics Richard Chase and Lionel Trilling, Hawthorne's formulation of the romance novel distinction in *The House of the Seven Gables* became the touchstone for a specifically national theory of style. "American writers of genius have not turned their minds to society," Lionel Trilling argues in *The Liberal Imagination* (1950). "Hawthorne was acute when he insisted that he did not write novels but romances—he thus expressed his awareness of the lack of social texture in his work."[34] Trilling's argument that the absence of "social texture" is characteristic of "great" American literature was influential to the idea that romance is a, if not *the,* definitive American genre. According to the "romance theory of American literature" initially developed by Chase and Trilling, unlike British literature (in which social realism reigned supreme), American authors turned away from the social world to the fantastical realm of romance, "a world elsewhere," liberated from the constraints of mimesis, but also, for that very reason, politically suspect.[35]

The nationalization of romance in Americanist literary criticism is both curious and ironic. Hawthorne never formulates romance as a symbolic extension of the United States. Indeed, he insistently emphasizes the epistemic and political foreignness of romance.[36] For example, in the preface to Hawthorne's last completed romance, *The Marble Faun* (1860), which follows U.S. expatriate artists in Italy, he suggests that the relative youth of the United States makes it a uniquely unsuitable subject for romance. "No author, without a trial," Hawthorne writes, "can conceive of the difficulty of writing a romance about a country where there is no shadow, no antiquity, no mystery, no picturesque and gloomy wrong, nor anything but a common-place prosperity, in broad and simple daylight, as is happily the case with my dear native land."[37] Seen in relationship to remarks like this, Hawthorne's characterization of "romance" as treason (which we will return to later) is simply an exceptionally polemical formulation of his reoccurring theorization of the extralegality of "romance"—a foreignness that, in a national frame-work, doubles as un-Americanness.

When we speak of literature as national—or local, regional, hemispheric, or global—we engage in the type of literalistic contextualization that the authorial invocation of "romance" is meant to forestall. To "assign an actual locality to the imaginary events of this narrative," Hawthorne warns in the second half of the preface to *The House of the Seven Gables,* "exposes the romance to an inflexible and exceedingly dangerous species of criticism, by bringing his fancy-pictures almost into positive contact with the realities of the moment" (*HSG,* 3). The preface ends with an entreaty that the "book may be read strictly as a Romance, having a great deal more to do with the clouds overhead than with any portion of the actual soil of the County of Essex" (*HSG,* 3). Hawthorne is insistent in his differentiation of "romance" from geopolitical imaginaries like the county of Essex, the state of Massa-chusetts, and the United States. The illocality of romance is fundamental to it.[38] It is thus a remarkable testament to the ideological allure of literary nationalism that Hawthorne's definitions of romance have played such an integral role in shaping a specifically national theory of literary form.[39]

For inheritors of the romance thesis, romance is a genre with recogniz-able attributes—not, as I am arguing, a *theory* of fiction that seeks to iso-late its distinguishing feature: its departure from the descriptive regime of the indicative.[40] "Romance" did not reliably designate a fully articulated concept in the early United States; instead, it was a hyperbolic term for the nonmimetic prerogatives of fiction.[41] Even the more specialized quasi-generic use of it (by Walter Scott, William Gilmore Simms, and Hawthorne) is shaped by this more generalized sense of the term. By bracketing the cir-cuitous self-referential definitions of genre, we can understand "romance" and "novel" in Hawthorne not as coherent genres, but as politically charged theories of the proper relationship between the world and text, experience and the imagination, citizen and community, locality and universality. In this spirit, I use "romance" in Hawthorne's peculiar sense of it, not to insist that it constitutes a consolidated genre or as a quintessentially national aesthetic, but rather as an exemplary formulation of the continual interplay between the renunciative impulse of fiction and the world it inhabits.

Romance, as Hawthorne conceives it, is not national, local, or even cos-mopolitan, rather, it nominates the irresolvable gap between terrestrially bound institutions and political ideals. Neither strictly terrestrial nor wholly ideal, romance, for Hawthorne, names a liminal mode, at once alien and civic. Romance conjures an image of unbounded liberty, but—like the wilds of the sea in Frederick Douglass's novelistic allegory of natural rights—romance's political import is comparative rather than substitutive. The comparative qualifications that structure the separation between romance and locality—"having a great deal *more* to do," "the *actual* soil"— define romance negatively in relationship to the terra. The clouds of romance do not escape referential relation to the "actual soil of the County of Essex": they are positioned comparatively, "overhead," a proximal location that forces us to imagine romance through the worldly perspective it ostensibly transcends.[42] The insistent grammatical relays between the clouds of romance and the territories of politics, as we will see, are central to the nostalgic form of civic longing that Hawthorne uses the extralegal realm of "romance" to cultivate.

Hawthorne's refusal to "assign an actual locality to the imaginary" is part of what allows him to conceive of romance as a special sphere for exercising "rights" and citizenship. The "alienable" character of rights—the extent, that is, to which rights are understood as transferable rather than innate—depends on the abstract character of the rights-bearing subject, which is itself an artifact of fiction. The precedent for natural rights, as Thomas Paine argues in *The Rights of Man* (1791), is not bound to "antiquity" or even historical time (as Edmund Burke maintains); it is fabled, "the origin of man."[43] The perfect coincidence between "man" and rights is itself mythic. Even a citizen cannot practically embody the ideals the category names.[44] The universal and the concrete subject of rights remain out of sync. The very ideality of rights makes them alien to experience.[45]

Rights are postulated in opposition to lived politics—both its failed histories and insufficient institutions.[46] This oppositional impulse is characteristic of the liberalist underpinnings of U.S. political thought, in which, as John Dewey argues, the "revolt against established forms of government" was "converted, intellectually, into the doctrine of independence of any and all association."[47] Yet to read Hawthorne's representation of romance as a simple expression of the negativity of liberalism would be as unsatisfying in the end as an attempt to assess it solely according to terrestrially determined models of the political. Among other things, Hawthorne's writing, far from repudiating tradition, tends to privilege the past over the present, even if it does so in mythical terms.[48] In this respect, the trajectories of the Burke and Paine debate—tradition versus myth, circumstance versus abstraction, historical versus natural rights—are of only limited import for understanding Hawthorne's formulation of fictional license. Rights, for

Hawthorne, are neither solely grounded in actual historical circumstances, nor natural principles. They are unnatural artifacts of the illocal world of letters.

"Romance" may be little more than the name Hawthorne gives to the renunciative potential of fiction, but his defensive celebration of fictional license in the charged language of "rights" foregrounded the politicized connotations of evolving theories of literary autonomy. As Edward Cahill eloquently observes in *Liberty of the Imagination* (2012), "American writers who considered the problems of aesthetic theory were sensitive to the homology of aesthetic and political liberty and ambitious in their persistence of its implications for both the pleasures of the imagination and the forms of national polity."[49] Cahill's study ends with a discussion of Emerson in the 1830s, when he suggests that "the concern about the imagination's tendency toward rebellion" was offset by a sense that "any constraint on the imagination was thought to be a greater moral threat than its potential for excess." This revaluation of the imagination, Cahill suggests, was matched by a new comfort with political liberty. Cahill's account of republican aesthetics operates in a very different methodological register than seminal accounts of the "liberal aesthetic," but his periodization of the "problem of liberty" reinforces the same mistaken assumption that liberty came to seem an innocuous if not virtuous ideal in the increasingly distant wake of the American Revolution.[50]

Hawthorne's writing helps illuminate another side of this story. Writers continued to use the trope of aesthetic autonomy to explore the political problem of freedom in the antebellum United States, but the meaning of this trope changed as political disaffiliation assumed a host of newly divisive meanings. In debates over expatriation and state sovereignty, the language and tropes of the American Revolution were invoked to defend a host of cultural and ideological practices that had little in common with the ideology of the founding era. These more contentious political appropriations of the trope of political independence began to infiltrate the metaphor of the imagination's epistemic autonomy. Thus instead of celebrating fiction's freedom from historical and political concerns, Hawthorne found himself in the position of defending it as a "right." Hawthorne's several definitions of "romance" may leave much to be desired if we treat them as formulations of a distinct genre. Yet as we will see in the following sections, they are incredibly prescient when understood as meditative reflections on the variable political implications that the romantic trope of literary autonomy took on in the turbulent era of citizenship's formative conceptualization.[51]

## On the Politics of "Neutrality"

The romantic celebration of fictional license resulted in a kind of double vision of representational norms, wherein the departure from a mimetic representational order seemed at once socially irresponsible and politically ideal. Evolving theories of the connection between world and text offered a convenient microcosm for theorizing and testing the dangers and benefits of an affiliatory order that gave increasing prominence to individual desire over and above communal need. Scholars have been attentive to the connections between romanticism and liberal individualism, but teleological narratives—about the reclamation of fictionality, in aesthetics, and the shift from republicanism to liberalism, in American politics—have foregrounded the celebratory ethos of the so-called liberal aesthetic without exploring the equally politicized effects of the residual affiliatory anxieties it conjured. It is this double impulse (aesthetic triumphalism and defensiveness) that Hawthorne's writing captures so nicely and that has made it possible for different generations of critics to alternately view him as a paragon of aestheticism and a cultural and political theorist of the antebellum era.[52] Each view has a degree of validity, but the discrete theorization of these "Hawthornes" in different eras of scholarship has preserved the quasi-mythological narrative of art's separation from politics that Hawthorne strategically manipulated to bolster his dual careers in letters and political office.

An 1847 review that places Hawthorne "in the first rank of American authors" laments, "It is a waste of kind of genius, which we can not well spare, to shut up Nathaniel Hawthorne in a custom house."[53] The shortage of distinguished native-born authors, the reviewer suggests, made Hawthorne's literary career more urgent than any role he could play in political office. In a reversal of the common opposition of political utility and aesthetic excess, it is Hawthorne's political career that lacks strategic utility. Authorship was the higher endeavor, in this case. Hawthorne would himself soon echo this sentiment when the election of Whig president Zachary Taylor cost Hawthorne (a Democrat) his appointed position as surveyor of the Salem Custom House. Writing to Henry Wadsworth Longfellow in June 1849, when his deposal seemed imminent but was not yet certain, an outraged Hawthorne invoked his standing as an author as a protection from the partisan-based hostilities of the spoils system. "I must confess it, it stirs up a little the devil within me, to find myself hunted by these political blood-hounds. If they succeed in getting me out of office, I will surely immolate one or two of them," Hawthorne declares.[54] His counterattack, he continues to explain, will not be "an act of individual vengeance, but in your behalf as well as mine, because he will have violated the sanctity of the priesthood to which we both, in our different degrees, belong. I do not claim to be poet; and yet I cannot but feel that some of the sacredness of that character adheres to me, and ought to be respected in me, unless I step out if its immunities."[55] The letter is fascinating for its double posturing. On the one hand, Hawthorne elevates the poetic, broadly understood, above politics and, in so doing, reinforces a sense of their incompatibility. The benefit of this trope of separation, as Lawrence Buell observes in a discussion of New England literary culture, is that "by dignifying the creative imagination as a source of quasi-divine authority, Romanticism gave the artist the central position in society and converted the author's sense of alienation from societal norms from a mark of shame to a badge of honor."[56] Hawthorne wields the "sacredness" of authorship to justify his immunity from political attack, but he does so here to authorize the *continuation* of his political career. Hawthorne's status as author, in other words, sets him above partisan politics, but it also helps him position himself firmly within its inner rung, as an appointed political officer.

It is this latter narrative about the entwined nature of his two careers that falls out of view in Hawthorne's better-known, and widely circulated, complaint about the political spoils system, "The Custom-House," the fictionalized autobiographical sketch that introduces *The Scarlet Letter* (1850). "The Custom-House" is regularly approached through the interpretative lens of *The Scarlet Letter*—and there is certainly good reason for this. Not only were these texts bound in print, but "The Custom-House" includes a fictional anecdote of the *Scarlet Letter*'s origins, in which "Hawthorne" is said to have found a scarlet embroidered *A* along with Surveyor Pue's "explanation of the whole affair" in a heap of lumber at the Custom House.[57] Yet there are equally good reasons for treating "The Custom-House" as a sketch about the relationship between antebellum letters and politics, which, only *secondarily,* serves as a preface to *The Scarlet Letter.* For one, "The Custom-House" was initially intended and written as a preface to a collection that included other short pieces (like "Main Street").[58] Hawthorne even briefly considered using "The Custom-House" as the principal title to this alternate/unrealized volume.[59] Second, the popularity of the volume when it first appeared, as Hawthorne himself recognized, was due, in part, to the excitement sparked by "The Custom-House," whose partisan-laced passages elicited both disapprobation and delight.

The formative Cold War–era readings of Hawthorne emphasize the more traditionally "literary" aspects of "The Custom-House," including

Hawthorne's famous characterization of romance as a "neutral territory"—a remark that for many has seemed to confirm the essentially apolitical and evasive tendencies of romance.[60] However, for many of Hawthorne's contemporaries, the keen interest that "The Custom-House" elicited was directly connected to its entanglement in partisan politics. A local review of *The Scarlet Letter* in *The Salem Register* lamented Hawthorne's unbecoming partisanship, exclaiming that "while reading this chapter on the Custom House, we almost began to think that Hawthorne had mistaken his vocation—that, instead, of indulging in dreamy transcendentalism, and weaving exquisite fancies to please the imagination and improve the heart, he would have been more at home as a despicable lampooner."[61] For other reviewers, this was the very appeal of "The Custom-House." A review of *The Scarlet Letter* in *Holden's Dollar Magazine* that isolated Hawthorne's "perfect" sketch of the "Old Inspector," declared, "No picture that we remember in Addison or Goldsmith excels it. Hawthorne was a Custom House officer that he might draw the "Old Inspector."[62] So, the reviewer concludes, "though humanity might lose a poet in the Custom House . . . we are benefitted by those who turned him out."[63]

Like his pilloried protagonist, it is the public character of "Hawthorne" that is on trial in "The Custom-House." The peculiarity of "The Custom-House," understood as a political essay, is that (in keeping with Hawthorne's letter to Longfellow) it invokes the romantic concept of art's separation from politics *in order to* authorize its highly poeticized political parries. Hawthorne may have cultivated an "aura of detachment" about his removal from office, but as Stephen Nissenbaum stresses, he resented the attacks on his reputation and did everything he could to garner support for his reinstatement.[64] Hawthorne wrote several letters to his friend George Hillard, who wrote to two prominent Massachusetts Whigs, Daniel Webster and Edward Everett, in the hope that they would intercede. In his response to Hillard, Everett avows that he has little "sympathy for men like Hawthorne, who give the weight of their name & influence to a party to which they cannot in heart belong," but he agrees to do what he can since "Hawthorne claims the credit of having abstained from all political action."[65] Everett proceeded to write to the secretary of the treasury on Hawthorne's behalf, but two days later he wrote to withdraw his letter, explaining that he has since discovered that "Mr. Hawthorne has been, while in office, the agent of party measures of the most objectionable character; acting perhaps rather as the instrument of others than from his own impulses, but in such a way as to *destroy all claim to the plea of neutrality.*"[66] It was, in the end, the inability to claim neutrality that ensured Hawthorne's removal from politics.

Hawthorne was unable to lay "claim to the plea of neutrality" to save his career in the Salem Custom House, but his efforts did not end in this important but little discussed epistolary claim. Hawthorne resurrects this claim in "The Custom-House," in which he famously characterizes romance as "a neutral territory, somewhere between the real world and fairy-land, where the Actual and Imaginary may meet, and each imbue itself with the nature of the other" (*SL*, 36). If romance enables a convergence between the material and the ideal, which is often taken as indicative of the reconciliatory nature of Hawthorne's aesthetic, such an intersection, it is worth stressing, is made possible by dislocating objects from their native, and too familiar, contexts.[67] To experience the world through the medium of romance is to relate to it on the condition of estrangement. It does not entail an absolute abnegation of the "real world," but instead structures identification on the model of removal. Romance, in this sense, is not a strictly autonomous realm; it derives its character from its relation to what it relinquishes. Neutral" thus operates primarily in its etymological sense, "not either": it does not name a "commons," but a form of epistemic dislocation, "*between* the real world and fairy-land."[68]

Hawthorne's use of "neutral territory" is typically seen as minor variation on what Scott calls the "neutral ground" in his own series of prefatory reflections on "romance," but its meaning is quite different—and it cannot be fully understood apart from the partisan contest that inspired Hawthorne's influential preface. For Scott, the "neutral ground" names the "manner and sentiments which are common to us, or which, arising out of the principles of our common nature, must have existed alike in either state of society."[69] For Hawthorne, the political force of romance is not the communion of individuals through fiction, but its differential relationship to the material world—and its interrelated suspension of political customs.

To see neutrality as the absence of politics is to miss its centrality to the republican ideal of political disinterestedness. As Everett's refusal to petition for Hawthorne's reinstatement reminds us, the refusal of *partisanship* is not the same as a retreat from *politics*. Partisan interest, after all, was seen as the enemy of good politics. Indeed, as Michael Warner and others have argued, viewed from the perspective of the republican ideal of political disinterestedness, "impersonality" and political neutrality are valorized as preconditions for political authority and democratic representativeness.[70] Understood thus, Hawthorne's characterization of romance as a "neutral territory" is not a celebration of political withdrawal. It is, instead, Hawthorne's defensive attempt to theorize the literary as a virtual realm defined by the idealized form of political disinterestedness that he himself had been found wanting. In these iconic lines, Hawthorne reclaims the differential episteme of fictionality—which previously had been maligned as a social threat—as a detached area in which partisan citizens might cultivate and achieve the republican ideal of disinterestedness. When Hawthorne characterized romance as "a neutral territory," he relocated the ideal of republican disinterestedness in the extralegal realm of the literary.[71]

The debates surrounding Hawthorne's deposal are crucial to understanding the special but admittedly peculiar political charge of romance in "The Custom-House." They also point us toward aspects of romanticism and transcendentalism that have been difficult to appreciate within the framework of the "liberal imagination." We often treat the republican ideal of citizenship as if it were a periodizable ideal of the early, pre-Jacksonian republic, which would soon give way to a more self-interested liberal citizen. However, the republican ideal had staying power, and it is crucial to understanding the complex political projects that romanticism and transcendentalism both mimicked and furthered. Take, for example, a rather banal appeal to the republican ideal of disinterestedness in a 1851 essay on citizenship, which argues that "a certain *disinterestedness*" is the "primary moral law" of democracy, because the state was not established for "any one person" or "class," "but for all."[72] Is this not the impersonal "I" of Ralph Waldo Emerson and Walt Whitman—writers who are regularly and rather reductively cast, like Hawthorne, as purveyors of the liberal imagination?[73] In highlighting the historical and conceptual overlap between republicanism and liberalism, my point is not that we can now safely redeem Hawthorne from a liberal worldview that critics have been understandably eager to distance themselves from in recent years. Instead, these moments illuminate the interpretive limits of liberalism, which has long invited generalized assumptions about citizenship and romantic aesthetics that eclipse the historical peculiarities of each.

## Literary Expatriation

To read "The Custom-House" as a political essay as much as a theory of the artist's role in antebellum politics is to return it to its intellectual and political origins. Partisanship was not an asset for surviving the mini revolutions of the spoils system, but (with the exception of Hawthorne's late writings during the Civil War) it was arguably an asset to his literary career. When *Literary World* editor Evert Duyckinck received an advanced copy of *The Scarlet Letter* in March 1850, he selected for advanced publication the satiric sketch of the "Old Inspector" that ultimately incited many of the most impassioned reviews.[74] Duyckinck was clearly alive to the political tenor of the volume and to its publicity potential. This is the same Duyckinck who, in a later review, insisted that *The Scarlet Letter* was "a psychological romance," not a "novel"—a distinction that in the hands of Trilling and many twentieth-century critics has been treated as code for an apolitical formalism.[75] Whether Duyckinck recognized that the preface—as much as *The Scarlet Letter* proper—contains romantic tropes, he understood that Hawthorne's quarrel with local politics would play a key role in the novel's success.[76] From this perspective, it was Hawthorne's provincial politicking that launched him to a new level of national and transatlantic prestige—universalizing arenas that had little investment in the local politics that facilitated his rise in the republic of letters.

With the complex interrelationship between local politics and the differential theory of the literary in mind, we can better understand the dramatic scene of symbolic denaturalization that brings "The Custom-House" to a close. Embittered that the election of a new president has cost him his position as surveyor, "Hawthorne" renounces the city that has served him so poorly.

> Soon, likewise, my old native town will loom upon me though the haze of memory, a mist brooding over and around it; as if it were no portion of the real earth, but an overgrown village in cloud-land, with only imaginary inhabitants to people its wooden houses, and walk its homely lanes, and the unpicturesque prolixity of its main street. Henceforth, it ceases to be a reality of my life. I am a citizen of somewhere else. (*SL*, 44)

Hawthorne's often-quoted declaration "I am a citizen of somewhere else" conceptualizes the formal project of romance as coterminous with a refashioning of political allegiance. If in privileging the renunciative character of fiction, Hawthorne would seem to disavow politics in the more everyday sense, what is striking in this formulation is that citizenship becomes the organizing figure for romantic alienation (rather than its antithesis). "Hawthorne" identifies as a "citizen" at the very moment he relinquishes his political allegiance to Salem for the imagined terms of a kind of literary citizenship.

In claiming to be "a citizen of somewhere else," Hawthorne aligns his authorship within a notion of the "literary" that was lauded in a transatlantic context, but that, as we will see, was also increasingly deprecated in the sectional crises that came to a head in the Civil War.[77] Hawthorne's "declaration of independence," as Dan McCall terms his formulation of literary citizenship, is often glossed in relation to the French and American Revolutions—contexts evoked by Hawthorne's recourse to the "metaphor of the political guillotine" *(SL,* 43).[78] But in the antebellum period, the trope of revolution was not reducible to the political histories of the late eighteenth century; it assumed a variety of contentious meanings in debates over the right of expatriation, nullification, and secession. Rather than read "I am a citizen of somewhere else" as a belated homage to events that preceded it by more than seventy years, this gesture, I suggest, needs to be understood in a more proximate context—one evoked so strongly by "Hawthorne's" metaphoric disentanglement with his ancestral soil as well as the imagery of romance's *latitudinal* separation (in the clouds)—debates about the right to expatriate.

When Hawthorne figuratively styled himself a "citizen of somewhere else," he was not laying claim to a well-established legal principle, but tacitly involving his aesthetic project in ongoing political controversies about the voluntary and so defeasible character of allegiance. Despite its inaugural significance for political membership during the American Revolution, the right to expatriate was a source of continued legal debate until the passage of "An Act concerning the Rights of American Citizens in Foreign States" in 1868. In Hawthorne's native state of Massachusetts—as with all states in this period (excepting Virginia and Kentucky)—there was no formal recognition of the right to expatriate.[79] Indeed, in one of the more definitive rulings against the right to expatriate in *Ainslee vs. Martin* (1813), the Massachusetts Supreme Court emphatically affirmed the British Common Law doctrine of natural and perpetual allegiance, and stressed the juridical links between British subjecthood and citizenship in Massachusetts. Framing the state of Massachusetts as sovereign successor to the king, the court concluded that "by the common law no subject can expatriate himself."[80] In the early United States, citizens could not presume their authority to "dissolve the relationship between themselves and the state" (to adopt Thoreau's phrasing).[81] However, the state nonetheless reserved the right to punitively expatriate disloyal citizens.[82] The state, in this respect, monopolized the ostensibly voluntary character of the relation between individuals and the state in a democratic government.

Hawthorne's belabored emphasis on romance's symbolic break from the terra firma provides the tropological underpinnings of his complex engagement with ongoing debates about the right to refuse allegiance. The question of the primacy of the land as the origin and site of political allegiance is at the heart of the question of expatriation. Take, for example, *Talbot vs. Janson* (1795), a Supreme Court case in which questions concerning expatriation, neutrality, and treason collided in a contest that centered on an alleged breach of U.S. neutrality during the Fourth Anglo-Dutch War. Virginia native William Talbot was charged with colluding with Captain

Edward Ballard (another Virginia native) to arm an "American built vessel" to capture a Dutch brigantine and cargo. Talbot's defense hinged on his contested citizenship status. Talbot claimed that when he was admitted as a citizen of the French Republic in 1793, he had exercised his right to expatriate and thus no longer owed allegiance to the United States.[83] As a native of Virginia, one of the only states to explicitly recognize the right to expatriated in this period, Talbot was better positioned to claim the right to expatriate than citizens in most of the several states. Yet, in the end, despite Virginia's unambiguous recognition of the right to expatriate, the Supreme Court concluded that Talbot's French naturalization did not release him from his native allegiance. The decision reached in *Talbot vs. Janson* is not especially noteworthy in itself; after all, the Supreme Court routinely ruled against the right to expatriate in the period treated in this book. However, this case bears special mention here, because the language Talbot's defense marshaled in support of the right to expatriate can help us better understand the political significance of Hawthorne's theorization of the autonomous character of romance—and its symbolic separation from the terra.[84] According to Talbot's defense,

> [T]he abstract right of individuals to withdraw from the society of which they are members is recognized . . . by every writer, ancient and modern; by the civilian as well as by the common-law lawyer; by the philosopher as well as the poet. . . . With this law, however, human institutions have often been at variance; and no institutions more than the feudal system, which made the tyranny of arms, the basis of society; chained men to the soil on which they were born; and converted the bulk of mankind into villeins, or slaves of a lord, or superior.[85]

Here the right to "withdraw from society" is abundantly evident in the works of writers, philosophers, and poets; it is only "human institutions" that have failed to consistently recognize "this law." As this disaggregation of the language of the "law" from the institutions of governance underlines, defenses of the right to expatriate in this period depended upon the extralegal authority of higher law discourse—an authority that, in this case, derives its cultural self-evidence from its recognition "by every writer." Within this framework, to refuse the right to expatriate is to defect from a higher law and to return to a feudal conception of allegiance, which, as the defense figuratively renders it, "chained men to the soil on which they were born." It is this tie to the soil—the symbolic site of the political obligations born of *jus soli*—that "The Custom-House" so relentlessly rends over the course of its pages.[86]

The central political drama that "The Custom-House" unfolds with such acuity is not the liberal dream of autonomous self-governance but the relational fantasy of the affective reciprocity of political allegiance. If, as Brook Thomas puts it, the text of *The Scarlet Letter* "places its protagonists in the space of civil society between the public and the private," discursively speaking, Hawthorne locates the extra-governmental sphere of voluntary affiliation in the epistemic modality of fiction.[87] The fictional contract between author and readers offers one formal mechanism for voluntary allegiance, but so, too, does fictionality itself. The process of fictionalization deprives nativity of the appearance of *naturalness*, which is instrumental to its ineluctable power. Thus, by the end of the scene of willed forgetting that facilitates Hawthorne's transformation of the locale of Salem into the imagined "Salem" of "The Custom-House," his "old native town" has lost its ability to command his civic affections. As "Hawthorne's" life at the Custom House recedes into the haze of recollection, the process of fictionalization provides the occasion for a figurative reversal of his ejection from office. The "venerable personages" of the Custom House, the narrator expresses with evident satisfaction, "are but shadows in my view; white-headed and wrinkled images, which my fancy used to sport with, and has now flung aside for ever" (*SL,* 44). In this metaphoric reversal of Hawthorne's dismissal, it is he who lightly dispatches the occupants of the Custom House. As with the voluntary posturing of the closing renunciation, "I am a citizen of somewhere else," this fanciful expulsion of the aged custom officers is both defensive and retributive. Read in the context of the narrative of "The Custom-House" and the history of deposal it retells, these meta-reflections on aesthetic disaffiliation are not untroubled enactments of liberal agency, but overdetermined responses to the circumstantial loss of control. To identify as a "citizen of somewhere else," thus, is not to affirm the sovereignty of the individual, so much as to understand the denaturalization of native allegiance as the basis for the kind of voluntary communities made and unmade in fiction.

If, as one critic argued in *The Edinburgh Review* in 1847, "intellectual expatriation" is always "requisite to the historical novelist," this distance at once epistemic and cultural is fundamental to fiction as Hawthorne theorizes it.[88] The affiliatory problem Hawthorne stages in his reflections on fiction is not the imaginative pull of another era, per se, but rather the evaluative power of viewing the political present from "somewhere else." Understood as a poetic solution to the persistence of the British doctrine of perpetual allegiance in the early United States, the airy clouds of romance take on unexpected figurative weight. As Henry James, the veritable expatriate of the American romantic tradition, suggestively puts it in his often-quoted definition of romance in the 1907 preface to the New York edition of *The American* (1876–1877), romance is "experience liberated, so to speak; experience disengaged, disembroiled, disencumbered, exempt from the conditions that we usually know to attach to it and, if we wish so to put the matter, drag upon it."[89] This "sacrifice of community," he continues, is best achieved with a sleight of hand in which the "cable" tying fiction "to the earth" is cut without arousing the reader's suspicions.

> The balloon of experience is in fact of course tied to the earth, and under that necessity we swing, thanks to a rope of remarkable length, in the more or less commodious car of the imagination; but it is by the rope we know where we are, and from the moment that cable is cut we are at large and unrelated: we only swing apart from the globe—though remaining as exhilarated, naturally, as we like, especially when all goes well. The art of the romancer is, "for the fun of it," insidiously to cut the cable, to cut it without our detecting him.[90]

Both James and Hawthorne are invested in the liberties of romance, untethered from the necessities of real life, but Hawthorne uses the label of "romance" to alert readers to the distance between "fairyland" and the "real world"—a difference that James would rather go undetected. These differential authorial performances of fiction lead readers to *expect* different degrees of referentiality, but they do not necessarily correlate to the actual plausibility of the works themselves. (Hawthorne's self-designated "romances" are not nearly as fanciful as his prefaces make out.) However, these variations in readerly cues prove consequential, because as we have already begun to see in "The Custom-House," open fictionality and fictionalization are instrumental to the denaturalization of nativity—a form of virtual disaffiliation that, as imagined by Hawthorne, need not end in unqualified Jamesian disengagement. Romantic fictionality, as we will see in Hawthorne's exilic sketches of fantasy, can also provide the occasion for a more ardent re-affiliation with the material world fiction seems to place under erasure.


## Exilic States of Fantasy

In the modernist tradition, expatriation is often invoked in the context of the mythos of the artist in exile. "Expatriation," in such cases is used as a loose synonym for "exile." As historian Nancy Green observes in her discussion of modernism, "There have been many expatriates, but few people have legally expatriated. Living abroad is one thing; losing one's citizenship is another."[91] The ability to formally expatriate, as we have seen, was contested in the period in which Hawthorne wrote, but the autobiographically determined sense of artistic exile with which this term is associated in modernism is certainly germane to the early United States. Melville spent time at sea; Washington Irving, James Fenimore Cooper, and Hawthorne held official posts abroad—and in all three cases, this time in Europe left them with a new sense of the provinciality and cultural shortcomings of their native countries.[92] These careers, and Hawthorne's in particular, can easily be seen as precursors to the modernist tradition of artistic exile.[93] Indeed, when James Baldwin described his time writing in Turkey, he turned to Hawthorne to explain his own sense of dislocation on returning to the United States. "I am an American artist, and I know exactly what Nathaniel Hawthorne meant when he wrote, from England, around 1861, that 'the United States may be fit for many purposes, but they are not fit to live in.' Nearly all American artists have felt this, and for very good reasons; but we have all—usually, anyway—gone home. The danger of being an expatriate is that you are very likely to find yourself living, in effect, nowhere."[94] The practice of artistic exile is a fascinating subject of its own, but I mention this familiar trope here to clarify my discussion of expatriation's figurative importance for literary citizenship in Hawthorne's writings. While it is possible to see antebellum authorship through the autobiographically determined lens of the expatriated artist, my focus here concerns a related way of thinking about fiction explored by Hawthorne and evoked in Baldwin's wonderfully Hawthornian invocation of "nowhere." In Hawthorne, the imaginative retreats of genius and the possibilistic worlds of fiction are themselves figured as expatriated spaces of political refashioning, riven between utopian longings and mundane disappointments.

Hawthorne's prefaces are well recognized by scholars for the insight they offer into antebellum theories of fiction and reading. His allegorical sketches on fantasy in his earlier magazine fiction offer another important but underutilized resource for understanding the theory of fiction that he later articulates more systematically in the language of romance. Hawthorne's allegorical retelling of the state of nature in "The New Adam and Eve," published in the *United States Democratic Magazine and Review* in 1843, offers an especially lucid formulation of fiction's denaturalizing power. The tale is prefaced by a paragraph that theorizes the stakes of the possible worlds that fiction births and brings into view. "We, who are born into the world's artificial system, can never adequately know how little in our present state and circumstances is natural, and how much is merely the interpolation of the perverted mind and heart of man. . . . It is only through the medium of the imagination that we can loosen those iron fetters, which we call truth and reality, and make ourselves even partially sensible what prisoners we are."[95] The liberty of the imagination, as it is conceived here, has less to do with the liberty to invent—the fictional license of "romance"—than with the liberating *effects* of the imagination that Ralph Waldo Emerson associates with poetry.[96] Fiction is liberating not as an escape from the real, but as a comparative episteme that facilities a reassessment of the "present state" as one possibility among many.

To achieve a more encompassing denaturalization, one that extends beyond home and town to address the world at large, "The New Adam and Eve" extends the trope of romantic estrangement to its existential limits by reapproaching it through its eschatological cousin: the millennial apocalypse. The reader is led into the story with the invitation to imagine "for instance" that "good Father Miller's interpretation of the prophecies have proved true. The Day of Doom has burst upon the globe, and swept away the whole race of men" ("NA," 146). "Then to inherit and repeople this waste and deserted earth, we will suppose a new Adam and a new Eve to have been created . . . with no knowledge of their predecessors" ("NA," 247). This conceit of a world begun anew places Adam and Eve not at the origins of creation, per se, but as alien spectators of the human-centered, postlapsarian world that, according to the mythology of Genesis, Eve's transgressive hunger for worldly knowledge ushered in. "Such a pair," Hawthorne assures us, "would at once distinguish between art and nature" ("NA," 248). Aligning the readers' perspective with the couple who initiated the split between "art and nature" that romanticism and transcendentalism both sought to overcome, Hawthorne's sketch seeks to elicit astonishment at the strangeness of an artificial society that, through the habits of custom, we might otherwise view as "natural" and inevitable.

For Hawthorne, the negativity of representation is treated so literally that it comes to simulate the apocalypse, a hyperbolic figure for the end of worldly affiliation that draws its epistemic force from Christianity theology's existential devaluation of the sphere of worldly attachments. One of the significant differences between aesthetic and theological modes of disaffiliation, Hawthorne suggests, is that fiction's temporary disengagement from the worldly ultimately invites a nostalgic reinvestment in the world. This is the lesson of Hawthorne's "The Hall of Fantasy" (1843), published in *The Pioneer* the subsequent year and later revised for inclusion in *Mosses from an Old Manse* (1846). When the tale opens, the narrator finds himself in a place that he had last been transported "unawares, while [his] mind was busy with an idle tale."[97] When the narrator asks a bystander where he is, he is told that he is "in that mystic region, which lies above, below, or beyond the Actual, may here meet, and talk over the business of their dreams."[98] This "place of refuge" is populated not only by artists but an "endless . . . herd of real or self styled reformers" who are "united" in their pursuit of "a better and purer life than had yet been realized on earth."[99] The narrator finds Father Miller surrounded by "a crowd of deeply attentive auditors . . . announc[ing] that the destruction of the world was close at hand."[100] The apocalypse Miller prophesies, according to the sketch, already has begun in a more mundane way for all who frequent the hall of fantasy, which is characterized as an almost heretical space of creation in which "man's disembodied spirit may recreate Time and the World for itself."[101] In a cautionary denouement, the sketch forewarns that "for those who waste all their days in the Hall of Fantasy, good Father Miller's prophecy is already accomplished and the solid earth has come to an end."[102] Faced with the prospect of a disappearing earth, which has been replaced by its virtual proxy in the "hall of fantasy"—and so now "exist[s] merely in idea"—the narrator responds by defiantly reclaiming the real world anew: "Come what may, I will never forget [the earth]! Neither will it satisfy me to have her exist merely in idea. I want her great, round, solid self to endure interminably."[103] It is the presentation of fantasy's apocalyptic effects that brings the narrator to his ardent defense of the "poor old earth."

"The Hall of Fantasy" is fascinating for its proto-environmentalist treatment of the refusal of excessive fantasy as a precondition for valuing the earth. Equally instructive is its suggestion that, in moderation, fantasy can actually elicit a reinvestment in the world—precisely because of its imagined distance from it. Thus, when the narrator considers relinquishing all ties to the soil for a virtual home—in the republic of letters or the heavenly city—he is overcome with civic longing. "[T]he root of human nature strikes down deep into this earthly soil; and it is but reluctantly that we submit to be transplanted, even for a higher cultivation in Heaven."[104] As this "even" highlights, the epistemic draw of fiction cannot quite match the more intensely motivated pull of heaven as telos. However, it is precisely the incomplete nature of this fictive cathexis, I would argue, that leaves fiction open to a decidedly nostalgic reinvestment in the earthly.

The implied similarity between religious and aesthetic disaffiliation that structures Hawthorne's allegories of the allure and dangers of fantasy speaks to the quasi-sacred character that the "literary" acquired in this period, which Melville captures so beautifully in *The Confidence-Man*. "It is with fiction as with religion: it should present another world, and yet one to which we feel the tie," the narrator observes.[105] Melville's remark comes at the close of a series of ironic reflections on the conflicting desires of readers who turn to fiction seeking diversion from a "real life" that has become "dull," and "yet demand of him who is to divert his attention from it, that he should be true to that dullness."[106] These arguments appear in the middle of chapter 33, "Which May Pass for Whatever It May Prove to Be

Worth," a meta-fictive interlude addressed to any naysaying readers, who might be frustrated by the unreality of the plot. The gambit of the chapter is to appease any readers who are outraged by the lack of realism, but its disruption of the narrative only makes it harder for readers to bracket these objections and to enjoy the pleasures of "poetic faith," the proverbial Coleridgean "suspension of disbelief."[107] In quietly rejecting the earlier, ambivalent cushioning of fictionality in novels that presented themselves as "founded in fact," Melville's chapter offers a philosophical defense of fictionality, but it also refuses its seductive effects—pulling the curtain back to insist on the artifice of fiction.[108]

Hawthorne's several prefatory theorizations of romance embrace this artifice even more wholeheartedly than Melville, forewarning readers that the romancer has "insidiously . . . cut the cable" that might otherwise anchor the otherworld of fiction. It is this unrelenting performance of the fictionality of the "other world" of fiction, I want to suggest, that marks one of the most substantive differences between the form of extralegal political critique traced in this chapter and in Chapter 2. "Citizenship in heaven" may be counterfactual in its relation to everyday politics, but for the believers who adhere to the metaphysical truths of theology, the otherworldly kingdom of heaven is not a fictive state but a theological reality. In announcing the virtuality of the worlds it projects, the open fictionality that Hawthorne theorizes under the rubric of "romance," invites a more provisional form of disaffiliation than its theological counterpart. Unlike Christian theology, in which the promise of heavenly citizenship offers a relatively stable imaginative substitute for active political membership, the artifice and ephemerality of fictive worlds makes it difficult to see fiction as an *end* in itself. It is, thus, by virtue of its clear demarcation of fiction's unreality that the label "romance" obtains its unlikely political salience. By announcing the fictionality of fiction, the designation "romance" reminds readers of the unsustainability of the fantastic worlds it projects. The presentation of fiction's artifice and its ephemerality—emblematized by the figure of disintegrating "castles in the air"—awakens readers to the nostalgic appeal of the worldly.[109] For whatever their temporary draw, readers occupy the clouds of "romance" knowing that they will (and must) leave them.

In Hawthorne's quasi-didactic allegories of fantasy, the literary imagination does not ultimately enable escape but rather reorientation. Hawthorne uses the romantic conceit of literary autonomy to highlight the affiliatory losses that haunt "citizen[s] of somewhere else." Hawthorne's allegorical theorizations of the virtuality of fiction explore the benefits of a sporadic literary denizenship—one in which occasional readerly retreats to the "halls of fantasy" temporarily suspend and recontextualize the affiliatory demands of state power, without leaving readers permanently stranded in fantastic imaginings. If, as Alexis de Tocqueville observes in the second volume of *Democracy in America* (1840), the "fantastic creatures" of the imagination "cause us sometimes to yearn for the world of reality," Hawthorne's theorizations of romance identify the civic longing borne of the exilic states of literature as the affective gravity that brings us back into the nostalgic spell of worldly affiliation.[110] By temporarily occupying the unmoored, renunciative extremes of fantasy, Hawthorne suggests, we are ultimately reeducated in the irreplaceable value of worldly affiliation—in all its imperfections. Understood in these terms, it is tempting to reinterpret Tocqueville's indictment of the poetic imagination as an unintended insight into its power as a medium of political reeducation.

## "A Kind of Treason"

When Hawthorne returned to the question of the politics of romance at the end of his career, twelve years after "The Custom-House," in "Chiefly about War-Matters" (1862), he found it increasingly difficult to valorize the romantic conceit of literary autonomy in a country newly polarized by disagreements over the renunciative rights of its citizens. Four months before "Chiefly about War-Matters" appeared in *The Atlantic Monthly,* Kentucky, one of the two states to explicitly acknowledge the right of expatriation in its original constitution, passed a bill declaring that anyone who joins or supports the Confederates "shall be deemed to have expatriated themselves, and shall no longer be a citizen of Kentucky."[111] Then, in July 1862, the month Hawthorne's essay appeared, Congress passed the Second Confiscation Act, just a few days before Lincoln surprised his cabinet with a draft of the Emancipation Proclamation. The Second Confiscation Act included a provision that anticipated the proclamation by declaring that all slaves who escape and "take refuge within the lines of the [Union] Army . . . shall be forever free," but its principal aim was to "suppress Insurrection" and "punish Treason and Rebellion."[112] From the perspective of the federal government, the confederates were not expatriates—whose allegiance can be narrated in the past tense—but "enemy" nationals. This latter distinction was critical to the U.S. government because, as one representative urged in a subsequent debate about the status of rebel officers, "a person cannot commit treason if he is not a citizen."[113] To recognize the right to relinquish citizenship, or even to revoke the civic protections of Confederates, would have amounted to an acknowledgment of the legitimacy of secession.

For Hawthorne, whose literary project relies so heavily on the rhetoric of disaffiliation, the increasing conflation of expatriation and treason during the Civil War only magnified the basic political predicament posed by the renunciative effects of fiction.

At the opening of "Chiefly about War-Matters," Hawthorne represents his literary project as a casualty of war, doomed, as it were, to the grave.

> There is no remoteness of life and thought, no hermetically sealed seclusion, except, possibly, that of the grave, into which the disturbing influences of this war do not penetrate. Of course, the general heart-quake of the country long ago compelled me, reluctantly, to suspend the contemplation of certain fantasies, to which, according to my harmless custom, I was endeavoring to give a sufficiently life-like aspect to admit of their figuring in a romance. ("CWM," 43)

The suggestion that the grave may be the only space that remains untouched by the war is strange, if not perverse. To imagine the grave as the last refuge from the encroaching realities of contemporary violence requires a *pure* metaphoricity, one that is apparently unburdened, for example, by any thought of the proliferation of graves for soldiers. Oddly, the casualty of the war here is not the soldier, but the space of fantasy itself. The endeavor to give these "fantasies" a "sufficiently *life-like aspect* to admit of their figuring in a romance," represents the relationship between "fairyland" and the "real world" as one of revivification, a resurrection from the dead. If fully detached from the real, "fantasies," Hawthorne suggests, are not utopian; their abstraction is moribund. In this way, the affective losses of the war begin to infiltrate the logic of romance at precisely the moment at which the grave appears to be metaphorized so decidedly against the grain of its literal function.

The metaphoric link between imaginative license and political liberty made it increasingly easy to see aesthetic disaffiliation as a form of political defection. As a mode of disaffiliation, fiction, for Hawthorne, is both vulnerable to the charge of treason and continually faced with the specter of its own demise. The impulse to withdraw is no longer portrayed as a "neutral" right—even of romance. After lamenting the war's intrusion on romance, Hawthorne remarks, "But I magnanimously considered that there is a kind of treason in insulating one's self from the universal fear and sorrow, and thinking one's idle thoughts in the dread time of civil war; and could a man be so cold and hard-hearted, he would better deserve to be sent to Fort Warren than many who have found their way thither on the score of violent, but misdirected sympathies" ("CWM," 43). If neutrality is the precondition for representation in "The Custom-House," in the context of the Civil War the rejection of partisanship, Hawthorne suggests, is *worse* than the Confederate sympathies held by those imprisoned in Fort Warren. The remote retreats of romance, here, are not only comparable to secession—they are more reprehensible for their very dispassion. Although recent criticism on Hawthorne's previously little-discussed essay has tended to focus on the treacherous character of sympathy, a sentiment idealized for its ethical sociability in earlier novels like *Uncle Tom's Cabin*, part of the problem Hawthorne identifies here is the increasing unavailability of neutrality as a viable political stance.[114] Neutrality, as we have seen, is not an apolitical perspective for Hawthorne; it inheres in a doubleness of vision—an occupation of discrepant perspectives—which is itself tantamount to disloyalty when Unionism becomes not only an ethos, but the only culturally legible signpost of loyalty in the North.[115]

Hawthorne is surely being somewhat tongue-in-cheek in his characterization of himself as both the magnanimous judge and the perpetrator of treason, but the suggestion that isolation constitutes "a kind of treason," is a source of manifest anxiety. It is worth noting, for example, that the agent of this treason is made impersonal: the first person is replaced midsentence with "one." There is an attempt to contain this charge, to disavow it, at the same time that Hawthorne is compelled to defend it. This defensiveness does nothing to dispute the charge of treason. Instead, it dramatizes, all the more, the treasonous logic of Hawthorne's aesthetic. A retreat into the realm of letters becomes the sign of a defected citizenship, a form of citizenship that resists integration into the ideal unity of the body politic.

For readers of *The Atlantic Monthly*, a magazine committed to the Union cause, Hawthorne's comparison of "romance" to secession, coupled with the proposition that Confederates, while "violent," were victims of "misdirected sympathies," would itself have appeared tantamount to disloyalty. This figurative transgression did not go unnoticed. A review of "Chiefly about War-Matters" in *The Liberator* explicitly charged the article with "treasonable sentiments."[116] Hawthorne anticipated the essay's charged reception. After submitting the manuscript of the essay and learning that Fields had submitted it directly to the printer unread, he wrote to Ticknor to express his regret, since he "wanted the benefit of somebody's opinion . . . as to the expediency of publishing two or three passages in the article."[117] Hawthorne explains that he has already left out "whole pages of freely expressed opinion" that he "doubted whether the public would bear," and he maintains that the "remainder is tame enough in all conscience" but urges, still, that he does not want "to foist an article upon you that might anywise damage the Magazine."[118] Despite his reservation on this point, he continues to argue that "the Magazine has been getting too deep a black Republican tinge, and that there is a time pretty near at hand when you will be sorry for that."[119] This continual shift between apologetic regret and the disparagement of Republican principles is characteristic of the article itself, which counterbalances the flippant appraisals of the Northern cause in the body of the essay with the footnoted rebuffs of a censorial "editor."

When Hawthorne first submitted the article to Fields, he explains that he "affixed some editorial foot-notes, which I hope you will have no hesitation in adopting, they being very loyal. For my own part, I found it quite difficult not to lapse into treason continually; but I made manful resistance to the temptation."[120] Hawthorne adapts the compositional hierarchy between text and footnote to stage a satirical debate between two regionally identified authorial personae: the treacherous essayist (with Southern sympathies) and the "very loyal" Northern censor.[121] Ironically, these footnotes, though devised as a "censorship hoax," as James Bense notes in a comprehensive account of the essay's composition, assumed new verisimilitude when, following Hawthorne's alert to Ticknor, he was asked to revise his irreverent characterization of "Uncle Abe" and to allow Fields to excise expressions that "outrage the feelings of many Atlantic readers."[122] Hawthorne decided to cut the offending passage about Lincoln altogether and to simply revise an existing footnote.[123] In the original manuscript, the footnote reads, "We hesitated to admit the above sketch, and shall probably regret our decision in its favor. It appears to have been written in a benign spirit, and perhaps conveys a not inaccurate impression of its august subject, but it lacks *reverence,* and it pains us to see a gentleman of ripe age, and who has spent years under the corrective influence of foreign institutions, falling into the characteristic and most ominous fault of Young America."[124] In the printed, revised version, Hawthorne replaces the opening language of personal hesitation with censorial interference: "We are compelled to omit two or three pages, in which the author describes the interview, and gives his idea of the personal appearance and deportment of the President. The sketch appears to have been written in a benign spirit" ("CWM," 47n). With a censorial frame already in place, we are thus invited to imagine the omitted material and, in all likelihood, invest it with treacherous qualities that exceed the original passages.

Many of the footnotes in "Chiefly about War-Matters" offer this type of satirical critique, but the interplay between text and footnotes is complicated by the political character of the two personae: the treacherous essayist (with southern sympathies) and the "very loyal" Northern censor (to recall Hawthorne's own characterization of the dynamic). In each case, Hawthorne portrays loyalty negatively: in the Northern propriety that the writer lacks, and in the principle of censorship, with its privileging of the unsaid. But if loyalty appears abstract and impervious to concrete expression, that is precisely Hawthorne's point. Following a defense of the "impulsive" passion of the rebels,[125] Hawthorne alleges that because national allegiance lacks the proximate allure of state affiliation, "treason" is inevitable:

> There never existed any other Government against which treason was so easy, and could defend itself by such plausible arguments as against the United States. The anomaly of two allegiances (of which that of the State comes nearest home to a man's feelings, and includes the altar and the hearth, while the General Government claims his devotion only to an airy mode of law, and has no symbol but a flag) is exceedingly mischievous in this point of view; for it has converted crowds of honest people into traitors, who seem to themselves not merely innocent, but patriotic, and who die for a bad cause with as quiet a conscience as if it were the best. ("CWM," 48)

Hawthorne narrates the conflict between state and national identity in the tropes of romance: the nation is a sort of "fairy-land," governed only by "an airy mode of law," while the state, which engenders a "physical love for the soil" (as he continues to say), comes closest to the "real world" (*SL*, 36; "CWM," 50). The nation is both experientially and symbolically impoverished ("no symbol but a flag"), while the state monopolizes the political "feelings" of its citizens. But it is the dilemma posed by the "anomaly of two allegiances" that is paramount. Bound by two logics of allegiance, the citizen is either irreparably torn between multiple allegiances or, in favoring one, suffers the loss of the other, as well as the potential allegation of treason. If in "The Custom-House" the liminality of "romance" expresses the intrinsic discrepancy between civic fantasy and practice, here the "anomaly of two allegiances" is the provisional expression of political crisis.

Treason, Hawthorne suggests, is not something that citizens commit, but a circumstance to which they are subject. By attributing the agency of treachery to the "anomaly of two allegiances"—"*it* converted crowds of honest people into traitors"—Hawthorne depicts secession as a force of nature, and the Confederates as victims rather than rebels. By portraying secession as an effect of local attachments that are so habitual as to be irresistible, Hawthorne counters the customary understanding of it as an expression of the voluntary character of political association. According to this latter view, "Underlying all the doctrines of nullification, state sovereignty and secession, was the notion that the government of the United States was 'one of love, not of force'; that obedience to its laws was rather voluntary than compulsory."[126] Yet, as "Chiefly about War-Matters" suggests, even such love is not strictly voluntary; its coercive effects are merely more affective in character. Seen thus, the choice is not between political empowerment and subjection, but between two types of compulsion. The renunciation of national citizenship may have invoked the conceit of individual autonomy, but as a reactionary gesture, it also called attention to the unchosen aspects of allegiance—the affiliatory obligations that persist regardless of personal sentiments.

The issue, for Hawthorne, is less that of the respective sovereignty of the state and the nation, than of the incongruity between the limited scope of "man's feelings" and the vastness of the country.[127] As Hawthorne explains in a subsequent passage, the national landscape cannot be "occupied"; it exceeds even the most ambitious imaginings:

> In the vast extent of our country,—too vast by far to be taken into one small human heart,—we inevitably limit to our own State, or at farthest, to our own section, that sentiment of physical love for the soil which renders an Englishman, for example, so intensely sensitive to the dignity and well-being of his little island, that one hostile foot, treading anywhere upon it, would make a bruise on each individual breast. If a man loves his own State, therefore, and is content to be ruined with her, let us shoot him, if we can, but allow him an honorable burial in the soil he fights for. ("CWM," 48)

At the limit of Hawthorne's attempt to defend the position of secession, the terrestrial assumes uncharacteristic significance. But the unit of the "State" is not naturalized as a result. It only approximates the region encompassed by "that sentiment of physical love for the soil" ("our own State, *or* at farthest . . . our own section"). The boundaries of allegiance may be based in the soil here, but they are still fundamentally affective—not a foregone effect of institutional divisions of governance (the town, the state, the nation).

Significantly, it is the Englishman who encapsulates the ideal of political belonging. It is as if, for Hawthorne, the exemplary American *is* an Englishman. The English possess exactly what is practically unavailable during the Civil War—a consolidated political identity that can be embodied. The "anomaly of two allegiances" is troubling for Hawthorne because it marks the loss of this kind of singular political identity. Yet, if England becomes a proxy for consolidated allegiance, it represents a natural connection to the homeland that its postcolonial subjects lack (and cannot reclaim). As with Hawthorne's exilic sketches on fantasy, England's ideality is structured and sustained negatively in the tragic register of civic longing. This predicament is at the heart of Hawthorne's sketches about England, *Our Old Home* (1863), published on the heels of "Chiefly about

War-Matters." It also drives the plot of *The American Claimant,* where an American returns to England in the hope of claiming his ancestral estate.[128] That Hawthorne was unable to finish this narrative of political reclamation is fitting, for as the title of his English sketches signals, England is a privileged origin, but the "*old* home" is a constitutively absent ideal of belonging and historical continuity. This nostalgia underwrites a constitutively ambivalent identification between the United States and the Old World. As Hawthorne ominously reflects in the final section of *The Marble Faun* (1860)—when the protagonists, who are U.S. expatriates in Italy, prepare to return to America—"between two countries, we have none at all, or only that little space of either, in which we finally lay down our discontented bones."[129] "Betweens" proliferate in Hawthorne, persistent reminders of an ideal but hypothetical form of political belonging that can only be posited negatively in the mode of tragedy.

For Hawthorne, the "rebel" epitomizes this tragedy of politics. Hawthorne is not invested in the success of the Confederates—despite his evident skepticism about the value of emancipation ("whoever may be benefited by this war, it will be the present generation of negroes" ["CWM," 50]).[130] It is, instead, the expectation that the Confederates will be "ruined" by their defection that makes them romantic for Hawthorne.[131] His insistence that all men who love their state deserve "an honorable burial in the soil [they] figh[t] for," memorializes the projected defeat of the South, not its prospective success. In so doing, Hawthorne turns the "ruined" rebels into an inverted symbol for an ideal of political belonging that is constitutively absent (both spatially and temporally). With this idealization of unredeemed fatalism in mind, it is possible to more fully understand the parameters of Hawthorne's famous denunciation of John Brown toward the end of the essay. While John Brown's militant raid on the federal arsenal at Harper's Ferry made him a hero among abolitionists, Hawthorne takes evident pleasure in countering the narrative of Brown as prophet. "I shall not pretend to be an admirer of old John Brown, any farther than sympathy with Whittier's excellent ballad about him may go; nor did I expect to shrink so unutterably from the apothegm of a sage . . . as from that saying . . . that the death of this blood-stained fanatic has 'made the Gallows as venerable as the cross!' Nobody was ever more justly hanged. He won his martyrdom fairly, and took it firmly. He himself, I am persuaded, (such was his natural integrity,) would have acknowledged that Virginia has a right to take the life which he had staked and lost" ("CWM," 54). Despite the apparent stridency of this remark, the essay as a whole implicitly qualifies Hawthorne's indictment of Brown. Hawthorne does not question the "integrity" of Brown; it is his status as national *savior* that he disputes. Brown's importance for the abolitionist movement is no doubt part of the reason for Hawthorne's demure. Yet to see this as a simple expression of Hawthorne's hostility to the cause would be to miss the extent to which Hawthorne idealizes romance precisely as an aesthetic of defection.

Brown is a romantic figure for Hawthorne, not as an "immortal" symbol (as for Thoreau), but as a testament to the nullity of idealism.[132] Thus if "just[ice]" here means martyrdom within the rule of law, it is the very inevitability of reprisal that Hawthorne relishes. He continues, "[A]ny common-sensible man, looking at the matter unsentimentally, must have felt a certain intellectual satisfaction in seeing him hanged, if it were only in requital of his preposterous miscalculation of possibilities."[133] It is precisely as a model for the "miscalculation of possibilities" that Hawthorne elaborates his theory of "romance." The "neutral ground" may facilitate provisional intersections between the real and the ideal, but "romance," for Hawthorne, is neither essentially reconciliatory nor redemptive.[134] Indeed, Hawthorne's poeticizing of the unsustainability of idealism is one of the defining features of his reflections on romance.[135] The "failure" of romance in Hawthorne is never incidental to it; it is what gives it its quasi-tragic force—and also its specifically nostalgic affiliatory potential.

The censorious terminology of "Chiefly about War-Matters" is extreme. However, seen in relationship to Hawthorne's several theorizations of the renunciative dimension of fiction, his figurative recourse to treason is not a deviation from his better-known definitions of romance; it is an exceptionally hyperbolic formulation of fiction's strange affiliatory pull and its ability to denaturalize the bond between citizens and the state.[136] Hawthorne was wonderfully attuned to the negativity of the literary imagination. His writings on romance insistently explore the renunciative dimension of fiction, the world it leaves behind, and the disappointments that motivate it. Hawthorne used the conceit of literary autonomy to explore the allure and dangers of political disaffiliation. As an aesthetic of disaffiliation—alternately conceived as a form of expatriation and treason—romantic fictionality denaturalizes the basis of allegiance, structuring civic identification on the nostalgic model of exile. Understood thus, the exilic states of romance are not ends in themselves, but catalysts for civic longing. The political orientation of the aesthetics of disaffiliation is wayward. It articulates the moral and affective pull of association negatively—by likening the epistemic isolation of fiction to political defection, and then doubling back nostalgically on the empirical and social domains from which it has ostensibly withdrawn. The tragic model of relationality that emerges in Hawthorne is too negative to be associative in any traditional sense. For Hawthorne, as for Baldwin and so many other writers, the angst of exile lends meaning to a form of political membership that is not seen as particularly attractive in and of itself.[137] Through the nostalgic prism of exile, citizenship appears an essentially tragic ideal, which can only be represented negatively through the symbols of its failure.

The Civil War brought residual anxieties about defeasible allegiance in this period to the surface. It left little room for the double perspective of "neutrality"—its betweens and not eithers—and this time, Hawthorne's partisan reprisal brought his own racially myopic imagination of citizenship into view. Hawthornian "romance" is not a particularly Union-friendly theory of fiction. Yet it is not the ideological content of his writings that distinguishes Hawthorne's contribution to the intellectual history of citizenship.[138] Instead, his insistent attention to the affiliatory predicament posed by romantic fictionality guided his insight into the political possibilities of a newly differentiated literary realm. Hawthorne's theorizations of fiction's affiliatory allure and denaturalizing power provided a conceptual resource for a model of political allegiance that was still in the process of gaining broader cultural legitimacy: defeasible allegiance—a form of allegiance that was subject to political revision and that recognized affiliation as an imaginative art fueled by desire as much as obligation.

The doctrine of literary autonomy was a mere conceit, but it was a resonant conceit that spoke to a political mythology and a need. Romantic theorists of literary autonomy may have celebrated literature's separation from real political conditions, but in a culture preoccupied with a Revolutionary ideal of consensual "citizenship" that was still deeply contested, this renunciative impulse analogized and extended the logic of the very political debates it ostensibly rose above. In the early United States, the negativity of political fantasy was not only a theoretical abstraction (associated with the idealized nowhere of *utopos*); it evoked a range of ambivalently localized debates about the nature and perpetuity of political allegiance.[139] The result of the odd but persistent tropological convergence between literary and political autonomy was that the negativity of the literary realm came to seem the fulfillment of an otherwise unrealized Revolutionary ideal of citizenship at precisely the moment in which authors most insistently disavowed their engagement with U.S. politics.

The trope of literary autonomy provided a relatively safe testing ground for exploring the limits of political allegiance, but the analogy between aesthetic and political autonomy cut both ways. The rhetoric of political liberty provided a culturally resonant idiom for revaluing fiction, but political autonomy was not itself seen as an unconditional good. Understood as a medium that structures and refashions political allegiance, the danger and value of fiction are one and the same: the fabricated ties that connect readers to fictional worlds temporarily derealize the imaginative regime of state power and, in so doing, provide a formal mechanism for a more consensual form of affiliation. Insofar as the increasingly robust and self-consciousness theorization of fiction laid bare the artifice and fragility of the human-made world of law, it mimicked the critical effects of "higher law" discourses. However, unlike divine law and natural law, fictionality did not offer an alternate set of "natural" truths to repair the political world. It traded artifice for artifice, "legal fictions" for literary fictions.

# CHAPTER FIVE

# Stateless Fictions

## *Negative Instruction and the Nationalization of Citizenship*

> A great obstacle to good education is the inordinate passion prevalent for novels, and the time lost in that reading which should be instructively employed. When this poison infects the mind, it destroys its tone and revolts it against wholesome reading. Reason and fact, plain and unadorned, are rejected. . . . The result is a bloated imagination, sickly judgment, and disgust towards all the real businesses of life.
>
> —Thomas Jefferson to Nathaniel Burwell (1818)

> We repeat the idea which we have already expressed, that even viewed as sources of amusement only, [novels] may indirectly, if not directly, have their share of influence in making us "better men and better citizens."
>
> —Anon., Review of Robert Montgomery Bird's *Robin Day* (1839)

IN AN 1880 REVIEW of Henry James's now-famous biography of Hawthorne (1879), novelist Elizabeth Stuart Phelps laments the "remarkable process of denationalization which has gone on in this undoubtedly talented and cultivated writer."[1] As we saw in the previous chapter, Phelps's charge of "denationalization" might easily have been leveled at Hawthorne, who theorized romance as a potentially treacherous, secessionist realm "elsewhere." However, Phelps's remarks do not concern the subject of James's biography, but James himself. James's "cosmopolitan culture," Phelps fears, has doomed him to the stateless plight of Philip Nolan, the protagonist of Edward Everett Hale's didactic allegory of Confederate secession, "The Man Without a Country" (1863). "This clever and petted young man [James]," Phelps declares, "has, indeed, become 'A Man Without a Country.' By a deterioration subtler, but hardly less sad than that which fastened upon poor Phillip Nolan, our fastidious cosmopolitan has been slowly smoothing away the still sturdy and respectable, if a little angular qualities of love and reverence for home."[2] Unlike the protagonist of Hale's tale, who is sentenced to unending exile at sea after he has been tried and convicted of treason, James's denationalization, as Phelps narrates it, is not measured by his geographic separation from his native country. Phelps does not discuss the time James had recently spent abroad, writing as an expatriate in Paris.[3] Instead, Phelps focuses on James's estranged relationship to U.S. literature—a cultural estrangement she locates in his condescending characterization of Hawthorne as "provincial." Phelps casts James's irreverence for Hawthorne as a form of disloyalty to the nation (whose literature has become its metonym).[4] Phelps's censorious characterization of James's literary defection from "the King of Romancers" marshals the basic conceit of literary nationalism: the notion that the literature authored in and about a country is synonymous with the nation, as such. Within this analogical paradigm, literary taste is never merely aesthetic; it is a charged cultural barometer of the political loyalties of individual writers and readers.

In the wake of the transnational turn, literary critics are now more likely to celebrate James's cosmopolitanism than to censure it. The "nation" and nationalism look very different to us in the twenty-first century than they did for Phelps and her contemporaries—who witnessed and facilitated the precarious birth of modern nationalism in the wake of the Civil War.[5] Despite these differences in perspective and judgment, Phelps's guiding assumption is not unfamiliar to us today. Phelps expresses a way of understanding the relationship between literature and citizenship that is still alive in the twenty-first-century U.S. academy: the notion that literature is an ideal didactic resource for training students to be active, national citizens. Within this view, as Woodrow Wilson powerfully articulated it in 1894, two decades before his presidency, "the only means of schooling [students'] spirits for their common life as citizens" is "by instruction in that literature which contains the ideals of its race . . . and thought of the nation."[6] The model of civic education that Phelps and Wilson voiced at the end of the nineteenth century has had long-lasting effects. It helped galvanize the institutional growth of liberal arts education in the twentieth-century United States. It also quickly became a touchstone in humanistic defenses of liberal education. To the question "What is the purpose of education?"—as Eleanor Roosevelt reflected in the 1930s— "good citizenship" has become a de facto answer.[7]

The civic faith in literature's power to shape the inner life of a national citizenry is so familiar to us today that these remarks might feel a bit obvious or even trite. Yet, as Wilson acknowledges in his essay, the specifically nationalist model of university training he advocates was still a relatively novel notion in the late nineteenth century: "We ask ourselves, Do we even want universities of a distinctly American type? It is the first impulse of most scholarly minds to reply with a plain and decided negative. Learning is cosmopolitan. . . . Let the common schools smack of the soil, if they must, but not the universities."[8] Wilson ventriloquizes and dismisses a universalist ideal of education that many writers discussed in the previous chapters would have defended. As we have seen, from the perspective of the higher law traditions of citizenship, U.S. laws and culture were only meaningful if and when they expressed universal truths that transcended the provinciality of custom. However, in the aftermath of the Fourteenth Amendment, a homegrown culture that "smack[s] of the soil" was no longer an ill to be avoided; it was a cultural ideal that resonated deeply with the territorial theory of identity that underwrites modern birthright citizenship. Universities, as much as citizens, Wilson suggests, should bear the political imprint of the soil that surrounds them. Studying "literature which contains the ideals of its race," for Wilson and for many after him, seemed like a reasonable strategy for cultivating the student-turned-citizen's allegiance to the nation.

Wilson's confidence in the civic utility of literature would have sounded strange to many in the early United States—including former president Thomas Jefferson. As we saw in Chapter 4, anxieties about the political effects of novel reading continued well into the nineteenth century, and anxieties about fiction gained new cultural traction when the romantic trope of literary autonomy was analogized to contested figures of political autonomy like secession. How did literature become a privileged resource for a citizenry that increasingly understood itself in national terms? The broad tenets of liberal arts education date back to the classical era, but Wilson voices three relatively modern assumptions that only gained traction in the United States toward the end of the period covered in this book:[9] (1) the comfort with fiction as a didactic medium; (2) the nationalization of the republic of letters; and (3) the preeminence of federal citizenship as a form of political membership that encompasses and transcends affiliatory ties to a particular region, state, county, or city. In first half of the nineteenth century, literature that contains the "thought of the nation" was hard to come by in the United States both because of the continued popularity of British literary texts and genres and because of the late arrival of full-fledged nationalism in U.S. politics.[10] Many writers and critics in the late eighteenth and early nineteenth centuries were eager for a national literary tradition—whose authors were "native" in themes as much as birth. Yet for all their enthusiasm, there were as yet many obstacles to literary and political nationalism.

Literary nationalism was no more inevitable than the colonies' tortuous political break from the British Crown. This point bears special emphasis in any account of citizenship in the early United States because it defamiliarizes a nationalist theory of the relationship between literature and citizenship that is now so deeply engrained that it is difficult to appreciate its historical unlikeliness. This chapter looks forward to the almost reflexive belief in literature's power to shape the inner life of a national citizenry. The chapter concludes this study by showing how the extralegal discourses of early citizenship that *Civic Longing* traces were domesticated during the Civil War to solidify a newly secularized form of Christian nationalism, in which national citizenship was itself articulated as a transcendent sacral ideal. Rather than generalizing about this shift across a number of texts that happened to be published at similar times or that enjoy similar canonical stature, I examine the conceptual problems endemic to this shift as they are dramatized by the changing reception of a popular Civil War tale that enjoys a special place in the history of American civic education: Hale's patriotic allegory of Confederate secession, "The Man Without a Country." Phelps's invocation of "The Man Without a Country" in her review of James, as we will see, typifies the insistently national conceptions of literature and citizenship that Hale's popular tale helped establish during the Civil War—and that it helped to reinforce during subsequent periods of political turmoil for over a century.

Though long relegated to little more than a footnote in literary criticism, "The Man Without a Country" has been widely reprinted since its first appearance in *The Atlantic Monthly* in 1863, has inspired plays and films, and most notably served for years as a standard text in secondary education.[11] For approximately a century after its publication, "The Man Without a Country" was a touchstone for educating students as citizens in the classroom. Even before the appearance of school editions of "The Man Without a Country" in the 1890s, the tale had already attained an almost mythical pedagogical status.[12] One reviewer in 1868, remarking on the story's "strange power to bring [patriotism] to the light of consciousness," recalls transformative classroom readings of the 1863 edition of the story: "We have known that story, when read in school from the pages of the *Atlantic Monthly,* to draw tears from the eyes of young men who but a few months later answered the call for 'three hundred thousand more' [soldiers]."[13] This fabled conviction in the tale's power to transform readerly pathos into patriotic enthusiasm secured a place for "The Man Without a Country" in the classroom well into the 1970s, when it gradually fell out of the curriculum.[14]

The remarkable cultural endurance and political adaptability of Hale's tale, I argue, bespeaks Hale's successful adaptation of a didactic model that, in many respects, was uniquely suited to the definitional problems that surrounded citizenship in the early United States. "The Man Without a Country" is an exemplar of a widespread but under-analyzed model of civic education: "negative" (nonimitative) models of civic instruction, which inspire patriotism by representing the pathos of political exclusion.[15] Drawing parallels with earlier didactic tales of seduction and treason, as well as Aaron Burr's iconic treason trial in 1807, "The Man Without a Country" represents the ideal meaning of citizenship through those persons deprived of its protections: the traitor, the exile, and the slave. Hale's recourse to negative instruction allows him to recast the meaning of the renunciative tropes that shaped the idealization of citizenship from its outer limits in the preceding decades: the renunciative ethos of Christian estrangement, the extraterritorial wilds of the sea, the elsewhere of fiction. Reimagined in the cautionary mold of didacticism, these exilic figures became flashpoints for a unified and national citizenry.

Hale's exilic idealization of citizenship provided a rather simple but powerful solution to the basic definitional problem that haunted citizenship in the early United States: by presenting the meaning of citizenship negatively—from the perspective of loss and longing—Hale sidestepped the difficult question of enumerating the essential, defining features of citizenship, the rights it conferred, its scope, and the perpetuity of allegiance. "The Man Without a Country" used the plight of its exilic protagonist to redirect the aspirational ideals of citizenship to a nostalgically idealized "nation" that, for Civil War readers, was still very much in the process of emergence.[16] The ideals of political life, of course, are never fully seated in the state as it *is*, but by the end of the Civil War, the aura of ideality that surrounded "citizenship" increasingly was reimagined as an extension of the state, and more specifically of the nation. The sacralization of the nation during and after the Civil War facilitated the late nationalization of citizenship, but it did not happen seamlessly from above. The architects of national citizenship negotiated this difficult transition by self-consciously rechanneling the renunciative aspects of the early, extralegal discourses of citizenship.[17]

## Negative Instruction

Portraits of patriots abound in republican literature. From the archetypal writings of founders and statesmen to the fabled political heroes of primers, tales, and elegies, there is no shortage of citizens "fit to be imitated," to quote Benjamin Franklin.[18] The exemplary patriot was not, however, the only model for citizenship in the early United States, nor was it arguably the most compelling one. Amid the several trials of uncertain and divided loyalties that mark the early history of citizenship—the Alien and Sedition

Acts in 1798, the War of 1812, the Nullification Crisis, and Confederate secession—citizens also found uniquely instructive analogues in representations of traitors, expatriates, and slaves. The treacheries of Benedict Arnold and Aaron Burr, for example, were didactic touchstones for early patriotic literature. As William Gilmore Simms observed in *Views and Reviews in American Literature, History and Fiction* (1845), "The fate and fortunes of Benedict Arnold . . . , beyond all others, seem meant 'to point the moral and adorn the tale.' "[19] Simms was by no means alone in this sentiment. To name just a few notable examples: Arnold's treason drives William Dunlap's 1798 play *André*, parts of which were incorporated into *The Glory of the Columbia—Her Yeomanry* (1803), a patriotic drama that became a "July fourth staple"; historian and educator Jared Parks, who became the President of Harvard in 1849, published *The Life and Treason of Benedict Arnold* in 1835; passages from George Lippard's sketch of the "hideous phantom known by history as—Arnold the Traitor" in *Washington and His Generals; or, Legends of the American Revolution* (1847) were reprinted in several classroom recitation books in the late nineteenth and early twentieth centuries and, most recently, in *The Moral Compass* (1995), published by conservative pundit William J. Bennett, who was the U.S. Secretary of Education during Ronald Reagan's second term.[20] The list goes on.[21]

Republican and antebellum authors regularly set aside the figure of the body politic, with its ideal of organic incorporation, to explore the ardent pathos of disenfranchised subjects and alienated citizens. Tales of treason offered ready allegories for patriotic citizenship, while episodes depicting the agonies of exile and slavery underscored the benefits of political inclusion and freedom. In Royall Tyler's fictional Barbary narrative, for example, the hero can only appreciate the "rich blessings" of citizenship after being cast into slavery in Algiers. Tyler's narrative closes by using the travails of his enslavement to school readers in the value of their citizenship, which they are wont to take for granted. "Let those of our fellow citizens, who set at nought the rich blessings of our federal union, go like me to a land of slavery, and they will then learn how to appreciate the value of our free government," the narrator reflects at the close of the tale.[22] For the doubting "fellow citizens" addressed, it is not necessary or even desirable to "go *like* [Underhill] to a land of slavery"; the novel offers this knowledge of dispossession by proxy. In the tradition of negative instruction, the pathos of political exclusion is used to lend affective meaning to the prospect of political membership, understood as a privilege rather than a circumstantial fact.[23]

Negative instruction readily addressed an aspect of citizenship that politicians and legislators have always struggled to control: the inner habits of allegiance. Unlike imitative models of civic instruction, the tradition of negative instruction is concerned foremost with regulating sentiments toward citizenship, rather than the actions of citizens. In both models of civic instruction, sentiment and actions are seen as mutually reinforcing, but the trajectory in each is quite different: whereas the imitative model moves from concrete actions to the ideals they embody (think of the chart of thirteen virtues in Franklin's *Autobiography,* as well as the Puritan self-evaluation it parodies), negative instruction separated the meaning of citizenship from its still as yet ambiguous legal significance. Citizenship, in the tradition of negative instruction, does not concern the protocols of civic life, but the abstract ideals that give political membership its emotive meaning. Negative instruction might thus be seen as a unique response to what several critics have referred to as the abstracting logic of citizenship.[24] Negative didactic models harnessed the inherent negativity of political ideals and also transformed persistent characterizations of the (presumptively dangerous) virtuality of fiction into a potential asset for civic instruction.[25] Tales of negative instruction offered writers and readers a relatively safe, virtual realm for playing out (and staving off) lingering doubts about the precise meaning of citizenship, as well as resistance to the national form it was beginning to take.

Hale adapted the well-established didactic tradition of negative instruction to address the debates over the scope of citizenship brought to a head in the Civil War. Hale, a Boston writer and Unitarian pastor,[26] published "The Man Without a Country" in *The Atlantic Monthly* at the height of the Civil War to encourage patriotic support for the Union by showing "young Americans of to-day what it is to be A MAN WITHOUT A COUNTRY," as he notes at the opening.[27] Like several earlier tales of treachery, Hale's "The Man Without a Country" evokes the example of Aaron Burr as "a beacon to warn all young men that the way of virtue is the only way to honor."[28] Burr's status as a "fallen founder" gave added poignancy to his downfall.[29] At the height of his political career, Burr served as the vice president during Thomas Jefferson's first term (1801–1805), but he soon became an icon of infamy. Burr not only shot and killed his political rival, Alexander Hamilton, in a duel in 1804, he was arrested and tried for treason in 1807.[30] Jefferson accused his former vice president of being "the prime mover" in "designs" in the western territories that were "unlawful and unfriendly to the peace of the Union."[31] Burr was not convicted, but the vague allegations of treason lingered and took on new life in the fictionalized portraits of Burr in didactic literature. Burr, as legal historian Robert Ferguson observes, "provided the object lesson in how *not* to behave—a lesson that brought new urgency and definition to westward expansion."[32]

In the context of the Civil War, Burr's defection no longer appeared exceptional; it offered a convenient figure for secession. To add didactic force to his political lesson, Hale presents the story as a forgotten history, pieced together by the narrator, a naval officer named Captain Ingham.[33] When the tale proper opens, it is 1805 and Philip Nolan, a young officer, has fallen under the fascination of Aaron Burr. Burr, "a disguised conqueror," "seduce[s]" Nolan, who is subsequently tried for treason ("M," 666). During the trial, Nolan exclaims in a "fit of frenzy," "D—n the United States! I wish I may never hear of the United States again!" ("M," 666–667). The officers of the court, many of whom "served through the Revolution," decide, in a gesture of poetic justice, that Nolan's punishment will be just that: he is sentenced "never [to] hear the name of the United States again" and never again to "see the country which he has disowned" ("M," 668). To carry the sentence out, Nolan, ever so aptly named as it turns out (no-land), is kept in a state of perpetual dislocation, confined onboard a series of ships.[34] In the piecemeal reconstruction of Nolan's imprisonment that follows, Ingham presents scenes of Nolan's education into the meaning of patriotism. During a battle in the War of 1812, for example, Nolan throws himself into the line of fire to save from destruction the ship on which he is a prisoner. Despite Nolan's repentance and fervent patriotism, however, the captain and Ingham fail to obtain his pardon from the government. Nolan dies at sea in 1863, ardent in his love for a country from which he has long been an outcast.

Hale, who seems to have been quick to equate national critique with disloyalty, wrote the tale following announcements that Ohio Copperhead Clement Vallandigham was running as a candidate for governor. Earlier that year, Vallandigham had been convicted by a military tribunal for publicly "declaring disloyal sentiments."[35] Lincoln commuted Vallandigham's sentence from imprisonment to banishment to the Confederacy—a gesture all the more peculiar for its procedural recognition of the discrete sovereignty of the Confederacy, the very thing Lincoln was so insistent in resisting. Hale hoped the story would provide his "'testimony' to the principles involved" in the "autumn elections."[36] Vallandigham is only mentioned once in the story itself, but in subsequent prefaces to "The Man Without a Country," Hale invokes Vallandigham to explain the urgency of the tale's patriotic lesson to postbellum readers "who hardly understan[d] that such a lesson was ever needed."[37] As Brook Thomas notes in one of the first of a flurry of recent accounts of "The Man Without a Country," by inaccurately portraying Vallandigham as "having denounced his country"—Hale "helped Lincoln win the historical spin on how to interpret the Vallandigham affair" (implicitly justifying Lincoln's policies for detaining political prisoners under martial law during the war).[38] Hale evinces little sympathy for Vallandigham's predicament; instead, as in Thomas Nast's emotive 1863 political depiction of the affair shown in Figure 3, "The Man

FIGURE 3. Thomas Nast, "A Hard Case—Vallandigham's Reception by His Friend Jeff" (1863). Courtesy of the American Antiquarian Society.

Without a Country" uses Vallandigham's exilic plight as a cautionary against rash disloyalty. Hale intends to offer a cautionary tale, a "warning to young Nolans and Vallandighams and Tatnalls of today of what it is to throw away a country" ("M," 677).

Hale's unsympathetic depiction of Vallandigham allows him to reduce the affair to a dogmatic illustration of patriotism, but the story itself expresses unexpected sympathy for Nolan's similar plight. The narrative leads us to expect and desire Nolan's formal pardon, when he heroically throws himself in the line of fire during a battle in the War of 1812 to regain control of the Navy's artillery. The captain presents Nolan with "his own sword of ceremony" and writes "a special letter to the Secretary of War" asking for Nolan's pardon. "But nothing ever came of it. As I said, that was about the time when they began to ignore the whole transaction at Washington, and when Nolan's imprisonment began to carry itself on because there was nobody to stop it without any new orders from home" ("M," 672). Nolan's imprisonment is upheld by neither reason nor justice. Once issued, his sentence is carried out automatically by an unaccountable government without intention or memory.[39] The government lacks the very thing that the narrative generates: sympathy for Nolan.[40] Nolan's patriotism, in the end, is a one-way love affair. This short-circuiting of the reciprocal model of allegiance that citizenship promised played a key role in the peculiarly mixed reception history of Hale's patriotic allegory. As we will see, the undercurrent of sympathy the story generates for its hapless protagonist, ultimately opened "The Man Without a Country" to a much wider range of political uses than Hale initially envisioned.

## "Poor Nolan"

The downfall of Philip Nolan, like many other characters in the tradition of negative instruction, is seduction. It is no surprise that seduction features prominently in the tradition of negative instruction. Seduction (from *se-* 'away, apart' + *ducere* 'to lead') is an etymological derivation of education; it is education's ill-behaved twin.[41] Hale reimagines the well-worn tropes of seduction fiction to narrate Nolan's defection, without disclosing the exact nature of Nolan's treachery. Nolan, we are told, meets Aaron Burr in 1805 and is immediately "fascinated" ("M," 666). He writes Burr "[l]ong, high-worded, stilted letters" but receives no response "from the gay deceiver."

> The other boys in the garrison sneered at him, because he sacrificed in this *unrequited affection* for a politician the time which they devoted to Monongahela, hazard, and high-low-jack. . . . But one day Nolan had his revenge. . . .

Burr had not been at the fort an hour before he sent for him. That evening he asked Nolan to take him out in his skiff, to show him a canebrake or a cotton-wood tree, as he said,—*really to seduce him;* and by the time the sail was over, Nolan was enlisted body and soul. From that time, though he did not yet know it, he lived as A MAN WITHOUT A COUNTRY. ("M," 666, emphasis added)

Cast in the sentimental tropes of "unrequited affection" and innocent deceit, the language of seduction here conjures up more than rhetorical persuasion. However, the tension between rhetorical and physical seduction remains unresolved. The scene of Nolan's transgression, in fact, is absent: the narrative jumps abruptly from the disclosure of Burr's future intentions to the aftermath ("by the time the sail was over").

Nolan's "seduction" can signal his denationalization because seduction and treachery implicitly operate as synonymous terms for the loss of civic virtue within the genre that Hale invokes. Burr's reputation as a traitor and seducer made explicit one of the seduction novel's central premises.[42] To be seduced, as Jan Lewis observes, "is to surrender republican virtue and to flirt is to commit an act of treason."[43] The equation of flirtation with treason is perhaps too hyperbolic, but the basic paradigm holds: the distribution of erotic attachments doubles for the structure of civic affiliations more generally. This is explicit in Harriet Beecher Stowe's *The Minister's Wooing* (1859), where Aaron Burr appears as the seducer of a married French aristocratic woman, whose "feelings" he uses "to carry his plans" of "founding a state."[44]

Seduction narratives helped establish virtue as a defining characteristic of republican citizenship. However, they also denigrated the more promiscuous forms of affiliation associated with democracy. For if, as John Adams remarked, "Democracy is Lovelace and the people are Clarissa," part of the implicit lesson of the seduction novel in the early republic was to apprise citizens of the perils of democracy.[45] A representative democracy might confer power on the people, but it does not ensure the discerning exercise of this power. The lesson of the seduction narrative was at once to cultivate a virtuous citizenry and to foster skepticism toward the rhetorical wiles of aspiring demagogues. Seduction narratives, in this way, address the basic volatility of democratic citizenship: by censuring licentious expressions of sociability, they seek to curtail the transgressive potential of democracy.

The prolific literature of seduction in the early republic—shaped so intimately by conservative, if not explicitly monarchical, models of virtue—tended in consequence to give way to deeply ambivalent political identifications. In Susanna Rowson's *Charlotte Temple* (1791), the most popular of these novels,

Montraville's seduction of Charlotte separates her not only from her previous virtue but also from her native country (as she follows Montraville from England to America).[46] The pathos of seduction in Rowson's novel thus becomes a trope for colonial nostalgia—in which England doubles for a virtue now lost, and America for seduction and homelessness. Hale remaps the conflation of virtue and nationality that structures *Charlotte Temple* in more strictly national terms in "The Man Without a Country," where U.S. nationality and exile are the only options.[47] In both narratives, the effects of unwise affiliations, with Burr and Montraville, are never merely personal; they result in a broader dislocation from home and homeland. Though the homeland is associated with different territories in each narrative (Britain and America), it is an essentially nostalgic construction in both cases. "The Man Without a Country," indeed, establishes nostalgia—which in its initial conceptualization in the seventeenth century described "pathological homesickness"—as the representative standard of patriotism, rather than its aberration.[48]

Rowson's and Hale's narratives both caution against developing personal attachments that depart from broader communal loyalties, whether familial or national, but "The Man Without a Country" more symptomatically associates the threat of social alienation with Nolan's ambiguously narrated homoerotic alliance with Burr. Nolan's frenzied denunciation of the state during his trial—"Damn the United States! I wish I may never hear of the United States again!" ("M," 667)—may provide the rationale for his sentence, but his affiliation with Burr constitutes the fundamental treachery in the narrative. Even when Nolan is tried as a conspirator to treason, we are told little more than that "there was evidence enough—that he was sick of the service, had been willing to be false to it, and would have obeyed any order to march any-whither with anyone . . . *had the order been signed, 'By command of his Exc. A. Burr'*" ("M," 666, emphasis added). Nolan's real treachery is an excessive loyalty to Burr. Nor is this a paradox. The crime of treason consists foremost in developing affiliations not aligned with the interests of the state. According to article III of the Constitution, which provided the primary precedent for treason law in the antebellum period, the commission of treason consists in either "levying War" against the United States or "adhering to their [the states'] Enemies, giving them aid and comfort."[49] The fictional treason committed by Hale's hero falls into this latter category of adherence.[50] The fact that Nolan's treachery is secondary, and not primary as with Burr, is crucial to the tale's didactic project because it allows Hale to manage the tenuous balance between conveying Nolan's error and yet making him a sympathetic character.[51]

The tale's apparent success at figuring Nolan's loyalty as a form of treachery may derive, in part, from the heteronormative assumptions that underwrite the common analogy between marriage and the social contract and, in turn, political legitimacy. But if so, this remains unspoken in the story, which makes more of the structure of seduction than of gender itself. Seduction becomes a form of criminality in "The Man Without a Country" foremost because it draws Nolan away from his duties to the nation as an army officer. In this respect, the court's decision to sentence Nolan to confinement at sea merely literalizes, in spatial terms, the affective distance instantiated in the barely narrated scene of seduction—which itself occurs on a boat. Nolan forfeits his nationality as soon as he leaves the country's terra firma, but—and this proves pivotal—he is not a fully cognizant or autonomous actor in this forfeiture.

Nolan may be naive and rash, but his guilt is secondary. He is an unwitting victim of Burr's machinations—not a prototypical figure of defiant masculinity. This dynamic replays one of the most rhetorically fraught aspects of Burr's trial for treason in 1807. During Burr's trial, as Nancy Isenberg argues, the prosecution employed Burr's infamous reputation as a seductive libertine to compensate for insufficient material evidence.[52] Since Burr was hundreds of miles away from the alleged scene of treason—Blennerhassett's island—his guilt could only be imputed by making treasonous influence, rather than actions, the principle offense. Burr's real crime, the prosecution implied, is seduction: Burr, it was said, "attempted the seduction of the officers and men, at the several forts and garrisons . . . which . . . were too weak to have resisted with effect," and most importantly, he seduced Harmon Blennerhassett, drawing him into the center of the conspiracy.[53] In a famous speech in the trial, reproduced in primers and guides to rhetoric, William Wirt, a lawyer for the prosecution, vividly renders Blennerhassett's seduction as the fall from "the state of Eden when the serpent [Burr] entered its bowers." "This unfortunate man . . . thus *seduced from the paths of innocence* and peace . . . this man, thus ruined and undone and made to play a *subordinate part in this grand drama of guilt and treason,* this man is to be called the principle offender, while he by whom he was thus plunged into misery is *comparatively innocent,* a mere accessory! . . . Sir, neither the human heart nor the human understanding will bear a perversion so monstrous and absurd!"[54] Despite his physical removal from the alleged scene of treason, Burr, according to the prosecution, remains the primary agent of treason. By privileging influence over actions, Blennerhassett (like Nolan), though "ruined," appears "comparatively innocent."

In both the trial and its reconfiguration in "The Man Without a Country," the language of seduction is employed to minimize the political culpability of "secondary" traitors—whose relatively *passive* guilt makes them ideal figures for civic instruction. The seduction tradition, as Nina Baym observes, reinforces a "spectacle of victimized innocence" that denies "that innocence was compatible with agency."[55] The seduction tradition is certainly not without its limitations as a genre of political instruction. However, the suggestion of passivity is precisely what allows seduction narratives to mitigate the culpability of their heroes/heroines and, in turn, to make their protagonists instructive exemplars. The protagonist in a seduction narrative must be both guilty and innocent to support the divided identification requisite to negative instruction. Protagonists need to be sympathetic enough to sustain readerly identification, but not *so* sympathetic that they inspire imitation.

The trope of seduction facilitates negative instruction by modeling a form of hybrid agency—between autonomy and susceptibility, guilt and innocence. Nolan, who is "guilty enough" on "evidence enough," is exemplary in this respect ("M," 666). "Poor Nolan," as the narrator often refers to him, is both fallen and virtuous, traitor and patriot, but the balance between these positions is precarious in the story. For if Nolan appears too innocent, his punishment is unjust—and the state unworthy of devotion—but, alternately, if his treachery is unredeemable, he is neither instructive nor worthy of sympathy. Seduction, then, does not resolve the problem of identification in the narrative. Rather, the ambiguity inherent in the rhetoric of seduction forestalls any decisive judgment of Nolan's character, allowing the tale to cultivate patriotic sentiments through a compromised protagonist who, despite his ardent reform, can only exemplify the love of a country that he has already lost.

Hale's patriotic recasting of the seduction genre stakes a claim integral to Unionism and the national citizenry it hopes to normalize. Like Lincoln, Hale is unwilling to recognize the autonomy of the Confederacy—and, in this case, the misled youths whose affections have been drawn away from the Union. Rather than present these "traitors" as informed and autonomous dissenters, Hale's enervated characterization of the "young Nolans and Vallandighams and Tatnalls of today" delegitimizes secession by presenting secessionists not as willful agents capable of *informed* consent, but as hapless victims of their own miseducation. Framed as a problem of political education, the ultimate "solution" to secession is not military force but civic reeducation. This moved Hale away from Lincoln's short-term solution for containing the threat Vallandigham symbolized and toward a new program of civic reeducation, which, as we will see in the concluding pages, was just as urgent after the Civil War as it was during it.

## An Education in Exile

In a preface written after the first school book edition, in which Hale explicitly rededicates the story to "the boys and girls who also are citizens of the United States," he remarks that he wrote "The Man Without a Country" with the "single purpose of teaching young Americans *what it is to have a country.*"[56] This comment establishes an apparently perfect inverse relationship between the moral of the tale and the basic situation of the narrative, as encapsulated in the title. "The Man Without a Country," that is, promises a myth of national possession ("hav[ing] a country"), but offers instead a narrative of dispossession. "The Man Without a Country" uses its protagonist's punitive exile from the nation to reconceive of patriotism as a form of national longing. In "The Man Without a Country," patriotism becomes a substitute for having a country, rather than the fulfillment of active national citizenship.

Negative instruction offered a reparative response to the ongoing sectional crisis, but the didactic tradition Hale adapts presented challenges in a culture in which—prior to transcendentalism—imitation long had been seen as the most effective means of education.[57] For those invested in the rote recitation-based model of education that the Lockean conception of "the mind as an empty tablet" helped popularize, the basic didactic conceit of negative instruction seemed a bit ludicrous.[58] In Lydia Maria Child's "Advice concerning Books" in *The Mother's Book* (1831), she attacks negative instruction as an unwarranted danger to young, impressionable readers. A moral that is solidified only at end of a book, Child cautions, is not enough to overturn its narrative thrust.

> The morality should be *in* the books, not tacked upon the *end* of it. Vices the juvenile reader never heard of, are introduced, dressed up in alluring characters, which excite their admiration, their love, their deepest pity; and they are told that these heroes and heroines were very naughty, and that in the end they were certain to die despised and neglected.
>
> What is the result? The generous bosom of youth pities the sinners, and thinks the world was a cruel world to despise and neglect them. Charlotte Temple has a nice good moral at the end, and I dare say was written with the best intention, yet I believe few works do so much harm to girls of fourteen or fifteen.
>
> I doubt whether books which represent vice, in any way, are suitable to be put into the hands of those whose principles are not formed. It is better to paint virtue to be imitated, than vice to be shunned.[59]

For Child, imitative instruction is preferable to negative instruction because young readers, insufficiently versed in social codes, sympathize with the protagonists and blame the society that failed them. The loyalties of the impressionable reader, Child assumes, form in direct imitation of the sentiments modeled in a work of literature—in part, because sympathy itself is a form of affinity. Within the terms of imitation, the negative portrayal of vice will always be a less efficacious means of instructing virtue, not only because the very knowledge of it is seen as potentially dangerous, but because narration is recognized as a force of readerly seduction.

Child articulates the danger inherent in negative instruction—that readers will sympathize too much with the plights of unprincipled protagonists and so imitate their actions—but she superimposes the assumptions of imitative instruction onto a genre that proceeds from very different premises. In negative instruction, the lesson appended to the main drama does not finally address the protagonist, who inevitably learns it too late, but the reader, imagined as the text's moral afterlife or embodied sequel. Negative instruction enlists the reader to translate the world of fiction (rendered as tragedy) into an ideal but civic-minded hermeneutics. Through the virtual experience attained through fiction, negative instruction seeks to educate readers in the vices and deceptions practiced by others, without their ever acquiring such knowledge through infelicitous actions. In an argument about the educative nature of novels in William Hill Brown's *The Power of Sympathy* (1789) that doubles as a defense of the text's own seduction plot, Mr. Holmes argues that books that record the "faithfulness of friendship—the constancy of *true love,* and even that honesty is the best policy" lead readers to place undeserved "confidence in the virtue of others." "Unsuspicious of deceit, she [the reader] is easily deceived—from the purity of her own thoughts, she trusts the faith of mankind, until experience convinces her of errour."[60] Literature that represents vice educates the reader in the necessity of skepticism. Readers can preserve civic virtue precisely through exposure to characters that err in their stead.

Child omits to consider negative instruction in its own terms. However, her concern that the clarity of its lesson depends on unpredictable reading practices—whether the imperatives of imitation or excessive sympathy—is suggestively born out in the uneven reception history of Hale's tale. Despite the tale's reputation for patriotic indoctrination, not all readers of "The Man Without a Country" have found its moral either convincing or successful. In 1864 the London *Observer* invoked the story as an "illustration" of their belief that "democracy, too, has its abuses, and the representatives of the free states are found to be guilty of acts as tyrannical as those committed by irresponsible despots."[61] Shortly thereafter, the *New York Observer* denounced Hale's story "as *contra bonos mores* [against good morals], inasmuch as it professed to be a truthful record of a passage in

American history, and was fitted to cast odium upon the government."[62] The central term of the *New York Observer*'s critique, *contra bonos mores*, extends beyond an accusation that the story engenders antipathy for the government; in its legal definition, *contra bonos mores* entails the "incentive to crime."[63] The *New York Observer*'s critique presumes that the relationship between fiction and reality is fundamentally imitative: not only will readers imitate the work, but the work itself ought to be based on reality, or in the very least it should not substitute verisimilitude for truth by "profess[ing] to be a truthful record of a passage in American history." This articulation of the proper relation of fiction to history presumes that representational fidelity (to American history) determines a story's political loyalty. The *New York Observer*'s suggestion is less that all fiction should be restricted to the domain of historical record, than that patriotic tales should be faithful to American history, while also reflecting favorably on the government.

In Hale's several responses to the *Observer* in subsequent prefaces and articles, he formulates the national character of literature in very different terms. Drawing on the homonym between "writes" and "rights," Hale variously defends the "rights of the writer of fiction" and contends that he has "taken *no liberties* with history other than such as every writer of fiction is privileged to take."[64] For Hale, the "rights of the writer of fiction" are no more absolute than they are for Hawthorne. Hale pivots between defending the "rights of the writer of fiction" and acknowledging the writer's "duty" to provide clues to a story's fictional status—a duty that, he acknowledges, he may not have successfully discharged in writing "The Man Without a Country."[65] Hale's qualified formulation of the "rights of the writer of fiction" captures the ambivalently political character of transcendentalism and romantic fictionality—which recoil from history, but in so doing (as we saw in Chapter 4), they also appropriate the pervasive rhetoric of disaffiliation that shaped contemporaneous debates about the voluntary and so defeasible nature of political allegiance. Negative instruction is structured by a similar dynamic, but more than any of the extralegal traditions discussed in the foregoing chapters, it aspires to domesticate this renunciative impulse by turning exile into the occasion for an expressly nationalized form of civic longing. Thus, unlike Hawthorne's formulation of the "rights" of the romancer in *The House of the Seven Gables*, for Hale the rhetoric of "rights" carries the unmistakable symbolism of the nation. Hale counters the mimetic, tradition-bound conception of literary nationalism upon which the *New York Observer*'s critique depends by insisting that the rejection of historical tradition is itself a recognizably national (and even Whiggish) trait.

These scattered critiques of the antipatriotic character of "The Man Without a Country" did little to dislodge the story's reputation for patriotism in the nineteenth century. As we will see at the end of this chapter, that shift came much later. Hale and his fabled protagonist quickly became icons of a newly nationalized conception of American citizenship. When Hale died in 1909, the obituary in the *Washington Post* framed his life as an allegory of national citizenship. "What Bayard was to the history of France, Edward Everett Hale was to American citizenship. No thought of personal advancement ever disturbed him, but every pulsation of his heart was for his country and humanity."[66]

Hale's contribution to the modern, nationalized conception of literature's role in civic education was twofold. In addition to the remarkable longevity of "The Man Without a Country" in the classroom, Hale actively theorized literature's role in civic education. In Hale's 1887 address "Democracy and a Liberal Education," he argues that "if a man is an American, let him remember one thing as he reads. . . . The man best fitted by his education to do the manly and godly service expected of an American citizen is not by that fortune [of his education], in any jot separated from the people. No! he is bone of their bone, and life of their life. The people can lead him just as much as his books can teach the people."[67] Any attempt to separate oneself from the people, Hale maintains, results in social death: "Anyone who separates himself from the race of which he is a part, at that moment death begins."[68]

Hale began articulating this populist form of literary nationalism several years before the Civil War had begun in a review of Whitman's *Leaves of Grass*. Although Whitman's *Leaves of Grass* was not particularly well received when it first appeared in 1855, Hale was one of its early enthusiasts. In an 1856 review of *Leaves of Grass* in the *North American Review,* Hale champions Whitman's populism. "Walter Whitman, an American,—one of the roughs,—no sentimentalist,—no stander above men and women, or apart from them,—no more modest than immodest,—has tried to write down here, in a sort of prose poetry, a good deal of what he has seen, felt, and guessed at in a pilgrimage of some thirty-five years."[69] Given Whitman's own investment in literary nationalism and his earlier dabbling in didactic tales like "Death in a School Room. A Fact" (1841), it is easy to imagine that this sense of intellectual sympathy was reciprocal. Yet whatever Whitman may or may not have thought about Hale's most popular tale, he understood literature's role in civic education in similar terms. For Whitman and Hale, U.S. authors and politicians share a common representational aspiration—one that made both writers natural supporters of Abraham Lincoln—to be "of the people, by the people, and for the people."[70]

Literature, Hale and Whitman suggest, is the only medium capable of developing and sustaining the spiritual cohesion necessary to a unified citizenry that is of the people in spirit, as well as in name. In *Democratic Vistas* (1871), Whitman's most sustained philosophical treatment of literature's role in preparing a new generation for the challenges of citizenship, he argues, "It is not enough that the new blood, new frame of democracy shall be vivified and held together merely by political means, superficial suffrage, legislation &c.," the reform must be "deeper" and "ge[t] at least as firm and as warm a hold in men's hearts, emotions and beliefs" (*DV*, 9). Whitman's sense of the peripheral character of the law, and its inadequacy as a medium of political reform, made him question the basic conceit of Reconstruction: that legislation could provide a satisfactory foundation for a new (and more inclusive) body politic.[71] "Two or three really original American poets," Whitman argues, "would give more compaction and more identity . . . to these States than all its Constitutions, legislative and juridical ties, and all its hitherto political, warlike, or materialistic experiences" (*DV*, 9). Whitman derides the fantasy that the law, in itself, can create and sustain meaningful forms of political attachment. For Whitman, as with many writers in the preceding generation, legal edicts cannot guarantee the inner revolutions of affiliation requisite to political consent and voluntary association.

Literature's facility at addressing things "invisible and of the spirit" (to recall Wilson) defines its integral role in civic education as Hale and Whitman understand it. In the opening pages of *Democratic Vistas,* Whitman promises, "I will not gloss over the appalling dangers of universal suffrage in the United States. In fact, it is to admit and face these dangers that I'm writing" (*DV*, 4). Yet in many respects, it is precisely this amnesia that the text approximates in its relentlessly future-oriented vision of democracy. "We have frequently printed the word Democracy. Yet I cannot too often repeat that it is a word the real gist of which still sleeps, notwithstanding the resonance and the many angry tempests out of which its syllables have come, from pen or tongue. It is a great word, whose history, I suppose, remains unwritten, because that history has yet to be enacted" (*DV*, 37). After "submit[ting] . . . that the fruition of democracy, on aught like a grand scale, resides altogether in the future," Whitman exclaims, "Thus we presume to write, as it were, upon things that exist not, and travel by maps yet unmade, and a blank" (*DV*, 34). Whitman's insistence on rewriting democracy as a "blank," a sanctified space unmarred by the history of democracy's failed enactments, evinces a need to purify language of any reference to the history of citizenship in the United States. The past is unusable, present only in the fragments left behind the "tempests" of history: the bare "syllables" of the word "democracy," whose meaning—like "citizenship" itself—remained deeply speculative.

The subjunctive orientation of literature—its freedom from history as it already is—Whitman suggests, allows it to embody an ideal of citizenship that is on the political horizon but has not yet been realized in U.S. history. In an unpublished fragment drafted as a preface to *Democratic Vistas*, Whitman expresses interest in what democracy would actually look like: "I have been curious to see how Democracy would appear in the emotional and speculative and aesthetic concrete—in human forms & action and life— on the battlefield, and among the wounded & dying afterward—in the presence of sky, fields, woods, waters—or in estimating poets, or their works—and how it would face and construe all those themes."[72] Whitman's curiosity to "see" democracy calls attention to the gap between the ideal of "Democracy" (an abstractness signaled in the capitalization) and the everyday world of embodied experience. Democracy, indeed, remains insistently withdrawn from view here. This is both the argument and the problem posed in *Democratic Vistas*. For while the text laments the discontinuities between the failed historical enactments of democracy and the great potential latent in the concept, it also dramatizes the extent to which the fulfillment of democracy is, on a fundamental level, only imaginable in the aspirational terms of a hitherto unrealized future. This is not to suggest that *Democratic Vistas* does not work toward such a future, but rather to emphasize that the structure of futurity is constitutive of Whitman's celebration of citizenship. In *Democratic Vistas*, Whitman's secular reimagining of the expressly theological formulations of "citizenship in heaven" (discussed in Chapter 2), the future of democracy stands in for a form of unqualified belonging that can only be imagined.

Literature, the medium Hale and Whitman propose to instruct citizens in the kind of autonomy necessary for this future democracy, must itself become the "aesthetic concrete" of democratic citizenship. Whitman, as we have seen, domesticates the aspirational impulse of the higher law traditions of citizenship by anchoring the "truth" of the nation in the future to come. Hale takes a somewhat different tact in domesticating the aspirational dimension of the higher law traditions of citizenship. He uses the premise of Nolan's exile to separate the idea of the United States from the institutional norms of everyday practice. In Hale's strategic sleight of hand, the nation itself becomes the experientially unavailable ideal horizon of political belonging. The fact that Nolan's exile is linguistic as well as spatial is crucial in this respect. Nolan's linguistically enforced exile from the country he has denounced turns the very name "United States" into the absent symbol of belonging.

"The Man Without a Country" thematizes what Hawthorne treats as an ontological problem: the exilic character of fiction, whose remove from the real world holds out as a possibility—but not a guarantee—affiliatory repatriation in a political world seen anew with civic longing. In "The Man Without a Country," Nolan becomes increasingly patriotic not by reading about the United States, but by experiencing its discursive and sensorial loss.[73] In keeping with Nolan's punishment ("never [to] hear the name of the United States again"), naval officers are only "permitted to lend him books, if they were not published in America and made no allusion to it" ("M," 669). The plan adopted for Nolan's reading presumes that foreign literature is safely free of "national" content, as it consists in American references, but in the sensitive situation of Nolan's discursive deprivation, the sentiment of patriotism itself becomes an allusion to the country Nolan denounced.[74] In a pivotal scene that triggers Nolan's patriotic reform during his sentence, he reads aloud passages from Walter Scott's nationalist poem, *Lay of the Last Minstrel* (1805), which impart to him, for the first time, the full pathos of his exile:

> "Breathes there the man, with soul so dead,
> Who never to himself hath said,"
> . . . Poor Nolan himself went on, still unconsciously or mechanically,—
> "This is my own, my native land!"
> Then they all saw something was to pay; but he expected to get through,
>     I suppose, turned a little pale, but plunged on,—
> "Whose heart hath ne'er within him burned
> As home his footsteps he hath turned
> From wandering on a foreign strand?
> If such there breathe, go, mark him well."
> . . . "For him no minstrel raptures swell;
> High though his titles proud his name,
> Boundless his wealth as wish can claim,
> Despite these titles, power and pelf,
> The wretch concentrated all in self,"
> and here the poor fellow choked, could not go on, but started up,
>     swung the book into the sea. ("M," 669–670)

The minstrel's eloquent patriotism stands in stark contrast to Nolan's rash denunciation of his country, and it is the import of his forfeiture that Nolan realizes as he chokes out these lines.

Nolan and the minstrel inspire patriotism in a similar manner. In Scott's poem, the minstrel, though patriotic, is fundamentally alienated from the

Scottish nationalism he nostalgically idealizes. He is "the last of the race . . . supposed to have survived the Revolution."[75] Even the minstrel's impassioned verse here—which in the poem constitutes his response to the suggestion that his skills would be better rewarded in "the more generous southern land" (England) than in the "poor and thankless soil" of Scotland—works according to a negative model of patriotism.[76] Scott's lines draw their fervency from the hypothetical figure of a soulless "wretch" devoid of national attachment. Indeed, patriotism is supposed to grow in direct accordance with geographical distance from one's country, such that nothing is more abject than a person " 'Whose heart hath ne'er within him burned/As home his footsteps he hath turned/From wandering on a foreign strand.' "

Like Scott, Hale insistently distinguishes the ideal of a country from the government and territory that define it at any given moment. In keeping with its etymology, "country" is truly a negative phenomenon in "The Man Without a Country," where patriotism is forged in the comparative grammar of exile.[77] The tale's insistently negative fabrication of a national literature and citizenry comes to a dramatic climax in Hale's representation of the annexation of Texas—the target of Burr's alleged attempt to raise his own empire. "[W]hen Texas was annexed, there was a careful discussion among the officers, whether they should get hold of Nolan's handsome set of maps and cut Texas out of it,—from the map of the world and the map of Mexico. The United States had been cut out when the atlas was bought for him. But it was voted, rightly enough, that to do this would be virtually to reveal to him what had happened, or, as Harry Cole said, to make him think Old Burr had succeeded" ("M," 676). Despite the officer's decision, Nolan becomes curious at the sudden absence of any references to Texas, which were all "painfully cut out of his newspapers," and finally asks "what has become of Texas." An officer bluntly responds, "Texas is out of the map, Mr. Nolan" ("M," 676). The acquisition of Texas thus registers as a loss for Nolan, another linguistic gap.[78]

Nolan ultimately finds himself in a situation not unlike that of Irving's somnolent protagonist Rip Van Winkle, who sleeps through the American Revolution and awakes, twenty years later, bewildered to discover that "instead of being a subject of his majesty George the Third, he was now a free citizen of the United States."[79] As with the hero of Irving's strange political bildungsroman, Nolan's knowledge of the Civil War is retroactive. However, unlike Rip, Nolan never physically returns to the changed world of his nativity. Nolan's imaginative occupation of the re-territorialized United States is fundamentally mediated by language and narrative. In this sense, narrative does not merely crystallize and retroactively lend meaning to political transformations that have already taken place in the law. Narrative, in "The Man Without a Country," offers the only access to a unified nation and citizenry that—in the story, and in the war-torn country for which it was written—was very clearly a thing of fiction.

Patriotism in "The Man Without a Country" is not a natural extension of political belonging; it is a sentiment conditioned by the imagination of exile. When, toward the close of the story, Nolan points from his deathbed to a "great map of the United States, as he had drawn it from memory" and sadly exclaims, "Here, you see, I have a country!" ("M," 677), it is clear that this imaginative possession comes at the cost of its material presence. The officer, Danforth, who witnesses this scene, comforts Nolan in these final hours by agreeing to tell him about the recent history of the United States, despite the prohibition in Nolan's sentence. Danforth draws the boundaries of newly incorporated states into Nolan's map, but he cannot bring himself to "tell him a word about this infernal Rebellion" ("M," 678–679). Nolan thus spends his final moments elated in the knowledge of the nation's progress, while ignorant of the Civil War that threatens it with disunity and collapse. Danforth's selective history may be characteristic of what Lauren Berlant refers to as the "typically amnesiac American," but for the reader the specter of the "infernal Rebellion" has been recalled.[80] The lesson of Hale's story is not to forget the nation's failures, but to render these failures as tragedies that individuals have the power to ameliorate and prevent. Patriotism, as an exuberant form of unwavering allegiance, emerges as the emotive answer to the institutional failure of unity that the Civil War marked.

To a degree, the didactic importance of exile in "The Man Without a Country" might seem to undercut Hale's investment in national unity. As Colin Pearce observes, "Hale ends up making a very strong case for the ennobling effects on the individual of exclusion from full membership in the community."[81] Pearce is right. "The Man Without a Country" does make a strong case for the educative value of statelessness. However, Hale did not confuse the imagination of statelessness with the lived experience of statelessness; he saw the former as a safeguard against the latter.[82] Hale's recourse to negative instruction allowed him to very self-consciously differentiate his exilic plot from his collectivist moral. Hale's gambit, indeed, is to present his readers with a fictive tale of statelessness *so* that they do not thoughtlessly enact the secessionist drama that "The Man Without a Country" allegorizes. The unmoored virtuality of fiction is crucial in this respect. It allows readers to witness Burr and Nolan's downfall without actually becoming *like* them. In effect, "The Man Without a Country" seeks to convert its readers into patriots by transforming what Hawthorne identifies as the quasi-treacherous unreality of fiction into the foundation of its value as a medium of civic instruction. This is the implicit insight of an allusion to Hale's story in the 1890s in the context of a custody battle that involved the divorce proceedings between a native-born U.S. citizen (Mr. Bagaley) and an Italian Countess. "Mr. Bagaley's living in Europe did not terminate his citizenship in Washington unless he acknowledged allegiance there. He could no more drop his citizenship than he could drop his shadow. He must be a citizen somewhere. A man without a country can only exist in fiction."[83] Statelessness was best left for fiction.

## The Changing Meaning of Statelessness

Legally speaking, Nolan's political outsiderness is defined by his treacherous defection from the state. However, the emotive force his exile assumes in "The Man Without a Country" reflects its subtle incorporation of a set of tropes developed outside the tradition of negative instruction in the genre of the slave narrative. The negative construction of national citizenship in "The Man Without a Country" hinges on analogies between two very different forms of statelessness: punitive exile and slavery.[84] The pathos of Nolan's imprisonment at sea derives its cultural recognizability from its symbolic overlay with the horrors of the Middle Passage. Hale develops the emotive meaning of Nolan's exile proximately through a pivotal scene set "in the first days after our Slave-Trade treaty, while the Reigning House, which was still the House of Virginia, had still a sort of sentimentalism about the suppression of the horrors of the Middle Passage, and something was sometimes done that way" ("M," 673).

The narrator, Ingham, we are told, "first came to understand anything about 'the man without a country' one day when we overhauled a dirty little schooner which had slaves on board" ("M," 673).[85] An officer takes charge of the ship but, without the help of a translator, is unable to communicate to the slaves that they are free. The captain asks if anyone can speak Portuguese, and "Nolan stepped out and said he would be glad to interpret" ("M," 673). Most of the scenes in the story are presented as legends of Nolan that Ingham has heard from other officers, but this is one of the few passages in which the narrator participates dramatically. Ingham accompanies Nolan to the schooner and witnesses a "scene as you seldom see, and never want to" ("M," 674). When Nolan translates that the slaves "are free," "there was such a yell of delight, clinching of fists, leaping and dancing, kissing of Nolan's feet" ("M," 674). However, when Nolan proceeds to inform them that they will all be taken to Cape Palmas, "this did not answer so well. Cape Palmas was practically as far from the homes of most of them as New Orleans or Rio Janeiro was; that is, they would be eternally separated from home there" ("M," 674). The parallel to Nolan's own exile becomes painfully evident as he translates the objections of the slaves back into English. Nolan explains, "He says, 'Not Palmas.' He says, 'Take us home, take us to our own country, take us to our own house, take us to our own pickaninnies and our own women.' He says he has an old father and mother, who will die, if they do not see him. . . . And this one says," choked out Nolan, "that he has not heard a word from his home in six months, while he has been locked up in an infernal barracoon" ("M," 674). The captain, moved to pity as "Nolan struggled through this interpretation," declares that all the slaves will be returned to their individual homes: "Tell them yes, yes, yes; tell them they shall go to the Mountains of the Moon, if they will. If I sail the schooner through the Great White Desert, they shall go home!" The slaves rejoice at this news, but Nolan "could not stand it long" ("M," 674–675). As Brook Thomas notes, the "contrast between these Africans allowed to return home and Nolan never allowed to return is too great to bear" (*CM,* 65). Nevertheless, the pathos comes precisely from the analogy that underwrites this contrast. Nolan is himself a captive exile. The scene receives coherence from the basic comparison between Nolan's homelessness and the domestic dispossession attendant on the offer to grant the slaves freedom in Cape Palmas, away from their homes. The analogy between Nolan and the slaves particularizes the generic promise of freedom, revealing its geographical and familial contingencies.

By prioritizing negative exemplars of citizenship, "The Man Without a Country" makes the virtual experience of statelessness a precondition for the patriotism of the protagonist and reader alike. As a result, Hale's seemingly simple allegory of loyalty interrogates the categories of political belonging—expanding readerly sympathy to the nation's outcasts as well as its heroes. The comparison between Nolan and the slaves extends the reader's sympathy and patriotic identifications to include those denied political autonomy. Hale uses the scene with the African slaves to represent a possibility of political reconciliation that is unavailable within the divisive terms of domestic slavery. For the Africans in the story, enslavement is the product of foreign abduction, not the judgment of their native governments. As such, the prospect of returning to their *native* countries carries the full symbolic weight of political reconciliation and reunification. If Hale had focused on domestic slavery instead of the slave trade, he would have lost this symmetry. As a condition of natal alienation, domestic slavery institutes a formal separation between nativity and citizenship that confounds narratives of the nation as home.

Strangely, "The Man Without a Country" comes the closest to addressing the problem that domestic slavery posed for the definition of U.S. citizenship through its representation of Nolan's exile. Nolan is a captive of the nation, deprived of autonomy and without viable legal redress. So, although Hale's story does not explicitly engage with the issue of *domestic* slavery, it plays on the generic range of the designation "the man without a country" to represent different forms of statelessness.[86] Indeed, in one of the uncanny echoes so characteristic of the story, Hale later reconstructed the tale as an abolitionist fable. In one of his many prefaces, Hale recounts with pleasure receiving a "memorandum of the death of 'Philip Nolan,' a black man from Louisiana, to whom the *war gave a country*." Hale hypothesizes that "this 'Philip Nolan' was named from the same Philip Nolan who gave a name to [his] hero"—a horse-trader shot by the Spaniards in Texas in 1801—but he suggests that this black solider was a much more fitting analogue to his fictive hero.[87] Framed thus, the fulfillment of the story is not only the engendering of patriotism, but the extension of citizenship. Negative instruction may entail ambiguities both categorical and formal, but the conflicting sympathies it elicits unsettle the exclusions that organize political belonging—revealing the pathos of dispossession at the heart of civic longing. By presenting dispossession as a common plight of political life, tales of negative instruction explore the disparity between personhood and citizenship, allegiance and rights, longing and belonging.

## Citizenship and Statelessness after the Fourteenth Amendment

The exilic scaffolding of negative instruction made it an ideal didactic tradition for facilitating the uneasy birth of a newly national, but in many ways deeply abject vision of a national citizenry. The didactic conceit of Nolan's reeducation through exile also brought political nuance and historical pliancy to what might easily have been aggressively Unionist propaganda with a very short life span.[88] The negatively formulated exilic plot of "The Man Without a Country" made it easy to adapt Hale's didactic tale to a range of different political crises. In the context of the Civil War, Nolan's treason allegorized the wayward defection of Confederate secessionists, and his subsequent enforced exile resonated with the unchosen plight of statelessness borne of the international slave trade—and systematized in the domestic institution of chattel slavery. For subsequent generations, statelessness took on a host of new meanings that changed how readers perceived the political lesson of "The Man Without a Country."

The predicament of global statelessness heralded by World War II brought into relief the most conservative aspects of Hale's tale. In a fervent critique of "The Man Without a Country" published in 1949 in *The English Journal,* the publication of the National Council of Teachers in English, Beatrice Oxley controverts the prevalent myth of "the historicity of Philip Nolan" and urges the story's antidemocratic character. Alluding to Nolan's unending confinement at sea, she contends that "if a reader will only disengage his mind from the idea that this is history, it will appear at once that such a sentence and such circumstances can occur only in a dictator state, and that the whole tale does not accord with our theses of justice and democracy."[89] The article is meant to "set [teachers] right" about Hale's famous story, both as to its fictional character and more importantly to suggest that "The Man Without a Country" is not patriotic but a tale of an unforgiving government that banishes a man whose "voyage seems actually to ache with his regret."[90] In a nation newly defined against the inhumanities of totalitarianism, the didactic ambiguities of "The Man Without a Country" were more evident than ever.

In a response to the 1949 critique, published the following year, a high school teacher from Brooklyn concedes that Nolan's punishment is "unconstitutional" because it violates the Eighth Amendment protection against "cruel and unusual punishments" but maintains that it is important nonetheless: "The story demonstrates that man is not a rootless creature but one that needs a home and a sense of belonging. It suggests to our generation the unintended conclusion that we should do all in our power to help the vast number of 'displaced persons,' who have been sentenced without guilt to become men without a country."[91] Sympathy for "displaced persons" may not have been the intended lesson of "The Man Without a Country," but the response highlights conflicting sympathies that are fundamental to Hale's strategic and truly timely adaptation of the tradition of negative instruction.

In light of these historically sensitive mid-twentieth-century revaluations of "The Man Without a Country," it is tempting to suggest that the story's precipitous disappearance from the curriculum during the Vietnam War proceeded from an increased emphasis on citizenship as a category of human rights, rather than a condition of allegiance.[92] In a moment in which the unglamorous spectacle of warfare was, for the first time, being directly broadcast into homes throughout the United States in the form of news footage, the United States was more palpably and unromantically present than ever. As a media event, the Vietnam War directly counteracted the strategic disappearing of the United States that structures the nostalgic form of patriotic citizenship that "The Man Without a Country" successfully established as a standard of civic education for roughly a century after its publication.

Vietnam catalyzed another momentous shift in the media-based constitution of citizenship. This shift bears emphasis, but as with any grand narrative of change, it is only part of the story. For as we already have seen, even at the height of the story's popularity its legibility as a patriotic tale was unstable, contingent on the identifications of its readers. Hale's foray into negative instruction helped him recast the renunciative impulse that runs throughout the extralegal traditions of citizenship as an exilic object lesson in patriotism. However, negative instruction also preserves some of the ambivalence toward institutional governance that characterized these early traditions. In effect, because "The Man Without a Country" successfully separates the fantasy of the United States from its experiential reality, readers who were not schooled in the negative aspirational paradigm of these early traditions easily mistook Hale's sacralization of the nation-state as a censorious portrait of a harsh and unforgiving government.

The negatively formulated political predicament of "The Man Without a Country" opened Hale's didactic tale to a range of widely divergent political uses. Educators who embraced "The Man Without a Country" as a didactic resource for schooling students as national citizens made a distinction that was lost on some of Hale's literalist readers: they did not mistake the tale's thematic plot for its political effects. Instead, they valued the stateless other worlds of fiction as nationalist training grounds. These readers did not mistake fiction for fact; they valued fiction for the new political realities it could help create. Ultimately, despite the long-standing wariness toward fiction discussed in Chapter 4, Nolan's treason was not instructive despite its fictionality, but because of it.

# Coda

## *Wong Kim Ark and "The Man Without a Country"*

IF CITIZENSHIP COULD be said to have a genre, that genre would be tragedy. The several exclusions that mar citizenship's inegalitarian history long have been narrated as the ever-disappointed and unrealized dream of equality. In addition to this familiar narrative of "delayed" inclusivity within individual eras, the idealization of citizenship has taken shape against and in direct response to its political unavailability to a large percentage of U.S. residents. The American dream of inclusion, as historian Judith Shklar and others have observed, gained its cultural meaning from the "nightmare" of political exclusion—which was an experiential reality for some and a terrifying prospect for others.[1] The structural importance of exclusion in defining the limits of community is something of a conceptual commonplace, but as we have seen, this negative definitional impulse played out in unique ways in the period before the Fourteenth Amendment.

When we idealize citizenship negatively, as the telos and denouement of the political struggles of the disenfranchised, we echo a way of thinking about citizenship that took shape in the extralegal traditions traced in the foregoing chapters. Precisely because the legal meaning of "citizenship" had not yet been formalized in the early United States, politicians and writers who sought to encourage civic devotion tended to focus on the *disadvantages* of political exclusion—rather than its as yet ambiguously narrated benefits. The negative idealization of citizenship in the early United States struck a deep cord with individuals who were denied a central role in early

U.S. politics. And as we saw in Chapters 4 and 5, exilic formulations of citizenship also resonated—albeit in cautionary terms—with those who enjoyed a presumptive claim to citizenship.

In a period that was fractured by conflicts over borders and loyalties, the prospect of dispossession held special meaning for both citizens and noncitizens. From the beginning, white, propertied men have enjoyed unequal power in U.S. politics. However, as the punitive repercussions faced by British loyalists in the late eighteenth century usefully remind us, even those whose presumptive claim to citizenship has historically been the least vexed were at times subject to the perils of disenfranchisement.[2] In addition, the numerous forms of "quasi citizenship" discussed in Chapter 1 muddied the line between inclusion and exclusion and gave far-reaching meaning to the prospect of political dispossession.[3] The speculative traditions of citizenship tapped into this widespread political anxiety. They did not celebrate the political privileges individuals already possessed. Instead, they idealized citizenship negatively by appealing to a distinctly tragic vision of political perfectibility—which was anchored in nostalgic narratives of a greatness that had never been and anticipatory visions of a future that had yet to be.

In the early United States, writers, reformers, and politicians turned to a number of highly speculative traditions—Christian theology, romantic philosophy, the literary imagination, and didactic literature—to authorize collectivist imaginaries that transcended the legal fictions of chattel slavery and feme covert. However, as with Judge Taney's landmark opinion in the *Dred Scott* case, the speculative interpretation of "citizenship" was also used to reinforce the complexly gradated political landscape of the republican and antebellum United States. By turning away from the letter of the law and invoking the "original intent" of the Constitution's authors, Taney and other originalists retroactively bound the still varied usages of "citizen" to the inegalitarian practices and assumptions of the founders.

Today, the meaning of citizenship is as fiercely contested as ever. However, twenty-first-century debates about citizenship take shape in fundamentally different ways by virtue of their complex textual mediation through the Constitution. As a way of looking toward the political present through the lens of the arguments unfolded in this book, this coda closes *Civic Longing* by examining a textual collision between the extralegal traditions of citizenship and the modern constitutional interpretation of birthright citizenship. As we saw in Chapter 5, Edward Everett Hale's "The Man Without a Country" (1863) is an important transitional text in the history of citizenship, one that helped manage and domesticate the renunciative impulses that structure the early, extralegal traditions of citizenship. So it is perhaps only fitting that Hale's allegory of secession later helped shape the constitutional interpretation of the form of national citizenship that Hale and other Unionists idealized amid the turmoil of the Civil War. The importance of "The Man Without a Country" as a cultural touchstone for changing conceptions of citizenship and statelessness is perhaps nowhere more dramatic than in a key allusion to Hale's tale in the 1898 U.S. Supreme Court decision in *United States vs. Wong Kim Ark*—a case that offered one of the first far-reaching interpretations of the Fourteenth Amendment's Citizenship Clause. The case involved the citizenship status of Wong Kim Ark, who was "born at San Francisco in 1873 to parents of Chinese descent and subjects of the Emperor of China, but domiciled residents at San Francisco."[4] Ark's U.S. citizenship was called into question following a trip to China. On returning to the United States, Ark was barred reentry under the Chinese Exclusion Act, passed by Congress in 1882 to prohibit the immigration of Chinese laborers to the United States.

Part of what complicated Wong's citizenship status from a legal standpoint was that the two primary paths to citizenship—citizenship by birthright and by naturalization—were governed by different laws, which restricted eligibility for citizenship in nonparallel terms. The path to citizenship by naturalization was relatively clear. The Chinese Exclusion Act echoed a form of racial exclusion that had even wider scope under general naturalization laws. The 1870 Naturalization Act "extended" the right to naturalize "to aliens of African nativity and to persons of African descent," but—since it built on earlier acts that limited naturalization to "white persons"—it did not deracialize naturalization. The revised scope of naturalization was now narrowly two-toned—and it would remain so until 1952.[5]

Since naturalization was not a viable path to citizenship for Ark, his claim to citizenship rested on the Fourteenth Amendment's Citizenship Clause: "All persons born or naturalized in the United States, and subject to the jurisdiction thereof, are citizens of the United States and of the State wherein they reside."[6] Was Wong Kim Ark a U.S. citizen by virtue of his birth within the physical borders of the United States? Or was he, like his parents, a Chinese subject under the legal jurisdiction of the emperor of China? What does it means to be "*in* the United States"? Is the United States a place, a jurisdictional imaginary, or a set of shared practices and beliefs?[7]

According to the attorney general, "although born in the city and county of San Francisco, State of California, United States of America," Wong "has been at all times, by reason of his race, language, color and dress, a Chinese person."[8] As Justice Gray observed, the "only adjudication that has been made by this court upon the meaning of the clause, "and subject to the jurisdiction thereof" was *Elk vs. Wilkins* (1884), which ruled that a Native

American, John Elk, though born on U.S. soil could not claim U.S. citizenship because he was born on a Native American reservation, which was sovereign and thus not subject to U.S. jurisdiction.[9] Since no similar excluding circumstance applied to Ark, the Supreme Court concluded, Ark must be a U.S. citizen.

The Court ultimately ruled in Ark's favor, but its rationale was not affirmative or celebratory. In Justice Gray's majority opinion, he channels Hale's popular story to formulate Ark's citizenship negatively through the process of elimination. "[D]ouble allegiance, in the sense of double nationality, has no place in our law, and the existence of a man without a country is not recognized."[10] Wong Kim Ark was saved from Philip Nolan's fate, but this strange application of Hale's tale was only possible because, as with the allusions discussed in Chapter 5, a new form of historical statelessness had once again changed what it meant to be a "man without a country." Slavery, immigration, refugeeism—again and again, the specter of statelessness has worked its negative power, lending urgency and meaning to the otherwise abstract (and in the early United States, juridically nominal) category of citizenship.

*Wong Kim Ark* occupies an important place in the history of citizenship after the Fourteenth Amendment. The Court's validation of Wong Kim Ark's citizenship status has made it possible for some to think of him as "the first 'Asian American'" citizen—one who significantly predates the reform of naturalization laws in 1952.[11] The decision was inaugural in a broader sense as well. It provided an early and precedent-setting clarification of the territorial scope of the Fourteenth Amendment's Citizenship Clause. The Court's belabored deliberations in *Wong Kim Ark* crystallized the new kinds of questions that would shape post–Civil War debates about citizenship. These debates would by necessity pivot on interpretations of the Fourteenth Amendment.[12]

The passage of the Fourteenth Amendment established the law as the primary discourse for citizenship moving forward. That did not mean that the extralegal traditions tracked in this book would cease to be resources for shaping and contesting citizenship in the years that followed. The impact that "The Man Without a Country" sustained in the classroom until the 1970s itself amply testifies to literature's continued importance to the cultural making of citizenship. However, in a way that was not true in the preceding years, post–Fourteenth Amendment formulations of political membership were developed in an interpretative field whose gravitational center was now very definitely located in the law and in the Constitution in particular.

The Fourteenth Amendment ushered in the modern form of national political membership that "citizenship" now names. It did not resolve all of the definitional questions that preceded them.[13] Yet, it did mark a decisive shift in the hermeneutics of citizenship: after its passage, the problem was no longer the absence of statutory definitions of citizenship, but how to interpret these complex legal precedents—whose meanings have become newly urgent in the contemporary debates borne of the speculative origins of U.S. citizenship.

Together, the twin legal reformations of 1868—the Fourteenth Amendment and the 1868 Expatriation Act—helped articulate the "what" of citizenship: the origins of political membership and the perpetuity of political allegiance. However, the "who" of citizenship has proven to be an even more enduring battle, one to which the 1920s brought some additional clarity with the Nineteenth Amendment's recognition of women's suffrage and the Indian Citizenship Act. By establishing the "citizen" as the preeminent personage of juridical privilege, the legal reformations of 1868 formalized the stakes of being recognized as a "citizen"—and ushered in an era newly fascinated with the language and jurisprudence of citizenship.

Contests over the scope of citizenship are ongoing, but the most urgent questions today are somewhat different than those asked in Attorney General Bates's 1862 opinion. To Bates's definitional queries, "Who is a citizen? What constitutes a citizen of the United States?" twenty-first-century debates about immigration raise fundamental questions about the desirability and effects of the Fourteenth Amendment's consequential identification of the "citizen" as the preferred designation and legal category of the rights-bearing personage.[14] Viewed from the perspective of the early debates about citizenship, the Fourteenth Amendment's formalization of birthright citizenship marked an important (albeit partial) legal victory for previously enslaved persons and persons of African descent, whose path to political membership long had been impeded by the hereditary bonds of *jus sanguinis*. However, in the United States today, the nativist logic of birthright citizenship has become a conspicuous stumbling block for undocumented residents, whose protections are limited and subject to the judgments and actions of a wide range of official and unofficial actors. Considered in light of today's debates about immigration, perhaps the Bill of Rights's omission of the language of "citizenship"—and its use of the more inclusive language of the "person"—is not a historic oversight, but a political opportunity. In a culture beholden to the letter of the law, the elevation of the "person" in the Bill of Rights might help us rethink the preconditions for enjoying full political protections through and beyond the textual history of "citizenship."

# Appendix

*Bible Translations*

*Appendix* Bible Translations

| Title [colloquial in brackets] | Translator or editor | Year | Printed | Translation of Phil. 3:20 |
|---|---|---|---|---|
| [Wycliffe's Bible] *The Newe Testament* | John Wycliffe William Tyndale | c. 1382–1395 1526 | n/a London | But oure lyuyng is in heunes; But oure conuersacion is in hevẽ, |
| *Biblia: The Bible . . . Translated in to the English* | Anon. [Myles Coverdale] | 1535 | London | But our conuersacion is in heaven, |
| *The Byble . . . Translated into Englysh by Thomas Matthew* | Thomas Matthew [pseudonym of John Rogers] | 1537 | London | But oure conuersaciõ is in heauen/ |
| [Great Bible] *The Most Sacred Bible* | Rychard Tavener | 1539 | London | But oure conuersacion is in heauen, |
| [Geneva Bible] *The Bible and Holy Scriptures* | Anon. [William Whittingham] | 1560 | Geneva | But oure conuersacion is in heauen, |
| [Bishop's Bible] *The Holie Bible* | Matthew Parker | 1568 | London | But oure conuersacion is in heauen, |
| [Douay-Rheims Bible] *The Holy Bible Faithfully Translated* | Multiple | NT 1582; OT 1609 | NT: Rheims; OT: Douay | But our conuersacion is in heauen; |
| [King James Version] *The Holy Bible* | Multiple | 1611 | London | But oure conuersacion is in heauen; |
| *The New Testament in Greek and English* | Daniel Mace | 1729 | London | But we are the denisons of heaven, |
| *Explanatory Notes upon the New Testament* | John Wesley | 1755 | London | For our conversation is in heaven; |

| Title | Translator | Year | Place | Text |
|---|---|---|---|---|
| A New and Literal Translation . . . of the Old and New Testament | Anthony Purver | 1764 | London | For our Conversation is in Heaven, |
| A Translation of the New Testament | Gilbert Wakefield | 1791 | London | But we are citizens of heaven; |
| An Attempt toward Revising Our English Translation of . . . the New Covenant of Jesus Christ | William Newcome | 1796 | London | For our citizenship is in heaven; |
| The Holy Bible, Containing the Old and New Covenant | Charles Thomson | 1808 | Philadelphia | But we are citizens of heaven, |
| The Sacred Writings of the Apostles | Alexander Campbell | 1826 | Bethany, VA | But we are citizens of heaven, |
| [Young's Literal Translation] The Holy Bible | Robert Young | 1863 | Edinburgh | For our citizenship is in the heavens, |
| Holy Scriptures, Translated and Corrected by the Spirit of Revelation | Joseph Smith | 1867 (c. 1830–1833) | Philadelphia | For our conversation is in heaven; |
| The New Testament of Our Lord | Anon. [Julia Evalina Smith Parker] | 1876 | Hartford, CT | For our citizenship is in the heavens; |
| [Revised Standard KJV] | Charles Ellicott | 1885 | Cambridge | For our citizenship is in heaven; |
| [American Standard Version] | Multiple | NT 1900; OT 1901 | New York | For our citizenship is in heaven; |
| [New American Standard Bible] | Multiple | NT 1963; OT 1971 | NT: La Habra, CA; OT: New York | For our citizenship is in heaven, |

# Notes

## Introduction

1. For a methodologically attuned overview of the recent critical "unsettling" of "what constitutes 'America'" in nineteenth-century U.S. literary criticism, see Dana Luciano and Ivy Wilson's introduction to their edited collection, *Unsettled States: Nineteenth Century American Literary Studies* (New York: New York University Press, 2014), esp. 5.
2. U.S. Constitution (1789).
3. For a compelling discussion of the inaugural status of the Civil Rights Act, see Eric Foner's *The Story of American Freedom* (New York: Norton, 1998), 105.
4. U.S. Constitution, amendment 14, section 1.
5. This basic definition of "citizenship" has, for a century and a half, been the presumptive starting place for a host of more fine-grained debates about political membership.
6. Governmental entities did not provide the dominant imaginative paradigms for the speculative traditions of citizenship, which this book examines. However, the "state" and the federation remain important units of analysis for this book because of their importance in shaping the uneven juridical conceptualization of citizenship.
7. Madison made this remark in a congressional session that sought to determine whether William Smith of South Carolina was eligible for a seat in the House of Representatives—a question that hinged on "whether he has been seven years a citizen of the United States or not" (James Madison, "May 22: Citizenship of the United States," in *The Writings of James Madison 1787–1790*, ed. Gaillard Hunt [New York: J. P. Putnam and Sons, 1904], 365).

8. Madison, *Writings,* 365.

9. As historian Linda Kerber observes in a summation of the tortuous legal history of citizenship, "the meanings of citizenship have been inconsistent from the beginning" (Linda K. Kerber, "The Meanings of Citizenship," *Journal of American History* 84, no. 3 [1997]: 833–854, esp. 836).

10. I characterize this process of imaginative fabrication as a form of "speculation" in keeping with the language of Attorney General Edward Bates's 1862 instructive opinion on citizenship, which I discuss at length in Chapter 1. In the absence of a constitutional definition of citizenship, Bates recognized, citizenship remained "open to argument and to speculative criticism" (Edward Bates, *Opinion of Attorney General Bates on Citizenship* [Washington, DC: Government Printing Office, 1862], 3).

11. My treatment of the politics of language focuses on written language rather than oral transmission not because the latter is not politically impactful (it is), but because written documents enable different forms of audience participation. The accessibility of written documents is delimited in a number of crucial ways, including circulation and literacy, but the materiality of these "inscriptions" is instrumental to their concretization of what is thinkable and possible at any given moment in history. As Jacques Rancière argues in his theorization of the historicity of the textual realities archived in writing, written rights "are inscriptions of the community as free and equal. As such they are not only the predicates of a non-existent being. Even though actual situations of rightlessness may give them the lie, they are not only an abstract ideal, situated far from the givens of the situation. They are also part of the configuration of the given. What is given is not only a situation of inequality. It is also an inscription, a form of visibility of equality" (Jacques Rancière, "Who Is the Subject of the Rights of Man?" *South Atlantic Quarterly* 103 [Spring/Summer 2004]: 297–310, esp. 302–303). For complementary studies of early U.S. literature and politics that center on speech and orality, see Jay Fliegelman, *Declaring Independence: Jefferson, Natural Language, and the Culture of Performance* (Stanford, CA: Stanford University Press, 1993); Christopher Looby, *Voicing America: Language, Literary Form, and the Origins of the United States* (Chicago: University of Chicago Press, 1996); and Sandra Gustafson, *Eloquence Is Power: Oratory and Performance in Early America* (Chapel Hill: University of North Carolina Press, 2000).

12. The shifting terrain of political affiliation in a newly global era, as well as recent debates over U.S. immigration, have only heightened a long-standing scholarly interest in citizenship.

13. Citizenship has elicited an extraordinarily robust body of scholarship across the humanities. Citizenship's broad scholastic allure is closely tied to a language-centered, qualitative conception of humanistic study. Within this paradigm, as Marc Kruman and Richard Marback nicely articulate it, literature is a site of cultural self-discovery and authorship: "Language, literature, art—the media through which people express who they are—these are the means by which communities define themselves, placing humanistic study at the very center of the study of citizenship" (Richard Marback and Marc W. Kruman,

eds., "Introduction," in *The Meaning of Citizenship* [Detroit: Wayne State University Press, 2015], 3).

14. For an example of the trans-historicization of citizenship that is all the more striking because of the piece's conceptual nuance, see Lauren Berlant's entry on "citizenship" in Bruce Burgett and Glen Hendler's *Keywords for American Cultural Studies*. Berlant's entry offers a rich overview of several questions and problems citizenship has organized, but it does not even mention the Fourteenth Amendment, so the historically contingent meanings of "citizenship" fall out of view (Lauren Berlant, "Citizenship," in *Keywords for American Cultural Studies*, ed. Bruce Burgett and Glen Hendler [New York: New York University Press, 2007], 37–42).

15. For a seminal account of what political scientist Rogers Smith succinctly designates as the "inegalitarian ascriptive traditions of Americanism"—which "assigned political identities . . . on the basis of such ascribed characteristics as race, gender"—see Rogers M. Smith, *Civic Ideals: Conflicting Visions of Citizenship in U.S. History* (New Haven, CT: Yale University Press, 1997), esp. 3. Other pivotal historiographical reassessments of citizenship include Edmund S. Morgan, *American Slavery, American Freedom* (New York: W. W. Norton, 1975); James H. Kettner, *The Development of American Citizenship, 1608–1870* (Chapel Hill: University of North Carolina Press, 1978); Judith Shklar, *American Citizenship: The Questions for Inclusion* (Cambridge, MA: Harvard University Press, 1991); Linda K. Kerber, *No Constitutional Right to Be Ladies: Women and Obligations of Citizenship* (New York: Hill & Wang, 1998); Foner, *Story of American Freedom*; Nancy Isenberg, *Sex and Citizenship in Antebellum America* (Chapel Hill: University of North Carolina Press, 1998); David Waldstreicher, *Slavery's Constitution: From Revolution to Ratification* (New York: Hill & Wang, 2009); Douglas Bradburn, *The Citizenship Revolution: Politics and the Creation of the American Union, 1774–1804* (Charlottesville: University of Virginia Press, 2009); Christopher Tomlins, *Freedom Bound: Law, Labor, and Civic Identity in Colonizing English America, 1580–1865* (New York: Cambridge University Press, 2010); Theresa Anne Murphy, *Citizenship and the Origins of Women's History in the United States* (Philadelphia: University of Pennsylvania Press, 2013); and Peter Thompson and Peter S. Onuf, eds., *State and Citizen: British America and the Early United States* (Charlottesville: University of Virginia Press, 2013).

Insightful, extended treatments of the racialized, gendered, and imperial ideologies that shaped the practical boundaries of citizenship in early U.S. literature include Gillian Brown, *Domestic Individualism: Imagining Self in Nineteenth-Century America* (Berkeley: University of California Press, 1990); Michael Warner, *The Letters of the Republic: Publication and the Public Sphere in Eighteenth-Century America* (Cambridge, MA: Harvard University Press, 1990); Eric J. Sundquist, *To Wake the Nations: Race in the Making of American Literature* (Cambridge, MA: Harvard University Press, 1993); Priscilla Wald, *Constituting Americans: Cultural Anxiety and Narrative Form* (Durham, NC: Duke University Press, 1995); Lauren Berlant, *The Queen of America Goes to Washington City: Essays on Sex and Citizenship*, Series Q

(Durham, NC: Duke University Press, 1997); Saidiya V. Hartman, *Scenes of Subjection: Terror, Slavery, and Self-Making in Nineteenth-Century America* (New York: Oxford University Press, 1997); Robert S. Levine, *Martin Delany, Frederick Douglass, and the Politics of Representative Identity* (Chapel Hill: University of North Carolina Press, 1997); Bruce Burgett, *Sentimental Bodies: Sex, Gender, and Citizenship in the Early Republic* (Princeton, NJ: Princeton University Press, 1998); Dana Nelson, *National Manhood: Capitalist Citizenship and the Imagined Fraternity of White Men* (Durham, NC: Duke University Press, 1998); Russ Castronovo, *Necro Citizenship: Death, Eroticism, and the Public Sphere in the Nineteenth-Century United States* (Durham, NC: Duke University Press, 2001); Russ Castronovo and Dana Nelson, eds., *Materializing Democracy: Toward a Revitalized Cultural Politics* (Durham, NC: Duke University Press, 2002); Gregg D. Crane, *Race, Citizenship, and Law in American Literature* (New York: Cambridge University Press, 2002); David Kazanjian, *The Colonizing Trick: National Culture and Imperial Citizenship in Early America*, Critical American Studies Series (Minneapolis: University of Minnesota Press, 2003); Elizabeth Maddock Dillon, *The Gender of Freedom: Fictions of Liberalism and the Literary Public Sphere* (Stanford, CA: Stanford University Press, 2004); Stephen Best, *The Fugitive's Properties: Law and the Poetics of Possession* (Chicago: University of Chicago Press, 2004); Joanna Brooks, "The Early American Public Sphere and the Emergence of a Black Print Counterpublic," *William and Mary Quarterly* 62, no. 1 (January 2005): 67–92; Edlie Wong, *Neither Fugitive nor Free: Atlantic Slavery, Freedom Suits, and the Legal Culture of Travel* (New York: New York University Press, 2009); Jason Frank, *Constituent Moments: Enacting the People in Postrevolutionary America* (Durham, NC: Duke University Press, 2010); Jennifer Greiman, *Democracy's Spectacle: Sovereignty and Public Life in Antebellum American Writing* (New York: Fordham University Press, 2010); Ivy G. Wilson, *Specters of Democracy: Blackness and the Aesthetics of Nationalism* (New York: New York University Press, 2011); Jeannine DeLombard, *In the Shadow of the Gallows: Race, Crime, and American Civic Identity* (Philadelphia: University of Pennsylvania Press, 2012); Hoang Gia Phan, *Bonds of Citizenship: Law and the Labors of Emancipation* (New York: New York University Press, 2013); Mark Rifkin, *Settler Common Sense: Queerness and Everyday Colonialism in the American Renaissance* (Minneapolis: University of Minnesota Press, 2014); Edlie Wong, *Racial Reconstruction: Black Inclusion, Chinese Exclusion, and the Fictions of Citizenship* (New York: New York University Press, 2015); Dana Nelson, *Commons Democracy: Reading the Politics of Participation in the United States* (New York: Fordham University Press, 2015). Given the vast amount of scholarship that deals with citizenship within and outside of literary criticism, I stagger my engagement with different subsets of this scholarship throughout this book to selectively highlight the material that deals at length with specific elements of the much broader body of scholarship on citizenship.

16. *Civic Longing* is not an account of the Fourteenth Amendment's cultural inevitability; it tells the story of citizenship before its late legal codification. For

an alternate account of the cultural and literary imagination of citizenship that uses the Fourteenth Amendment as its anchoring point, see Deak Nabers's *Victory of Law,* which treats the Fourteenth Amendment as a triumphal expression of already implicit legal principles (Deak Nabers, *Victory of Law: The Fourteenth Amendment, the Civil War, and American Literature, 1852–1865* [Baltimore: Johns Hopkins University Press, 2006]). The somewhat teleological character of Nabers's account reflects his concerted effort to understand how John Bingham, the Fourteenth Amendment's principal framer, was able to present the amendment as a fulfillment of the Constitution as it was originally conceived.

17. In the United States and other representative democracies, laws carry additional evidential value, because they double as indirect expressions of the will of "the people," who are both the electors and subjects of state actors.

18. As Jeannine DeLombard observes in her far-reaching account of the criminalization of African American personhood, "American writers rushed to fill the Constitution's awkward silence over slavery and citizenship" (DeLombard, *Shadow of the Gallows,* 53).

19. Recent work on settler colonialism offers one of the most trenchant and far-reaching critiques of citizenship. As Mahmood Mamdani powerfully observes, "Unlike all previous exclusions—ethnicity, race, and gender" work on "the native question" offers "a far more fundamental challenge to the celebration of citizenship in America" (Mahmood Mamdani, "Settler Colonialism: Then and Now," *Critical Inquiry* 41, no. 3 [Spring 2015]: 596–614, esp. 602). This book builds on revisionist reassessments of U.S. politics to bring into focus coercive aspects of citizenship itself, which has indelibly shaped the disappointments that have accompanied the entrance into citizenship as well as the exclusion from it. As we will see, the ambiguities that surrounded early debates about citizenship had a number of different effects, both politically and culturally. As I discuss in Chapter 1, they enabled the emergence of gradated and nominal forms of "quasi citizenship." However, as we will see, they also left openings for developing and authorizing a number of different models of political membership in experiments that ranged across a number of genres.

20. The definitional question of citizenship in the early United States is typically framed in terms of scope: Were women deemed citizens? Free blacks? Native Americans? And, if so, under what conditions? The question, in this historiographical tradition, as James Kettner succinctly poses it in the most comprehensive legal account of citizenship to date, is "Who are 'the people'?" (Kettner, *Development of American Citizenship,* 285).

21. Citizenship, when discussed in this narrow, technical sense, generates categorical claims. Either one is a citizen, or one is not a citizen. The line between citizen and noncitizen has not always been as explicitly delineated as it is today, but the stakes of this distinction always have been high—both legally and symbolically. As a result, the definitional borders of citizenship elicited an extraordinary amount of debate from the very beginning.

22. As one writer reflected in 1846 in an eloquent treatment of the politics of fiction, it is no surprise that "the most efficient politico-ethical writers have written under adverse circumstances; nay, under circumstances which are in glaring contrast with the principles they advocated. . . . These very circumstances may have given the motive, and their amelioration may have been the aim" (J. Sullivan Cox, "Imaginary Commonwealths," *United States Magazine and Democratic Review,* September 1846, 175–185, esp. 175).

23. *Civic Longing* does not recount the familiar identity-based contours of citizenship in the early United States, but instead explores the residual ambivalence of its underlying terms. For a particularly compelling theorization of the limitations of identity politics, see Wendy Brown's *States of Injury* (Princeton, NJ: Princeton University Press, 1995).

24. This historical focus helps bring into relief aspects of the early history of citizenship that do not readily accord with its current meaning and that have, as a result, largely been eclipsed by these late connotations.

25. This book is interdisciplinary in its scope but disciplinary in its methods. In contradistinction to Richard Posner's influential, if notorious, claim that "the study of literature has little to contribute to the interpretation of statutes and constitutions," *Civic Longing* argues that we cannot fully understand the development of citizenship in the early United States unless we take seriously the varied cultural forms through which its meaning was provisionally made and remade in a period of exceptional turmoil. Law, after all, draws its rhetorical authority as much from cultural precedents as it does from legal ones. And this is especially true in areas of emergent legal interest, in which the law needs to justify its reach rather than simply sustain an existing logic.

    As Brook Thomas argues in a lucid formulation of the interpretative gains of what he refers to as a "law-and-literature approach to citizenship," "selected works of literature . . . [can] help us identify the civic myths implied by citizenship laws, while citizenship laws help us to identify the civic aspects of various myths that literary stories work on/with" (Brook Thomas, *Civic Myths: A Law-and-Literature Approach to Citizenship* [Chapel Hill: University of North Carolina Press, 2007], 13). Moreover, as Jeffory Clymer and others stress, "Law, like literature, exists within rather than outside or above culture more generally" (Jeffory A. Clymer, "Family Money: Race and Economic Rights in Antebellum US Law and Fiction," *American Literary History* 21, no. 2 [2009]: 211–238, esp. 213). See Richard A. Posner, "Law and Literature: A Relation Reargued," *Virginia Law Review* 72, no. 8 (1986): 1351–1392, esp. 1351.

    This book engages interdisciplinary scholarship at the crossroads of law and literature, but it also expands its focus beyond this dyad to address a number of other nonlegal discourses that played a key role in the development of citizenship—including theological texts, which address themselves to the unseen and the unseeable. Law-centered accounts of citizenship easily obscure part of what makes early U.S. citizenship uniquely illustrative: namely, that the fundamentally contested meaning of "citizenship" in early U.S. law made it possible for fictional representations of political membership to enjoy a cultural authority rarely associated with literature as an imaginative art form. The secular purview of legal history also has tended to overshadow the political work of theological tropes like "citizenship in heaven," which, as we will see in Chapter 2, helped shape an ambivalence toward active political membership that is too often explained by way of liberalism alone.For excellent work on citizenship at the crossroads of law and literature, see Thomas, *Civic Myths;* Crane, *Race, Citizenship, and Law;* Wong, *Neither Fugitive nor Free;* DeLombard, *Shadow of the Gallows;* Caleb Smith, *The Oracle and the Curse: A Poetics of Justice from the Revolution to the Civil War* (Cambridge, MA: Harvard University Press, 2013; and Phan, *Bonds of Citizenship.* Along similar lines, Karla Holloway uses the legal history of chattel slavery to examine racial identity as a "legal fiction," but unlike the other studies I have listed here, Holloway's textual focus is weighted in twentieth- and twenty-first-century literature (Karla F. C. Holloway, *Legal Fictions: Constituting Race, Composing Literature* [Durham, NC: Duke University Press, 2014], 5). I have also found Priscilla Wald's discussion of what she terms "official stories" instructive for thinking within and beyond law and literature. Wald uses official stories broadly to designate the legal, political, and literary "stories through which a nation—'a people'—spoke itself into existence" (Wald, *Constituting Americans,* 2). In spirit, the trans-generic account of citizenship I offer in *Civic Longing* works along similar lines, but I use "official" more narrowly to distinguish statutory law. This distinction allows me to foreground the unique narrative possibilities that marked the era before citizenship's formal codification.

26. Kettner, *Development of American Citizenship;* Shklar, *American Citizenship;* Kerber, *No Constitutional Right to Be Ladies;* Foner, *Story of American Freedom;* Isenberg, *Sex and Citizenship;* Smith, *Civic Ideals;* Bradburn, *Citizenship Revolution;* Tomlins, *Freedom Bound.*

27. Lyman Cobb, ed., *The North American Reader: Containing a Great Variety of Pieces in Prose and Poetry from Highly Esteemed American and English Readers* (Zanesville, OH: J. R. and A. Lippitt, 1835), v–vi.

28. James Fenimore Cooper, *The American Democrat; or, Hints on the Social and Civic Relations of the United States of America* (Cooperstown, NY: H. and E. Phinney, 1838), 139.

29. My use of the term "extralegal" is inspired by Cooper's use of the term. However, as I explained earlier in this introduction, I use "extralegal" in two senses: both descriptively, to identify a number of nonlegal traditions, and also structurally, to theorize the negative, exilic ways of imagining citizenship that helped sustain its distinctly tragic cultural allure.

30. Here I am drawing on Hannah Arendt's distinction between social and political practices. Society, Arendt argues, is normative, not political, because it expects a certain type of behavior from its members. Arendt's distinction is useful, but I disagree with her claim that the novel is an entirely social art form (Arendt, *The Human Condition*, ed. Margaret Canovan [Chicago: University of Chicago Press, 1998], esp. 39, 40).

31. John Dewey, *Democracy and Education: An Introduction to the Philosophy of Education* (New York: Free Press, 1944), 4.

32. Dewey, *The Public and Its Problems* (New York: H. Holt, 1927; repr., Athens: Ohio University Press, 1954), 184.

33. For a different performative theory of citizenship, see Lauren Berlant's discussion of what she terms "Diva Citizenship," moments "of risky dramatic persuasion" that offer opportunities for political renewal. According to Berlant, "Diva Citizenship occurs when a person stages a dramatic coup in the public sphere in which she does not have privilege. Flashing up and startling the public, she puts the dominant story into suspended animation . . . calling on people to change the social and institutional practices of citizenship" (Berlant, *The Queen of America Goes to Washington City*, 223). Berlant offers a powerful theorization of moments of narrative insurgency, strident demands that counter the norms of citizenship and transform the public in the process. However, as we will see, civic counter-possibilities are not always neatly tied to recognizable categories of outsiderness, nor are they always linked to assertive modes of protest. Often enough, individuals whose social status presumptively guarantees their political satisfaction prove affectively resistant to the equanimity they otherwise seem destined to enjoy.

34. The emotive world of allegiance is often marginalized in the public sphere tradition associated with Jürgen Habermas. For Habermas, citizenship is rooted in forms of cultural expression and deliberation that are *outside* the official sphere of the law. However, this deliberative approach to democracy finds its telos in "the public use of *reason*" (Jürgen Habermas, *The Structural Transformation of the Public Sphere*, trans. Thomas Burger and Frederick Lawrence [Cambridge, MA: MIT Press, 1991], 28). As Elizabeth Maddock Dillon and Caleb Smith both stress in their reassessments of Habermas, desire as much as reason underwrites our relation to the public. As Dillon eloquently puts it, the public is not governed by disinterestedness, but by desire—"the desire of subjects to emerge into the space of subjectivity or social recognition" (Dillon, *Gender of Freedom*, 6). See also Smith's *The Oracle and the Curse*. For a somewhat different theorization of the subjective depths of citizenship, see Christopher Castiglia's fascinating discussion of the human interior as a displaced realm for resolving the democratic struggles of the early United States. For Castiglia, the fascination with political interiority marks a melancholic redirection of social drives that are properly external and developed in communion with others (Christopher Castiglia, *Interior States: Institutional Consciousness and the Inner Life of Democracy in the Antebellum United States* [Durham, NC: Duke University Press, 2008]). While I agree that such a shift is evident in this period, I see it less as a departure from democratic sociality than an ambivalent expression of it, because consensual allegiance requires a new attention to the subjective life of the subject-citizen.

35. *Congressional Record*, 31st Congress, 1st session, 260–269.

36. For two excellent book-length accounts of the higher law tradition in early U.S. fiction and politics, see Smith's *Oracle and the Curse* and Crane's *Race, Citizenship, and Law*.

37. In literary criticism, we often talk about how a particular text "revises" the cultural norms that govern political membership in the period in which it was written. These comparative claims require a clear understanding of what these definitional norms were. This knowledge is typically assumed to be relatively easy to come by. After all, the early United States was riven by very clear political inequalities, which were brought to a head in debates over chattel slavery, women's suffrage, and Native American sovereignty. Yet these extreme disparities have made it easy to overlook another interrelated aspect of the contentious history of citizenship: its remarkably undefined legal character in the ninety years between the Declaration of Independence and the Fourteenth Amendment.

38. For a discussion of the "limitations and possibilities of political critique in the Emersonian tradition of aesthetic dissent," see John Carlos Rowe, *At Emerson's Tomb: The Politics of Classic American Literature* (New York: Columbia University Press, 1997), esp. 1–5.

39. *Civic Longing* joins new scholarship on the aesthetics of politics, including Russ Castronovo, *Beautiful Democracy: Aesthetics and Anarchy in a Global Era* (Chicago: University of Chicago Press, 2007), Cindy Weinstein and Christopher Looby, eds., *American Literature's Aesthetic Dimensions* (New York: Columbia University Press, 2012), and Smith, *The Oracle and the Curse*. In dialogue with this renewed interest in aesthetics as a question "not of what aesthetics is but what it can do" (Luciano and Wilson, *Unsettled States,* 13), *Civic Longing* examines the aesthetics of citizenship—the interested fantasies of affiliation and disaffiliation through which individuals forged their subjective relation to the law.

40. If "context is not optional" for literary critics, as Rita Felski has argued, it is in part because of "a cultural studies methodology that sees contextualization as the quintessential virtue" (Rita Felski, "Context Stinks!" *New Literary History* 42 [Autumn 2011]: 573–591, esp. 573).

41. Eric Slauter, Alison Games, Bryan Waterman, Eliga Gould, and Elizabeth Maddock Dillon, "The 'Trade Gap' in Atlantic Studies: A Forum on Literary and Historical Scholarship," *William and Mary Quarterly* 65, no. 1 (January 2008): 135–186.

42. Intradisciplinary dynamics are admittedly difficult to shift, but the methodologies that underwrite these dynamics offer meaningful opportunities for identifying and reimagining the unique contributions that different disciplines bring to topics like citizenship—which has inspired an impressive body of scholarship in multiple fields of study. For a fuller account of my take on the limitations of historical contextualization, see my reassessment of the historiographical controversy surrounding the Denmark Vesey Conspiracy, where I use the peculiarity of conspiratorial crime (and the linguistic forms of evidence on which it necessarily relies) to develop a performative model for understanding the historicity of linguistic utterance (Carrie Hyde, "Novelistic Evidence: Denmark Vesey and Possibilistic History," *American Literary History* 27, no. 1 [Spring 2015]: 26–55).

43. Popular literature, as Eric Slauter compellingly argues, needs to be understood "not simply as in dialogue with but as part of the history of political thought" (Eric Slauter, *The State as a Work of Art: The Cultural Origins of the Constitution* [Chicago: University of Chicago Press, 2009], 240). As Jane Tompkins simi-

larly stresses in her influential reassessment of popular genres like the sentimental novel, "novelists have designs upon their audiences, in the sense of
wanting to make people think and act in a particular way" (Jane Tompkins,
*Sensational Designs: The Cultural Work of American Fiction, 1790–1860*
[New York: Oxford University Press, 1985], xi).

44. While legal mandates are traditionally exempted from the broader subordination of rhetoric—because of the coercive power of the imperatives they institute—
imaginative writing is often seen through the diminutive lens of *mere* rhetoric.

45. As legal historian Steven Wilf observes in his discussion of the popular imagination of criminal law during the American Revolution, "The law is imagined before it is enacted." Wilf justifies his attention to the wide-ranging, largely unofficial theorizations of criminal law as "aspirational visions of the law"—an
aspirational impulse that I theorize somewhat differently in terms of the "political subjunctive" (Steven Wilf, *Law's Imagined Republic: Popular Politics and
Criminal Justice in Revolutionary America* [New York: Cambridge University
Press, 2010], 7–8). The political subjunctive, as I am theorizing it here, is aspirational, but its politics does not depend on the law as telos. The political subjunctive is not, by definition, "before" the law—its cultural precursor; it is a
mode that cuts across a number of semiofficial and imaginative discourses.

46. In a characteristic formulation of this fantasy of future political perfectibility,
Whitman explains that he "assum[es] Democracy to be at present in its em-
bryo condition, and that the only large and satisfactory justification of it resides
in the future" (Walt Whitman, *Democratic Vistas: The Original Edition in
Facsimile,* ed. Ed Folsom [Iowa City: University of Iowa Press, 2010], 36–37. I
discuss the insistently futural structure of Whitman's romance of democracy at
greater length in Chapter 5.

47. Bates, *Opinion,* 3.

## 1. The Retroactive Invention of Citizenship

1. Nathaniel Hawthorne, *The Scarlet Letter,* Centenary Edition of the Works of
Nathaniel Hawthorne (Columbus: Ohio State University Press, 1968), 1:44.

2. Edward Bates, *Opinion of Attorney General Bates on Citizenship* (Washington,
DC: Government Printing Office, 1862), 4.

3. The terminological distinction between "subject" and "citizen" continues to organize many discussions of citizenship—including those that seek to complicate
each term. Thus in Cathy Davidson and Michael Moon's excellent collection on
the topic, *Subjects and Citizens* (1995), they evoke two interlocking ways of
understanding "subject," but they do not discuss the variable historical meanings of "citizenship." "In juxtaposing the terms 'subject' and 'citizen' in the title,
we have chosen to emphasize some of the historical and political continuities
between the traditional political and social meanings of 'subject' (one who is
placed under the authority of a monarch and governed by his law, as well as the
wife who was enjoined to be 'subject' to her husband as servants—or slaves—

were to their masters) and the term 'subject' in its contemporary sense (a person considered as the sum of the psychic effects of his or her interactions with the laws of language and other institutions that are formative of culture)" (Cathy Davidson and Michael Moon, eds., *Subjects and Citizens: Nation, Race, and Gender from Oroonoko to Anita Hill* [Durham, NC: Duke University Press, 1995], 1–2). As Brook Thomas emphasizes, "Even though the word 'citizen' resonates with thoughts of self-governance and freedom from subjection, citizens remain subjects of the state," so "even if not all subjects are citizens, all citizens are subjects" (Brook Thomas, *Civic Myths: A Law-and-Literature Approach to Citizenship* [Chapel Hill: University of North Carolina Press, 2007], 9).

4. In the comparative framework of American Independence, citizenship gains its significance differentially through assumptions about its structural difference from British subjecthood (assumptions that are inflected by a celebratory account of U.S. founding).

5. David Ramsay, *A Dissertation of the Manners of Acquiring the Character and Privileges of a Citizen of the United States* (n.p., 1789), 3.

6. Ramsay, *Dissertation,* 4.

7. Ramsay, *Dissertation,* 4.

8. John Locke, *Second Treatise on Government,* ed. C. B. Macpherson (Indianapolis: Hackett, 1980), 111.

9. Most famously, the Declaration adapts and revises Locke's enumeration of the basic rights to "life, liberty, and *estate*" as "life, liberty and the pursuit of *happiness*" (Pauline Maier, ed., "Introduction," in *The Declaration of Independence and the Constitution of the United States* [New York: Bantam, 1998], 10). The inclusion of "happiness" is believed to indicate Jefferson's debt to George Mason's Declaration of Rights of Virginia.

As Bernard Bailyn observes, "In pamphlet after pamphlet the American writers cited Locke on nature rights and on the social and governmental contract" (Bernard Bailyn, *Ideological Origins of the American Revolution,* enlarged edition [1967; Cambridge, MA: Belknap Press of Harvard University Press, 1992], 27). T. H. Breen has argued that explicit references to Locke only partially capture his tremendous cultural impact. Breen contends, "[E]ven when the name of the great philosopher did not appear, his ideas still powerfully informed popular public consciousness" (T. H. Breen, "Ideology and Nationalism on the Eve of the American Revolution: Revisions Once More in Need of Revising," *Journal of American History* 84, no. 1 [June 1997]: 13–39, esp. 37). In an instructive alternative to this Locke-centered view, Robert Ferguson has insightfully argued that "if the language of self-evidence and equality seems to come from John Locke's Second Treatise of Civil Government (1690), it can be found just as easily in Algernon Sidney's *Discourses Concerning Government* (1698), and, by the 1770s everywhere in colonial America" (Robert A. Ferguson, *The American Enlightenment, 1750–1820* [Cambridge, MA: Harvard University Press, 1994], 126). For another excellent, in-depth treatment of the broader political culture that shaped the Declaration of Independence, see Pauline Maier,

*American Scripture: Making the Declaration of Independence* (New York: Vintage Books, 1998).

10. By 1865 Ramsay's *History of the American Revolution* had gone through six American editions as well as multiple foreign reprintings (Arthur Schaffer, *To Be an American: David Ramsay and the Making of the American Consciousness* [Columbia: University of South Carolina Press, 1991], 1).

11. Lockean liberalism is a pervasive point of reference in American political historiography and literary criticism. Gillian Brown's *Consent of the Governed* offers a lucid distillation of the intellectual importance (and, as she argues, continued political promise) of Lockean social contract theory in the United States (Gillian Brown, *Consent of the Governed: The Lockean Legacy in Early American Culture* [Cambridge, MA: Harvard University Press, 2001]). As Gail Murray notes, Jay Fliegelman's influential *Prodigals and Pilgrims* (1985) "reasserted Locke's formative influence" amid a renewed attention to civic republicanism spurred by J. G. A. Pocock's *The Machiavellian Moment* (Princeton, NJ: Princeton University Press, 1975). Gail S. Murray, "Reviewed Work: *The Consent of the Governed: The Lockean Legacy in Early American Culture* by Gillian Brown," *Journal of the Early Republic* 21, no. 4 (Winter 2001): 700–703, esp. 700. While influential, Fliegelman's *Prodigals and Pilgrims* is somewhat atypical in its approach to Locke. Fliegelman shifts his focus away from the well-trodden terrain of *Second Treatise* to examine the reception of the model of "parental responsibility and filial freedom set forth by Locke in *Some Thoughts Concerning Education*" (Jay Fliegelman, *Prodigals and Pilgrims: The American Revolution against Patriarchal Authority, 1750–1800* [New York: Cambridge University Press, 1985], 5).

12. Locke uses "citizen" once in *An Essay Considering Human Understanding* and once in his *Four Letters Concerning Toleration*. In *An Essay* Locke treats "citizen" as synonymous with "burgher" ("A citizen or a burgher"), and in *Letters* he speaks of it in relation to the Bible—which, as I discuss in Chapter 2, continued to be one of the primary texts for conceptualizing the meaning of citizenship in the nineteenth century. Locke also uses "citizen" in passing in "A Letter from a Person of Standing to His Friend in the Country," where Locke complains of the "vanities" of a "pert citizen." To find these isolated, nominal uses of "citizen" in Locke, I searched through the Liberty Fund's nine-volume collection of Locke's writing (http://oll.libertyfund.org/people/john-locke).

13. Jean-Jacques Rousseau, *On the Social Contract*, in *Basic Political Writings*, ed. and trans. Donald A. Cress and Peter Gay (Indianapolis, IN: Hackett, 1987), 148–149n.

14. Ramsay's definition of U.S. citizenship was doubly timely. Ramsay published the pamphlet the same year he contested the results of a failed congressional run. When William Smith of South Carolina bested Ramsay's pursuit of a seat in the House of Representatives, Ramsay contested Smith's eligibility, arguing that Smith was not eligible for the position—a question that hinged on "whether he has been seven years a citizen of the United States or not." Smith's situation was admittedly a peculiar one. His parents had died before the American Revolution and, although he was born in South Carolina, Smith was studying abroad

at the time of the Declaration of Independence. However, Ramsay's effort to disqualify Smith failed. The dispute spurred the congressional debate about citizenship discussed in the Introduction (see Madison's remarks about the legal ambiguities surrounding citizenship). Madison ultimately concluded in Smith's favor, but the circumstances of Smith's citizenship were too idiosyncratic for the decision to constitute a major precedent. As Madison observed, "If we are bound by the precedent of such a decision as we are about to make . . . I still think we are not likely to be inundated with such characters" (James Madison, "May 22: Citizenship of the United States," in *The Writings of James Madison, 1787–1790,* ed. Gaillard Hunt [New York: J. P. Putnam and Sons, 1904], 369).

15. In a deft formulation of pre-Revolutionary usages of "subject" and "citizen," Peter Onuf emphasizes that "before 1776, the distinction between subject and citizen would have been meaningless to most Anglo-Americans: they were citizens *because* they were subjects" (Onuf, "Introduction: State and Citizen in British America and the Early United States," in *State and Citizen: British America and the Early United States,* ed. Peter Thompson and Peter S. Onuf [Charlottesville: University of Virginia Press, 2013], 3). As legal historian Maximilian Koessler similarly notes, "Even in the period immediately before the American Revolution, there was no such difference in connotation between 'subject' and 'citizen' as would predicate reserving the status of 'citizen' to the people of a republic and 'subject' to those under the sovereignty of a monarch." Koessler, like many others, overemphasizes the decisiveness of this terminological shift when she argues that "the term 'subject' was brushed aside as a leftover from the feudal law" with the "enactment of the Federal Constitution" (Maximilian Koessler "'Subject,' 'Citizen,' 'National,' and 'Permanent Allegiance,'" *Law Journal Company* 56, no. 1 [November 1946]: 59, 60). The terminological distinction between citizen and subject, I want to stress, did not solidify in the immediate aftermath of the American Revolution (as the frequent recourse to 1776 to periodize this shift implies). Instead, the gradual colloquial differentiation of "subject" and "citizen" found its most unqualified precedents in the French tradition—first in Rousseau and later in the French Declaration of the Rights of Man and of the Citizen (1789).

16. As Ohio representative Philemon Bliss observed in January 1859, in a congressional speech contesting Taney's ruling in the *Dred Scott* case, "Confusion in the meaning of the term citizen is often created by referring to its use in the old Republics." "But we use not the word in its legal sense. . . . It no longer means electors or those enrolled in the national or city guards, but is a simple transfer of, or substitute for, the word subject" (Philemon Bliss, *Citizenship: State Citizens, General Citizens* [Washington, DC: Buell and Blanchard, 1858], 2).

17. As Douglas Bradburn remarks, scholarly "emphasis on national identity and the 'making of American nationalism' obscures the non-national, highly federal character of citizenship in the United States before the Civil War" (Douglas Bradburn, "The Problem of Citizenship in the American Revolution," *History Compass* 8, no. 9 [2010]: 1093–1113, esp. 1101).

18. Raymond Williams, *Marxism and Ideology* (New York: Oxford University Press, 1977), 134.
19. The Fourteenth Amendment is pivotal to current understandings of citizenship—and the meanings to which it helped give rise understandably shape our encounter with this term in the republican and antebellum archive.
20. Bates, *Opinion,* 4.
21. Bates, *Opinion,* 3–4.
22. Bates, *Opinion,* 26.
23. Bates, *Opinion,* 15.
24. I discuss this abolitionist reading strategy at greater length in my discussion of David Walker's *Appeal* in Chapter 2.
25. Not everyone shared Bates's conviction about the national character of allegiance. This aspect of Bates's definition bespeaks the relatively late date of this pamphlet and Bates's official role in the regional conflict that spurred Chase's question. As an attorney general in Lincoln's administration during the Civil War, it was politically necessary for Bates to presume the primacy of *national* allegiance—and, by implication, the illegitimacy of the seceded Confederated States. Yet as the war itself dramatized, many in the early United States understood themselves, first and foremost, as members of the individual states in which they resided (Bates, *Opinion,* 7).
26. In an 1851 speech on the Fugitive Slave Law, Douglass attacks this conceit directly. "The basis of allegiance is protection. We owe allegiance to the government that protects us, but to the government that destroys us, we owe no allegiance" (Frederick Douglass, "Freedom's Battle at Christiana," in *Frederick Douglass: Selected Speeches and Writings,* ed. Philip Sheldon Foner and Yuval Taylor [Chicago: Lawrence Hill, 1999], 179–182, esp. 181).
27. The term was not always used with expectant optimism, but Bates's definition can easily and usefully be adopted to include conceptions of allegiance and protection that were marked by their *failure* to meet the reciprocal promise of citizenship.
28. Jurists and legal historians continue to disagree about which provision of the Fourteenth Amendment requires the states to protect the federal rights enumerated in the Bill of Rights. For a longer discussion of these debates, see Kurt T. Lash's extensive account of historical interpretations of the Privileges and Immunities Clause. As Lash notes, "Initially the Supreme Court rejected the idea that the Fourteenth Amendment forces the states to follow the federal Bill of Rights" (Kurt T. Lash, *The Fourteenth Amendment and the Privileges and Immunities of American Citizenship* [New York: Cambridge University Press, 2014], viii). U.S. Constitution, amendment XIV, section 1.
29. U.S. Declaration of Independence (1776).
30. A handful of states recognized the right to emigrate, but as several early U.S. politicians pointed out, emigration (or permanent relocation) did not in itself dissolve the juridical ties between citizens and their native state (see George Hay's important *A Treatise on Expatriation* [Washington, DC: A. & G. Way, 1814], 2). State constitutions that include language about emigration include Pennsylvania (1776), Vermont (1776), Louisiana (1812), Indiana (1816), Alabama (1819), and Mississippi (1819) (Ezra Seaman, *Commentaries on the*

*Constitutions and Laws, Peoples and History, of the United States: And upon the Great Rebellion and Its Causes* [Ann Arbor, MI: Printed for the Author, at the Journal Office, 1863], 107). Thomas Jefferson, "A Bill Declaring Who Shall Be Deemed Citizens of the Commonwealth," in *Thomas Jefferson: Writings* (New York: Library of America, 1984), 374–375,

31. See I-Mien Tsiang, *The Question of Expatriation in America Prior to 1907* (Baltimore: Johns Hopkins University Press, 1942), 61–70.

32. The resolution to form a committee for this purpose was put forward by Robertson on December 13, 1817. *Annals of Congress,* 15th Congress, 1st session, 448.

33. The principle of natural and perpetual allegiance was established in Sir Edward Coke's influential decision in Calvin's Case (1608). Johnson of Virginia eloquently critiqued the proposed adherence to this British precedent, proclaiming: "Introduce but the doctrine of perpetual allegiance, that baleful scion from the odious stock the feudal system, and you have tooled the death bell to the liberties of the people of this country" (*Annals,* 15th Congress, 1st session, 1065). For more on natural allegiance and Calvin's Case, see James H. Kettner, *The Development of American Citizenship, 1608–1870* (Chapel Hill: University of North Carolina Press, 1978), 13–28.

34. As Representative Cobb of Georgia noted, to counter this argument, Congress has the right to regulate naturalization, so it should have the right to regulate expatriation as well (since the two are correlative). *Annals,* 15th Congress, 1st session, 1068.

35. The latter suggestion was made by Mr. McLane, a representative of Delaware and an eloquent opponent of the bill. *Annals,* 15th Congress, 1st session, 1060.

36. A notable geographic bias can be discerned in the votes for and against the bill. According to Tsiang's tabulation, New England representatives voted 2 to 1 in opposition to the right of expatriation, and middle states representatives were only slightly inclined to oppose the right, whereas southern representatives voted in favor of the bill by over 2 to 1, and the new western representatives favored it by a striking margin of about 3 to 1 (Tsiang, *Question of Expatriation,* 61). Interestingly, although the passage of the bill would have effectively buttressed the *national* character of citizenship (by subjecting it to congressional regulation), southern representatives, on the whole, were more favorable toward the bill. Other than Tsiang's exhaustive account of expatriation prior to 1907, there is only a handful of criticism that discusses expatriation debates in "the years of confusion," as Roche appropriately terms it (John P. Roche, "Loss of American Nationality: The Years of Confusion," *Western Political Quarterly* 4, no. 2 [June 1951]: 268–294). Rising Lake Morrow, "The Early American Attitude toward the Doctrine of Expatriation," *American Journal of International Law* 26, no. 3 (1932): 552–564.

37. Act of July 27, 1868. 15 Stat. 223.

38. Coke ruled that persons born in Scotland after the Union of the Crowns in 1603 owed the British Crown allegiance and were entitled to the king's protection. As legal historian Polly Price observes in her discussion of the Fourteenth

Amendment, "The roots of United States conceptions of birthright citizenship lie deep in England's medieval past" (Polly Price, "Natural Law and Birthright Citizenship in Calvin's Case [1608]," *Yale Journal of Law and the Humanities* 9, no. 1 [2013]: 73–145, esp. 73).

39. For an excellent theoretical treatment of the blood logic of chattel slavery, see Nancy Bentley, "The Fourth Dimension: Kinlessness and African American Narrative," *Critical Inquiry* 35 (Winter 2009): 270–292.

40. U.S. Congress, Sess. II, Chap. 3; 1 stat 103. 1st Congress; March 26, 1790.

41. See Linda K. Kerber, "Meanings of Citizenship," *Journal of American History* 84, no. 3 (1997): 839.

42. See Kerber, "Meanings of Citizenship," 839.

43. U.S. Constitution, article I, section 8, clause 4.

44. U.S. Congress, Sess. II, Chap. 3; 1 stat 103. 1st Congress; March 26, 1790.

45. As Coviello observes, "the relation of the social category called 'race' to property and to the possessive states of self-relation is profoundly unsettled in late-eighteenth century America" (Coviello, *Intimacy in America: Dreams of Affiliation in Antebellum Literature* [Minneapolis: University of Minnesota Press, 2005], 34).

46. Bates, *Opinion*, 5.

47. U.S. Constitution, article IV, section 2.

48. The problem, as James Kettner observes, is that "the comity clause placed a constitutional obligation on the states to confer 'all Privileges and Immunities of Citizens' upon the 'Citizens of each State'—but who was to determine what those privileges and immunities were?" (Kettner, *Development of American Citizenship,* 231). The Fourteenth Amendment, it is worth stressing, does not itself explicitly enumerate all of the privileges and immunities of citizenship. However, the 1866 Civil Rights Act to which it is closely tied specified that "citizens, of every race and color . . . shall have the same right, in every State and Territory in the United States, to make and enforce contracts, to sue, be parties, and give evidence, to inherit, purchase, lease, sell, hold, and convey real and personal property, and to full and equal benefit of all laws and proceedings for the security of person and property, as is enjoyed by white citizens . . ." (Civil Rights Act, 14 Stat. 27 [1866]). In addition, as the Fifteenth Amendment's subsequent clarification of the right to vote attests, by putting into place a working constitutional definition of citizenship, the Fourteenth Amendment set the foundation for an increasingly substantive constitutional understanding of these privileges and immunities in the following years.

49. James Wilson, "Pennsylvania Ratifying Convention, Nov. 28 & Dec. 4 1787," in *The Debates in the Several State Conventions on the Adoption of the Federal Constitution,* ed. Jonathan Elliott, 5 vols., 2:434–437, 453–454, http://press-pubs.uchicago.edu/founders/documents/v1ch14s27.html. I would like to thank Hunt Howell for a helpful question and conversation about the Bill of Rights, following a talk I gave on citizenship at the Mahindra Humanities Center at Harvard University in November 2016.

50. For a lucid account of the Constitution's complex interrelationship to "extra-textual sources such as judicial opinions, executive practices, legislative enact-

ments, and American tradition," see Akhil Reed Amar's *America's Unwritten Constitution: Its Precedents and the Principles We Live By* (New York: Basic Books, 2012), xiii. I find Amar's argument about the Constitution's fundamental interdependence on a host of precedents outside of its textual limits compelling. I also find his heuristic characterization of these precedents as an "unwritten Constitution" evocative. However, the heuristic has its limits, since (as Amar acknowledges) many of the precedents he discusses do appear in written form. For the purposes of clarity, I would recast what he terms "extra-textual" as extra-constitutional, because, as I argue in this book, there was no shortage of textual treatments of citizenship. Moreover, this revised phrasing can help us to distinguish between questions that were extraordinarily under-conceived within the law *writ large* (such as citizenship) and the many questions that were not addressed in the Constitution proper but *were* addressed at length in other legal documents.

51. As historian Douglas Bradburn observes in his account of the debates that surrounded citizenship in the thirty years after the Declaration of Independence, "In law there was very little national uniformity to American citizenship: states controlled the extent and limits of the franchise; some states possessed religious establishments; states followed different derivations of the English Common law; one state (Louisiana) possessed a completely alien legal code . . . and numerous minor differences complicated the civil and political rights of citizens and non-citizens throughout the United States" (Douglas Bradburn, *The Citizenship Revolution: Politics and the Creation of the American Union, 1774–1804* [Charlottesville: University of Virginia Press, 2009], 1–2).

52. The North Carolina Constitution holds that "every foreigner, who comes to settle in this State having first taken an oath of allegiance to the same, may purchase, or, by other means, acquire, hold, and transfer land, or other real estate; and after one year's residence, shall be deemed a free citizen" (North Carolina Constitution [1776], XL).

53. The Pennsylvania Constitution (and the 1777 Constitution of Vermont after it) mentions citizenship once in the context of religious freedom (Pennsylvania Constitution [1776], II).

54. "The enigma," as historian Nancy Isenberg frames it, is that "freeborn women had the appearance of citizenship but lacked the basic rights to be real citizens" (Nancy Isenberg, *Sex and Citizenship in Antebellum America* [Chapel Hill: University of North Carolina Press, 1998], esp. xii, 24). The problem, as Linda Kerber aptly frames it, is that "if a citizen had to possess civic rights, then women were not citizens, for they did not vote except briefly in New Jersey" (Linda Kerber, "'May All Our Citizens Be Soldiers, and All Our Soldiers Citizens': The Ambiguities of Female Citizenship in the New Nation," in *Arms at Rest: Peacemaking and Peacekeeping in American History,* ed. J. R. Challinor and R. L. Beisner [New York: Greenwood Press, 1987], 5). See also Kerber's extended treatment of these questions in her seminal study, *No Constitutional Right to Be Ladies: Women and Obligations of Citizenship* (New York: Hill & Wang, 1998).

55. This admittedly limited form of women's suffrage came to an end with the 1807 New Jersey Constitution, which restricted suffrage to white men. See

Judith Apter Klinghoffer and Lois Elkis, "'The Petticoat Electors': Women's Suffrage in New Jersey, 1776–1807," *Journal of the Early Republic* 12, no. 2 (Summer 1992): 159–193; Jan Ellen Lewis, "Rethinking Women's Suffrage in New Jersey, 1776–1807," *Rutgers Law Review* 63, no. 3 (August 2011): 1017–1035.

56. Theresa Anne Murphy, *Citizenship and the Origins of Women's History in the United States* (Philadelphia: University of Pennsylvania Press, 2013), 115.

57. Laurel A. Clark, "The Rights of a Florida Wife: Slavery, U.S. Expansion, and Married Women's Property Law," *Journal of Women's History* 22, no. 4 (Winter 2010): 39–63, esp. 40.

58. "The First Constitution of the Great State of Tennessee, 1796," http://www .tngenweb.org/law/constitution1796.html; "State of Tennessee Constitution of 1835," http://www.tngenweb.org/law/constitution1835.html.

59. "The Second Constitution of New York, 1821," http://www.nycourts.gov /history/constitutions/1821_constitution.htm.

60. By 1855, only Massachusetts, Vermont, New Hampshire, Maine, and Rhode Island did not exclude or restrict black suffrage. Amid these increasingly explicit racial exclusions, black reformers seized new forms and modes of political participation. As Derrick Spires argues in his discussion of the printed proceedings of black state conventions, "unofficial modes of participatory politics" provided "viable, visible, and potentially revolutionary modes of direct intervention in a civic sphere in which voting was just becoming accessible to masses of white men" (Derrick R. Spires, "Imagining a Nation of Fellow Citizens: Early African American Politics of Publicity," in *Early African American Print Culture,* ed. Lara L. Cohen and Jordan A. Stein [Philadelphia: University of Pennsylvania Press, 2012], 274–289, esp. 275).

61. Dana Nelson succinctly captures and dismantles this persistent teleological narrative in her reexamination of democracy. "One of the cornerstones of the United States' self-image," Nelson writes, "is a story of how its orderly political freedom matured over time into 'the world's leading democracy'" (Nelson, *Commons Democracy: Reading the Politics of Participation in the United States* [New York: Fordham University Press, 2015], 24). As with this book's prehistory of citizenship, Nelson's genealogy of democracy turns its focus from the official mandates of the law (what Nelson glosses in terms of "formal democracy") to examine the informal practices that helped to shape the uneven development of political thought in the early United States.

62. S. Croswell and R. Sutton, "Speech of Mr. Cornell, on Colored Suffrage," in *Debates and Proceedings in the New-York State Convention, for the Revision of the Constitution* (Albany, NY: S. Croswell and R. Sutton, 1846): 904–907, esp. 906, emphasis in original. For another discussion of this instructive speech, see Jeannine DeLombard's *In the Shadow of the Gallows: Race, Crime, and American Civic Identity* (Philadelphia: University of Pennsylvania Press, 2012), 51–52).

63. As Bates emphasized in his 1862 pamphlet, it is a "common error" to think that "the right to vote for public officers is one of the constituent elements of American citizenship" (Bates, *Opinion,* 4). The uncertain link between citizen-

ship and suffrage is suggested by the very existence of the Fifteenth Amendment (1870). If voting had been practically recognized as an incontrovertible right of all citizens, the Fourteenth Amendment's extension of citizenship to black men should have been sufficient to guarantee black suffrage. Even the Fifteenth Amendment did not fully clarify this issue. In declaring that the "right of citizens of the United States to vote shall not be denied or abridged by the United States or by any State on account of race, color, or previous condition of servitude," the Fifteenth Amendment makes it clear that the right to vote is *only* enjoyed by citizens, but it does not unequivocally establish suffrage as a right enjoyed by *all* citizens (U.S. Constitution, amendment XV, section 1).

64. As Sophia Rosenfeld observes in a different context, Wilson is "best known for his attachment to the ideal of common sense as the bedrock of republican government (Sophia Rosenfeld, *Common Sense: A Political History* [Cambridge, MA: Harvard University Press, 2011], 176).

65. William Apess, *Indian Nullification of the Unconstitutional Laws of Massachusetts Relative to the Marshpee Tribe; or, the Pretended Riot Explained,* in *On Our Own Ground: The Writings of William Apess, a Pequot,* ed. Barry O'Connell (Amherst: University of Massachusetts Press, 1993), 166–274, esp. 183.

66. This is a good example of what Mark Rifkin refers to as a "settler common sense" (Mark Rifkin, *Settler Common Sense: Queerness and Everyday Colonialism in the American Renaissance* [Minneapolis: University of Minnesota Press, 2014]). Rifkin discusses Apess through the lens of his "Eulogy on King Philip's War" (1836), where Apess describes Congress "disenfranchising us as citizens" (William Apess, "Eulogy on King Philip's War," in *On Our Own Ground,* 277–310, esp. 306).

67. To further solidify his analogical defense of tribal sovereignty, Apess situates the Maspee Revolt in relationship to Massachusetts's own history of dissent: its role as "the boasted cradle of independence" in the Boston tea party, and the later revolt of white farmers against the state government during the Constitutional Convention in Shay's Rebellion (Apess, *Indian Nullification,* 195, 237).

68. U.S. Constitution, amendment XIV, section 1.

69. Within this double standard, as it was set out in Justice Marshall's majority ruling, "[Indians] are considered as within the jurisdictional limits of the United States, subject to many of those restraints which are imposed upon our own citizens," but "they are in a state of pupilage" (Richard Peters, ed., *The Case of the Cherokee Nation against the State of Georgia,* University of Michigan Library facsimile reprint [Philadelphia: John Grigg, 1831], 161).

70. For another treatment that stresses the limits of citizenship for discussing Native politics and agency, see Audra Simpson's account of the Mohawk efforts to maintain political sovereignty by refusing American or Canadian citizenship (Audra Simpson, *Mohawk Interruptus: Political Life across the Borders of Settler States* [Durham, NC: Duke University Press, 2014]). As Mishuana Goeman observes, the Indian Act reflects the settler nation's investment in "mold[ing] a particular citizenship, in which a 'person [is] an individual other than an Indian'" (Mishuana Goeman, *Mark My Words: Native Women Mapping Our Nations* [Minneapolis: Minnesota University Press, 2013], 41).

71. See Josh Blackman, "Original Citizenship," *University of Pennsylvania Law Review* 159, no. 95 (2010): 95–126, esp. 125.

72. *Dred Scott v. Sandford: A Brief History with Documents,* ed. Paul Finkelman (New York: Bedford, 1997), 63.

73. *Dred Scott,* 63.

74. *Dred Scott,* 64.

75. As David Bromwich emphasizes, "There was a reason why Lincoln called [Taney's] finding 'an astonisher in legal history.'" His decision "presented a new theory about the meaning of the Constitution" (David Bromwich, *Moral Imagination* [Princeton, NJ: Princeton University Press, 2014], 19).

76. Philemon Bliss, *Citizenship,* 1.

77. Bliss, *Citizenship,* 1.

78. Tomlins's discussion of citizenship in the United States appears after nine chapters on the colonies, so his treatment of Taney's decision stands in for the broader debates about citizenship in the early United States—debates that, as I argue here, usefully bring into focus the decision's peculiarities as well as its continuities with previous legal precedents (Christopher Tomlins, *Freedom Bound: Law, Labor, and Civic Identity in Colonizing English America, 1580–1865* [New York: Cambridge University Press, 2010], 510, 534, emphasis added).

79. For a powerful discussion of this analogy, see Karen Sanchez-Eppler, "Bodily Bonds: The Intersecting Rhetorics of Feminism and Abolition," *Representations* 24 (1988): 28–59.

80. Here I want to echo Robert Ferguson's trenchant critique of our misplaced confidence in our understanding of the early republican terminology: "When modern wielders of early republican phraseology think they are using the same language, they do so only in a literal sense. The words themselves often held different meanings when first expressed, and every original expression came in a context now lost to easy comprehension" [Robert A. Ferguson, *Reading the Early Republic* (Cambridge, MA: Harvard University Press, 2004), 9–10).

81. For a discussion of these interpretative theories in relation to the Fourteenth Amendment, see Bret Boyce's call for a return to the common-law approach to constitutional adjudication in the present (Bret Boyce, "Originalism and Fourteenth Amendment," *Wake Forest Law Review* 33, no. 4 [1996]: 909–1034, esp. 909).

## 2. "Citizenship in Heaven"

1. Isaac Kramnick and Laurence Moore, *The Godless Constitution: A Moral Defense of the Secular State,* updated ed. (New York: W. W. Norton, 2005).

2. "In marked contrast with their federal counterpart," as political scientist Alan Tarr notes, "most early state constitutions expressly recognized the existence of God, and most later state constitutions acknowledged the state's dependence on God's favor" (Alan Tarr, "Religion under State Constitutions," *Annals of the American Academy of Political and Social Science* 946 [March 1988]: 65–75, esp. 67).

3. New Jersey Constitution (1776), article XIX.

4. North Carolina Constitution (1776), article XXXII.

5. *Journal of the Convention, Called by the Freemen of North-Carolina, to Amend the Constitution of the State* (Raleigh, NC: Gales and Sons, 1835), 47.

6. To facilitate my comparative review of the several state constitutions, I used Yale Law's Avalon Project (avalon.law.yale.edu).

7. As we saw in the Introduction, this territorial understanding of citizenship distinguishes birthright citizenship as it was belatedly formalized with the Fourteenth Amendment.

8. *Oxford English Dictionary Online*, s.v. "Citizen," 3.n, accessed December 19, 2014, http://www.oed.com/view/Entry/33513.

9. Exegetical treatments of Philippians 3:20 were also popular in the seventeenth century, as Allison Hurley observes in her discussion of "conversation." The passage "was popular across doctrinal divides for admonishing Christians to live and act on earth as if they had already been received into the community of saints in heaven" (Allison Hurley, "Peculiar Christians, Circumstantial Courtiers, and the Making of Conversation in Seventeenth-Century England," *Representations* 111, no. 1 [2011]: 33–59, esp. 42). Hurley's focus is the importance of the term "conversation"; she does not analyze the turn to the language of citizenship in later modernized translations.

10. Unless otherwise noted, I use the recension of Philippians 3:20 in the first U.S. translation of the Bible by Charles Thomson as the primary point of reference for modernized versions, because it offers a historically important and yet understudied alternative to the King James Version. Charles Thomson, trans., *The Holy Bible, Containing the Old and New Covenant, Commonly Called the Old and New Testament: Translated from the Greek* (Philadelphia: Jane Aitken, 1808), Phil. 3:19–21, emphasis added.

11. As I discuss in the second section, the King James Version continued to be widely reprinted and adapted amid this surge of new translations.

12. In the words of Peter 2:11, "As strangers and pilgrims, [Christians] abstain from fleshly lusts, which war against the soul" (KJV).

13. This is a common formulation. As one writer observes in a British editorial, "To be a Christian at the time when the gospels was formed, was voluntarily to exclude themselves from their former connexions. . . . The name of a Christian was one of reproach,—it brought no honors,—it conferred no titles,—it had no distinctions, they were as the Apostles say, 'In the world but not of the world'" ("To the Editor," *Republic*, September 1, 1820, 18).

14. Important modernized translations of the Bible that used citizen/citizenship to render Philippians 3:20 include the following: Gilbert Wakefield's *A Translation of the New Testament* (London: London Philanthropic Press, 1791); William Newcome's *An Attempt toward Revising Our English Translation of the Greek Scriptures, or the New Covenant of Jesus Christ* (Dublin: John Exshaw, 1796); and Charles Thomson's 1808 *The Holy Bible;* and George Campbell, James Macknight, and Philip Doddridge, trans., *The Sacred Writings of the Apostles and Evangelists of Jesus Christ, Commonly Styled the New Testament*, ed. Alexander Campbell (Buffaloe, VA: Alexander Campbell, 1826).

15. Even beyond the U.S. political context, the theological usages of "citizen" are rarely mentioned in the otherwise robust body of scholarship on citizenship. In a partial exception to this general omission, Augustine's use of "citizenship" in relationship to heaven is noted in the entry on citizenship in Bryan Turner, "Citizen," in *New Keywords: A Revised Vocabulary of Culture and Society,* ed. Tony Bennett, Lawrence Grossberg, and Meaghan Morris (Malden, MA: Blackwell, 2005), 29–32, esp. 29. This brief allusion to the theological use of "citizen" is atypical, but the inclusion of this information in a term-centered study is fitting. It underlines just how different citizenship looks when it is treated as a term and when it is treated as a concept, i.e., political membership.

16. This chapter uses the fascinating and unexamined turn to the language of citizenship in post-Revolutionary recensions of Philippians to build a bridge between religious history and the traditionally secular purview of political history. For a pioneering collection of work in new religious studies, see Justine Murison and Jordan Alexander Stein, eds., "Methods for the Study of Religion in Early American Literature," *Early American Literature* 45, no. 1 (2010): 1–29; see also Jared Hickman, *Black Prometheus: Race and Radicalism in the Age of Atlantic Slavery* (New York: Oxford University Press, 2016).

17. Revolution, expatriation, and secession—these are the negative grammars of relation through which citizenship was alternately contested and idealized.

18. Harriet Beecher Stowe, *Uncle Tom's Cabin; or, Life among the Lowly,* ed. Elizabeth Ammons, Norton Critical Editions (New York: W. W. Norton, 1994), 362.

19. Tom's celebratory exclamation adopts the economic bonds of chattel slavery as a figure for theological affiliation, even as it privileges the comparative desirability of heaven.

20. Phillis Wheatley, "On Being Brought from Africa to America," in *Complete Writings,* ed. Vincent Carretta (New York: Penguin, 2001), 13. In addition to Wheatley's thematic engagement with the broader cultural trope of heavenly citizenship in her poetry, her participation in this tradition is evident in the circulation of her poetry. Her elegy on Whitefield was appended to the printing of a 1770 Boston sermon on Whitefield's death that explicitly engages this exegetical tradition. Ebenezer Pemberton, *Heaven the Residence of Saints: A Sermon Occasioned by the Sudden and Much Lamented Death of the Rev. George Whitefield . . . To Which Is Added, an Elegiac Poem on His Death, by Phillis, a Negro Girl* (Boston: C. Dilly, 1771).

21. For the definitive, secular account of the fatalistic figuration of liberty that passages like Stowe's typify, see Russ Castronovo's *Necro Citizenship: Death, Eroticism, and the Public Sphere in the Nineteenth-Century United States* (Durham, NC: Duke University Press, 2001). As Castronovo observes in his insightful analysis of liberalism's impossibly abstract (and moribund) universal "citizen," "the metaphor of death as freedom saturates nineteenth-century culture" (Castronovo, *Necro Citizenship,* 36). The metaphoric link between liberty and death, as Castronovo emphasizes, structures a troublingly limited vision of the possibilities for freedom in the world. The exegetical cultural history of "heavenly citizenship" brings into focus the eschatological *dureé* that gave figurative life—and political force—to this otherwise merely fatalistic trope. By

necessity, an exegetical treatment of citizenship brings us outside the secular interpretive regime of liberalism, whose nationalistic temporality tends to eclipse the theological beliefs that made even literal death seem as much a *beginning* as an end.

22. As New York abolitionist pastor Joseph Thompson observes in his 1848 sermon "The Duties of the Christian Citizen," since "the Gospel is to regulate our civil, as well as our social and our religious conduct, it is important to inquire what duties the New Testament prescribes for the Christian *as a citizen*" (Joseph Parrish Thompson, *The Duties of the Christian Citizen: A Discourse, by Joseph P. Thompson, Pastor of the Broadway Tabernacle Church* [New York: S. W. Benedict, 1848], 4).

23. John Mason, *The Voice of Warning, to Christians, on the Ensuing Election of a President of the United States* (New York: G. F. Hopkins, 1800), 26.

24. Mason, *Voice of Warning*, 26–27.

25. Mason was "one of the most noted clerical critics" of Jefferson (Dumas Malone, *Jefferson and the Ordeal of Liberty* [Boston: Little, Brown, 1962], 3:482).

26. Mason, *Voice of Warning*, 9. "The approaching election of a President is to decide a question not merely of preference to one eminent individual, or particular views of policy," Mason warned, "but what is infinitely more, of an national regard or disregard for the religion of Jesus Christ" (Mason, *Voice of Warning*, 8).

27. John Mason, "Politics and Religion," in *A Compendium of American Literature*, ed. Charles Dexter Cleveland (Philadelphia: J. A. Bancroft, 1859), 167–168.

28. Jefferson made this comment in a response to the Danbury Baptists in January 1802, but his general position on the relationship between church and state was well established before this, and it was this general principle that Mason's sermon expounds on with concern. See Thomas Jefferson to Nehemiah Dodge, Ephraim Robbins, and Stephen S. Nelson, a committee of the Danbury Baptist association in the state of Connecticut, January 1, 1802, accessed January 1, 2017, http://www.loc.gov/loc/lcib/9806/danpre.html.

29. As Amanda Porterfield observes, "The spike in religion's popularity around 1800 coincided with political upheaval and new forms of political organization" (Porterfield, *Conceived in Doubt: Religion and Politics in the New Nation* [Chicago: University of Chicago Press, 2012], 5).

30. Here I am playing on the evocative title of *Varieties of Secularism in a Secular Age*, ed. Michael Warner, Jonathan VanAntwerpen, and Craig Calhoun (Cambridge, MA: Varieties of Secularism, 2010).

31. This is how Sacvan Bercovitch characterizes the dual modality of the "American Jeremiad" (Sacvan Bercovitch, *The American Jeremiad* [Madison: University of Wisconsin Press, 1978], xi).

32. In particular, see Mark A. Noll, "The Bible and Slavery," in *Religion and the American Civil War*, ed. Randall M. Miller, Harry S. Stout, and Charles Reagan Wilson (New York: Oxford University Press, 1998), 43–73; Mitchell Snay, *Gospel of Disunion: Religion and Separatism in the Antebellum South* (New York: Cambridge University Press, 1993); and Mark A. Noll, *The Civil War as*

*a Theological Crisis,* Steven and Janice Brose Lectures in the Civil War Era (Chapel Hill: University of North Carolina Press, 2006).

33. Abraham Lincoln, "Second Inaugural Address," in *Lincoln's Selected Writings,* ed. David S. Reynolds (New York: Norton, 2015), 364–368, esp. 367.

34. Augustine argues that the material blessings and hardships are experienced by the "godless and godly" alike, but he also characterizes the desire for "good things" as a sign of fallenness: "[H]e has willed that these temporal goods and temporal evils should befall good and bad alike, so that the good things should not be too eagerly coveted, when it is seen that the wicked also enjoy them" (Augustine of Hippo, *Concerning the City of God against the Pagans,* trans. Henry Bettenson [New York: Penguin, 2003], 49, 13).

35. Horace Bushnell, "American Politics," *American National Preacher,* December 1840, 189. Hereafter cited parenthetically as "AP."

36. There is an immense body of scholarship describing Christian nationalism, but comparatively little dealing with residual tensions between religion and politics. The historiography, in this respect, tends to naturalize the univocity and developmental telos immanent to Christian nationalism itself. Mark Hanley's *Beyond a Christian Commonwealth* is one of the few exceptions to this trend. Hanley argues that "Protestant praise for the Republic in the decades before the Civil War, was accompanied by a countervailing 'critical republican vision' " that "denounced the confounding of civilization and Christianity as an attack upon religion itself." Hanley offers illustrative excerpts from sermons in this countervailing tradition, but the book sometimes lacks the persuasiveness of the examples it marshals (Mark Y. Hanley, *Beyond a Christian Commonwealth: The Protestant Quarrel with the American Republic, 1830–1860* [Chapel Hill: University of North Carolina Press, 1994], 56, 87).

37. Nevin's central argument that the "true destination of man . . . lies beyond the present world" is explicitly framed as a rejoinder to Christian nationalism. After noting, "We hear much said, in glorification of the present age. . . . The genius of the age is emphatically the genius of this rising republic," Nevin continues to dismiss the idea: "Never was there, however, under such plausible form, a more perfect delusion. The age is *not* thus infallible and safe. On the contrary, it is made up, to a terrible extent, beyond most ages that have been, of falsehood and error, sophistry and sham" (John Nevin, "Man's True Destiny," *Mercersburg Quarterly Review,* October 1853, 492–521, esp. 493, 510–511).

38. These remarks appear in an essayistic account of the theological implications of Bishop George Berkeley's "strange conceit in opposition to the common sense of mankind, that there was no external world" (Melancthon, "No External World," *Millennial Harbinger,* September 1853, 509, emphasis added).

39. Among other things, the emphasis on America's special role in the millennium facilitated defenses of imperial expansion. In Lyman Beecher's *Plea for the West,* for example, he reiterates Jonathan Edwards's conviction that "the millennium would commence in America," but he emphasizes that the "religious and political destiny of our nation is to be decided in the West" (Lyman

Beecher, *A Plea for the West,* 2nd ed. [Cincinnati: Truman and Smith, 1835], 9–11).

40. Ansel Doane Eddy, *The Christian Citizen: The Obligations of the Christian Citizen; With a Review of High Church Principles in Relation to Civil and Religious Institutions* (New York: J. S. Taylor, 1843), 20.

41. Hollis Read, *The Hand of God in History; or, Divine Providence Historically Illustrated in the Extension and Establishment of Christianity* (Hartford, CT: H. E. Robins, 1856), 2:181, emphasis added.

42. James Albert Ukawsaw Gronniosaw, *A Narrative of the Most Remarkable Particulars in the Life of James Albert Ukawsaw Gronniosaw, an African Prince, as Related by Himself,* in *Pioneers of the Black Atlantic,* ed. Henry Louis Gates Jr. and William L. Andrews (Washington, DC: Civitas, 1998), 52–53.

43. Gronniosaw, *Narrative,* 59.

44. Henry David Thoreau, "Resistance to Civil Government," in *Aesthetic Papers* (New York: G. P. Putnam, 1849), 189–211, esp. 192.

45. Orestes Brownson, "Art. IV.—A Tale of the Real and Ideal, Blight and Bloom," *Brownson's Quarterly Review,* July 1, 1846, 369–399, esp. 371.

46. Brownson, "Tale of the Real and Ideal," 370.

47. Robert Govett, "May Christians Be Politicians? To the Editor of the 'Baptist Magazine,'" in *Baptist Magazine for 1868,* vol. 60, ed. W. G. Lewis (London: Elliot Stock, 1868), 794.

48. The writer "direct[s] the attention of the restless millions of earth to the Glory regions of the better land." The version I cite here was "revise[d] . . . for an American edition," but the prefatory note about the Gold Rush appears in the author's original 1853 preface (Jeremiah Dodsworth, *The Better Land; or, The Christian Emigrant's Guide to Heaven,* revised by Thomas O. Summers [Nashville, TN: E. Stevenson and F. A. Owen, 1857], ix, see also introductory note).

49. The successive chapter titles in *The Better Land* capture the book's attempt to overcome the uncomfortable gap between the speculative fabulation of the heavenly state and the semblance of certainty that it enjoys within the extraempirical episteme of Christian theology: "The Future State . . . It Is Necessary . . . It is Requisite . . . It is Desirable . . . It is Possible . . . It is Probable . . . It is Certainly Revealed." (Dodsworth, *Better Land,* table of contents). Not surprisingly, the most polemical formulation of the relationship between political and heavenly citizenship appears in "It is Certainly Revealed." In an argument that crystallizes the antipolitical potential of religious faith that famously drew Karl Marx's reproach, the section argues that the greatest "acts of self-denial" and "heroism" in history were all buttressed "by the firm belief of the doctrine of full reward. . . . [S]o strong was their faith in the doctrine of a future state of recompense, that they resolved rather to sacrifice their privileges as citizens of this world . . . than to give up their hopes of immortality" (Dodsworth, *Better Land,* 57).

50. As Dodsworth notes in a subsequent publication, *The Better Land* was in "extensive demand"; by 1858, he had already sold fifteen thousand copies of *The Better Land* (Jeremiah Dodsworth, *The Eden Family: Shewing the Loss of Our Paradise Home* [London: Partridge, 1858], iii). Dodsworth, *Better Land,* 11.

51. Hale's personal copy of the Bible is now housed at the American Antiquarian Society. I am grateful to Thomas Knoles, the head librarian at the Antiquarian Society, for his help confirming that the Greek characters Hale scrawled were a transliteration of *politeuma*. Edward Everett Hale, [Annotations], in *The New Testament . . . Conformed to Griesbach's Standard Greek Text* (Boston: William L. Lewis, 1828). The Edward Everett Hale Papers, 1855–1906, American Antiquarian Society, Worcester, MA.

52. After referring to this "unhappy translation," Cumming proceeds to explain that "conversation" "is the old Saxon word, meaning not talking, but citizenship; the literal translation is, 'Your citizenship is in heaven.' If you blot out the word 'conversation' in your Bible and put in 'citizenship,' you have the exact and true idea" (John Cumming, *The Millennial Rest; or, The World as It Will Be* [London: Richard Bentley, 1862], 200).

53. In keeping with these remarks, Campbell's edition renders Philippians 3:20 as "we are citizens of heaven." Alexander Campbell, "General Preface: An Apology for a New Translation," in Campbell, Macknight, and Doddridge, *The Sacred Writings of the Apostles and Evangelists of Jesus Christ*, 3–10, esp. 4.

54. Hannah Arendt, *The Human Condition*, ed. Margaret Canovan (Chicago: University of Chicago Press, 1998), 198.

55. Arendt, *Human Condition*, 14, emphasis added.

56. Thompson posits a categorical distinction between positive and divine law, but he also defuses its oppositional implications by suggesting that the Christian citizen is obliged to obey the laws of the Gospel and the government. Thompson, *Duties of the Christian Citizen*, 3.

57. Edward Bates, *Opinion of Attorney General Bates on Citizenship* (Washington, DC: Government Printing Office, 1862), 7.

58. While "eschatology" is sometimes used interchangeably with "millennialism," the term refers to the part of theology concerned with the last four things: death, judgment, heaven, and hell. I use it in its broad meaning to foreground the relationship between these concepts. For one thing, as Ann Douglas points out, millennial writers in the period "increasingly confused the millennial period with the heavenly afterlife" (Ann Douglas, *The Feminization of American Culture* [New York: Knopf, 1977], 221). The doubling of these concepts is particularly explicit in readings of Philippians 3, since the passage on "citizenship in heaven" is followed almost immediately with the promise that "The Lord is at Hand" (Thomson, trans., *Holy Bible*, Phil. 4.4). *Oxford English Dictionary Online*, s.v. "Eschatology," 1.a, accessed December 1, 2014, http://www.oed .com/view/Entry/64274.

59. As I discuss in Chapter 1, "citizen" was still used interchangeably with "subject" in this period. The significance of the Declaration of the Rights of Man and of the Citizen, in this respect, was not the crystallization of the term's differential usage in the preceding years, but its role in giving this specialized usage new global visibility.

60. "Introduction," in *The New Testament, in an Improved Version, upon the Basis of Archbishop Newcome's New Translation: With a Corrected Text and Notes Critical and Explanatory* (London: Richard Taylor, 1808), 2.

61. As the introduction to an 1808 "improved" edition of the New Testament explains, republication efforts were subsequently resumed by "another Society in the West of England," but they proved abortive due to Wakefield's untimely death ("Introduction," *The New Testament in an Improved Version*, 2).

62. Robert Wakefield, trans., *A Translation of the New Testament* (Cambridge, MA: University Press, 1820).

63. *The New Testament: The Version Set Forth A.D. 1611, Revised A.D. 1881* (Oxford, UK: Oxford University Press, 1881), 455. *The New Covenant Formerly Called the New Testament . . . Newly Edited by the American Revision Committee* (New York: Thomas Nelson and Sons, 1901), 430.

64. The two translators to whom I am referring here are Gilbert Wakefield and Charles Thomson. (I discuss Thomson's engagement with this key passage later in this chapter.)

65. "Wakefield to Rev. Mr. Gregory, Feb. 27, 1781," in *Memoirs of the Life of Gilbert Wakefield*, 2 vols. (London: J. Johnson, 1804), 1:432–433.

66. As Mason Lowance observes in his excellent collection of speeches and sermons that shaped the terms of the slavery debate in the United States, the story of Sarah and Hagar was one of two biblical sources that proslavery advocates routinely invoked (Mason I. Lowance, ed., *A House Divided: The Antebellum Slavery Debates in America, 1776–1865* [Princeton, NJ: Princeton University Press, 2003], 51).

67. The first part of the line is identical in these two editions, but the second clause is different. Thomson's recension, "But we are citizens of heaven; *whence indeed we are expecting a deliverer*," is only slightly different from Wakefield's, which reads, "But we are citizens of heaven, *from which we earnestly expect a savior*" (Thomson, *Holy Bible*, Phil. 3:20; Wakefield, *New Testament*, Phil. 3:20). Kendrick Grobel argues that Thomson is indebted "to Wakefield for striking—and often fantastic—suggestions," but he does not mention Philippians 3:20 in his discussion of these parallels (Kendrick Grobel, "Charles Thomson, First American N. T. Translator: An Appraisal," *Journal of Bible and Religion* 11, no. 3 [1943]: 145–151).

68. Charles Thomson, Original manuscript of Thomson's translation from the Greek of *The New Covenant Commonly Called the New Testament*, Historical Society of Pennsylvania, Philadelphia.

69. U.S. Library of Congress, "Hyperspectral Imaging by Library of Congress Reveals Change Made by Thomas Jefferson in Original Declaration of Independence Draft," July 2, 2010, http://www.loc.gov/today/pr/2010/10-161.html.

70. For Hatch, the democratization of Christianity "has less to do with the specifics of polity and governance and *more with the incarnation of the church into popular culture*" (Nathan O. Hatch, *The Democratization of American Christianity* [New Haven, CT: Yale University Press, 1989], 9).

71. Thomas Jefferson, "To Charles Thomson," January 11, 1808, in *The Writings of Thomas Jefferson*, vol. 9, 1807–1815, ed. Paul Leicester Ford (New York: G. P. Putnam's Sons, 1898), 173, emphasis added.

72. Paul Gutjahr, *An American Bible: A History of the Good Book in the United States, 1777–1880* (Stanford, CA: Stanford University Press, 1999), 6.

73. Gutjahr, *American Bible*, 191, 193.
74. According to Noll, "Only 6% [of these new editions] were Catholic translations. . . . The rest represented unsuccessful efforts by Protestants to improve upon the King James Version." Noll's assumption of the cultural insignificance of these volumes is reinforced by his evaluative characterization of them as failed attempts at improving the King James Version (Mark A. Noll, *America's God: From Jonathan Edwards to Abraham Lincoln* [New York: Oxford University Press, 2002], 372).
75. As literary historian Paul Gutjahr somewhat playfully observes, "Scholars have paid stunningly little attention to 'the book' when considering 'the Book' " (Gutjahr, *American Bible*, 3). Compared to the King James Version, revised Bibles occupied a relatively modest portion of the market, but when we are talking about the bestselling book of the nineteenth century, 10 percent is not an insignificant number of volumes. The percentage of volumes published, moreover, is an imperfect barometer of cultural importance.
76. Gutjahr, *American Bible*, 4.
77. Noll, "Bible and Slavery," 44, 45.
78. The arguments advanced in *The City of God* attempt to explain the sacking of Rome and the apparent success of the "enemies of God." Despite Augustine's insistence on the distinct nature of the earthly and heavenly city, like later proslavery proponents, he is still quick to equate the condition of enslavement with spiritual fallenness. Recalling Galatians in his discussion of the subordination of Ishmael to his half-brother Isaac, Augustine explains, "The slave-woman's son was born in the course of nature, the free woman's son as a result of promise. . . . 'The son of the slave shall not be joint-heir with the son of the free woman.' . . . *Sarah, the free woman, stood for the free city, which the shadow, Hagar, for her part served to point in another way*" (Augustine, *City of God*, 597–598, emphasis added). When it comes to actual captives, Augustine misses the potentially revolutionary implications of his larger argument. For a description of the circumstances in which Augustine wrote *The City of God*, see the preface by G. R. Evans. "Introduction" to *The City of God*, esp. ix, xiv.
79. "The Bible, Our True Magna Charta," in *The Bible and Its People for 1851: A Growing Manual of Principles and Investigation, for Doubters, Enquirers, and Intelligent Believers* (London: Ward, 1851), 1:146, 151.
80. As a result of these tensions, the higher law traditions of reforms are uniquely totalizing in their claims. As Wai Chee Dimock insightfully observes in a critique of the "adversarial grammar" of "natural and immanent" rights, this "adversarial grammar . . . can resolve conflict only by a verdict of 'total justice,' only be resolving the world into a residueless language: a syntax of uncompromising and all-liquidating absolutes" (Wai Chee Dimock, *Residues of Justice: Literature, Law, and Philosophy* [Los Angeles: University of California Press, 1996], 190).
81. Scottish common sense philosophy promised "a touch of the real," as John Lardas Modern evocatively observes in his discussion of the "metaphysics of secularism" (John Lardas Modern, *Secularism in Antebellum America* [Chicago: University of Chicago Press, 2011], 24). Modern's definition of secu-

larism as "that which conditioned not only particular understandings of the religious but also the environment in which these understandings became matters of common sense" is capacious enough to include the expressly theological common sense I discuss here (Modern, *Secularism*, 7). However, the explicitly theological nature of Walker's polemic bears special emphasis because it highlights Walker's epistemic departure from the iconic form of political common sense associated with reflexively secular writers like Thomas Paine, who leveraged rationalism as a guarantor of truth—and the new kinds of faith that circulated around this ostensibly universal epistemic ideal.

82. David Walker, *Appeal to the Coloured Citizens of the World,* ed. Peter Hinks (University Park: Pennsylvania State University Press, 2003), 78. Unless otherwise indicated, this is the version of *Appeal* used throughout.

83. For an excellent discussion of the politically charged typography of Walker's *Appeal,* see Marcy Y. Dinius's "'Look!! Look!! at This!!!!' The Radical Typography of David Walker's *Appeal,*" *PMLA* 126, no. 1 (2011): 55–72.

84. Walker, *Appeal,* 74.

85. Walker, *Appeal,* 78–79.

86. Walker, *Appeal,* 22.

87. For a nuanced account of the legal ramifications of Walker's *Appeal* in the plantation South, see Edlie Wong's discussion of David Walker in relation to the cosmopolitanism of free black sailors—whose movements were increasingly restricted in the anxious years that followed the insurrectionary scares of Denmark Vesey and Nat Turner (Edlie Wong, *Neither Fugitive nor Free: Atlantic Slavery, Freedom Suits, and the Legal Culture of Travel* [New York: New York University Press, 2009], esp. 235–238).

88. Walker, *Appeal,* 2, emphasis added.

89. Brooks's essay extends and rethinks Michael Warner's theorization of counterpublics in order to attend to the special challenges and forms of collectivity developed in early African American print culture (Michael Warner, *Publics and Counterpublics* [New York: Zone Books, 2002]). Brooks's focus is on the late eighteenth century, but it is helpful for understanding Walker's slightly later strategies in *Appeal* (Joanna Brooks, "The Early American Public Sphere and the Emergence of a Black Print Counterpublic," *William and Mary Quarterly* 62, no. 1 [January 2005]: 67–92, esp. 73).

90. Brooks, "Black Print Counterpublic," 82.

91. As Robert Levine observes in his productively speculative account of Walker's possible indebtedness to Vesey, "The published version of the [Vesey] trial transcript itself, ironically enough, provided Walker and other African Americans with a model of resistance in which black revolutionism and community were conceptualized both within and beyond the U.S. nation" (Robert S. Levine, *Dislocating Race and Nation: Episodes in Nineteenth-Century American Literary Nationalism* [Chapel Hill: University of North Carolina Press, 2008], 73). For my take on the complex historiographical questions surrounding the Denmark Vesey conspiracy, see Carrie Hyde, "Novelistic Evidence: Denmark Vesey and Possibilistic History," *American Literary History* 27, no. 1 (Spring 2015): 26–55. Although Christian theology is central in the extant records of the

Vesey conspiracy, the court's special preoccupation with Gullah Jack also suggests the additional threat associated with religious practices related to African theologies and conjuring.

92. This question and anxiety, as I discuss toward the end of this chapter, is by no means unique to scholarship. It is one with which influential nineteenth-century abolitionists like Martin Delany and Frederick Douglass also struggled.

93. This letter is reprinted in Hink's excellent edition (Walker, *Appeal,* 98).

94. See the letter from James F. McKee, magistrate of police in Wilmington, North Carolina, to the North Carolina governor John Owen, which discusses jailing the agent who distributed Walker's "seditious book" (reprinted in Walker, *Appeal,* 105).

95. Walker, *Appeal,* 26, 5.

96. Reprinted in Walker, *Appeal,* 107.

97. Jane P. Tompkins, *Sensational Designs: The Cultural Work of American Fiction, 1790–1860* (New York: Oxford University Press, 1985), 132.

98. Christianity authorized reform, but it did so within an extended theological timeframe and in terms deeply ambivalent about the significance of the material circumstances of lived experience.

99. In Harry Stout's succinct formulation of the Civil War's importance as a key turning point in secularization, he characterizes the war as "the birthing of a fully functioning, truly national, *American* civil religion" (Harry S. Stout, *Upon the Altar of the Nation: A Moral History of the American Civil War* [New York: Viking, 2006], xvii).

100. Beecher clearly communicated his religious zeal as effectively at home as he did from the pulpit. Stowe's several brothers went on to become men of the cloth, and Stowe followed her calling with the pen.

101. R. C. De Prospo, "Afterword/Afterward: Auntie Harriet and Uncle Ike—Prophesying a Final Stowe Debate," in *The Stowe Debate: Rhetorical Strategies in Uncle Tom's Cabin,* ed. Mason Lowance, Ellen Westbrook, and R. C. De Prospo (Amherst: University of Massachusetts Press, 1994), 289, 3.

102. Susan Ryan, "Charity Begins at Home: Stowe's Antislavery Novels and the Forms of Benevolent Citizenship," *American Literature* 72, no. 4 (December 2000): 751–782, esp. 751. Ryan's discussion of what she calls "benevolent citizenship—a way of thinking about national membership and national character through the paradigm of doing good"—is nuanced (Ryan, "Charity," 752). However, as with many other excellent readings of Stowe, her emphasis on the domestic familiarity of Stowe's politics eclipses what I speak of later in this chapter as the alienating effects of what we might usefully think of as a "theological uncanny."

103. James Baldwin, "Everybody's Protest Novel," in *Notes of a Native Son* (Boston: Beacon Press, 1984), 18.

104. In Vernon Parrington's *Main Currents in American Thought* (1927), one of the earliest scholarly treatments of *Dred,* he suggests that if *Dred* is "a weaker story" than *Uncle Tom's Cabin,* it is also "a better sociological study" (Vernon Louis Parrington, "Harriet Beecher Stowe: Daughter of Puritanism," in *The*

*Romantic Revolution in America, 1800–1860*, vol. 2 of *Main Currents in American Thought*, ed. Bruce Brown [New Brunswick, NJ: Transaction Publishers, 2012], 377). Parrington's characterization of *Dred* as a "weaker story" than *Uncle Tom's Cabin* resonates with frustration voiced in early reviews of *Dred* (which I discuss later in the chapter). More to my purposes, I agree with Parrington's emphasis on its special sociological insights, which are especially clear in *Dred*'s more complex treatment of Christian abolitionism.

105. As Robert Levine observes, Stowe's incorporation of an icon of black abolitionist resistance makes it possible to see *Dred* "as an African American-inspired revision of *Uncle Tom's Cabin*" (Robert S. Levine, "Heap of Witness: The African American Presence in Stowe's *Dred*," in *Martin Delany, Frederick Douglass, and the Politics of Representative Identity* [Chapel Hill: University of North Carolina Press, 1997], 170).

106. In Caleb Smith's account of the Nat Turner rebellion and the broader exhortatory tradition of national sin and condemnation in which it and *Dred* both participate, he rightly underlines the truly "remarkable" and consequential "difference between Dred's dark prophesies and Uncle Tom's modest entreaties" (Caleb Smith, *The Oracle and the Curse: A Poetics of Justice from the Revolution to the Civil War* [Cambridge, MA: Harvard University Press, 2013], 151–152).

107. According to Lisa Whitney, "Stowe sets up a tension in the novel, which is never resolved, between a feminine New Testament vision of meekness, submission, and forgiveness and a masculine Old Testament vision of power, self-assertion, and retribution" (Lisa Whitney, "In the Shadow of Uncle Tom's Cabin: Stowe's Vision of Slavery from the Great Dismal Swamp," *New England Quarterly* 66, no. 4 [1993]: 552–569, esp. 567). The presumed coherence of this biblical tension (and of its personification in Milly and Dred) has made character analysis appear as the decisive key to the novel's politics. Thus, countering an earlier critique of *Dred*, Robert Levine stresses that "Dred's desire to 'smite' . . . along with his claims to leadership, retain a privileged place in [*Dred*] not even to be annulled by Milly's Christlike insistence on patience" (Levine, "Heap of Witness, 109). Lynn Sadler and Theodore Hovet also discuss the characters as personifications of the New and Old Testament, but Hovet locates this tension between Dred and Nina, rather than Milly (Lynn Veach Sadler, "The Samson Figure in Milton's *Samson Agonistes* and Stowe's *Dred*," *New England Quarterly* 56, no. 3 [1983]: 440–448; Theodore R. Hovet, *The Master Narrative: Harriet Beecher Stowe's Subversive Story of Master and Slave in Uncle Tom's Cabin and Dred* [Lanham, MD: University Press of America, 1989], esp. 46–48). Justine Murison's treatment of Milly is a notable exception to this prevalent reading of her similarity to Uncle Tom. Sojourner Truth, Murison convincingly suggests, may have been a "source" for Stowe's portrait of Milly (Justine Murison, *The Politics of Anxiety in Nineteenth-Century American Literature* [New York: Cambridge University Press, 2011], 107–135, esp. 123–124).

108. Harriet Beecher Stowe, *Dred: A Tale of the Great Dismal Swamp,* ed. Robert S. Levine (Chapel Hill: University of North Carolina Press, 2000), 460. Hereafter cited parenthetically as *D.*

109. "Milly had drawn herself up, in the vehemence of her narration, and sat leaning forward, her black eyes dilated, her strong arms clenched before her, and her powerful frame expanding and working with the violence of her emotion. She might have looked, to one with mythological associations, like the figure of a black marble Nemesis in a trance of wrath" (Stowe, *D,* 181). This trance, as Murison observes, positions Milly as a "prophetess" in her own right (Murison, *Politics of Anxiety,* 124).

110. The word "dreadful," and to a lesser extent "dread," appear with noticeable frequency in the novel. As Clare Cotugno observes, "True to its title, *Dred* offers a grim message to its readers; well before the novel's end the characters Dred and Nina are dead, and by the end of the novel, all the remaining noble black and white characters have fled to the North, where they can at least lead productive and progressive lives" (Clare Cotugno, "Stowe, Eliot, and the Reform Aesthetic," in *Transatlantic Stowe: Harriet Beecher Stowe and European Culture,* ed. Denise Kohn, Sarah Meer, and Emily Todd [Iowa City: University of Iowa Press, 2006]: 111–130). For more on Stowe's original title and the conditions in which she changed it, see Noel B. Gerson, *Harriet Beecher Stowe: A Biography* (New York: Praeger, 1976), 105–106.

111. In the postscript to this letter, Stowe herself remarked on the popular appeal of such a title, noting, "As things now are, the very title will sell thousands of copies. Dred is in reality the hero of the book, the Dismal Swamp the theater" (quoted in Gerson, *Harriet Beecher Stowe,* 105).

112. *Dred*'s insurrectionary theological force, it might be said, was doomed to come to naught as soon as it was renamed in the enervated idiom of the law: Dred. Stowe could not have predicted the precise outcome of the *Dred Scott* case, but as her abolitionist novels make clear she was deeply skeptical about the morality of the law and its efficacy in addressing racial injustice.

113. Samuel Otter argues, "Unlike the self-indulgent, superstitious fear of damnation that Baldwin sees in the earlier book, the 'theological terror' in *Dred* is moored in the histories of slavery and revolution" (Samuel Otter, "Stowe and Race," in *The Cambridge Companion to Harriet Beecher Stowe,* ed. Cindy Weinstein [New York: Cambridge University Press], 35). In Cynthia Hamilton's words, "a terror of damnation and horror of blackness . . . stalks the white community in the form of Dred's unrealized apocalyptic potential." According to Hamilton, "Stowe pulls back in horror from a vision of black retributive justice and insurgency. For all his charisma, intelligence, strength, and righteousness, Stowe cannot fully recognize the Promethean potential of her black hero" (Cynthia S. Hamilton, "'Dred': Intemperate Slavery," *Journal of American Studies* 34, no. 2 [2000]: 257–277, esp. 277).

114. Jacob Stratman, "Harriet Beecher Stowe's Preachers of the Swamp: Dred and the Jeremiad," *Christianity and Literature* 57, no. 3 (2008): 379–400, 380.

115. Michael Johnson's influential reinterpretation of the Vesey conspiracy in *The William and Mary Quarterly* in 2001 helped bring this skeptical account of

the Vesey affair into historiographical prominence (Michael P. Johnson, "Denmark Vesey and His Co-Conspirators," *William and Mary Quarterly* 58, no. 4 [2001]: 915–976).

116. See Hyde, "Novelistic Evidence."

117. As Robert Levine suggests in a similar spirit, it is possible to understand *Dred*'s abortive revolutionary plot as a reflection on the many obstacles that limited the number of successful revolutions. "What prevents Dred from putting his desires into action, in addition to his apprehension of God's silence at this particular moment, is what prevented other slaves from leading successful rebellions: the state's brutal legal and policing authority" (Levine, "Heap of Witness," 170).

118. Harriet Beecher Stowe, "Dred: A Tale of the Great Dismal Swamp," *Christian Examiner and Religious Miscellany*, November 1856, 60, 3. *American Periodical Series Online.*

119. Reflecting on the tragic character of *Dred,* Lawrence Buell argues, "The momentum of Stowe's work from *Uncle Tom's Cabin* to *Dred* suggests that she came increasingly to sense that the only legitimate path for a grand national fiction in the age of slavery had to be tragic rather than comic" (Lawrence Buell, "Harriet Beecher Stowe and the Dream of the Great American Novel," in *The Cambridge Companion to Harriet Beecher Stowe,* ed. Cindy Weinstein [New York: Cambridge University Press, 2004], 190–202, esp. 200). In a subjunctive formulation of this claim, Mason Lowance observes, "Stowe's Millennial Vision of America's decline is staged against the backdrop of America's potential greatness, so that throughout there is a tension between what *is* and what *ought to be*" (Mason I. Lowance Jr., "Biblical Typology and the Allegorical Mode: The Prophetic Strain," in *The Stowe Debate: Rhetorical Strategies in Uncle Tom's Cabin* [Amherst: University of Massachusetts, 1994], 159–184, esp. 159).

120. For a detailed account of the original source of this remark and its incorporation into subsequent editions of *Uncle Tom's Cabin,* see Claire Parfait, *The Publishing History of Uncle Tom's Cabin, 1852–2002* (Burlington, VT: Ashgate, 2007), 178.

121. Edward declares that he has caught glimpses of the "deeper part" of her nature and believes that he is "the only person in the world that ever touched it at all" (*D,* 20–21). Edward's double function as lover/minister is explicated in the analogy he draws between his infatuation and that of a local pastor (*D,* 20).

122. As Deak Nabers observes, "If *Dred* repeatedly reminds us that God alone will not solve the problems of slavery, however, it never quite specifies what will" (Deak Nabers, "The Problem of Revolution in the Age of Slavery: 'Clotel,' Fiction, and the Government of Man," *Representations,* no. 91 [2005]: 84–108, esp. 85).

123. For discussions of the novel's engagement with specific legal cases, see Jeffory A. Clymer, "Family Money: Race and Economic Rights in Antebellum US Law and Fiction," *American Literary History* 21, no. 2 (2009): 211–238; Laura H. Korobkin, "Appropriating Law in Harriet Beecher Stowe's *Dred,*" *Nineteenth-Century Literature* 62, no. 3 (2007): 380–406; and Gregg Crane, "Stowe and

the Law," in *The Cambridge Companion to Harriet Beecher Stowe,* ed. Cindy Weinstein (New York: Cambridge University Press, 2004), 154–170. Brook Thomas also briefly discusses *Dred*'s debt to *State v. Mann* (1830) in *Cross Examinations of Law and Literature* (New York: Cambridge University Press, 1987), 133–135.

124. The review originally appeared in 1856. George Eliot, "Review of Dred: A Tale of the Great Dismal Swamp," *Westminster Review,* 1856; reprinted in *Critical Essays on Harriet Beecher Stowe,* ed. Elizabeth Ammons (Boston: G. K. Hall, 1980), 44.

125. Jeannine Marie DeLombard, "Representing the Slave: White Advocacy and Black Testimony in Harriet Beecher Stowe's 'Dred,' " *New England Quarterly* 75, no. 1 (2002): 80–106.

126. The scene of Dickson's lynching—which as Stowe notes in the appendix draws on material from *A Key to Uncle Tom's Cabin* (*D,* 593)—appears to be a composite of accounts of two separate lynchings. Stowe lifts some of the dialogue used at the opening of the encounter from an account of the lynching of Reverend Jesse McBridge, but the whipping itself is taken from an article on John Cornutt who, like Dickson, "refused to renounce his abolition sentiments" and was subsequently "stripped, tied to a tree, and whipped" (Harriet Beecher Stowe, *A Key to Uncle Tom's Cabin: Presenting the Original Facts and Documents upon Which the Story Is Founded. Together with Corroborative Statements Verifying the Truth of the Work* [Cleveland: John P. Jewett, 1853], 189–190, 191–192). As several critics remark, *A Key to Uncle Tom's Cabin* is as much a "key" to *Dred* as to her previous novel (Judie Newman and Karen L. Kilcup, "Was Tom White? Stowe's *Dred* and Twain's *Pudd'nhead Wilson,*" in *Soft Canons: American Women Writers and Masculine Tradition,* edited by Karen L. Kilcup [Iowa City: University of Iowa Press, 1999], 67–81, esp. 70; Samuel Otter, "Stowe and Race," in *The Cambridge Companion to Harriet Beecher Stowe,* ed. Cindy Weinstein [New York: Cambridge University Press, 2004], 15–38, esp. 29).

127. As John Carlos Rowe remarks in a similar spirit, Stowe "levels a devastating critique at the pedantic sophistry and internal cavils of nineteenth-century Christianity, attributing the inaction of the Church to personalities like Shubael Packthread and Aunt Nesbit who typify the very sins they are so intent upon condemning." Rowe argues, "In the place of the hypocritical and powerless white Christianity, Stowe invokes the millenarian rhetoric and political activism of the African American Church as a potential resource for renewing religious credibility in the U.S." (John Carlos Rowe, "Stowe's Rainbow Sign: Violence and Community in *Dred: A Tale of the Great Dismal Swamp* (1856)," *Arizona Quarterly* 58, no. 1 [2002]: 37–55). This opposition, nonetheless, is only provisional in the novel. Dred's millenarian prophecy is never enacted and, in fact, typifies the type of inaction implicit in Christian expectation. As Martha Schoolman notes, Dred himself "embodies a confrontation of prophetic Christianity with the pragmatics of organized religion" (Martha Schoolman, "White Flight: Maroon Communities and the Geography of Antislavery in Higginson and Stowe," in *American Literary Geographies: Spatial*

*Practice and Cultural Production, 1500–1900,* ed. Martin Brückner and Hsuan Hsu [Newark: University of Delaware Press, 2007], 259–278).

128. In *Uncle Tom's Cabin,* as George Fredrickson remarks, "women and negroes are almost interchangeable in their natural virtues"—virtues that find their superlative expression in the art of dying" (George Fredrickson, *The Black Image in the White Mind: The Debate on Afro-American Character and Destiny, 1817–1914* [New York: Harper and Row, 1971], 113).

129. Robert Perceval Graves, *Our Heavenly Citizenship; or, The Heavenly Elements of Earthly Occupations: A Sermon . . .* (London: Whittaker, 1862), 7.

130. Henry Ward Beecher, *Morning and Evening Exercise: Selected from the Published and Unpublished Writings of Henry Ward Beecher,* ed. Lyman Alcott (New York: Harper and Brothers, 1871), 409, emphasis in original.

131. Graves, *Our Heavenly Citizenship,* 9, emphasis added.

132. For a treatment of "higher law" in *Dred* that is more secular in its focus, see Gregg Crane's *Race, Citizenship, and Law in American Literature* (New York: Cambridge University Press, 2002), 56–86.

133. Nina's dread of Christianity derives, in part, from her sense that faith is borne of suffering: "'I wish I were like Milly,' said Nina. 'She's a Christian, I know but she has come to it by dreadful sorrows. Sometimes I'm afraid to ask my heavenly Father to make me good, because I think it will come by dreadful trials if it does" (*D,* 261).

134. In her discussion of the "domestication of death," Douglas argues that recurring images of "saintly dead hovering around their old haunts" and "[c]hanging funerary practices" that treated the dead as if they "still 'cared,'" "rob[bed] death of its proverbial sting," presenting death as both familiar and benign. Douglas does not discuss Eva in her chapter on the domestication of death, but the narrative proceeds implicitly from her opening reading of *Uncle Tom's Cabin* (Douglas, *Feminization of American Culture,* 4).

135. Stowe, *Uncle Tom's Cabin,* 257–258.

136. Catherine Beecher and Harriet Beecher Stowe, *The American Woman's Home; or, The Principles of Domestic Science: Being a Guide to the Formation and Maintenance of Economical, Healthful, Beautiful, and Christian Homes* (New York: J. B. Ford, 1869), 18.

137. Beecher and Stowe, *American Woman's Home,* 19.

138. The convention includes a resolution, "That inasmuch as man, while claiming for himself intellectual superiority, does accord to woman moral superiority, it is pre-eminently his duty to encourage her to speak, and teach, as she has an opportunity, in all religious assemblies" ("Declaration of Sentiments and Resolutions, Seneca Falls," in *Feminism: The Essential Historical Writings,* ed. Miriam Schneir [New York: Random House, 1972], 77–82, esp. 81). Domesticity, as Gillian Brown suggests in her reading of *Uncle Tom's Cabin,* places women in contradictory positions, "regarding them simultaneously as the embodiment of transcendent principles and the primary support of the social system" (Gillian Brown, *Domestic Individualism: Imagining Self in Nineteenth-Century America* [Berkeley: University of California Press, 1990], 28). This tension, I would stress, stems from Stowe's insistent prioritization

of the heavenly home. The "family state," according to Stowe and Beecher, is the "aptest earthly illustration of the heavenly kingdom," but it is only a metaphor at that (Beecher and Stowe, *American Woman's Home,* 19).

139. After Nina's death, Clayton finds in Dickson "what he had seen in Nina—a soul swayed by attachment to an invisible person, whose power over it was the power of personal attachment, and who swayed it, not by dogmas or commands, merely, but by the force of a sympathetic emotion. Beholding, as in a glass, the divine image of his heavenly friend" (*D,* 490).

140. Although Nina is still living when Edward reaches the house, Dred's prophecy is soon fulfilled by her sudden death. It is, indeed, the only prophecy made by Dred that comes to pass in the novel.

141. Review of *Dred,* by Harriet Beecher Stowe, *Methodist Quarterly Review,* January 1857, 156. According to the *New Englander,* "after the death of Nina, the interest of the reader rapidly declines" ("Mrs. Stowe's New Novel," *New Englander,* November 1856, 515).

142. Stowe's permission is noted on the title page. John Broughman, *Dred or the Dismal Swamp: A Play in Five Acts,* French's American Drama (New York: Samuel French, 1856).

143. Broughman, *Dred: A Play,* 43.

144. Broughman, *Dred: A Play,* 35.

145. Review of *Dred, Methodist Quarterly Review,* emphasis in original.

146. The novel presumes the value of death and wonders instead at the point of life. As Dred asks of Harry, in a provocation to resistance, "'Die?—Why not die? Christ was crucified! Has everything dropped out of you, that you can't die—that you'll crawl like worms for the sake of living?'" (*D,* 341).

147. Christian estrangement, I would suggest, provided an expressly theological model for the kind of alternative humanism that literary critic Lloyd Pratt has identified as an ethical alternative to the quasi-narcissistic, hierarchical structure of sympathy. Pratt does not discuss Stowe, presumably because she is typically seen as the paragon of the model of sympathy he seeks to leave behind. See Lloyd Pratt, *The Strangers Book: The Human of African American Literature* (Philadelphia: University of Pennsylvania Press, 2016).

148. Elizabeth Stuart Phelps, *The Gates Ajar* (Boston: Fields, Osgood, 1868), 73.

149. Phelps, *Gates Ajar,* 217.

150. Phelps, *Gates Ajar,* 218.

151. Phelps, *Gates Ajar,* 220.

152. Edward Everett Hale, "The Bible and Its Revision: Three Addresses (Boston: A. Williams, 1879), 33.

153. As Cindy Weinstein argues in her discussion of *The Gates Ajar,* "Death in *Uncle Tom's Cabin* is final." Consolation literature, as she suggests, hinges on a linguistic achievement—to make the absent present (Cindy Weinstein, "Heaven's Tense: Narration in *The Gates Ajar,*" *Novel* 45, no. 1 [Spring 2012], 56–70, esp. 56–58).

154. Leslie A. Fiedler, "Home as Heaven, Home as Hell: *Uncle Tom's* Canon," in *Rewriting the Dream: Reflections on the Changing American Literary Canon,* ed. W. M. Verhoeven (Atlanta: Rodopi, 1992), 22–42.

155. Fiedler, "Home as Heaven," 27.
156. Fiedler, "Home as Heaven," 28.
157. Tiff continues to explain, in a remark at once melodramatic and emblematic, "Diss yer world is mighty well as long as it holds out; but, den, yer see, it don't last forever! Tings is passing away!" (*D, 336*).
158. Andrew P. Peabody, *Our Conversation in Heaven, Jan. 23, 1859; Being the Sunday after the Death of Mary Lyman Lothrop, Wife of the Pastor of the Church . . . Printed for Private Distribution* (Boston: John Wilson and Son, 1859), 7.
159. Martin Delany, *Blake; or, The Huts of America* (Boston: Beacon Press, 1970), 16.
160. To Delany's complaint that Stowe "*knows nothing about us,*" Douglass replied that this critique "shows us Bro. Delany knows nothing about Mrs. Stowe" (Robert S. Levine, ed., *Martin R. Delany: A Documentary Reader* [Chapel Hill: University of North Carolina Press, 2003], 224, 226). For a more extended treatment of these debates, see Robert Levine's *Martin Delany, Frederick Douglass, and the Politics of Representative Identity* (Chapel Hill: University of North Carolina Press, 1997). As Robert Levine trenchantly argues in his rehistoricization of *Uncle Tom's Cabin* through its reception in *Frederick Douglass' Paper*, "An important index of the novel's relative success or failure, particularly when it is viewed . . . in a socio-historical context should be its reception by those who had the most at stake in its reformatory social program: the free and enslaved blacks of the 1850s" (Robert Levine, "Uncle Tom's Cabin in Frederick Douglass' Paper: An Analysis of Reception," *American Literature* 64, no. 1 [March 1992]: 71–93, esp. 72).
161. Fredric Jameson, *The Political Unconscious: Narrative as a Socially Symbolic Act* (Ithaca, NY: Cornell University Press, 1981), 118.
162. Frederick Douglass, *Narrative of the Life of Frederick Douglass, an American Slave*, in *Narrative of the Life of Frederick Douglass, an American Slave, and Incidents in the Life of a Slave Girl*, ed. Kwame Anthony Appiah (New York: Modern Library, 2000), 118–119, 107.

### 3. Citizens of Nature

1. John Jay, "Number II: Concerning Dangers from Foreign Force and Influence," in *The Federalist Papers*, by James Madison, Alexander Hamilton, and John Jay (1788; reprint, New York: Penguin, 1987), 91.
2. John Jay to George Washington, July 25, 1787, in *Correspondence and Public Papers of John Jay, 1782–1793*, vol. 3, ed. Henry Johnston (New York: G. P. Putnam's Sons, 1891), 250. Jay's first contribution to *The Federalist Papers*, "Federalist No. 2," was published in October 1787.
3. Jay's claim that "this country and this people" were "made for each other" participated in a broader fantasy of the United States as a "natural nation." For an extended historical account of the role of nature in shaping the formation of the United States from 1713 to 1789, see James D. Drake, *The Nation's*

*Nature: How Continental Presumptions Gave Rise to the United States of America* (Charlottesville: University of Virginia Press, 2011). Drake discusses this passage in Federalist No. 2 as part of a longer tradition that called on "administrators to organize a commercial empire in harmony with natural geographic systems" (Drake, *Nation's Nature*, 295).

4. U.S. Constitution, article I, section 2.

5. In judge Jill Pryor's reassessment of the Natural-Born Citizen Clause, she argues that the clause needs to be understood in relation to "the naturalization powers clause of Article 1, as modified by section one of the Fourteenth Amendment" (Jill Pryor, "The Natural-Born Citizen Clause and Presidential Eligibility: An Approach for Resolving Two Hundred Years of Uncertainty," *Yale Law Journal* 97, no. 5 [April 1998]: 881–899, esp. 883).

6. James H. Kettner, *The Development of American Citizenship, 1608–1870* (Chapel Hill: University of North Carolina Press, 1978), 301. See also Devon W. Carbado, "Racial Naturalization," *American Quarterly* 57 (September 2005): 633–658, esp. 648. Article II, section 1.

7. Indigenous peoples occupied a similarly liminal juridical status in the early United States: they were neither full members of the body politic nor aliens. However, in many respects, the juridical battles surrounding indigeneity in the early United States were fundamentally different from those faced by enslaved people and married women. As with *Cherokee Nation vs. Georgia* (1831), indigenous tribes sought to establish their rights by maintaining that they were *not* natives of the United States but sovereign *foreign* nations— which were geographically surrounded by the United States but not subject to U.S. jurisdiction.

8. The territorial paradox of early U.S. citizenship, as Frederick Douglass put it in an 1853 speech, was that "[colored persons] are far less esteemed than the veriest stranger and sojourner. Aliens are we in our native land" (Frederick Douglass, "The Present Condition and Future Prospects of the Negro People," in *Frederick Douglass: Selected Speeches and Writings*, ed. Philip Sheldon Foner and Yuval Taylor [Chicago: Lawrence Hill, 1999], 251). "Alienated from all 'rights' or claims of birth," Patterson observes, a slave "ceased to belong in his own right to any legitimate social order. All slaves experienced, at the very least, a secular excommunication" (Orlando Patterson, *Slavery and Social Death: A Comparative Study* [Cambridge, MA: Harvard University Press, 1982], 5).

9. William Goodell, *National Charters: For the Millions* (New York: J. W. Alden, 1863), 50.

10. In addition to the tropic and epistemological differences between these two traditions, natural theorists could not invoke the cultural authority of a cohesive, well-known written tradition. There was no obvious canon of natural law classics—and, compared to the Bible, the readership of even "classic" works of political philosophy was relatively small. Unlike the exegetical tradition of heavenly citizenship, which found its textual grounding in the Bible, natural law writers could only speak metaphorically of a "book of nature." In a discussion of the trope of the "book of nature" in the context of children's citizenship and slavery, Courtney Weikle-Mills suggests that "the belief in the legibility of

the book of nature was perhaps one of the major influences upon political philosophy's attempt to locate the origin of society in the state of nature." My point here is that the "book of nature" is a tenuous metaphor that tries to cover over the troubling illegibility of higher law. Thus, to recast Weikle-Mills's point, I would suggest that the philosophical fascination with the state of nature was part of a broader attempt to give content to an otherwise abstract moral conceit. See the fifth chapter of Courtney Weikle-Mills's *Imaginary Citizens: Child Readers and the Limits of American Independence, 1640–1868* (Baltimore: Johns Hopkins University Press, 2012), esp. 181.

11. The ship has been integral to Atlantic studies as an icon of this extra-national circulation. Paul Gilroy's landmark study, for example, invokes the "image of the ship in motion across the spaces between Europe, America, Africa, and the Caribbean as the organizing symbol" of the "black Atlantic," because it focuses "attention on the middle passage, on the various projects for redemptive return to an African homeland" (Paul Gilroy, *The Black Atlantic: Modernity and Double Consciousness* [New York: Verso, 1993], 4). The ship is the very image of fluidity, transition, and transculturation, but the nationality of vessels was rigorously imposed and managed in the period.

12. There is not nearly as much criticism on the revolt on the *Creole* as there is on the *Amistad*, but there are a few extended discussions of it: Howard Jones, "The Peculiar Institution and National Honor: The Case of the *Creole* Slave Revolt," *Civil War History* 21, no. 1 (1975): 28–50; Edward D. Jurvey and C. Harold Hubbard, "The Creole Affair," *Journal of Negro History* 65, no. 3 (Summer 1980): 196–211; and Maggie Montesinos Sale, *The Slumbering Volcano: American Slave Ship Revolts and the Production of Rebellious Masculinity* (Durham, NC: Duke University Press, 1997), 120–145. The introduction to the new stand-alone edition of *The Heroic Slave* offers one of the most far-ranging treatments of the revolt and its literary reception, and it will, presumably, help bring further attention to the revolt and Douglass's novella alike (Robert S. Levine, John Stauffer, and John R. McKivigan, eds., "Introduction," *The Heroic Slave*, by Frederick Douglass [New Haven, CT: Yale University Press, 2015], xi–xxxvi).

13. As Daniel Webster summarily acknowledges in a letter to Lord Ashburton (that was subsequently collected and printed as a Senate document), "The facts in the particular case of the 'Creole' are controverted: positive and officious interference by the colonial authorities to set the slaves free being alleged on the one side and denied on the other" (Senate Document 1: Message from the President . . . December 7, 1842, 27th Congress, 3rd Session, 116; hereafter cited parenthetically as Doc. 1). The correspondence, protests, and individual testimonies of the white crew were collected in an earlier Senate document for the review of Congress (Senate Document 51: Message from the President . . . January 20, 1842, 27th Congress, 2nd Session, 1–46; hereafter cited as Doc. 51). There were also several insurance cases after the liberation of the slaves in Nassau.

14. Phillip Troutman describes the insurrectionists' evident knowledge of the geopolitics of slavery and freedom—and their familiarity with the compass—as a

form of "geopolitical literacy" (Phillip Troutman, "Grapevine in the Slave Market: African American Geopolitical Literacy and the 1841 *Creole* Revolt," in *The Chattel Principle: Internal Slave Trades in the Americas,* ed. Walter Johnson [New Haven, CT: Yale University Press, 2004], 203–233).

15. The second protest belabors the distinction between the nineteen active mutineers and the other slaves: "The nineteen said, all they had done was for their freedom: the others said nothing about the affair; they scarcely dared to say anything about it, they were so much afraid of the nineteen" (Doc. 51, 41). Part of the reason for this emphasis, as the subsequent insurance cases make clear, is that the master was considered "responsible for the wrong doing of his slaves" and "must bear the loss thus incurred" (Supreme Court, *E. Lockett versus the Merchants' Insurance Company. Brief of Slidell, Benjamin, and Conrad for Defendants* [New Orleans: n.p., 1842], 35).

16. Five slaves "who had hidden in the hold of the *Creole* would eventually return to the United States" (Jones, "Peculiar Institution," 32).

17. This quote comes from a summary of the parliamentary consideration of the case (and of the Earl of Aberdeen's comments in particular) printed in the Philadelphia *Niles National Register.* "The Creole Case," *Niles National Register,* March 19, 1842. The British *Anti-Slavery Reporter,* which referred to the *Creole* revolt as a "second Amistad" in an article in January, subsequently reprinted an excerpt from the chief justice's conclusion stating that "no British court could try a foreigner for an offence committed against another foreigner on the high seas, except for the crime of piracy" ("Case of the Creole," *Anti-Slavery Reporter* [January 1842], 12; "Case of the Creole," *Anti-Slavery Reporter* [August 1842], 132).

18. Capel Lofft, ed., "Somerset *against* Stewart," in *Reports of Cases Adjudged in the Court of King's Bench* (Dublin: James Moore, 1772), 20.

19. Lofft, "Somerset," 20, emphasis in original.

20. William M. Wiecek, "Somerset: Lord Mansfield and the Legitimacy of Slavery in the Anglo-American World," *University of Chicago Law Review* 42 (Autumn 1974): 86–146, esp. 87.

21. Wiecek, "Somerset," 145.

22. Wiecek, "Somerset," 118.

23. Lofft, "Somerset," 2.

24. Wiecek, "Somerset," 143. Quoted in Steven M. Wise, *Though the Heavens May Fall: The Landmark Trial That Led to the End of Human Slavery* (Cambridge, MA: Da Capo Press, 2005), 189.

25. Wise, *Though the Heavens May Fall,* 27.

26. "[O]ur mild and just constitution," Hargrave explains, "is ill adapted to the reception of arbitrary maxims and practices" (Lofft, "Somerset," 3).

27. William Cowper, *The Task: A Poem . . . A New Edition* (Philadelphia: Thomas Dobson, 1787), 30. Wise suggests that Cowper's poem may have been a response to lines published in the *Morning Chronicle* and *London Advertiser* five days after the Somerset judgment: "Tyrants, no more the servile yoke prepare, / Fore breath of Slaves too pure in British air" (Wise, *Though the Heavens May Fall,* 191).

28. Robert Phillimore, *The Case of the Creole Considered in a Second Letter to the Right Hon. Lord Ashburton* (London: J. Hatchard and Son, 1842), 12–13.

29. Even as it became clear—to the "regret" of Virginia-born President John Tyler—that the British were unwilling to "enter into a formal stipulation" for resolving the principles involved in the Creole case, Webster attempted to reach an understanding that would prevent similar jurisdictional disputes (Doc. 1, 116). Although Britain refused to include any stipulations resolving the *Creole* affair, in his response to Webster's letter, Ashburton said that he "can engage that instructions shall be given to the Governors of her majesty's colonies on the southern borders of the United States to execute their laws with careful attention to the wish of their government to maintain good neighborhood, and that there shall be no officious interference with American vessels driven by accident or by violence into those ports" (Doc. 1, 124).

30. As quoted in Jones, "Peculiar Institution," 45.

31. The full title of the treaty, now commonly referred to simply as the Webster-Ashburton Treaty, is "A Treaty to Settle and Define the Boundaries between the Territories of the United States and the Possessions of Her Britannic Majesty, in North America: For the Final Suppression of the African Slave Trade: and for the Giving Up of Criminals Fugitive from Justice, in Certain Cases" (8 Stat. 572 [August 9], 1842).

32. The *Creole* case provided a limit case for elaborating subsequent understandings of the doctrine of force majeure, which holds that vessels driven into a port by irresistible force (war, crime, or weather) are immune to foreign interference even when in extra-national waters. See, for example, Gustavus H. Robinson, *Handbook of Admiralty Law in the United States* (St. Paul: West, 1939), 358n.

33. As Webster remarks elsewhere in this letter, while a ship on the "high seas" is "regarded as part of the territory of the nation to which she belongs," ships that come within "a marine league from the shore" are generally considered to have entered territorial waters and, as such, are subject to foreign jurisdiction (Doc. 1, 117).

34. As one definition of the doctrine notes, "the term *vis major* (superior force) is used in the Civil Law in the same way that the words 'act of God' are used in the Common Law" (Joseph Angell, *A Treatise on the Law of Carriers of Goods and Passengers, by Land and by Water,* 2nd ed. [Boston: Charles C. Little and James Brown, 1851], 154).

35. As Robert Levine, John McKivigan, and John Stauffer observe in their discussion of the Southern claimants' success in claiming remuneration, Douglass "emphasized that fiction was more effective than law in representing the truth of the *Creole* affair" (Levine, McKivigan, and Stauffer, "Introduction," xxvi). *Report of Decisions of the Commission of Claims under the Convention of February 8, 1853, between the United States and Great Britain Transmitted to the Senate by the President of the United States, August 11, 1856,* ex. doc. no. 103 (Washington, DC: A. G. P. Nicholson, 1856), 52.

36. Frederick Douglass, "America's Compromise with Slavery," April 6, 1846, in *The Frederick Douglass Papers; Series One: Speeches, Debates and Interviews,*

*1841–1846,* ed. John W. Blassingame, 5 vols. (New Haven, CT: Yale University Press, 1979), 1:211–212.

37. For a discussion of the Anglophilic dimensions of abolitionism, see Elisa Tamarkin's "Black Anglophilia; or, The Sociability of Antislavery," *American Literary History* 14, no. 3 (2002): 444–478.

38. Frederick Douglass, "Meaning of July Fourth for the Negro," in *Selected Speeches,* 188–206, esp. 205.

39. Frederick Douglass, "Freedom's Battle at Christiana," in *Selected Speeches,* 179–182, esp. 182.

40. In "Slavery, the Slumbering Volcano" (1849), Douglass mentions Webster's earlier letter to Edward Everett, as well as Ashburton's role in the dispute. Douglass also mentions Webster explicitly in "American and Scottish Prejudice against the Slave: An Address Delivered in Edinburgh, Scotland, on 1 May 1846." Douglass refers to Madison in "American Prejudice against Color" (1845), "America's Compromise with Slavery" (1846), "American and Scottish Prejudice against the Slave" (1846), "The Slaves' Right to Revolt" (1848), and "Slavery, the Slumbering Volcano" (1849). See *The Frederick Douglass Papers; Series One: Speeches, Debates and Interviews, 1841–1846,* ed. John W. Blassingame, 5 vols. (New Haven, CT: Yale University Press, 1979), 1:67–69; 1:211–212; 1:245; 2:153–158. Several scholars discuss Douglass's break from Garrison in relation to Douglass's novelistic treatment of Madison Washington in *The Heroic Slave* (1853). Cynthia Hamilton, for example, argues that "'The Heroic Slave' was, in part, Douglass's response to Garrison's efforts to strangle *Frederick Douglass' Paper* financially and to silence Douglass's independent voice" (Cynthia S. Hamilton, "Models of Agency: Frederick Douglass and 'The Heroic Slave,'" *Proceedings of the American Antiquarian Society: A Journal of American History and Culture through 1876* 114, no. 1 [2004]: 87–136, esp. 113). Also see Robert Stepto, "Storytelling in Early Afro-American Fiction: Frederick Douglass' 'The Heroic Slave,'" *Georgia Review* 36, no. 2 (1982): 355–368, esp. 355–357.

41. Douglass wrote "The Heroic Slave" as his contribution to *Autographs for Freedom*—an annual published on behalf of the Rochester Ladies' Anti-Slavery Society by John P. Jewett, the publisher of *Uncle Tom's Cabin*—and reprinted the novella in parts in *Frederick Douglass' Paper,* beginning on March 4, 1853. The Rochester Ladies' Anti-Slavery Society released a second volume (through a different press) with the same title the subsequent year. Robert Stepto argues that *Autographs for Freedom* was a "fundraising mechanism for Douglass's paper" (Stepto, "Storytelling," 357). The respective chronology of the two printings, which occasionally has been reversed in criticism, is preserved in the newspaper version, which prefaces the novella's title with an attribution: "From the *Autographs for Freedom.*" An advertisement for *Autographs* appears in *Frederick Douglass' Paper* on January 21, 1853.

42. As I will discuss later, the irony in this case is produced both by the link between Britain and freedom and by the racist bias of the white seaman, Tom Grant, who hesitantly compares the *Creole* revolt to the American Revolution (Frederick Douglass, "The Heroic Slave," in *Autographs for Freedom* [1853],

Michigan Historical Reprint Series [Ann Arbor, MI: Scholarly Publishing Office, 2005], 238; hereafter cited parenthetically as "HS").

43. The Fugitive Slave Act remapped the geopolitics of freedom in national terms, but the question of whether slaves could claim freedom by virtue of travel to free territories was not itself new. For an account of the legal culture of free black travel, see Edlie Wong, *Neither Fugitive nor Free: Atlantic Slavery, Freedom Suits, and the Legal Culture of Travel* (New York: New York University Press, 2009).

44. "From the Friend of Man. Madison Washington. Another Chapter in His History," *Liberator,* June 10, 1842. In a footnote to "Slavery, the Slumbering Volcano," John Blassingame suggests that "Douglass's information concerning Madison Washington's early life may have come, in fact, from this piece in the *Liberator*" (Douglass, *Frederick Douglass Papers,* 2:154n).

45. Fittingly, the revolt is precisely "but one chapter" in Douglass's fictional history of Madison.

46. Maggie Sale, for example, argues that "Douglass disarms gendered, racialist discourses that would figure Washington as a 'black murderer' or raging savage" (Maggie Sale, "To Make the Past Useful: Frederick Douglass' Politics of Solidarity," *Arizona Quarterly: A Journal of American Literature, Culture, and Theory* 51, no. 3 [1995]: 25–60, esp. 51–52). However, the evasion of violence has led many critics to suggest that the tale is too conciliatory in its address. Richard Yarborough observes that Douglass "strips his fictional slave rebel of much of his radical, subversive force," while Ivy Wilson argues that by narrating the revolt indirectly through a white sailor, the story reproduces the authenticating logic of the white abolitionist preface (Richard Yarborough, "Race, Violence, and Manhood: The Masculine Ideal in Frederick Douglass's 'The Heroic Slave,'" in *Frederick Douglass: New Literary and Historical Essays,* ed. Eric J. Sundquist [New York: Cambridge University Press, 1991], 166–188, esp. 181; Ivy G. Wilson, "On Native Ground: Transnationalism, Frederick Douglass, and 'The Heroic Slave,'" *PMLA* 121, no. 2 [2006]: 453–468, esp. 461). Without ignoring these tensions, I argue that this indirection is not a symptomatic omission confined to the depiction of insurrectionary violence, but something that Douglass insists on self-consciously throughout "The Heroic Slave"—and that informs his conception of the project of liberty.

47. The novella opens, "The State of Virginia is famous in American annals for the multitudinous array of her statesmen and heroes. She has been dignified by some the mother of statesmen. History has not been sparing in recording their names, or in blazoning their deeds. . . . Yet not all the great ones of the Old Dominion have, by the fact of their birth-place, escaped undeserved obscurity. By some strange neglect, *one* of the truest, manliest, and bravest of her children . . . lives now only in the chattel records of his native State" ("HS," 174–175).

48. Hamilton, "Models of Agency," 130.

49. Robert Stepto, for example, writes, "'The Heroic Slave' is not an altogether extraordinary piece of work. . . . Still, after dismissing the florid soliloquies which unfortunately besmirch this and too many other anti-slavery writings, we

find that the novella is full of craft, especially of the sort which combines art-fulness with a certain fabulistic usefulness" (Stepto, "Storytelling," 360). In addition to unfavorable characterizations of the novella's style, scholarship on "The Heroic Slave" has expressed frustration with its elision of black agency (see note 46 above). Hamilton's article echoes these stylistic critiques, but unlike Stepto she is less concerned with the peculiar conceptualization of Madison as a "character" than with the tone and genre of the text. Ham-ilton thus concludes that "The Heroic Slave" "exposes the implications of the cultural politics of benevolence," but "the rhetoric of sentimental vic-timization had come to seem so 'natural' that the techniques Douglass used to expose this discourse did not register" (Hamilton, "Models of Agency," 130, 136).

50. As Stepto was the first to point out, Listwell "is indeed a 'Listwell' in that he *en-lists* as an abolitionist and does *well* by the cause—in fact he does magnificently. He is also a 'Listwell' in that he *listens* well" (Stepto, "Storytelling," 365).

51. Marianne Noble reads this gesture more affirmatively, arguing that "The He-roic Slave" "rejects the visual/corporeal model of persuasion . . . and promotes instead a complex idea of sympathy grounded in listening" (Marianne Noble, "Sympathetic Listening in Frederick Douglass's 'The Heroic Slave' and *My Bondage and My Freedom*," *Studies in American Fiction* 34, no. 1 [2006]: 53–68, esp. 59). See also John Stauffer, "Interracial Friendship and the Aesthetics of Freedom," in *Frederick Douglass and Herman Melville: Essays in Relation*, ed. Robert S. Levine and Samuel Otter (Chapel Hill: University of North Car-olina Press, 2008), 134–158.

52. The aggressive undertones of Listwell's overhearing are also suggested by the moment Listwell first hears Madison: he "*caught* the sound of a human voice" ("HS," 176, emphasis added).

53. Both Maggie Sale and Paul Jones read Douglass's prefatory remarks as acknowl-edging his limited archive (Sale, "To Make the Past Useful," 25–60, esp. 47; Paul Christian Jones, "Copying What the Master Had Written: Frederick Douglass's 'The Heroic Slave' and the Southern Historical Romance," *Southern Quarterly: A Journal of the Arts in the South* 38, no. 4 [2000], 78–92).

54. Also, if historical fidelity had been Douglass's primary concern, presumably more time would be devoted to depicting the actual revolt (which is better documented than Madison's life).

55. William L. Andrews, "The Novelization of Voice in Early African American Narrative," *PMLA* 105, no. 1 (1990): 23–34.

56. "The Hero-Mutineers," *New York Evangelist,* December 25, 1841, 206.

57. As Peter Meyers points out, Douglass's conceptualization of natural law as self-executing follows in part from his reading of George Combe, an influential Scottish phrenologist and natural law theorist (Peter C. Meyers, *Frederick Douglass: Race and the Rebirth of American Liberalism* [Lawrence: Univer-sity Press of Kansas, 2007], 15). In *Life and Times of Frederick Douglass,* Dou-glass remarks that Combe's *The Constitution of Man* "relieved my path of many shadows" (Frederick Douglass, *Life and Times of Frederick Douglass,* in *Douglass: Autobiographies* [New York: Library of America, 1994], 685).

Combe, it is worth noting, is himself attentive to the sporadic fulfillment of natural law in the political world. As he writes in a preface to *The Constitution of Man*, "The civil history of man equally proclaims the march, although often vacillating and slow, of moral and intellectual improvement" (George Combe, *The Constitution of Man Considered in Relation to External Objects*, 4th ed. [Boston: William D. Ticknor, 1835], 9–10).

58. "The noblest ministry of nature is to stand as the apparition of God," Emerson argued in this vein in *Nature* (1836) (Ralph Waldo Emerson, *Nature*, in *Essays and Poems* [New York: Library of America, 1996], 40).

59. In Emerson's 1841 speech, "The Transcendentalist," he (ambivalently) reclaimed this previously pejorative designation as a self-applied term for the movement, which initially had referred to itself as "the club of the like-minded" (Reverend James Freeman Clarke, quoted in Philip Gura's *American Transcendentalism: A History* [New York: Hill & Wang, 2007], 5).

60. Emerson, *Nature*, 9.

61. Stauffer, "Interracial Friendship," 134–135.

62. Douglas Jones gets at the Douglass–Emerson connection beautifully in a recent article that draws on Sharon Cameron's influential theorization of Emersonian impersonality (Sharon Cameron, "The Way of Life by Abandonment: Emerson's Impersonal," *Critical Inquiry* 25, no. 1 [Autumn 1991]: 1–31). Jones argues that "Douglass discerned this democratic ethic in Emerson's insistent searching and striving beyond 'the merely visible part of things,' and as he read and heard more Emerson from the late 1840s onward, he came to believe that the transcendentalist logic of essential and immutable human sameness might exert an antislavery pressure in the nation's collective consciousness that the realms of economics, law, and formal politics could not muster" (Douglas A. Jones, "Douglass' Impersonal," *ESQ* 61, no. 1 [2015]: 1–35 esp. 3–4). Jones does not discuss "The Heroic Slave," but his treatment of Douglass instructively elaborates the philosophical framework that shapes the ambivalence toward heroic individualism that I trace in this chapter and in the earlier article on which it builds (Carrie Hyde, "The Climates of Liberty: Natural Rights in the *Creole* Case and 'The Heroic Slave,'" *American Literature* 85, no. 3 [September 2013]: 475–504). For an alternate account of Douglass's complex renegotiation of a transcendentalist conception of "self," see Maurice Lee's treatment of *My Bondage and My Freedom*, which argues that Douglass "finally privileg[es] the material fact of race over transparent selfhood" (Lee, *Slavery, Philosophy, and American Literature, 1830–1860* [New York: Cambridge University Press, 2005], 113).

63. As Krista Walter observes, Grant's counterfactual example of ships floundering as a result of natural forces indicates that he can "plainly see the hand of Providence" in the revolt. Yet it is also important that Douglass conveys the providential character of the revolt without attributing (and thus restricting) this interpretation to Grant. By so doing, Douglass advances his critique as an unacknowledged contradiction inherent in the arguments that Webster and others employed to refute the authority of the slaves (Krista Walter, "Trappings of Nationalism in Frederick Douglass's *The Heroic Slave*," *African American Review* 34, no. 2 [2000]: 233–247, esp. 240).

64. The fact that Listwell allows himself to be mistaken as a slaveholder while in the South (in order to avoid disagreeable disputations with the locals) is one of several passages that emphasizes his self-interested complacency. "Having as little spirit of a martyr as Erasmus," Douglass writes, Listwell "concluded that it was wiser to trust the mercy of God for his soul than the humanity of slave-traders for his body. Bodily fear, not conscientious scruples, prevailed" ("HS," 214).

65. As Krista Walters notes, Grant functions as a "figure for the reluctant reader" (Walters, "Trappings," 239).

66. Before the actual revolt, the slaves on the *Creole* were, in fact, neither chained nor fettered.

67. The problem, as William Andrews phrases it, is the text's "rhetorical dependence on white precedents for the sanctioning of acts of black violence" (William L. Andrews, *To Tell a Free Story: The First Century of Afro-American Autobiography, 1760–1865* [Urbana: University of Illinois Press, 1988], 187). This issue is addressed in several readings, but Richard Yarborough offers the most comprehensive elaboration of this problem, observing that Douglass's "celebration of black heroism was subverted from the outset by the racist, sexist, and elitist assumptions upon which the Anglo-American male ideal was constructed" (Yarborough, "Race, Violence, and Manhood," 182).

68. That the use of retrospective narration is part of a deliberate representational strategy (and not a foregone conclusion) is further suggested by the fact that Douglass depicts the revolt more directly in earlier speeches. In "Slavery, the Slumbering Volcano," for example, Douglass remarks, "About twilight on the ninth day, Madison, it seems, reached his head above the hatchway, looked out on the swelling billows of the Atlantic, and feeling the breeze that coursed over its surface, was inspired with the spirit of freedom" (Douglass, *Frederick Douglass Papers,* 2:155).

69. Although there has been much discussion of Listwell's name, Grant's equally symbolic name has gone entirely unremarked upon by critics.

70. Criticism on "The Heroic Slave" often emphasizes that its representation of black agency is compromised by the centrality of the two white narrators, Listwell and Grant. However, little attention has been paid to the organizing displacement of Madison's agency onto nature in the novella. The one essay that examines the novella's use of natural imagery as a metaphor for natural rights—Lance Newman's "Free Soil and the Abolitionist Forests of Frederick Douglass's 'The Heroic Slave'"—does not even mention the novella's climatic representation of the *Creole* revolt. By only discussing the transcendentalist forest scenes—and not accounting for Douglass's idealization of the ocean as a site of freedom—the piece proffers a more conventional understanding of rights as founded on *landed* property. Newman argues that "the rights of life, liberty and the pursuit of happiness are meaningless without the right of access to the soil" (Lance Newman, "Free Soil and the Abolitionist Forests of Frederick Douglass's 'The Heroic Slave,'" *American Literature* 81 [March 2009]: 127–152, esp. 140).

71. Douglass, *Frederick Douglass Papers,* 2:158, emphasis added. The end of this passage evokes John Philpot Curran's famous defense of Hamilton Rowan in a 1793 trial for sedition, which Stowe uses as the epigraph to the "Liberty"

chapter in *Uncle Stowe's Cabin* (1852): "No matter with what solemnities he may have been devoted upon the altar of slavery, the moment he touches the sacred soil of Britain, the altar and the God sink together in the dust, and he *stands redeemed, regenerated, and disenthralled,* by the irresistible genius of universal emancipation" (Harriet Beecher Stowe, *Uncle Tom's Cabin; or, Life among the Lowly,* ed. Elizabeth Ammons, Norton Critical Editions [New York: W. W. Norton, 1994], 331, emphasis added).

72. Similarly, as we have seen, moral judgments are expressed indirectly in "The Heroic Slave," in the episodic character of the narrative itself, which is organized by the interruptions of a nature that is unsteady—and subject to unexpected delays and reversals.

73. William Boelhower argues that the *Creole* case and its depiction in "The Heroic Slave" have "become a flashpoint for tracing Atlantic-world trajectories" (William Boelhower, "The Rise of the New Atlantic Studies Matrix," *American Literary History* 20, no. 1 [2007]: 83–101, esp. 97). See also Ivy Wilson's reading of transnationalism in "The Heroic Slave" (Wilson, "On Native Ground"). There has been a commensurate surge of interest in the Atlantic contours of Douglass's career more generally—especially his lectures abroad and his late post as U.S. consul in Haiti. The 2009 *Cambridge Companion to Frederick Douglass,* for example, includes two pieces on the topic (Ifeoma C. K. Nwankwo, "Douglass's Black Atlantic: The Caribbean," and Paul Giles, "Douglass's Black Atlantic: Britain, Europe, Egypt," in *The Cambridge Companion to Frederick Douglass,* ed. Maurice Lee [New York: Cambridge University Press, 2009], 146–159 and 132–145). For an essay that self-consciously bridges the national and the hemispheric, see the fourth chapter of Robert Levine's *Dislocating Race and Nation: Episodes in Nineteenth-Century American Literary Nationalism* (Chapel Hill: University of North Carolina Press, 2008), 179–236.

74. Frederick Douglass, "Fighting Rebels with Only One Hand," in *The Frederick Douglass Papers; Series One: Speeches, Debates and Interviews, 1841–1846,* ed. John W. Blassingame, 5 vols. (New Haven, CT: Yale University Press, 1979), 3:478–479.

75. For these reasons, DeLombard argues that "criminal confessions provided a more viable route to autonomous liberal subjectivity than the path of virtue charted by spiritual autobiography" (Jeannine DeLombard, *In the Shadow of the Gallows: Race, Crime, and American Civic Identity* [Philadelphia: University of Pennsylvania Press, 2012], 14, 85).

76. William E. Channing, *The Duty of the Free States; or, Remarks Suggested by the Case of the Creole* (Boston: William Crosby, 1842), 28.

77. The absence of territorial boundaries at sea foregrounds the basic virtuality of the nation more generally.

78. Although some of the petitions are statewide (as in the case of Vermont), most are from local counties (in Illinois, New York, Ohio, Michigan, Pennsylvania, and Maine). See, for example, *U.S. House Journal,* 27th Congress, 2nd session, December 1841, 15, 76, 77, 79; January 7, 1842, 133, 138; April 16, 1862, 721–722.

79. After emphasizing that the British did not disregard the national laws of the United States—but only the local laws of the South—the article concludes, "How preposterous a war with Great Britain on such a question!" ("The Creole Heroes in New-York," *New York Evangelist*, April 7, 1842, 54).

80. William Jay, *The Creole Case, and Mr. Webster's Despatch; With the Comments of the N.Y. American* (New York: New York American, 1842), 11–12,

81. "The Creole Case," *Christian Reflector*, June 8, 1842.

82. "More British Outrage," *Louisiana American*, December 3, 1841, American Antiquarian Society. There are two related articles in this paper, as well as "Probability of War—the Whigs," [New Orleans] *Jeffersonian*, March 20, 1842. Sale discusses another Southern newspaper article that threatens war with Britain, noting that by representing British interference as a "new outrage," the *Mercury* sees the *Creole* as another incident of white victimization at the hands of England—and invokes "the trope of the revolutionary struggle, that is, the (property) rights for which one is willing to die" (Sale, *Slumbering Volcano*, 133).

83. Although Southern newspapers decried the British response to the revolt on the *Creole* as a form of rebellion against the United States, as Martha Schoolman points out in her brief discussion of William Ellery Channing's characterization of the *Creole* case, British authorities did not *actively* intervene on behalf of the enslaved people held on the ship. Instead, they refused to *act* on behalf of U.S. slaveholders. Thus, as Schoolman observes, the dispute was also readily figured by abolitionists as an emblematic expression of "antislavery *inaction*" (Martha Schoolman, *Abolitionist Geographies* [Minneapolis: University of Minnesota Press, 2014], 77).

84. Morgan famously argues, "To a large degree it may be said that Americans bought their independence with slave labor." Edmund S. Morgan, *American Slavery, American Freedom* (New York: W. W. Norton, 1975), 5. See also David Waldstreicher, *Slavery's Constitution: From Revolution to Ratification* (New York: Hill & Wang, 2009).

85. "Art. VIII.—Postscript to Article IV., On the Case of the Creole," *American Jurist and Law Magazine*, August 1842, 180.

86. Deak Nabers, *Victory of Law: The Fourteenth Amendment, the Civil War, and American Literature, 1852–1867* (Baltimore: Johns Hopkins University Press, 2006), 51.

87. Thomas Paine, *Rights of Man*, in *Rights of Man, Common Sense and Other Political Writings*, ed. Mark Philp (New York: Oxford University Press, 1995): 119.

88. The increasingly vitriolic tenor of proslavery arguments in the middle of the nineteenth century can itself be understood as a response to this definitional heterogeneity. The scientification of racism may have lent proslavery writers and politicians a new grammar of certitude for advancing their arguments, but it was precisely the anxious recognition of the growing institutional and regional strength of abolitionism that motivated this defensive appeal for legitimacy.

89. For excellent accounts of the antislavery origins of the Fourteenth Amendment, see William E. Nelson, *The Fourteenth Amendment: From Political Principle*

to *Judicial Doctrine* (Cambridge, MA: Harvard University Press, 1988), esp. 64–90; Michael Kent Curtis, *No State Shall Abridge: The Fourteenth Amendment and the Bill of Rights* (Durham, NC: Duke University Press, 1990); and William M. Wiecek, *The Sources of Antislavery Constitutionalism in America, 1760–1848* (Ithaca, NY: Cornell University Press, 1977).

## 4. The Elsewhere of Citizenship

1. U.S. Declaration of Independence (1776).
2. See M. H. Abrams's "Kant and the Theology of Art," *Notre Dame English Journal* 13, no. 3 (1981): 75–106, esp. 84. As Jared Hickman observes in an essay that discusses romance in terms of political theology, "The modern romance—explicitly distinguished as such by Walter Scott and others—has a secularization narrative built into its theoretical premises" (Jared Hickman, "Political Theology," in *The Routledge Companion to Literature and Religion*, ed. Mark Knight [New York: Routledge, 2016], 129).

   This chapter's reexamination of the politics of the romantic trope of literary autonomy in the early United States engages a differential conception of the literary that critics sometimes discuss in terms of deepening boundaries in the nineteenth century between the previously interconnected fields (and professions) of law and literature. In dialogue with a key passage from Brook Thomas's foundational account of law and literature, Caleb Smith argues that the "rise of a literature that could critique legal institutions . . . became possible only after 'the breakup of a configuration of law and letters' that had remained in place through the 1820s" (Caleb Smith, *The Oracle and the Curse: A Poetics of Justice from the Revolution to the Civil War* [Cambridge, MA: Harvard University Press, 2013], 29; see also Brook Thomas, *Cross-Examinations of Law and Literature: Cooper, Hawthorne, Stowe, and Melville* [New York: Cambridge University Press, 1987], esp. 16). "More and more estranged from the authority of legal institutions," Smith argues, "literary authors saw how the laws of God might summon a faction, igniting a conflict over the foundations of justice" (Smith, *Oracle*, 5). Smith's theorization of the higher law traditions of critique as a "poetics of justice" is instructive and nuanced, but this chapter seeks to rethink the politics of literature beyond the redemptive framework of justice—paying special attention to the defensive (and occasionally explicitly pejorative) figurations of politics that structured the ambivalent ideal of literary autonomy.
3. Martha C. Nussbaum, *Cultivating Humanity: A Classical Defense of Reform in Liberal Education* (Cambridge, MA: Harvard University Press, 1997), 97, 88.
4. Georg Lukács, "Realism in the Balance," in *Aesthetics and Politics,* trans. Rodney Livingstone (New York: Verso, 2007), 28–59, esp. 35, 37.
5. Frederic Jameson, *The Political Unconscious: Narrative as a Socially Symbolic Act* (Ithaca, NY: Cornell University Press, 1981), 20.
6. Jameson takes care to distinguish his methods from a positivistic historicism that presumes the existence of a pure, unmediated "Real." "History is inaccessible to

us except in textual form," Jameson acknowledges, and the "literary or aesthetic act" "draw[s] the Real into its own texture" (Jameson, *Political Unconscious,* 82, 36). These nuances are key to Jameson's lasting contribution, but his expansive theorization of history does not fully unseat the epistemological hierarchy that Lukács explicates in sharper terms.

7. Although "fictionality" is now closely associated with Catherine Gallagher's "The Rise of Fictionality," the term has been used sporadically by a number of critics since at least the 1930s. The influential defender of new criticism, René Wellek, uses the term in multiple pieces including "Style in Literature, Closing Statement," where he identifies "fictionality" as the "central quality of literature" (René Wellek, "Style in Literature, Closing Statement," in *Style in Language,* ed. Thomas A Sebeok [Cambridge, MA: Technology Press and John Wiley, 1960], 408–418, esp. 417). Gallagher uses "fictionality" more narrowly as a shorthand for the kind of "novelistic fictionality" that developed with the rise of the novel. Novelistic fictionality, for Gallagher, is characterized by an investment in "plausible stories" and "probability"—as distinguished from the non-referentiality of "romances, fables, allegories, stories, narrative poems," which Gallagher classes as "premodern genres" that cannot be distinguished from "fantasy" (Catherine Gallagher, "The Rise of Fictionality," in *The Novel,* vol. 1, edited by Franco Moretti [Princeton, NJ: Princeton University Press, 2006], 336–363, esp. 337). The distinction between premodern "fantasy" and modern "fictionality" allows Gallagher to recast her initial treatment of the emergence of a specifically "novelistic" form of fictionality as a more categorical account of the invention of fictionality—in which the novel and fictionality are all but synonymous representational regimes. This interpretative move is useful in establishing the broad strokes of a genealogy of the British novel. However, as we will see, the consignment of "romance" to the "premodern" raises special interpretative problems in the early U.S. literary tradition—both because "romance" is a common terminological touchstone for critiquing and defending fiction more broadly in the antebellum period, and because Americanist literary criticism (à la Nathaniel Hawthorne) has its own idiosyncratic terminological investment in the "romance" "novel" distinction. "Romance," as Hawthorne and many other antebellum authors used it, is not an *alternative* to fictionality (as it is for Gallagher); it is a term that calls attention to the artifice of fiction. To avoid terminological confusion with Gallagher's piece, I offer an additional term, "romantic fictionality," to describe the defensive formulations of "romance" in the nineteenth century that reclaimed the non-referential prerogatives of fictional license as a right. These transatlantic terminological distinctions are important, because as Thomas Koenigs observes, despite the flurry of new scholarship on fictionality in the British and French traditions, "the history of fictionality in early America has largely been ignored or casually dismissed" (Thomas Koenigs, "'Nothing but Fiction': *Modern Chivalry,* Fictionality, and the Political Public Sphere in the Early Republic," *Early American Literature* 50, no. 2 [2015]: 301–330, esp. 301).

8. The resistance to recognizing romantic aesthetics as something other than a tool of hegemonic coercion is even evident in the criticism that has done the

most to articulate the relationship between modern critique and aesthetics. In a typically ambivalent formulation of this problem, Terry Eagleton argues that "the aesthetic may be the language of political hegemony, and an imaginary consolation for a bourgeoisie bereft of a home but it is also, in however idealist a vein, the discourse of utopian critique of the bourgeois social order" (Terry Eagleton, "The Ideology of the Aesthetic," *Poetics Today* 9, no. 2 (1988): 327–338, esp. 337). As Caleb Smith observes in an insightful critique of the politicized wariness toward aesthetics, the assumption that "enchantment" invariably structures "submission" fails to take into account the many other power structures and possibilities it facilitates (Caleb Smith, "From the Critique of Power to the Poetics of Justice," *J19: The Journal of Nineteenth-Century Americanists* 1, no. 1 [Spring 2013]: 160–166).

9. The doctrine of literary autonomy also continued to play a prominent role in evolving theories of literary value well after the period treated in this book—most notably in the modernist ethos of art for art's sake.

10. "Echoes of the Dinner to Dr. Hale: Fact and Fiction in Historical Novels, and the Relation of Ethics to Book Making," *Critic* (January 8, 1898), 27.

11. "Aesthetic dissent," as Rowe defines it, refers to the "romantic idealist assumption that rigorous reflections on the processes of thought and representation constitutes in itself a critique of social reality and effects a transformation of the naive realism that confuses truth with social convention." Rowe is concerned as much with the limitations of aesthetic dissent as with its possibilities, at times emphasizing the "subordination" of "an aesthetic dissent" to "urgent political and social issues." His own reading, in this sense, explicitly foregrounds the hierarchical restrictions endemic to a criticism modeled on aesthetic dissent (John Carlos Rowe, *At Emerson's Tomb: The Politics of Classic American Literature* [New York: Columbia University Press, 1997], esp. 1–16).

12. Jonathan Arac, *Prose Writing, 1820–1865*, vol. 2 of *The Cambridge History of American Literature* (New York: Cambridge University Press, 1995), 693.

13. Nathaniel Hawthorne, *The Scarlet Letter,* Centenary Edition of the Works of Nathaniel Hawthorne, vol. 1 (Columbus: Ohio State University Press, 1968), 36; hereafter cited parenthetically as *SL*. Nathaniel Hawthorne, "Preface," in *The House of the Seven Gables,* Centenary Edition of the Works of Nathaniel Hawthorne, vol. 2 (Columbus: Ohio State University Press, 1971), 1; hereafter cited parenthetically as *HSG*. "Chiefly about War-Matters. By a Peaceable Man," *Atlantic Monthly,* July 1862, 43; hereafter cited parenthetically as "CWM."

14. As Sacvan Bercovitch and Myra Jehlen observe in their introduction to *Ideology and Classic American Literature*, "The paradox of an ideology that commanded transcendence seems almost to demand an ideological examination" (Sacvan Bercovitch and Myra Jehlen, eds., "Introduction: Beyond Transcendence," in *Ideology and Classic American Literature* [New York: Cambridge University Press, 1986], 14).

15. *HSG*, 1.

16. This phrasing appears in Emerson's "Montaigne; or, The Skeptic"—"The wise skeptic is a bad citizen"—but Emerson's most sustained treatment of the bad

citizenship of the transcendentalists appears in "The Transcendentalist." Ralph Waldo Emerson, "Montaigne; or, The Skeptic," in *Essays and Poems* (New York: Library of America, 1996), 702.

17. Act of July 27, 1868. 15 Stat. 223.

18. In Webster's 1828 dictionary, quoted here, this earlier use of "literature" as it broadly pertains to the field of letters is unaccompanied by the later, specialized usage of the term as an aesthetic designator of "elevated," highly stylized genres of writing ("Literature," Noah Webster's *American Dictionary of the English Language,* ed. Noah Webster, s.v. "Literature," accessed January 1, 2015, http://1828.mshaffer.com). I am intentionally using the "literary" here (a specific *theory* of what literature is and does), rather than speaking descriptively of literature as a category.

19. Within the romantic framework, art is defined by its discursive and cultural differentiation from (and resistance to) recognizable social norms.

20. The "novelty" of this new theory of art, Abrams thus concludes, "was not a novelty of content but of application" (Abrams, "Kant and the Theology of Art," 84). In New England, as Lawrence Buell and others note, Unitarianism played an especially prominent role in the conceptual development of the literary, such that "aesthetic questions and questions of religious and moral orientation became closely entwined" (Lawrence Buell, *New England Literary Culture: From Revolution through Renaissance* [New York: Cambridge University Press, 1986], 39).

21. *SL,* 44.

22. Jay Grossman situates this shift succinctly in his discussion of federalist antipathy to the "kinds of [noninstrumental] imaginative projections" that would later be "associated with much that is valuable in literature." Grossman's account, while short, is illustrative for my purposes here, because it is attentive to the "gradual" character of the reassessment of the imagination—an uneven development, which, as he suggests, prompts us to "approach Emerson and Whitman along with other writers of Matthiessen's Renaissance) from the other historical end, as it were, considering their writing as extensions of eighteenth-century textual and publishing practices rather than primary exemplars of Romantic and post-Romantic dicta" (Jay Grossman, *Reconstituting the American Renaissance: Emerson, Whitman, and the Politics of Representation* [Durham, NC: Duke University Press, 2003], esp. 28–74). In addition to being overly teleological, the narrative of fiction's reclamation in the nineteenth century tends to simplify the philosophical conceptualization of fiction in the eighteenth century. As Sarah Kareem argues, the "truism" that eighteenth-century literature is "distinguished by its realism and its air of probability" misses the period's abiding and conceptually significant investment in the "wondrous" (Sarah Kareem, *Eighteenth-Century Fiction and the Reinvention of Wonder* [Oxford: Oxford University Press, 2014], 1). For a sustained account of the rise of the literary in New England that treats its cultural and institutional catalysts at length, see Buell's *New England Literary Culture.*

23. The concern, as articulated in former Yale College president Timothy Dwight's relatively well-known critique of fiction, "Fashionable Education" (1821), is

that "after a succession of tales to which her misguided zeal leads her, [a novel reader] loses contact with reality; the world becomes to her a solitude and its inhabitants strangers, because her taste for living has become too refined, too dainty, to relish anything found in real life" (Timothy Dwight, Letter XLVII, in *Travels in New England and New York* [London: William Baynes and Son, 1823], 1:476).

24. Thomas Jefferson to Nathaniel Burwell, March 22, 1818, in *Thomas Jefferson: Writings* (New York: Library of America, 1984), 1411.

25. As Michael Davitt Bell observes, the dominant meaning of "romance" in the period was "fiction as opposed to fact, the spurious and possibly dangerous as opposed to the genuine" (Bell, *The Development of American Romance: The Sacrifice of Relation* [Chicago: University of Chicago Press, 1980], 9).

26. J. Doran, "Romance and Reality," *Gentleman's Magazine*, December 1855, 588.

27. Doran, "Romance and Reality," 589.

28. Doran, "Romance and Reality," 588.

29. For writers who embraced the romantic theory of the literary, the unmoored realm of the imagination was an idealized destination, whose allure depended on its refusal of the epistemic norms of empiricism and the market-driven currency of utility. In an exemplary formulation of this tradition in the preface to her transcendental novel, *Philothea: A Romance* (1836), Lydia Maria Child explains that "the practical tendencies of the age, and particularly of the country in which I lived, have so continually forced me into the actual, that my mind has seldom obtained freedom to rise into the ideal" (Lydia Maria Child, *Philothea: A Romance* [Boston: Otis, Broaders, 1836], vi).

30. Scholarly assessments of the political significance of the romantic aesthetic frequently pivot on interpretations of Hawthorne—whose several definitions of romance have been central to assessments of the political character of his work and of American literature more generally. "As a result of Hawthorne's status as America's first fully recognized artist of genius," Gordon Hutner observes, Hawthorne's "writing has always elicited a critical reaction that fairly well encapsulates the prevailing social tendencies and critical preoccupations" (Gordon Hutner, "Whose Hawthorne?" in *The Cambridge Companion to Nathaniel Hawthorne*, ed. Richard H. Millington [New York: Cambridge University Press, 2004], 251–265, esp. 252).

31. *HSG*, 1.

32. In Mark Rifkin's analysis of Hawthorne's preface to *The House of the Seven Gables* in *Settler Common Sense* (2014), he astutely observes that Hawthorne's "framing of 'the possible' in this preface has a "distinctly Lockean cast to it." Building on his analysis of the contested land claim that structures the plot of Hawthorne's *The House of the Seven Gables*, Rifkin reads Hawthorne's characterization of romance as an uninhabited space with "no possible owner" as an emblematic expression of settler common sense (Mark Rifkin, *Settler Common Sense: Queerness and Everyday Colonialism in the American Renaissance* [Minneapolis: University of Minnesota Press, 2014], 53). Hawthornian romance, as I argue somewhat differently here, is deeply Lockean—insofar as

it becomes a virtual space for theorizing and enacting a contractual form of political allegiance. However, as I argue in what follows, Hawthorne does not theorize romance as a *natural* "space of retreat/regeneration," as Rifkin suggests in his chapter "Romancing the State of Nature." Instead, as we will see most dramatically in Hawthorne's allegorical allegories of fantasy, Hawthorne insistently theorizes romance as an *artificial,* and even nihilistic, space—which does not offer the rejuvenation of a mythologized "nature," but instead presents readers with the *violence* of fantasy, which replaces the world with artificial and unsustainable illusions.

33. Walter Scott, "Essay on Romance," reprinted in *Essays on Chivalry, Romance, and Drama* (1824; repr., London: Frederick Warne, 1887), 65–108, esp. 65.

34. Lionel Trilling, *The Liberal Imagination: Essays on Literature and Society* (New York: Viking Press, 1950), 205–222.

35. In this scholarly tradition, "romance" serves a different heuristic function than "romantic." For, while "romantic" is often used to express the intellectual and textual concerns shared by transcendentalism and British romanticism, Trilling and Chase's formative studies established "romance" as a differential term for a distinctly America impulse. According to the nationalist account of romance, "American romance fiction . . . was an effort by a group of writers to produce what Noah Webster called 'an American tongue' " (Emily Miller Budick, *Nineteenth-Century American Romance: Genre and the Construction of Democratic Culture* [New York: Prentice Hall International, 1996], 20). The equation of romance with political evasion has proven persistent in the critical tradition that developed out of these formative readings of Hawthorne's distinction between romance and the novel. As Emily Budick observes in one of several discussions of the critical legacy of the romance thesis in the late twentieth century, the "idea developed by some of Chase's most important inheritors" is "that in evading the direct, mimetic representation of sociopolitical reality," romance "escapes direct engagement with political and ideological issues" (Emily Miller Budick, "Sacvan Bercovitch, Stanley Cavell, and the Romance Theory of American Fiction," *PMLA* 107, no. 1 [1992]: 78–91, esp. 79). Richard Poirer, *A World Elsewhere: The Place of Style in American Literature* (New York: Oxford University Press, 1966), 3.

36. As Nancy Glazner observes in her discussion of the romance novel distinction from the perspective of the realist tradition, romance was often "identified with un-American materials and techniques"—a usage that, as she stresses, departs from the way the term "has been reconstructed by most twentieth-century academic critics" (Nancy Glazner, *Reading for Realism: The History of U.S. Literary Institution* [Chapel Hill, NC: Duke University Press, 1997], 51). Charles Swann makes a similar point in an earlier discussion of *The Marble Faun,* noting, "If anything, Hawthorne implies that the natural American mode should be realism" (Charles Swann, "Hawthorne: History versus Romance," *Journal of American Studies* 7, no. 2 [August 1973]: 153–170, esp. 156).

37. Nathaniel Hawthorne, *The Marble Faun; or, The Romance of Monte Beni.* Centenary Edition of the Works of Nathaniel Hawthorne, vol. 4 (Columbus: Ohio State University Press, 1968), 3.

38. The community imagined in Hawthorne is foremost one of dislocation. As Edgar Dryden has argued, "Homelessness . . . becomes the original impulse or basic theme of Hawthornian Romance, and gives the familiar metaphor of the house of fiction a special ontological dimension" (Edgar A. Dryden, "Hawthorne's Castle in the Air: Form and Theme in *The House of the Seven Gables,*" *ELH* 38, no. 2 [1971]: 295).

39. Lauren Berlant brought new theoretical sophistication to nationalistic accounts of Hawthorne's aesthetic in *The Anatomy of National Fantasy* (1991), where she theorizes a "national symbolic" that is "not merely juridical, terrestrial (*jus soli*), genetic (*jus sanguinis*), linguistic, or experiential, but some tangled cluster of these" (Lauren Berlant, *The Anatomy of National Fantasy: Hawthorne, Utopia, and Everyday Life* [Chicago: University of Chicago Press, 1991], 4–5). However, even in its most complex articulations, the literalistic comparisons that make it possible to speak of "literary nationalism" to begin with miss just how insistently the aesthetic and national imaginaries are disarticulated in Hawthorne. For other influential nationalist readings, see Myra Jehlen, *American Incarnation: The Individual, the Nation, and the Continent* (Cambridge, MA: Harvard University Press, 1986), esp. 123–184; and Lawrence Buell, "Hawthorne and the Problem of 'American' Fiction: The Example of *The Scarlet Letter,*" in *Hawthorne and the Real: Bicentennial Essays,* ed. Millicent Bell (Columbus: Ohio State University Press, 2005), 70–87, esp. 80. In somewhat different terms, the national bent of Hawthorne criticism persists in transnational reassessments. For example, John Carlos Rowe argues that Hawthorne's "ability to 'Americanize' international and transnational" is what "makes him relevant to our present situation" (John Carlos Rowe, "Nathaniel Hawthorne and Transnationality," in *Hawthorne and the Real: Bicentennial Essays,* ed. Millicent Bell [Columbus: Ohio State University Press, 2005], 88–106, esp. 89). For other transnational readings of Hawthorne, see Frederick Newberry, *Hawthorne's Divided Loyalties: England and America in His Works* (Toronto: Fairleigh University Press, 1987); and Mark A. R. Kemp, "*The Marble Faun* and American Postcolonial Ambivalence," *Modern Fiction Studies* 43, no. 1 (1997): 209–236.

40. It is the assumption of the generic stability of romance that has allowed critics to attribute differential characteristics like American nationalism to it (traits that certainly could not be ascribed to fiction more broadly).

41. As Nina Baym emphasizes in her influential reassessment of the romance thesis, "romance" does not have the type of generic stability (even in Scott) that Hawthorne's use of the term in his prefaces seems to presuppose (Nina Baym, "Concepts of the Romance in Hawthorne's America," *Nineteenth-Century Fiction* 38 [March 1984]: 426–443). Baym is right to suggest the term's unstable link to genre, but Hawthorne's differential use of romance and the novel is not as idiosyncratic as she suggests. It had broad enough currency to be included in Noah Webster's 1828 definition of "romance": "Romance differs from the novel, as it treats of great actions and extraordinary adventures; that is, according to the Welch signification, it vaults or soars beyond the limits of fact and real life, and often of probability." (*American Dictionary of the English*

*Language,* ed. Noah Webster, s.v. "Romance," accessed January 1, 2015, web-stersdictionary1828.com). For an extensively documented (albeit polemical) account of other prominent uses of the romance/novel distinction in the nineteenth century, see G. R. Thompson and Eric Carl Link, *Neutral Ground: New Traditionalism and the American Romance Controversy* (Baton Rouge: Louisiana State University Press, 1999).

42. In his now classic essay "Romance and Real Estate," Walter Benn Michaels argues that by "figuring the romance as uncontested title and inalienable right," Hawthorne "has sought in the escape from reference" the "bare right" to property. Though this reading returns romance to recognizable terrestrial commitments, under the trope of property, I find Michaels's argument that the resistance to reference enables Hawthorne to understand romance as a right compelling. See Walter Benn Michaels, "Romance and Real Estate," in *The American Renaissance Reconsidered,* ed. Walter Benn Michaels and Donald E. Pease (Baltimore: Johns Hopkins University Press, 1985), 162.

43. Thomas Paine, *Rights of Man,* in *Rights of Man, Common Sense and Other Political Writings,* ed. Mark Philp (New York: Oxford University Press, 1998), 116.

44. As Michael Warner argues, the "abstract and universal" norms of "public discourse" are "available only to those occupants whose social role allows self-negation (that is, to persons defined by whiteness, maleness, and capital)." For Hawthorne, the abstracting logic of citizenship also means that its meaning is experientially unavailable. Michael Warner, *The Letters of the Republic: Publication and the Public Sphere in Eighteenth-Century America* (Cambridge, MA: Harvard University Press, 1990), 42.

45. The disconnection of political ideals from "reality" has come under important scrutiny. In the introduction to *Materializing Democracy,* for example, Russ Castronovo and Dana Nelson, noting the idea that the "romantic ideal of civic life" discourages "our participation in gritty dialogues about the political (pre) conditions for community," emphasize, instead, democracy as "material practice." Still, despite the inevitable limitations of civic ideals, they are an integral aspect of politics—which is, after all, a discursive practice even in its more mundane forms. Russ Castronovo and Dana Nelson, eds., "Introduction: Materializing Democracy and Other Political Fantasies," in *Materializing Democracy: Towards a Revitalized Cultural Politics* (Durham, NC: Duke University Press, 2002), 1–21. See also David Kazanjian, *The Colonizing Trick: National Culture and Imperial Citizenship in Early America,* Critical American Studies Series (Minneapolis: University of Minnesota Press, 2003).

46. As Hannah Arendt argues in her reassessment of the Burke Paine controversy in the aftermath of World War II, "From the beginning the paradox involved in the declaration of inalienable human rights was that it reckoned with an 'abstract' human being who seemed to exist nowhere." For Arendt, Burke was thus right to insist on inherited right; since we "are not born equal; we become equal as part of the group." Hannah Arendt, "Decline of Nation-State; End of Rights of Man," in *The Origins of Totalitarianism* (New York: Harcourt, 1976), 267–302.

47. Dewey argues that "born in revolt" democratic political forms "were deeply tinged by a fear of government," so the terms of its movement "had a negative

import even when they seemed to be positive" (John Dewey, *The Public and Its Problems* [Athens: Ohio University Press, 1954], 86–87).

48. Also, the liberalist tradition is too variable to consistently carry any particular political investments, apart from a general investment in the value of liberty and an anxiety about governance.

49. Edward Cahill, *Liberty of the Imagination: Aesthetic Theory, Literary Form, and Politics in the Early United States* (Philadelphia: University of Pennsylvania Press, 2012), 14.

50. Cahill argues, "Writers and critics had less need to use aesthetic theory to comprehend the problem of liberty because, in many ways, they saw liberty as less of a problem" (*Liberty of the Imagination*, 237; see also 14, 227).

51. In a limited way, my account of the political tenor of Hawthorne's defense of the extremities of fictional license echoes an aspect of Trilling's argument. For it is Hawthorne's emphasis on the renunciative dimensions of fiction that marks his vexed participation in a broader cultural dialogue about citizenship and affiliation that centered on disaffiliation. However, this impulse can only be called "national" in a collective sense. For, as becomes increasingly clear later in Hawthorne's career, disaffiliation in this period was linked to a specifically regional model of citizenship: a notion of state sovereignty brought to a head in both the nullification controversy and, later, Confederate secession. Disaffiliation, moreover, is a negative structural paradigm that does not lend itself to the traditional geographic analogies through which the political work of literature is so often conceived.

52. "As a result of Hawthorne's status as America's first fully recognized artist of genius," Gordon Hutner observes, Hawthorne's "writing has always elicited a critical reaction that fairly well encapsulates the prevailing social tendencies and critical preoccupations" (Hutner, "Whose Hawthorne?," 251–265, esp. 252).

53. "Nathaniel Hawthorne," *New Englander*, January 1847, 56.

54. Hawthorne to Longfellow, June 5, 1849, in Nathaniel Hawthorne, *The Scarlet Letter*, ed. John Stephen Martin, appendix C (New York: Broadview, 2004), 320.

55. Hawthorne to Longfellow, June 5, 1849.

56. Buell, *New England Literary Culture*, 69.

57. *SL*, 32. "The Custom-House" was not always published with *The Scarlet Letter*. The Riverside Literature series reprinted it along with "Main-Street," one of the sketches it was originally intended to accompany (Nathaniel Hawthorne, *The Custom House and Main Street*, Riverside Literature Series, vol. 138 [New York: Houghton, Mifflin, 1899]).

58. The internal textual connection to "Main Street" is preserved in the published version of "The Custom-House," which says that this "article" is "included in the present volume" (*SL*, 30).

59. Fredson Bowers, "Textual Introduction," in *SL*, xxii.

60. Sacvan Bercovitch influentially argues that the "overall tendency of [*The Scarlet Letter*] is toward evasion. Indeed, we might almost read Hester's counsel (after the letter has done its office) as a preview of Hawthorne's answer to the abolitionists" (Sacvan Bercovitch, "Hawthorne's A-Morality of Compromise,"

*Representations* 24 [Autumn 1988]: 1–27, esp. 8). In a similar vein, Jean Fagan Yellen argues, "The studied ambiguity of [Hawthorne's] works, usually understood as the result of deliberate artistic decisions, must also be considered as a strategy of avoidance and denial (Jean Fagan Yellen, "Hawthorne and the American National Sin," in *The Green American Tradition: Essays and Poems,* ed. H. Daniel Peck [Baton Rouge: Louisiana State University Press, 1980], 97).

61. Review of *The Scarlet Letter, The Salem Register,* March 21, 1850, reprinted in Benjamin Lease, "Salem vs. Hawthorne: An Early Review of the Scarlet Letter," *New England Quarterly* 44, no. 1 (March 1971), 110–117, esp. 113–117.

62. "*The Scarlet Letter:* A Romance," *Holden's Dollar Magazine* (June 1850), 337.

63. "*The Scarlet Letter:* A Romance."

64. Nissenbaum stresses that Hawthorne—far from rejoicing at his dismissal, as he suggests in "The Custom-House"—"initiated a campaign to win reinstatement" (Stephen Nissenbaum, "The Firing of Nathaniel Hawthorne," *Essex Institute Historical Collections* 114, no. 2 [1978]: 58).

65. Edward Everett to George Hillard, June 21, 1849, reprinted in "Edward Everett and Hawthorne's Removal from the Salem Custom House," ed. B. Bernard Cohen, *American Literature* 27, no. 2 (May 1955): 246–247.

66. Edward Everett to William Meredith, June 25, 1849, reprinted in "Edward Everett and Hawthorne's Removal," 248, emphasis added.

67. Michael Davitt Bell, for example, argues that "the domain of romance is a world of balance and reconciliation." Bell distinguishes Hawthornian romance, as a "fundamentally integrative mode," from the "radical lack of integration between the actual and imaginary" exemplified by James's understanding of romance. The paradigm of reconciliation is equally important to Sacvan Bercovitch's reading of *The Scarlet Letter* as "a story of socialization in which the point of socialization is not to conform, but to consent." Bercovitch's argument that *The Scarlet Letter* is complicit in the ideology of compromise (as exemplified by the 1850 Compromise Act) shows what a reconciliatory reading of Hawthorne's aesthetic looks like as a political model. Bell, *Development of American Romance,* 7–8. Sacvan Bercovitch, *The Office of "The Scarlet Letter"* (Baltimore: Johns Hopkins University Press, 1991), xiii.

68. "Neuter," the root of "neutral," signifies not one or the other. *Oxford English Dictionary Online,* s.v. "Neutral," "Neuter," accessed November 1, 2013, www .oed.com.

69. Walter Scott, "Dedicatory Epistle," in *Ivanhoe,* ed. Graham Tulloch (1819; reprint, New York: Penguin, 2000), 9.

70. The idealization of political disinterestedness, as Michael Warner has observed, made the performance of "impersonality" a governing condition for political legitimation in print (Warner, *Letters of the Republic,* 48).

71. "Thus, therefore, the floor of our familiar room has become a *neutral territory,* somewhere between the real world and fairy-land, where the Actual and Imaginary may meet, and each imbue itself with the nature of the other" (*SL,* 36, emphasis added).

72. "Art. III.—Citizenship," *Christian Examiner and Religious Miscellany* (September 1851), 51.

73. As Bryce Traister similarly emphasizes in his reading of "The Custom-House," the "concept of political neutrality defines the bureaucratic ideal" (Bryce Traister, "The Bureaucratic Origins of *The Scarlet Letter,*" *Studies in American Fiction* 29, no. 1 [Spring 2001]: 77–92, esp. 78). Traister's attention to the bureaucratic dimension of disinterestedness and neutrality—and their relevance for Hawthornian romance and transcendentalism—is instructive. However, as we will see in Hawthorne's writing during the Civil War, these disengaged affects were also closely associated with rhetorics of political disaffiliation (like secession) that were seen as anything but neutral. For another post-individualistic theorization of Hawthorne's fiction, see Stacey Margolis's analysis of a disembodied public in Hawthorne's short stories. Margolis argues that the almost contagious communication of public opinion in Hawthorne's tales can be understood in terms of a "network theory of power" (Margolis, *Fictions of Mass Democracy in Nineteenth-Century America* [New York: Cambridge University Press, 2015], 72–99).

74. This is the same passage isolated in the reviews in *The Salem Register* and *Holden's Dollar* discussed at the opening of this section. According to the headnote accompanying the selection, *The Scarlet Letter* was scheduled to be published that same week ("Advance Passages from New Books," *The Literary World*, March 16, 1850, 270).

75. Evert A. Duyckinck, [Great Feeling and Discrimination], reprinted in *The Scarlet Letter,* ed. Seymour Gross, Sculley Bradley, Richmond Croom Beatty, and E. Hudson Long (New York: Norton Critical Edition, 1988), 181.

76. As Bowers notes, "The sketch was extremely popular, as Fields knew it would be, and many readers preferred it to *The Scarlet* Letter, as the author predicted" (Bowers, "Textual Introduction," xxiii–xxiv).

77. In an instructive departure from Lauren Berlant's influential nationalist reading of "I am a citizen of somewhere else," Helen Deutch emphasizes that "the paradoxical relationship between personal depravity and its public exposure that Berlant links to claiming one's Americanness has roots elsewhere, in Hawthorne's imaginative inhabiting of [Samuel] Johnson's England" (Helen Deutch, "The Scaffold in the Market Place: Samuel Johnson, Nathaniel Hawthorne, and the Romance of Authorship," *Nineteenth-Century Literature* 68, no. 3 [December 2013]: 363–395, esp. 375). Hawthorne's imaginative link to Johnson's England, I would add, has as much to do with this desire to align himself with a certain notion of the "literary" as it does with England as such. For a transatlantic account of *The Scarlet Letter*'s exemplification of literary autonomy, see Joseph Rezek's *London and the Making of Provincial Literature.* In Rezek's discussion of this passage, he argues that "Hawthorne, like *The Scarlet Letter,* is 100 percent *New England*" (Joseph Rezek, *London and the Making of Provincial Literature: Aesthetics and the Transatlantic Book Trade, 1800–1850* [Philadelphia: University of Pennsylvania Press, 2015], 185–198, esp. 192). For the reasons elaborated throughout this account, this chapter departs from geopolitical accounts of the "elsewhere" of romance— whether they are national or regional in emphasis. However, Rezek's departure from the traditional nationalistic reading of this passage resonates with a

key dimension of Hawthorne's subsequent reimagining of the politics of romantic autonomy during the section crisis: as we will see, regional debates about state sovereignty very clearly inform Hawthorne's censorious characterization of romantic autonomy as "a kind of treason" ("CWM," 43).

78. See, for example, Douglas Anderson's comparison of "The Custom-House" to the Declaration of Independence. As Berlant and Rowe differently suggest, Hawthorne invokes these revolutionary traditions even as he deflates them by casting them in a "comic" light. Douglas Anderson, "Jefferson, Hawthorne, and 'The Custom-House,'" *Nineteenth-Century Literature* 46, no. 3 (1991): 309–329. Berlant, *Anatomy of National Fantasy*, 1–2. Rowe, "Nathaniel Hawthorne and Transnationality," 92–93. Dan McCall, *Citizens of Somewhere Else: Nathaniel Hawthorne and Henry James* (Ithaca, NY: Cornell University Press, 1999), 41.

79. See my overview of debates about expatriation in Chapter 1.

80. "[W]e are of opinion that his allegiance to that king was founded on his birth within his dominion of the province of *Massachusetts Bay;* and that upon his abdication, that allegiance accrued to the commonwealth, as his lawful successor" (*Ainslie vs. Martin*, 9 Mass. 454).

81. Henry David Thoreau, "Resistance to Civil Government," *Aesthetic Papers*, 1849, 189–211, 192.

82. Thoreau, "Resistance to Civil Government," 189–211, 192.

83. As a French citizen, Talbot averred, any collusion he engaged in with Ballard was "lawful as a stratagem of war" (*Talbot vs. Janson*, 3 U.S. 133 [1795]).

84. The Supreme Court avoided any definitive ruling on the right to expatriate, emphasizing instead the lack of definitive "evidence" that Talbot "ceased to be an American citizen" (*Talbot vs. Janson*).

85. *Talbot vs. Janson*.

86. The tropology of nativity pervades the opening pages of "The Custom-House," but the link between nativity and political allegiance is portrayed as a tragic bond that is best "severed" (*SL*, 11).

87. Brook Thomas, *Civic Myths: A Law-and-Literature Approach to Citizenship* (Chapel Hill: University of North Carolina Press, 2007), 50.

88. The reviewer argues that the French are unable to write good historical novels, because they are too domestic and so unfit for "that kind of intellectual expatriation which is so requisite to the historical novelist" (Review of *Les Rues de Paris*, ed. Louis Lurine, *Edinburgh Review,* January 1847, 74).

89. Henry James, *The American* (New York: Charles Scribner's Sons, 1907), xvii–xviii.

90. James, *The American,* xvii–xviii.

91. Henry James, as Green notes, is an exception in this respect: James legally expatriated in 1915 (Nancy L. Green, "Expatriation, Expatriates, and Expats: The American Transformation of a Concept," *American Historical Review* 114, no. 2 [April 2009]: 307–328, esp. 307).

92. In Cooper's fascinating but little-read *American Democrat* (1838), written after he had returned to the United States after several years abroad, he explains that "a long absence from home, ha[d] put the writer in the situation of a foreigner

in his own country" (James Fenimore Cooper, *The American Democrat; or, Hints on the Social and Civic Relations of the United States of America* [Cooperstown, NY: H. and E. Phinney, 1838], 5–6). Amanda Claybaugh discusses the "remarkable" number of political appointments enjoyed by prominent American writers in her discussion of Hawthorne's time as an American consul in England (Amanda Claybaugh, "The Consular Service and US Literature: Nathaniel Hawthorne Abroad," *Novel* 42, no. 2 (2009): 284–289.

93. Hawthorne's own relationship to expatriation can be discussed on two levels. On the one hand, as American consul in Liverpool (1853–1857), Hawthorne gained direct experience with the question of expatriation, in cases where he had to assess whether a claimant of the office had relinquished their native allegiance through prolonged allegiance abroad. Thus in June 1854, he decided that Captain Porter is an "Alien" (and so cannot be master of a U.S. ship) because, "although his Father may have been an American citizen, it is quite evident from the statements made to me that he was domiciled in the British provinces; and it is equally evident that Captain Porter, tho' he may have resided in the United States, never had any intention of considering himself an American Citizen." For Hawthorne here, allegiance can be voluntarily amended, but re-naturalization requires proof of "intention" (Nathaniel Hawthorne, "To Gibbs, Bright & Company," June 17, 1854, letter C49 of *The Consular Letters, 1853–1855*, Centenary Edition of the Works of Nathaniel Hawthorne, vol. 19 [Columbus: Ohio State University Press, 1988], 162). In more general terms, Hawthorne also often represents his period as American consul, and subsequent continental travels, as a period of exile (if not expatriation precisely). In a letter to Longfellow, written during his appointment as American consul, for example, Hawthorne characteristically remarks: "I am not particularly patriotic, myself;—indeed, I never considered myself at all so, at home; but, here [in England], among our ill-wishers and maligners, my heart warms a little. The English are intensely patriotic; their island being not too big to be taken bodily into each of their hearts; whereas, we must dilute and attenuate our patriotism till it becomes little better than none. We have so much country that we have really no country at all; and I feel the want of one, every day of my life" (Nathaniel Hawthorne, "To Henry Wadsworth Longfellow," October 24, 1854, letter 756 of *The Letters, 1853–1856*, Centenary Edition of the Works of Nathaniel Hawthorne, vol. 17 [Columbus: Ohio State University Press, 1987], 266).

94. "James Baldwin Breaks His Silence," *Atlas* 13 (March 1967): 47–49. Reprinted in *Conversations with James Baldwin*, ed. Fred L. Standley and Louis H. Pratt (Jackson: University Press of Mississippi, 1989), 60.

95. Nathaniel Hawthorne, "The New Adam and the New Eve," *Mosses from an Old Manse*, Centenary Edition of the Works of Nathaniel Hawthorne, vol. 10 (Columbus: Ohio State University Press, 1974), 247–267, esp. 247; hereafter cited parenthetically as "NA."

96. In "The Poet," Emerson refers to poets as "liberating gods" (Ralph Waldo Emerson, "The Poet," in *Essays and Poems* [New York: Library of America, 1996], esp. 462). Whitman develops this understanding of poetry to a degree, but he

also sees poetry as a relatively continuous *extension* of freedom. Thus, in the 1855 *Leaves of Grass,* he argues that "the rhyme and uniformity of perfect poems show the free growth of metrical laws and bud from them as unerringly and loosely as lilacs or roses on a bush" (Walt Whitman, *Leaves of Grass and Other Writings,* ed. Michael Moon [New York: Norton, 2002], 622).

97. Nathaniel Hawthorne, "The Hall of Fantasy," *Pioneer,* February 1843, 49–55, esp. 49.

98. Hawthorne, "Hall of Fantasy," 49.

99. Hawthorne, "Hall of Fantasy," 53.

100. Hawthorne, "Hall of Fantasy," 54.

101. Hawthorne, "Hall of Fantasy," 54.

102. Hawthorne, "Hall of Fantasy," 54.

103. Hawthorne, "Hall of Fantasy," 54.

104. Hawthorne, "Hall of Fantasy," 54.

105. Herman Melville, *The Confidence-Man* (New York: Norton, 1971), 158.

106. Melville, *Confidence-Man,* 157.

107. Samuel Taylor Coleridge, *Biographia Literaria,* in *The Major Works,* ed. H. J. Jackson (New York: Oxford University Press, 2008), 184.

108. The chapter follows directly on the heels of chapter 32, "Showing that the Age of Magic and Magicians Is Not Yet Over," which ends with the cosmopolitan's promise "to tell you the story of Charlemont, the gentleman-madman" (Melville, *Confidence-Man,* 157).

109. These exuberantly artificial worlds also provide a window into the artifice of the political customs that happen to prevail at any one moment in history.

110. The first volume of *Democracy in America* appeared five years before in 1835. Alexis de Tocqueville, *Democracy in America and Two Essays on America,* trans. Gerald Bevin, ed. Isaac Kramnick (New York: Penguin, 2003), 566–567.

111. This bill was part of Kentucky's attempt to establish its neutrality at the opening of the war. *Kentucky Opinions: Containing the Unreported Opinions of the Court of Appeals,* compiled by Hon. J. Morgan Chinn, vol. 1, 1864–1866 (Lexington, KY: Central Law Book Company, 1906), 105.

112. United States, *Statutes at Large, Treaties, and Proclamations of the United States of America,* vol. 12 (Boston, 1863), 589–592.

113. This objection was raised in the discussion of a provision in a bill that (like the Wade Davis Bill that Lincoln vetoed) declared a rebel officer "not to be a citizen." Following this objection, the offending line was struck from the bill, and the bill itself was subsequently passed. "To guarantee to certain States whose governments have been usurped or overthrown a republican form of government." U.S. Congress, *Congressional Globe,* 38th Congress, 2nd session, 299 (1865).

114. The problem, that is, is not sympathy in itself, but the improper extension of sympathy to politically unsanctioned rebel agents. For an excellent alternate account of "Chiefly about War-Matters" that situates the treacherous character of the piece as an effect of an excess of feeling, see Justine Murison's "Feeling out of Place: Affective History, Nathaniel Hawthorne, and the Civil

War," *ESQ* 59, no. 4 (2013): 519–551. See also Elizabeth Duquette's discussion of "Chiefly about War-Matters" in *Loyal Subjects: Bonds of Nation, Race, and Allegiance in Nineteenth-Century America* (New Brunswick, NJ: Rutgers University Press, 2010).

115. As Elizabeth Duquette observes in a discussion of allegiance that builds on "Chiefly about War-Matters," "The Civil War restructured assumptions about allegiance replacing sympathy with loyalty" (Duquette, *Loyal Subjects*, 3).

116. "The Thorn that Bears Haws," *Liberator* 32 (1862): 102. For a more extended discussion of the anger the piece incited in several contemporary reviews, see Murison's "Feeling out of Place."

117. Nathaniel Hawthorne, "To William D. Ticknor," May 17, 1862, letter 1200 of *The Letters, 1857–1864,* Centenary Edition of the Works of Nathaniel Hawthorne, vol. 13 (Columbus: Ohio State University Press, 1987), 456–457.

118. Hawthorne, "To William D. Ticknor."

119. Hawthorne, "To William D. Ticknor."

120. See "To James T. Fields," May 7, 1862, letter 1199 of *Letters, 1857–1864,* 455. Fields's letter to Hawthorne, May 21, 1862, is included in the footnote to letter 1200 of *Letters, 1857–1864,* 458n.

121. As James Bense notes, the original "humorous signal of satiric intent must have taken on a new semblance of irony for Hawthorne as he deleted" this line to revise the footnote (James Bense, "Nathaniel Hawthorne's Intention in 'Chiefly about War Matters,'" *American Literature* 61, no. 2 [1989]: 200–214).

122. Despite Bense's clarification that the footnotes were not only written by Hawthorne, but were part of his intentional scheme, in one of the only other extended treatments of "Chiefly about War-Matters," Grace Smith (on the premise of correcting Bense) perpetuates the misconception that the footnotes were added only after Fields's suggested revisions. Grace E. Smith, "'Chiefly about War Matters': Hawthorne's Swift Judgment of Lincoln," *American Transcendental Quarterly* 15, no. 2 (2001): 150–161.

123. That Hawthorne did, in fact, originally compose the essay to appear as if it had already been censored—including abrupt section breaks, ellipses, and the much debated footnotes—is manifestly clear in the manuscript.

124. Nathaniel Hawthorne, Manuscript 6249-g, Clifton Waller Barrett Library, University of Virginia.

125. Hawthorne suggests that "undoubtedly thousands of warm-hearted, sympathetic, and impulsive persons have joined the rebels, not from any zeal for their cause, but between two conflicting loyalties, they chose that which necessarily lay nearest the heart" ("CWM," 48).

126. "Nullification," in *Cyclopedia of Political Science, Political Economy, and of the Political History of the United States,* ed. John J. Lalor, vol. 2 (Chicago: Melbert B. Cary, 1883), 1051.

127. Hawthorne's own position, in his letters, is that the "Union [between North and South] is unnatural, a scheme of man, not an ordinance of God" ("To Henry A. Bright," December 17, 1860, letter 1144 of *Letters, 1857–1864,* 355). Hawthorne elaborates this sentiment most powerfully in an 1861

letter to Horatio Bridge: "For my part, I don't hope (nor, indeed, wish) to
see the Union restored as it was; amputation seems to me much the better
plan, and all we ought to fight for is, the liberty of selecting the point where
our diseased members should be lopt off. I would fight to the death for the
Northern slave-states, and let the rest go." "To Horatio Bridge," October 12,
1861, letter 1177 of *Letters, 1857–1864*, 412.

128. There is a passage in *The Ancestral Footstep* (the first draft of *The American
Claimant* manuscripts) that recalls the belated discovery of the Pyncheon
deed in *The House of the Seven Gables*. In this latter work, the American, finally face-to-face with the miniature mansion that he has been told about as
a child, opens its hidden compartment to find that all it holds has been reduced to "dust and ashes." Nathaniel Hawthorne, *The American Claimant
Manuscripts*, Centenary Edition of the Works of Nathaniel Hawthorne, vol.
12 (Columbus: Ohio State University Press, 1977), 29.

129. It is significant, in this respect, that Hilda and Kenyon never return to America within the space of the narrative. Even in the postscript, which reconnects
with the characters at a later point in time, they are still in Rome (Hawthorne, *The Marble Faun; or, The Romance of Monte Beni*. Centenary Edition of the Works of Nathaniel Hawthorne, vol. 4 [Columbus: Ohio State
University Press, 1968], 461).

130. For a more extended treatment of race and romance in Hawthorne's late
writings, see Nancy Bentley, "Slaves and Fauns: Hawthorne and the Uses of
Primitivism," *ELH* 57, no. 4 (1990): 901–937.

131. In a particularly pronounced example of this romanticization of the South (*in
its defeat*), Hawthorne compares the unexpected advance of the Union obtained by General McClellan to the defeat of a phantasmal enemy in "old
romances": "There are instances of a similar character in old romances
where great armies are long kept at bay by the arts of necromancers, who
build airy towers and battlements, and muster warriors of terrible aspect,
and thus feign a defense of seeming impregnability, until some bolder cham-
pion of the besiegers dashes forward to try to encounter with the foremost
foeman, and finds him melt away in the death-grapple." "CWM," 45.

132. Thoreau, stressing that he "plead[s] not for [John Brown's] life, but for his
character—his immortal life," continues to suggest that his death will do
more good than his life: "I almost *fear* that I may yet hear of his deliverance,
doubting if a prolonged life, if *any life*, can do as much good his death." For
Thoreau, it is only through death that Brown can become immortal. Thoreau's
emphasis on the power of failure attests to unexpected parallels between
Thoreau's and Hawthorne's representations of Brown. Henry David Thoreau,
"A Plea for Captain John Brown," in *Collected Essays and Poems* (New York:
Library of America, 2001), 416.

133. "CWM," 54.

134. Here I am departing from generic studies of romance, which read it as a mode
that subsumes losses (both psychical and political) into an ideal horizon of
promise and redemption. See Fredric Jameson, "Magical Narratives: Romance as Genre," *New Literary History* 7, no. 1 (Autumn 1975): 135–163.

The tragic element of Hawthorne's writing is not typically treated as a political paradigm, but in a broader sense, the tragic impulse in Hawthorne's writing is well known. See for example, F. O. Matthiessen's formative discussion of Hawthorne's "tragic vision" in *The American Renaissance: Art and Expression in the Age of Emerson and Whitman* (New York: Oxford University Press, 1968), 263.

135. Hawthorne, *Marble Faun,* 3.

136. In stressing the representative character of "Chiefly about War-Matters" as an articulation of Hawthorne's theory of romance, I depart from critics like Edward Wesp and Randall Fuller, who take Hawthorne's late remarks about his inability to write romance at face value. Given Hawthorne's several incomplete and fragmented manuscripts in this period, it is easy to confer special credibility on late lamentations like the one in *Our Old Home,* where Hawthorne says that the present "takes away not only my scanty faculty, but even my desire for imaginative composition, and leaves me sadly content to scatter a thousand peaceful fantasies upon the hurricane that is sweeping us all along with it, possibly, into a Limbo where our nation and its polity may be as literally the fragments of a shattered dream as my unwritten Romance" (Nathaniel Hawthorne, *The American Claimant Manuscripts,* Centenary Edition of the Works of Nathaniel Hawthorne, vol. 12 [Columbus: Ohio State University Press, 1977], 3–4). These late remarks are fascinating on a number of levels, but in the end they do not mark a fundamental departure from Hawthorne's long narrated plight as an artist whose imaginative works cannot survive contact with the ever-returning light of the present. See Randall Fuller, "Hawthorne and War," *New England Quarterly* 80, no. 4 (2007): 655–686, esp. 675; and Edward Wesp, "Beyond the Romance: The Aesthetics of 'Chiefly about War Matters,'" *Texas Studies in Literature and Language* 52, no. 4 (Winter 2010): 408–432, esp. 426.

137. George Kateb's iconic characterization of Thoreau, Emerson, and Whitman's marked ambivalence toward active citizenship might be extended to Hawthorne, albeit in a somewhat different register. "Though they are distant citizens, we may say they remain citizens. The citizenship, however, that is most congenial to them is participation by lecturing and writing" (George Kateb, "Democratic Individuality and the Claims of Politics," *Political Theory* 12, no. 3 [August 1984]: 331–360, esp. 356).

138. In light of Hawthorne's late writings, the tendency to view his aesthetic through the regional political culture of New England is simply not tenable. In a very explicit articulation of this premise, Bercovitch explains, "By 'Hawthorne's society' and 'antebellum ideology,' I mean the complex of social practices and cultural ideals that we associate with the liberal Northern United States from 1820 to the Civil War" (Bercovitch, *Office of "The Scarlet Letter,"* xiv).

139. As Carl Schmitt argues in a suggestive discussion of the strictly utopian character of the oceanic order, implicit in More's *Utopia* "and in the profound and productive formulation of the word *Utopia,* was the possibility of an enormous destruction of all orientations based on the old *nomos* of the earth. . . . Utopia

did not mean any simple and general nowhere (or erewhon), but a U-*topos*, which, by comparison even with its negation, A-*topos*, has a stronger negation in relation to *topos*" (Carl Schmitt, *The* Nomos *of the Earth in the International Law of the* Jus Publicum Europaeum, trans. G. L. Ulmen [New York: Telos Press, 2006], 178).

## 5. Stateless Fictions

1. Elizabeth Stuart Phelps, "The Man Without a Country," *Independent,* May 6, 1880, 1.
2. Hawthorne is exempt from Phelps's critique. She even contrasts James's "cosmopolitan culture" with what she characterizes as Hawthorne's "natural piety of patriotism"—a characterization of Hawthorne that would have perplexed readers familiar with his sympathetic portrait of Confederate secession in "Chiefly about War-Matters" (1862) (Phelps, "Man Without a Country," 1).
3. James wrote his classic tale of an American in Paris, *The American* (1877), while he was in Paris. For a discussion of this period of James's career, see Peter Brooks, *Henry James Goes to Paris* (Princeton, NJ: Princeton University Press, 2007), esp. 15.
4. Phelps, "Man Without a Country," 1.
5. The nation now enjoys a hegemonic institutional and political dominance that Phelps desired but had not actually experienced.
6. Woodrow Wilson, "University Training and Citizenship," *Forum,* September 1894, 107.
7. Eleanor Roosevelt, "Good Citizenship: The Purpose of Education," *Pictorial Review* 31 (April 1930): 4, 94, 97.
8. Wilson, "University Training," 107.
9. The classical association between political education and "literature"—in the earlier, more inclusive sense of the term as "learning" through an "acquaintance with letters or books"—was never particularly contested in the early United States. Even those who were openly critical of novels often recognized the civic utility of literature in this broader sense. Jefferson had himself voiced this classical understanding of literature's civic utility in an earlier letter in 1771. There, Jefferson argues that it matters little "whether the story we read be fiction or truth"; its utility hinges on its moral effects rather than its content-level veracity. "Our virtuous dispositions, and dispositions of the mind, like limbs of the body acquire strength by exercise," Jefferson observes, and when good deeds are presented to "either our sight or imagination, we are deeply impressed with its beauty and feel a strong desire in ourselves of doing charitable and grateful acts also" (Thomas Jefferson to Robert Skipwith, August 3, 1771; a digitized copy of the letter is available on the Library of Congress site: http://www.loc.gov/item/mtjbib000065/).
10. For four excellent accounts of the continued popularity of British literature and the delayed institutional development of a national literature, see Meredith

McGill, *American Literature and the Culture of Reprinting, 1834–1853* (Philadelphia: University of Pennsylvania Press, 2003); Trish Loughran, *The Republic in Print: Print Culture in the Age of U.S. Nation Building, 1770–1870* (New York: Columbia University Press, 2007); Elisa Tamarkin, *Anglophilia: Deference, Devotion, and Antebellum America* (Chicago: University of Chicago Press, 2008); and Joseph Rezek, *London and the Making of Provincial Literature Aesthetics and the Transatlantic Book Trade, 1800–1850* (Philadelphia: University of Pennsylvania Press, 2015).

11. The story's popularity in the classroom has never been matched by a comparable scholarly investment. Until quite recently, most of the writing on "The Man Without a Country" has been produced for introductions to new printings of the text. Brook Thomas's impressive chapter on "The Man Without a Country" was the first of several recent reconsiderations of Hale's important text (Brook Thomas, "'The Man Without a Country': The Patriotic Citizen, Lincoln, and Civil Liberties," in *Civic Myths: A Law-and-Literature Approach to Citizenship* [Chapel Hill: University of North Carolina Press, 2007], 55–101; hereafter abbreviated *CM* and cited parenthetically by page number). This chapter builds on an earlier treatment of Hale's story that I published in 2010 (Carrie Hyde, "Outcast Patriotism: The Dilemma of Negative Instruction in 'The Man Without a Country,'" *ELH* 77, no. 4 [2010]: 915–939). See also Jeannine DeLombard, *In the Shadow of the Gallows: Race, Crime, and American Civic Identity* (Philadelphia: University of Pennsylvania Press, 2012), 302–311; Caleb Smith, *The Oracle and the Curse: A Poetics of Justice from the Revolution to the Civil War* (Cambridge, MA: Harvard University Press, 2013), 208–211; Robert A. Ferguson, *The Trial in American Life* (Chicago: University of Chicago Press, 2007), 100–106; Colin Pearce, "The Wisdom of Exile: Edward Everett Hale's 'The Man Without a Country,'" *Interpretation* 22, no. 1 (1994): 91–109; Daniel Aaron, "'The Man Without a Country' as a Civil War Document," in *Geschichte und Gesellschaft in der amerikanischen Literatur,* ed. Karl Schubert and Ursula Müller-Richter (Heidelberg: Quelle and Meyer, 1975), 55–61; and Robert Levine, "Edward Everett Hale's and Sutton Griggs's Men Without a Country," in *Jim Crow, Literature, and the Legacy of Sutton E. Griggs,* ed. Tess Chakkalakal and Kenneth W. Warren (Athens: University of Georgia Press, 2013), 69–87. For a very early treatment, see Van Wyck Brooks, "Introduction," in *The First Book Edition of the Man Without a Country,* by Edward Everett Hale (New York: Franklin Watts, 1960), v–x.

12. Although previous editions of the story were likely used in schools, educational journals began reviewing schoolroom editions of the tale in the 1890s. See "Books Received," *School Review* (April 1893): 261–262. Also see "Advertisement 46—No Title," *Outlook,* August 19, 1893: 328.

13. "Book Table: If, Yes, and Perhaps," *The Independent . . . Devoted to the Consideration of Politics, Social and Econ. . . . ,* November 19, 1868, 6. The call for three hundred thousand more troops came on July 1, 1862, a year and a half before the publication of the story ("A Call for More Troops—Three Hundred Thousand More Men Wanted," *Philadelphia Inquirer,* July 7, 1862).

14. As Thomas observes, the tale "began to disappear from the literary canon around the time of the Vietnam War" (*CM*, 89). School editions of "The Man Without a Country" were produced and marketed until at least the late 1970s, but regular notices and order forms for the tale dropped off in 1978. After a few advertisements for its inclusion in two new media collections (Prentice Hall and *Master Story Tellers*), for example, it ceases to appear in *The English Journal*.

15. Hale distinguishes between negative and positive modes of civic instruction in a preface to "The Man Without a Country." He notes that "any lesson was well perceived by persons of conscience and patriotism, which *showed either positively or negatively* what the word 'Patriotism' means,—or what one's country is" (Edward Everett Hale, *The Man Without a Country and Its History* [Boston: J. Stilman Smith, 1897], 4, emphasis added; hereafter abbreviated *History*). "Its History" refers to Hale's most comprehensive prefatory note on "The Man Without a Country." It is one of several prefaces written after the tale's original publication in *The Atlantic Monthly*.

16. As we have seen, the extralegal traditions of citizenship all had an extraordinarily ambivalent relation to the nation-state and to the still-emergent institutional framework of juridical citizenship.

17. The romantic ideal of literature's separation from political concerns was a liability in a period of political strife. It was this volatile association of aesthetic autonomy with political defection, I argue, that subsequent writers invested in literature's utility for civic education had to address—and to reinvent as an asset.

18. Benjamin Franklin, *The Autobiography, and Other Writings* (New York: Signet Classics, 2001), 16.

19. William Gilmore Simms, *Views and Reviews in American Literature, History and Fiction* (New York: Wiley and Putnam, 1845), 49.

20. See Jeffrey Richards's discussion of the reception history and subsequent adaptation of Dunlap's *André* (Jeffrey H. Richards, ed., "André," in *Early American Drama* [New York: Penguin, 1997], 58–62; William Dunlap, *André; A Tragedy, in Five Acts,* in Richards, ed., *Early American Drama,* 58–108). For a discussion of Jared Parks's treatment of Arnold, see Brian F. Carso Jr., "*Whom Can We Trust Now?*": The Meaning of Treason in the United States, from the Revolution to the Civil War* (Boulder, CO: Lexington Books, 1991), esp. 150; George Lippard, *Washington and His Generals; or, Legends of the American Revolution* (Philadelphia: T. B. Peterson, 1847), 182–208, esp. 193. The line I quote from *Washington and His Generals* was not among the selected passages reprinted for use in recitations. The selections are included in an elocutionary series (*Brown's Popular Readings . . . for Readings and Recitations* [Chicago: A. Flanagan, 1893], 162–166). The line also appears in several editions of *The Speaker's Garland* (including Phineas Garett, ed., *The Speaker's Garland: Comprising One Hundred Choice Selections,* ed. Phineas Garett, vol. 5 [Philadelphia: Penn Publishing, 1910], 161–164). William J. Bennett, *The Moral Compass: Stories for a Life's Journey* (New York: Simon & Schuster,

1995). Lippard's sketch is listed as supplementary reading in a number of recitation books, including Caroline B. Le Row, comp., *Werner's Readings and
Recitations: America's Recitation Book,* no. 10 (New York: Edgar S. Werner,
1893), 2.

21. See, for example, William Bailey, "General Arnold," in *Records of Patriotism
and Love of Country* (Washington, DC: Drakard and Wilson, 1826), 169–
176; [Lafayette], *Stories about Arnold, the Traitor, Andre, the Spy, and
Champe, the Patriot: For the Children of the United States,* 2nd ed. (New
Haven, CT: A. H. Maltby, 1831); "The Spy and the Traitor," *Atheneum; or,
Spirit of English Magazines,* January 1833, 353; *The Cruel Boy, and Other
Pieces* (Worcester, MA: J. Grout, Jr. [1835?]), 3–6; R., "The Conspiracy,"
*Casket,* June 1840, 254; and [William C. Cutter], "Uncle Hiram's Pilgrimage,"
*Merry's Museum, Parley's Magazine, Woodworth's Cabinet, and the School-
fellow,* January 1, 1858, 174.

22. Royall Tyler, *The Algerine Captive; or, The Life and Adventures of Doctor Updike Underhill* (New York: Modern Library Classics, 2002), 124.

23. In the tradition of negative instruction, fantasies about citizenship are sustained
by the type of "negative pleasure" that Immanuel Kant associates with the sublime. The sublime, Kant stresses, "cannot be contained in any sensuous form,
but rather concerns ideas of reason, which, although no adequate presentation
of them is possible, may be aroused and called to mind by that very inadequacy
itself" (Immanuel Kant, *Critique of Judgment,* trans. James Creed Meredith
[New York: Oxford World Classics, 2008], 76).

24. Michael Warner offers the term "principle of negativity" to describe the "negation of persons in public discourse." My discussion of the negativity of citizenship, while related to this, focuses on negative modes of instruction, rather
than "tactic[s] of depersonalization" (Michael Warner, *The Letters of the Republic: Publication and the Public Sphere in Eighteenth-Century America*
[Cambridge, MA: Harvard University Press, 1990], 34–72, esp. 42–49). Also
see Lauren Berlant, *The Queen of America Goes to Washington City: Essays
on Sex and Citizenship,* Series Q (Durham, NC: Duke University Press, 1997);
and David Kazanjian, *The Colonizing Trick: National Culture and Imperial
Citizenship in Early America,* Critical American Studies Series (Minneapolis:
University of Minnesota Press, 2003), esp. 1–5.

25. I am using abstraction here in both its precise etymological sense—drawn
away (in this case from the real)—as well as to nominate the peculiar embodiment of the conceptual in literature. While anxieties about the ill effects of
reading fiction—especially so-called romances—were particularly prominent
in eighteenth-century letters, such concerns, as we saw in Chapter 4, persisted
in different forms throughout the antebellum period. Traditional enlightenment critiques of novels (as undermining the imperatives of rationality) continued to appear, often in Christian forums, but similar assumptions also
shaped the preoccupation with distinguishing between beneficial and deleterious forms of reading. See, for example, Frances Wright, "Novel Reading
Unchristian," *Christian Advocate and Journal,* January 3, 1834, 73; E. D.

Sanborn, "Article V. Moral and Literary Influence of Novels," *American Biblical Repository* (April 1843): 362; "Effect of Reading on Character," *New York Evangelist*, August 25, 1864, 6; and Lydia Maria Child, "Advice concerning Books," in *The Mother's Book* (Boston: Carther and Hendez, 1831), 86–97. As I will discuss later, defenses of novels that contend that they can educate readers in the dangers of vices, without requiring them to acquire such knowledge through infelicitous lived experiences, reinforce characterizations of the abstract nature of literature, but they also portray this quality as an advantage rather than a danger. "An Investigation of the Principal Causes which Have Led to the Condemnation of Novels," *Port Folio,* September 1820, 221.

26. Edward Everett Hale (1822–1909), the grandnephew of Revolutionary War hero Nathan Hale—who famously declared, "I only regret that I have but one life to lose for my country"—was a prolific writer. In addition to "The Man Without a Country," his most well-known writings include "My Double and How He Undid Me" (1859); "The Children of the Public" (1863); his collection of stories *If, Yes, and Perhaps* (1868), which reprints these and other stories; and his peculiar sequel to "The Man Without a Country," *Philip Nolan and His Friends* (1877). Hale married the niece of Harriet Beecher Stowe. For more on Hale's biography, see John R. Adams, *Edward Everett Hale,* Twayne's United States Authors Series (Boston: Twayne, 1977).

27. Edward Everett Hale, "The Man Without a Country," *Atlantic Monthly* (December 1863): 665–679, 666. Hereafter abbreviated "M" and cited parenthetically by page number.

28. Cutter, "Uncle Hiram's Pilgrimage," 174.

29. Nancy Isenberg uses this apt designation in her biography of Burr (Nancy Isenberg, *The Fallen Founder: The Life of Aaron Burr* [New York: Penguin, 2007]).

30. For an excellent treatment of Burr, see Isenberg, *Fallen Founder.*

31. Thomas Jefferson, "Special Message to Congress, Jan. 22, 1807," in *The Works of Thomas Jefferson,* ed. Paul Leicester Ford, vol. 9 (New York: J. P. Putnam's Sons, 1905): 14–20, http://oll.libertyfund.org/titles/806.

32. Ferguson, *Trial in American Life,* 99.

33. Hale went to great lengths to reinforce the narrative's historical premise. He spent an entire summer doing daily research at the American Antiquarian Society in preparation for the piece, pouring over the details of Aaron Burr's two voyages down the Mississippi, the proceedings of Burr's treason trial, Wilkinson's *Memoirs,* and newspapers from the period. See the preface to *History,* ix–xii. With the assistance of the staff at the American Antiquarian Society, I retraced some of Hale's initial research—using AAS's historical archival records and Hale's several accounts of his reading.

34. In an essay on the literature of conspiracy, Ursula Brumm also notes this echo with "no land" but emphasizes that Nolan's name also suggests "rejection (from Latin nolo, nolui, nolle)." See Ursula Brumm, "Consensus and Conspiracy in American Literature," *Yearbook of Research in English and American Literature* 11 (1995): 29–43, 34.

35. *The Trial of Hon. Clement L. Vallandigham, by a Military Commission . . .* (Cincinnati: Rickey and Carroll, 1863), 11, 34.

36. Despite Hale's intentions, the story did not appear until two months after the Ohio election, though it was of little consequence since Vallandigham was defeated. For a discussion of Lincoln's motivations in commuting Vallandigham's sentence from imprisonment to banishment, see James M. McPherson, "'As Commander-in-Chief I Have a Right to Take Any Measure which May Best Subdue the Enemy,'" in *This Mighty Scourge: Perspectives on the Civil War* (New York: Oxford University Press, 2007), 215–216. Hale's discussion of Vallandigham's election appears in subsequent prefaces. See Edward Everett Hale, "From the Ingham Papers," in *The Man Without a Country, and Other Tales* (Boston: Roberts Brothers, 1886), 3.

37. "The Civil War has taught its lesson so well that the average American of the year 1896 hardly understands that such a lesson was ever needed" (Edward Everett Hale, preface to *The Man Without a Country* [New York: H. M. Caldwell, 1897], iii). The prefaces vary, but in each Hale suggests that he does not expect his readers to remember Vallandigham.

38. *CM,* 89, 57.

39. Indeed, when Ingham (who is both the narrator and a character in the story) later tries to obtain Nolan's pardon, he finds "it was like getting a ghost out of prison. They pretended that there was no such man, and never was such a man. They will say so at the Department now. Perhaps they do not know. It will not be first thing in the service of which the Department appears to know nothing" ("M," 675). The government fails to properly adjudicate Nolan's punishment, not only because it does not grant a pardon seen by all immediately concerned as well deserved, but also because on an institutional level it ceases to acknowledge his very existence.

40. As Pearce notes, "The conduct of the government in his own case would appear to justify to some extent the young Nolan's initial attitude of contempt for the United States" (Pearce, "Wisdom of Exile," 92).

41. *Oxford English Dictionary Online,* s.v. "Seduction," n., accessed January 1, 2016, http://www.oed.com/viewdictionaryentry/Entry/11125.

42. Burr was a peripheral figure in sentimental writing. Leonora Sansay's epistolary novel, *Secret History; or, The Horrors of St. Domingo* (1808), for example, consists of a series of letters addressed to "Colonel Burr," who is the protagonist's intimate confidant. Sansay herself, in fact, is commonly thought to have been Burr's lover and was reputed to be a "coquette." Burr was also suspected, among others, of being the unnamed seducer of Elizabeth Whitman, whose fall and death served as the basis of *The Coquette.* For more on Sansay's reputation and relation to Burr, see Michael Drexler's introduction to Leonora Sansay, *Secret History; or, The Horrors of St. Domingo; and, Laura,* ed. Michael Drexler (Peterborough, ON: Broadview, 2007), 10–37. Though Burr was among those suspected of the seduction, Pierrepont Edwards was the primary suspect and model for Major Sanford. See Cathy Davidson, *Revolution and the Word: The Rise of the Novel in America,* expanded ed. (New York: Oxford University Press, 2004), 222.

43. Jan Ellen Lewis, "The Republican Wife: Virtue and Seduction in the Early Republic," *William and Mary Quarterly* 44 (1987): 689–721.

44. Burr accompanies Madame de Frontignac's "husband to explore the regions of the Ohio, where he had some splendid schemes of founding a state." When Madame de Frontignac realizes that Burr is *"using* [her] feelings to carry his plans," she leaves her life of cosmopolitan intrigue to stay with Mary Scudder—the devout and virtuous protagonist—in rural New England (Harriet Beecher Stowe, *The Minister's Wooing* [New York: Penguin, 1999], 225–226).

45. John Adams to William Cunningham, March 15, 1804, in *Correspondence between the Hon. John Adams, Late President of the United States, and the Late Wm. Cunningham, Esq.* (Boston: True and Greene, 1823), 19.

46. As Cathy Davidson argues, "Rowson's tale of a fifteen-year-old girl misled by a conniving French schoolmistress, seduced by a British solider, and abandoned in a strange new country, an ocean away from beloved (but perhaps paternalistic) parents" itself offers a compelling "allegory of changing political and social conditions in early America" (Cathy Davidson, "Introduction," in *Charlotte Temple*, by Susanna Rowson [New York: Oxford University Press, 1986], xi–xii).

47. As Nina Baym points out, even after the turn away from Richardsonian fiction in woman's writing, "Seduction continued to be a staple of sensational men's fiction" (Nina Baym, *Woman's Fiction: A Guide to Novels by and about Women in America, 1820–70,* 2nd ed. [Urbana: University of Illinois Press, 1993], 52).

48. The term "nostalgia" was proposed by Johannes Hoffer in 1688 (Johannes Hoffer, "Medical Dissertation on Nostalgia or Homesickness," trans. Carolyn Kiser Anspach, *Bulletin of the Institute of the History of Medicine* 2 [1934]: 376–391). Nolan's nostalgia, indeed, is shared by the sailors as well. As Ingham explains, "No mess liked to have him [Nolan] permanently, because his presence cut off all talk of home or of the prospect of return . . . cut off more than half the talk men like to have at sea" ("M," 668). Renato Rosaldo, "Imperialist Nostalgia," *Representations* 26 (1989): 108–109.

49. "The Constitution of the United States of America," in *The Federalist Papers,* ed. Isaac Kramnick (New York: Penguin, 1987), 491–508.

50. Hale's more pointed allegory of secession as a form of treachery also reflects Lincoln's redefinition of treason to include "any rebellion or insurrection against the authority of the United States" in the Second Confiscation Act, July 17, 1862.

51. Nolan's double status as villain *and* hero is particularly unstable in the scene following the judges' sentence, where the narrator explains that Nolan only denounced the United States because he was raised so much at the periphery of the States—spending half of his youth in Texas, then still Spanish territory—that the United States "was scarcely a reality." The narrator proceeds to explain, "I do not excuse Nolan; I only explain to the reader why he damned his Country, and wished he might never hear her name again" ("M," 667).

52. See Nancy Isenberg, "The 'Little Emperor': Aaron Burr, Dandyism, and the Sexual Politics of Treason," in *Beyond the Founders: New Approaches to the*

*Political History of the Early American Republic,* ed. Jeffrey L Pasley, Andrew W. Robertson, and David Waldstreicher (Chapel Hill: University of North Carolina Press, 2004), 129–158.

53. *Reports of the Trials of Colonel Aaron Burr, (Late Vice President of the United States) for Treason, and for a Misdemeanor . . . Taken in Shorthand by David Robertson, Counsellor at Law, in Two Volumes* (Philadelphia: Hopkins and Earle, Fry and Kammerer, 1808), 2:100.

54. *Reports,* 97–98, emphasis added. As Ferguson argues, "The image of Aaron Burr in 'The Man Without a Country' flows from the one that William Wirt created" (Ferguson, *Trial in American Life,* 101).

55. Baym, *Women's Fiction,* xxix.

56. Hale, "Preface," in *The Man Without a Country* (Boston: J. Stilman Smith, 1888), vii, vi, emphasis added.

57. Hale was by no means a pioneer in departing from the Lockean model of education. As Barbara Packer observes, transcendentalism developed its central precepts in a double "assault on Locke" (Barbara Packer, *The Transcendentalists* [1995; reprint, Athens: University of Georgia Press, 2007], esp. 20–31).

58. Packer, *Transcendentalists,* 20.

59. Lydia Maria Child, "Advice concerning Books," 90–91. *Charlotte Temple* anticipates critiques such as Child's in asides that defend the propriety of sympathizing with Charlotte's fallen state. Nonetheless, as the novel's subtitle, "A Tale of Truth," and its preface attest, the medium of fiction—its content aside—is seen as a threat to the text's didactic project.

60. William Hill Brown, *The Power of Sympathy,* in *The Power of Sympathy and The Coquette,* ed. Carla Mulford (New York: Penguin, 1996), 23.

61. "A Political Romance," *Observer,* January 3, 1864, 6.

62. This is how the *New York Observer* summarizes their initial critique of the story in a subsequent review of Hale's *If, Yes, and Perhaps.* "Literary," *New York Observer and Chronicle,* October 22, 1868, 341.

63. John Bouvier, *A Law Dictionary,* 15th ed., vol. 1 (Philadelphia: J. B. Lippincott, 1883), 391.

64. The article, which is subtitled "Fact and Fiction in Historical Novels, and the Relation of Ethics to Book-Making," includes letters from Hale and Paul Leicester Ford, written at the *Critic'*s request following "interesting remarks at the dinner given to Dr. Hale by the Aldine Club of New York." In Ford's accompanying letter in the article, he remarks that Hale has set "so high an ethical standard to our guild to book-makers." "Echoes of the Dinner to Dr. Hale: Fact and Fiction in Historical Novels, and the Relation of Ethics to Book Making," *Critic* (January 8, 1898), 27. Hale, "Ingham Papers," 5.

65. "Now, I say that it is the business of a writer of fiction to make it seem like the truth, and I say that writers of parables have very high authority for writing them so that people do not know how much hard fact there is, and how much is the play of the imagination. But I also say that the duty of the writer of fiction is to put his earmark . . . or if you please his 'totem,' on the narrative, which shall say to him who can understand, 'This is fiction.' I took the pains to do that in the story of 'The Man Without a Country.' . . . I tried to draw the

line—and I do not think I succeeded very well—as to the rights of the writer of fiction" ("Echoes," 27).

66. "Edward Everett Hale," *Washington Post,* June 11, 1909, 6, Proquest Historical Newspapers.

67. Edward Everett Hale, "Democracy and Liberal Education," in *Addresses and Essays on Subjects of History, Education, and Government,* The Works of Edward Everett Hale Library (Boston: Little, Brown, 1900), 8:61.

68. Hale, "Democracy and Liberal Education," 48.

69. Edward Everett Hale, Review of *Leaves of Grass* (1855), by Walt Whitman. *North American Review* 82 (January 1856): 275–277, http://www.whitman-archive.org/criticism/reviews/leaves1855/anc.00018.html. For a broader account of Whitman's initial reception, see David S. Reynolds's *Walt Whitman's America: A Cultural Biography* (New York: Vintage, 2011).

70. Whitman appropriates Abraham Lincoln's famous line from the Gettysburg Address to explain the representational ambitions of democratic literature in *Democratic Vistas* (Walt Whitman, *Democratic Vistas: The Original Edition in Facsimile,* ed. Ed Folsom [Iowa City: University of Iowa Press, 2010], 18; hereafter cited parenthetically as *DV*). For an in-depth discussion of Hale's idealization of Lincoln, see Thomas, *Civic Myths,* 55–101.

71. This skepticism of the law—and its bare premise of association—is part of what makes what Allen Grossman aptly terms Whitman's "poetics of union" so urgent in *Leaves of Grass*. Grossman uses this term to highlight the continuities between Whitman's poetics and Lincoln's policies of national unification (Allen Grossman, "The Poetics of Union in Whitman and Lincoln: An Inquiry toward the Relationship of Art and Policy," in *The American Renaissance Reconsidered: Selected Papers from the English Institute, 1982–83,* new series, no. 9, ed. Walter Benn Michaels and Donald E. Pease [Baltimore: Johns Hopkins University Press, 1985], 183–208).

72. Whitman's introductory remarks were first reproduced in facsimile form in the *Walt Whitman Review* in the 1960s. The original is held in the Feinberg Collection. For the facsimile version, see Walt Whitman, "Preface to Democratic Vistas," ed. William White, *Walt Whitman Review* 9 (September 1963): 71–72.

73. As Pearce similarly points out, "Nolan becomes a better citizen despite or because of the fact that the rule of his reeducation was that it be free from all content appertaining to his country" (Pearce, "Wisdom of Exile," 101).

74. The reference to the Bermudas, if somewhat playful, suggests another reason for this. Within the logic of manifest destiny, foreign territories appear as prospective extensions of the nation. The "anarchy of empire," to use Amy Kaplan's phrase, consists indeed in the essential non-consanguinity of the imperial nation, in which the line between the domestic and foreign is continually rewritten (Amy Kaplan, *Anarchy of Empire in the Making of U.S. Culture* [Cambridge, MA: Harvard University Press, 2002]).

75. Walter Scott, *The Lay of the Last Minstrel* (1805; reprint, New York: Woodstock Books, 1992), prefatory page.

76. Scott, *Lay of the Last Minstrel*, 156.
77. Country, as Brook Thomas observes, "comes from 'contrary' and implies a spatial relation" (*CM*, 85).
78. Burr's scheme, too, appears in a different light—the failed plan of Burr, when actualized, becomes demonstrative of national glory. Indeed, when the Republic of Texas was declared in 1836, Burr himself reportedly remarked, "I was only thirty years too soon. What was treason in me thirty years ago is patriotism today!" (James Parton, *The Life and Times of Aaron Burr* [New York: Mason Brothers, 1858], 319, quoted in Hsuan L. Hsu, "Contexts for Reading 'The Man Without a Country,'" in *Two Texts by Edward Everett Hale: "The Man Without a Country" and "Philip Nolan's Friends,"* ed. Hsuan Hsu and Susan Kalter [Lanham, MD: Lexington Press, 2010], 6.) I am indebted to Hsu for letting me read an early manuscript copy of his introduction, which traces how "Hale's historical allusions and subsequent commentaries on the story gradually reframed its nationalist object lesson to suit the increasingly expansionist outlook of American readers" (Hsu, "Contexts for Reading," 3).
79. Washington Irving, "Rip Van Winkle," in *The Sketch Book of Geoffrey Crayon. Gent.*, vol. 1 (London: John Murray, 1822), 88.
80. Lauren Berlant, *The Anatomy of National Fantasy: Hawthorne, Utopia, and Everyday Life* (Chicago: University of Chicago Press, 1991), 54.
81. Pearce, "Wisdom of Exile," 100.
82. Hale identified the imagination of exile as an impetus to active political membership.
83. "Bagaleys Are Divorced: Italian Countess' Daughter Given Custody of Her Children. Judge's Scathing Criticism," *Morning Times*, February 26, 1896, 8.
84. Slavery is not typically seen as a critical issue in the story's reception (*CM*, 99). The tale only explicitly addresses the slave trade, not domestic slavery, but the "man without a country" (deprived of home and homeland), I argue, doubles as a figure for slavery more generally.
85. This is key to my argument about "The Man Without a Country" in an earlier essay that provided the germ for this chapter (Hyde, "Outcast Patriotism," 915–939). DeLombard also stresses the importance of the story's depiction of the slave trade (DeLombard, *Shadow of the Gallows*, esp. 303).
86. In *Philip Nolan and His Friends*, Hale's peculiar sequel to "The Man Without a Country," this phrase finds a feminine corollary in "the girl without a country" (Edward Everett Hale, *Philip Nolan and His Friends: A Story of the Change of Western Empire* [New York: Scribner, Armstrong, 1877], 41).
87. Edward Everett Hale, "Preface," in *The Man Without a Country*, ed. Thomas Tapper (Boston: Page Company Publishers, 1917), xvii, emphasis added).
88. It is perhaps unfair to speak of propaganda in such a diminutive register because, as Russ Castronovo insightfully argues, propaganda played a truly formative role in the information landscape of the founding era (Russ Castronovo, *Propaganda 1776: Secrets, Leaks, and Revolutionary Communications in Early America* [New York: Oxford University Press, 2014]).

89. Here, the objection to the story's carefully constructed verisimilitude is not simply that it disguises fiction as fact but that the factual premise obscures the tale's ideological tensions.

90. Beatrice Oxley, "The Man Who Wasn't There," *English Journal* 38 (1949): 396–397.

91. Julian M. Drachman, "Significant despite Impossibilities," *English Journal* 39 (1950): 163. Historian Linda Kerber argues that the surge of editions of "The Man Without a Country" during wartime and following 9/11 exemplifies widespread trends in the "attention paid to the issue of statelessness" (Linda Kerber, "Toward a History of Statelessness in America," *American Quarterly* 57 [2005]: 727–749, esp. 728).

92. Given the persistent redaction of the story to national propaganda, during the Spanish-American War and two world wars, I agree with Thomas that shifting civic paradigms for readers help explain the story's marked decline (*CM*, 55–101).

# Coda

1. As historian Judith Shklar emphasizes in a short but trenchant account of citizenship, "from the first," Americans "defined their standing as citizens very negatively, by distinguishing themselves from their [political] inferiors, especially slaves and occasionally women" (Judith Shklar, *American Citizenship: The Questions for Inclusion* [Cambridge, MA: Harvard University Press, 1991], 15). Shklar helpfully isolates this broader dynamic in her nuanced analysis of the metaphorical use of "slave" to describe British colonialism before the American Revolution. As Shklar argues, intermediate forms of political subjection, like indentured servitude—while "far better" than chattel slavery—were terrifying enough "to engrave the terror of enslavement upon the minds of many." Slavery, Shklar poignantly concludes, was thus a "nightmare, though not a probability" for most whites in America (Shklar, *American Citizenship*, 40). The problem, as David Kazanjian eloquently observes, is that "the formal abstract equality of citizen-subjects was paradoxically qualified by the modern, 'invented tradition' of systematically enforced national identity, such that the putatively universal equality of national citizen-subjects depended on the systematic exclusion of various non-national subjects" (David Kazanjian, *The Colonizing Trick: National Culture and Imperial Citizenship in Early America*, Critical American Studies Series [Minneapolis: University of Minnesota Press, 2003], 4).

2. This point bears emphasis because loyalists made up a fairly significant portion of the populace. Loyalists are estimated to have comprised as much as one-third of the population. As Philip Gould notes in his recent and much-needed account of the literary culture of loyalism, estimates of the number of loyalists have varied widely in the historiography. For the most part, it simply was not in the interest of loyalists to publicize their allegiance (Philip Gould,

*Writing the Rebellion: Loyalists and the Literature of Politics in British America* [New York: Oxford University Press, 2013], 6).

3. S. Croswell and R. Sutton, "Speech of Mr. Cornell, on Colored Suffrage," in *Debates and Proceedings in the New-York State Convention, for the Revision of the Constitution* (Albany, NY: S. Croswell and R. Sutton, 1846), 904–907, esp. 906.

4. *United States vs. Wong Kim Ark,* 169 U.S. 649 (1898). Hsuan Hsu mentions this allusion in passing in his introduction to "The Man Without a Country" (Hsuan Hsu, "Contexts for Reading 'The Man Without a Country,'" in *Two Texts by Edward Everett Hale: "The Man Without a Country" and "Philip Nolan's Friends,"* ed. Hsuan Hsu and Susan Kalter [Lanham, MD: Lexington Press, 2010], 1, 12n2).

5. As historian Lucy Salyer observes, "Being white—or, after 1870, of African descent—would remain a requirement for naturalization until 1952" (Lucy E. Salyer, "Wong Kim Ark: The Contest over Birthright Citizenship," in *Immigration Stories,* ed. David A. Martin and Peter H. Schuck [New York: Foundation Press, 2005], 51–85, esp. 53). Act of July 14, 1870, 16 Stat. 254–256. 1st Congress; March 26, 1790.

6. U.S. Constitution, amendment 14, section 1.

7. These basic questions are ones with which scholars have long struggled. For an excellent reexamination of "America" that questions the "adequacy of a nation-based paradigm," see Wai Chee Dimock, "Introduction: Planet and America, Set and Subset," in *Shades of the Planet: American Literature as World Literature,* ed. Wai Chee Dimock and Laurence Buell (Princeton, NJ: Princeton University Press, 2007), 1–16. More than the other texts discussed in this study, the nation is key for understanding "The Man Without a Country"— precisely because of the unique role Hale's allegory played in facilitating a distinctly national imaginary. However, as we have seen, in keeping with the structure of negative instruction, "The Man Without a Country" nonetheless bears a remarkably ambivalent relationship to the nation. Among other things, the text lacks the kind of affirmative idealization that distinguishes the kind of jingoistic formulations of the nationalism that were simply not possible in the same way before the Civil War.

8. *United States v. Wong Kim Ark,* 650.

9. *United States v. Wong Kim Ark,* 680.

10. *United States v. Wong Kim Ark,* 721.

11. Hoang Gia Phan, "Imagined Territories: Comparative Racialization and the Accident of History," *Genre* 39 (Fall 2006): 21–38, esp. 22 and 22n.

12. For, as Justice Gray rightly reflects in the majority opinion, "The Constitution of the United States as originally adopted uses the words 'citizen of the United States,' and 'natural-born citizen' of the United States," but it "nowhere defines the meaning of these words . . . except in so far as this is done by the affirmative declaration [in the Fourteenth Amendment] that 'all persons born or naturalized in the United States, and subject to the jurisdiction thereof, are citizens of the United States'" (*United States v. Wong Kim Ark,* 655).

13. As legal historian Douglas Smith has observed, "Technically, the language of the first sentence of Section 1 does not provide a true "definition" of the term "citizen," but rather a statement of the conditions sufficient for attaining the status of 'citizen' of a state as well as of the United States" (Douglas G. Smith, "Citizenship and the Fourteenth Amendment," *San Diego Law Review* 34, no. 681 [1997]: 681–808, esp. 683).

14. Edward Bates, *Opinion of Attorney General Bates on Citizenship* (Washington, DC: Government Printing Office, 1862), 3.

# Bibliography

Aaron, Daniel. "'The Man Without a Country' as a Civil War Document." In *Geschichte und Gesellschaft in der amerikanischen Literatur,* ed. Karl Schubert and Ursula Müller-Richter, 55–61. Heidelberg: Quelle and Meyer, 1975.

Abrams, M. H. "Kant and the Theology of Art." *Notre Dame English Journal* 13, no. 3 (1981): 75–106.

Adams, John, and William Cunningham. *Correspondence between the Hon. John Adams, Late President of the United States, and the Late Wm. Cunningham, Esq.* Boston: True and Greene, 1823.

Adams, John R. *Edward Everett Hale.* Twayne's United States Authors Series. Boston: Twayne, 1977.

"Advance Passages from New Books." *Literary World,* March 16, 1850, 270.

"Advertisement 46—No Title." *Outlook,* August 19, 1893, 328.

Amar, Akhil Reed. *America's Unwritten Constitution: Its Precedents and the Principles We Live By.* New York: Basic Books, 2012.

Anderson, Douglas. "Jefferson, Hawthorne, and 'The Custom-House.'" *Nineteenth-Century Literature* 46, no. 3 (1991): 309–329.

Andrews, William L. "The Novelization of Voice in Early African American Narrative." *PMLA* 105, no. 1 (1990): 23–34.

———. *To Tell a Free Story: The First Century of Afro-American Autobiography, 1760–1865.* Urbana: University of Illinois Press, 1988.

Angell, Joseph. *A Treatise on the Law of Carriers of Goods and Passengers, by Land and by Water.* 2nd ed. Boston: Charles C. Little and James Brown, 1851.

Apess, William. *On Our Own Ground: The Writings of William Apess, a Pequot.* Edited by Barry O'Connell. Amherst: University of Massachusetts Press, 1993.

Arac, Jonathan. *Prose Writing, 1820–1865.* Vol. 2 of *The Cambridge History of American Literature.* New York: Cambridge University Press, 1995.

Arendt, Hannah. *The Human Condition.* Edited by Margaret Canovan. Chicago: University of Chicago Press, 1998.

———. *The Origins of Totalitarianism.* New York: Harcourt, 1976.

"Art. III.—Citizenship." *Christian Examiner and Religious Miscellany,* September 1851, 51.

"Art. VIII.—Postscript to Article IV., On the Case of the Creole." *American Jurist and Law Magazine,* August 1842, 180.

Augustine of Hippo. *Concerning the City of God against the Pagans.* Translated by Henry Bettenson. New York: Penguin, 2003.

"Bagaleys Are Divorced: Italian Countess' Daughter Given Custody of Her Children. Judge's Scathing Criticism." *Morning Times,* February 26, 1896, 8.

Bailey, William. "General Arnold." In *Records of Patriotism and Love of Country,* 169–176. Washington, DC: Drakard and Wilson, 1826.

Bailyn, Bernard. *Ideological Origins of the American Revolution.* 1967. Enlarged ed., Cambridge, MA: Belknap Press of Harvard University Press, 1992.

Baldwin, James. "Everybody's Protest Novel." In *Notes of a Native Son,* 13–23. Boston: Beacon Press, 1984.

Bates, Edward. *Opinion of Attorney General Bates on Citizenship.* Washington, DC: Government Printing Office, 1862.

Baym, Nina. "Concepts of the Romance in Hawthorne's America." *Nineteenth-Century Fiction* 38 (March 1984): 426–443.

———. *Woman's Fiction: A Guide to Novels by and about Women in America, 1820–70.* 2nd ed. Urbana: University of Illinois Press, 1993.

Beecher, Catherine, and Harriet Beecher Stowe. *The American Woman's Home; or, The Principles of Domestic Science: Being a Guide to the Formation and Maintenance of Economical, Healthful, Beautiful, and Christian Homes.* New York: J. B. Ford, 1869.

Beecher, Henry Ward. *Morning and Evening Exercise: Selected from the Published and Unpublished Writings of Henry Ward Beecher.* Edited by Lyman Alcott. New York: Harper and Brothers, 1871.

Beecher, Lyman. *A Plea for the West.* 2nd ed. Cincinnati: Truman and Smith, 1835.

Bell, Michael Davitt. *The Development of American Romance: The Sacrifice of Relation.* Chicago: University of Chicago Press, 1980.

Bennett, William J. *The Moral Compass: Stories for a Life's Journey.* New York: Simon & Schuster, 1995.

Bense, James. "Nathaniel Hawthorne's Intention in 'Chiefly about War Matters.'" *American Literature* 61, no. 2 (1989): 200–214.

Bentley, Nancy. "The Fourth Dimension: Kinlessness and African American Narrative." *Critical Inquiry* 35 (Winter 2009): 270–292.

———. "Slaves and Fauns: Hawthorne and the Uses of Primitivism." *ELH* 57, no. 4 (1990): 901–937.

Bercovitch, Sacvan. *The American Jeremiad.* Madison: University of Wisconsin Press, 1978.

———. "Hawthorne's A-Morality of Compromise." *Representations* 24 (Autumn 1988): 1–27.

———. *The Office of "The Scarlet Letter."* Baltimore: Johns Hopkins University Press, 1991.

———, and Myra Jehlen, eds. "Introduction: Beyond Transcendence." In *Ideology and Classic American Literature*, 1–18. New York: Cambridge University Press, 1986.

Berlant, Lauren. *The Anatomy of National Fantasy: Hawthorne, Utopia, and Everyday Life.* Chicago: University of Chicago Press, 1991.

———. "Citizenship." In *Keywords for American Cultural Studies,* ed. Bruce Burgett and Glen Hendler, 37–42. New York: New York University Press, 2007.

———. *The Queen of America Goes to Washington City: Essays on Sex and Citizenship.* Series Q. Durham, NC: Duke University Press, 1997.

Best, Stephen. *The Fugitive's Properties: Law and the Poetics of Possession.* Chicago: Chicago University Press, 2004.

"The Bible, Our True Magna Charta." In vol. 1 of *The Bible and Its People for 1851: A Growing Manual of Principles and Investigation, for Doubters, Enquirers, and Intelligent Believers.* London: Ward, 1851.

Blackman, Josh. "Original Citizenship." *University of Pennsylvania Law Review* 159, no. 95 (2010): 95–126.

Bliss, Philemon. *Citizenship: State Citizens, General Citizens.* Washington, DC: Buell and Blanchard, 1858.

Boelhower, William. "The Rise of the New Atlantic Studies Matrix." *American Literary History* 20, no. 1 (2007): 83–101.

"Books Received." *School Review* (April 1893): 261–262.

"Book Table: If, Yes, and Perhaps." *The Independent . . . Devoted to the Consideration of Politics, Social and Econ. . . . ,* November 19, 1868, 6.

Bouvier, John. *A Law Dictionary.* 15th ed. Vol. 1. Philadelphia: J. B. Lippincott, 1883.

Bowers, Fredson. "Textual Introduction." In vol. 1 of *The Scarlet Letter.* Centenary Edition of the Works of Nathaniel Hawthorne. Columbus: Ohio State University Press, 1968.

Boyce, Bret. "Originalism and Fourteenth Amendment." *Wake Forest Law Review* 33, no. 4 (1996): 909–1034.

Bradburn, Douglas. *The Citizenship Revolution: Politics and the Creation of the American Union, 1774–1804.* Charlottesville: University of Virginia Press, 2009.

———. "The Problem of Citizenship in the American Revolution." *History Compass* 8, no. 9 (2010): 1093–1113.

Breen, T. H. "Ideology and Nationalism on the Eve of the American Revolution: Revisions Once More in Need of Revising." *Journal of American History* 84, no. 1 (June 1997): 13–39.

Bromwich, David. *Moral Imagination.* Princeton, NJ: Princeton University Press, 2014.

Brooks, Joanna. "The Early American Public Sphere and the Emergence of a Black Print Counterpublic." *William and Mary Quarterly* 62, no. 1 (January 2005): 67–92.

Brooks, Peter. *Henry James Goes to Paris.* Princeton, NJ: Princeton University Press, 2007.

Brooks, Van Wyck. "Introduction." In *The First Book Edition of the Man Without a Country,* by Edward Everett Hale, v–x. New York: Franklin Watts, 1960.

Broughman, John. *Dred or the Dismal Swamp: A Play in Five Acts.* French's American Drama. New York: Samuel French, 1856.

Brown, Gillian. *Consent of the Governed: The Lockean Legacy in Early American Culture.* Cambridge, MA: Harvard University Press, 2001.

———. *Domestic Individualism: Imagining Self in Nineteenth-Century America.* Berkeley: University of California Press, 1990.

Brown, Wendy. *States of Injury.* Princeton, NJ: Princeton University Press, 1995.

Brown, William Hill. *The Power of Sympathy.* In *The Power of Sympathy and The Coquette,* ed. Carla Mulford, 1–103. New York: Penguin, 1996.

*Brown's Popular Readings . . . for Readings and Recitations.* Chicago: A. Flanagan, 1893.

Brownson, Orestes. "Art. IV.—A Tale of the Real and Ideal, Blight and Bloom." *Brownson's Quarterly Review,* July 1, 1846, 369–399.

Brumm, Ursula. "Consensus and Conspiracy in American Literature." *Yearbook of Research in English and American Literature* 11 (1995): 29–43.

Budick, Emily Miller. *Nineteenth-Century American Romance: Genre and the Construction of Democratic Culture.* New York: Prentice Hall International, 1996.

———. "Sacvan Bercovitch, Stanley Cavell, and the Romance Theory of American Fiction." *PMLA* 107, no. 1 (1992): 78–91.

Buell, Lawrence. "Harriet Beecher Stowe and the Dream of the Great American Novel." In *The Cambridge Companion to Harriet Beecher Stowe,* ed. Cindy Weinstein, 190–202. New York: Cambridge University Press, 2004.

———. "Hawthorne and the Problem of 'American' Fiction: The Example of *The Scarlet Letter.*" In *Hawthorne and the Real: Bicentennial Essays,* ed. Millicent Bell, 70–87. Columbus: Ohio State University Press, 2005.

———. *New England Literary Culture: From Revolution through Renaissance.* New York: Cambridge University Press, 1986.

Bunker, Gary. *From Rail-Splitter to Icon: Lincoln's Image in Illustrated Periodicals, 1860–1865.* Kent, OH: Kent State University Press, 2001.

Burgett, Bruce. *Sentimental Bodies: Sex, Gender, and Citizenship in the Early Republic.* Princeton, NJ: Princeton University Press, 1998.

Bushnell, Horace. "American Politics." *American National Preacher,* December 1840, 189.

Cahill, Edward. *Liberty of the Imagination: Aesthetic Theory, Literary Form, and Politics in the Early United States.* Philadelphia: University of Pennsylvania Press, 2012.

"A Call for More Troops—Three Hundred Thousand More Men Wanted." *Philadelphia Inquirer,* July 7, 1862.

Cameron, Sharon. "The Way of Life by Abandonment: Emerson's Impersonal." *Critical Inquiry* 25, no. 1 (Autumn 1991): 1–31.

Campbell, George, James Macknight, and Philip Doddridge, trans. *The Sacred Writings of the Apostles and Evangelists of Jesus Christ, Commonly Styled the New Testament*. Edited by Alexander Campbell. Buffaloe, VA: Alexander Campbell, 1826.

Carbado, Devon W. "Racial Naturalization." *American Quarterly* 57 (September 2005): 633–658.

Carso, Brian F., Jr. *"Whom Can We Trust Now?" The Meaning of Treason in the United States, from the Revolution to the Civil War*. Boulder, CO: Lexington Books, 1991.

"Case of the Creole." *Anti-Slavery Reporter*, August 1842, 132

"Case of the Creole." *Anti-Slavery Reporter*, January 1842, 12.

Castiglia, Christopher. *Interior States: Institutional Consciousness and the Inner Life of Democracy in the Antebellum United States*. Durham, NC: Duke University Press, 2008.

Castronovo, Russ. *Necro Citizenship: Death, Eroticism, and the Public Sphere in the Nineteenth-Century United States*. Durham, NC: Duke University Press, 2001.

———. *Beautiful Democracy: Aesthetics and Anarchy in a Global Era*. Chicago: University of Chicago Press, 2007.

———. *Propaganda 1776: Secrets, Leaks, and Revolutionary Communications in Early America*. New York: Oxford University Press, 2014.

Castronovo, Russ, and Dana Nelson, eds. *Materializing Democracy: Toward a Revitalized Cultural Politics*. Durham, NC: Duke University Press, 2002.

Channing, William E. *The Duty of the Free States; or, Remarks Suggested by the Case of the Creole*. Boston: William Crosby, 1842.

Child, Lydia Maria. "Advice Concerning Books." In *The Mother's Book*, 86–97. Boston: Carther and Hendez, 1831.

———. *Philothea: A Romance*. Boston: Otis, Broaders, 1836.

Clark, Laurel A. "The Rights of a Florida Wife: Slavery, U.S. Expansion, and Married Women's Property Law." *Journal of Women's History* 22, no. 4 (Winter 2010): 39–63.

Claybaugh, Amanda. "The Consular Service and US Literature: Nathaniel Hawthorne Abroad." *Novel* 42, no. 2 (2009): 284–289.

Cleveland, Charles, ed. "Politics and Religion." In *A Compendium of American Literature*, 167–168. Philadelphia: J. A. Bancroft, 1859.

Clymer, Jeffory A. "Family Money: Race and Economic Rights in Antebellum US Law and Fiction." *American Literary History* 21, no. 2 (2009): 211–238.

Cobb, Lyman, ed. *The North American Reader: Containing a Great Variety of Pieces in Prose and Poetry from Highly Esteemed American and English Readers*. Zanesville, OH: J. R. and A. Lippitt, 1835.

Cohen, B. Bernard, ed. "Edward Everett and Hawthorne's Removal from the Salem Custom House." *American Literature* 27, no. 2 (May 1955): 246–247.

Coleridge, Samuel Taylor. *Biographia Literaria*. In *The Major Works*, ed. H. J. Jackson, 155–482. New York: Oxford University Press, 2008.

Combe, George. *The Constitution of Man Considered in Relation to External Objects.* 4th ed. Boston: William D. Ticknor, 1835.

"The Conspiracy." *Casket,* June 1840, 254.

"The Constitution of the United States of America." In *The Federalist Papers,* ed. Isaac Kramnick, 491–508. New York: Penguin, 1987.

Cooper, James Fenimore. *The American Democrat; or, Hints on the Social and Civic Relations of the United States of America.* Cooperstown, NY: H. and E. Phinney, 1838.

Cotugno, Clare. "Stowe, Eliot, and the Reform Aesthetic." In *Transatlantic Stowe: Harriet Beecher Stowe and European Culture,* ed. Denise Kohn, Sarah Meer, and Emily Todd, 111–130. Iowa City: University of Iowa Press, 2006.

Coviello, Peter. *Intimacy in America: Dreams of Affiliation in Antebellum Literature.* Minneapolis: University of Minnesota Press, 2005.

Cowper, William. *The Task: A Poem . . . A New Edition.* Philadelphia: Thomas Dobson, 1787.

Cox, J. Sullivan. "Imaginary Commonwealths." *United States Magazine and Democratic Review,* September 1846, 175–185.

Crane, Gregg D. *Race, Citizenship, and Law in American Literature.* New York: Cambridge University Press, 2002.

———. "Stowe and the Law." In *The Cambridge Companion to Harriet Beecher Stowe,* ed. Cindy Weinstein, 154–170. New York: Cambridge University Press, 2004.

"The Creole Case." *Christian Reflector,* June 8, 1842.

"The Creole Case." *Niles National Register,* March 19, 1842. "The Creole Heroes in New-York." *New York Evangelist,* April 7, 1842, 54.

Croswell, S., and R. Sutton. "Speech of Mr. Cornell, on Colored Suffrage." In *Debates and Proceedings in the New-York State Convention, for the Revision of the Constitution,* 904–907. Albany, NY: S. Croswell and R. Sutton, 1846.

*The Cruel Boy, and Other Pieces.* Worcester, MA: J. Grout, Jr., [1835?].

Cumming, John. *The Millennial Rest; or, The World as It Will Be.* London: Richard Bentley, 1862.

Curtis, Michael Kent. *No State Shall Abridge: The Fourteenth Amendment and the Bill of Rights.* Durham, NC: Duke University Press, 1990.

[Cutter, William C.] "Uncle Hiram's Pilgrimage." *Merry's Museum, Parley's Magazine, Woodworth's Cabinet, and the Schoolfellow,* January 1, 1858, 174.

Davidson, Cathy. "Introduction." In *Charlotte Temple,* by Susanna Rowson, xi–xii. New York: Oxford University Press, 1986.

———. *Revolution and the Word: The Rise of the Novel in America.* Expanded ed. New York: Oxford University Press, 2004.

———, and Michael Moon, eds. *Subjects and Citizens: Nation, Race, and Gender from Oroonoko to Anita Hill.* Durham, NC: Duke University Press, 1995.

"Declaration of Sentiments and Resolutions, Seneca Falls." In *Feminism: The Essential Historical Writings,* ed. Miriam Schneir, 77–82. New York: Random House, 1972.

Delany, Martin. *Blake; or, The Huts of America.* Boston: Beacon Press, 1970.

DeLombard, Jeannine. *In the Shadow of the Gallows: Race, Crime, and American Civic Identity.* Philadelphia: University of Pennsylvania Press, 2012.

———. "Representing the Slave: White Advocacy and Black Testimony in Harriet Beecher Stowe's 'Dred.'" *New England Quarterly* 75, no. 1 (2002): 80–106.

De Prospo, R. C. "Afterword/Afterward: Auntie Harriet and Uncle Ike—Prophesying a Final Stowe Debate." In *The Stowe Debate: Rhetorical Strategies in Uncle Tom's Cabin,* ed. Mason Lowance, Ellen Westbrook, and R. C. De Prospo, 271–293. Amherst: University of Massachusetts Press, 1994.

Deutch, Helen. "The Scaffold in the Market Place: Samuel Johnson, Nathaniel Hawthorne, and the Romance of Authorship." *Nineteenth-Century Literature* 68, no. 3 (December 2013): 363–395.

Dewey, John. *Democracy and Education: An Introduction to the Philosophy of Education.* New York: Free Press, 1944.

———. *The Public and Its Problems.* New York: H. Holt, 1927. Reprint, Athens: Ohio University Press, 1954.

Dillon, Elizabeth Maddock. *The Gender of Freedom: Fictions of Liberalism and the Literary Public Sphere.* Stanford, CA: Stanford University Press, 2004.

Dimock, Wai Chee. "Introduction: Planet and America, Set and Subset." In *Shades of the Planet: American Literature as World Literature,* ed. Wai Chee Dimock and Laurence Buell, 1–16. Princeton, NJ: Princeton University Press, 2007.

———. *Residues of Justice: Literature, Law, and Philosophy.* Los Angeles: University of California Press, 1996.

Dinius, Marcy Y. "'Look!! Look!! at This!!!!' The Radical Typography of David Walker's *Appeal.*" *PMLA* 126, no. 1 (2011): 55–72.

Dodsworth, Jeremiah. *The Better Land; or, The Christian Emigrant's Guide to Heaven.* Revised by Thomas O. Summers. Nashville, TN: E. Stevenson and F. A. Owen, 1857.

———. *The Eden Family: Shewing the Loss of Our Paradise Home.* London: Partridge, 1858.

Doran, J. "Romance and Reality." *Gentleman's Magazine,* December 1855, 588.

Douglas, Ann. *The Feminization of American Culture.* New York: Knopf, 1977.

Douglass, Frederick. *Frederick Douglass: Selected Speeches and Writings.* Edited by Philip Sheldon Foner and Yuval Taylor. Chicago: Lawrence Hill, 1999.

———. *The Frederick Douglass Papers; Series One: Speeches, Debates and Interviews, 1841–1846,* ed. John W. Blassingame, 5 vols. New Haven, CT: Yale University Press, 1979.

———. "The Heroic Slave." In *Autographs for Freedom.* 1853. Michigan Historical Reprint Series. Ann Arbor, MI: Scholarly Publishing Office, 2005.

———. *Life and Times of Frederick Douglass.* In *Douglass: Autobiographies,* 453–1045. New York: Library of America, 1994.

———. *Narrative of the Life of Frederick Douglass, an American Slave.* In *Narrative of the Life of Frederick Douglass, an American Slave, and Incidents in the Life of a Slave Girl,* ed. Kwame Anthony Appiah, 1–114. New York: Modern Library, 2000.

Drachman, Julian M. "Significant despite Impossibilities." *English Journal* 39 (1950): 163.

Drake, James D. *The Nation's Nature: How Continental Presumptions Gave Rise to the United States of America.* Charlottesville: University of Virginia Press, 2011.

*Dred Scott v. Sandford: A Brief History with Documents.* Edited by Paul Finkelman. New York: Bedford, 1997.

Dryden, Edgar A. "Hawthorne's Castle in the Air: Form and Theme in *The House of the Seven Gables*." *ELH* 38, no. 2 (1971): 294–317.

Dunlap, William. *André: A Tragedy, in Five Acts*." In *Early American Drama*, ed. Jeffrey H. Richards, 58–108. New York: Penguin, 1997.

Duquette, Elizabeth. *Loyal Subjects: Bonds of Nation, Race, and Allegiance in Nineteenth-Century America.* New Brunswick, NJ: Rutgers University Press, 2010.

Duyckinck, Evert A. [Great Feeling and Discrimination]. Reprinted in *The Scarlet Letter,* ed. Seymour Gross, Sculley Bradley, Richmond Croom Beatty, and E. Hudson Long. New York: Norton Critical Edition, 1988.

Dwight, Timothy. Letter XLVII. In *Travels in New England and New York,* 1:476. London: William Baynes and Son, 1823.

Eagleton, Terry. "The Ideology of the Aesthetic." *Poetics Today* 9, no. 2 (1988): 327–338.

"Echoes of the Dinner to Dr. Hale: Fact and Fiction in Historical Novels, and the Relation of Ethics to Book Making." *Critic* (January 8, 1898): 27.

Eddy, Ansel Doane. *The Christian Citizen: The Obligations of the Christian Citizen; With a Review of High Church Principles in Relation to Civil and Religious Institutions.* New York: J. S. Taylor, 1843.

"Edward Everett Hale." *Washington Post,* June 11, 1909, 6. Proquest Historical Newspapers.

Edward Everett Hale Papers, 1855–1906. American Antiquarian Society, Worcester, MA.

"Effect of Reading on Character." *New York Evangelist,* August 25, 1864, 6.

Eliot, George. "Review of Dred: A Tale of the Great Dismal Swamp." *Westminster Review,* 1856. Reprinted in *Critical Essays on Harriet Beecher Stowe,* ed. Elizabeth Ammons, 43–48. Boston: G. K. Hall, 1980.

Emerson, Ralph Waldo. *Essays and Poems.* New York: Library of America, 1996.

Felski, Rita. "Context Stinks!" *New Literary History* 42 (Autumn 2011): 573–591.

Ferguson, Robert A. *The American Enlightenment, 1750–1820.* Cambridge, MA: Harvard University Press, 1994.

———. *Reading the Early Republic.* Cambridge, MA: Harvard University Press, 2004.

———. *The Trial in American Life.* Chicago: University of Chicago Press, 2007.

Fiedler, Leslie A. "Home as Heaven, Home as Hell: *Uncle Tom*'s Canon." In *Rewriting the Dream: Reflections on the Changing American Literary Canon,* ed. W. M. Verhoeven, 22–42. Atlanta: Rodopi, 1992.

Fliegelman, Jay. *Declaring Independence: Jefferson, Natural Language, and the Culture of Performance.* Stanford, CA: Stanford University Press, 1993.

———. *Prodigals and Pilgrims: The American Revolution against Patriarchal Authority, 1750–1800.* New York: Cambridge University Press, 1985.

Foner, Eric. *The Story of American Freedom*. New York: Norton, 1998.

Frank, Jason. *Constituent Moments: Enacting the People in Postrevolutionary America*. Durham, NC: Duke University Press, 2010.

Franklin, Benjamin. *The Autobiography, and Other Writings*. New York: Signet Classics, 2001.

Fredrickson, George. *The Black Image in the White Mind: The Debate on Afro-American Character and Destiny, 1817–1914*. New York: Harper and Row, 1971.

"From the Friend of Man. Madison Washington. Another Chapter in His History." *Liberator,* June 10, 1842.

Fuller, Randall. "Hawthorne and War." *New England Quarterly* 80, no. 4 (2007): 655–686.

Gallagher, Catherine. "The Rise of Fictionality." In *The Novel*, vol. 1, ed. Franco Moretti, 336–363. Princeton, NJ: Princeton University Press, 2006.

Garett, Phineas, ed. *The Speaker's Garland: Comprising One Hundred Choice Selections*. Vol. 5. Philadelphia: Penn Publishing, 1910.

Gerson, Noel B. *Harriet Beecher Stowe: A Biography*. New York: Praeger, 1976.

Giles, Paul. "Douglass's Black Atlantic: Britain, Europe, Egypt." In *The Cambridge Companion to Frederick Douglass*, ed. Maurice Lee, 132–145. New York: Cambridge University Press, 2009.

Gilroy, Paul. *The Black Atlantic: Modernity and Double Consciousness*. New York: Verso, 1993.

Glazner, Nancy. *Reading for Realism: The History of U.S. Literary Institution*. Chapel Hill, NC: Duke University Press, 1997.

Goeman, Mishuana. *Mark My Words: Native Women Mapping Our Nations*. Minneapolis: Minnesota University Press, 2013.

Goodell, William. *National Charters: For the Millions*. New York: J. W. Alden, 1863.

Gould, Philip. *Covenant and Republic: Historical Romance and the Politics of Puritanism*. New York: Cambridge University Press, 1996.

———. *Writing the Rebellion: Loyalists and the Literature of Politics in British America*. New York: Oxford University Press, 2013.

Govett, Robert. "May Christians Be Politicians? To the Editor of the 'Baptist Magazine.'" In *Baptist Magazine for 1868*, vol. 60, ed. W. G. Lewis, 461–464. London: Elliot Stock, 1868.

Graves, Robert Perceval. *Our Heavenly Citizenship; or, The Heavenly Elements of Earthly Occupations: A Sermon. . . .* London: Whittaker, 1862.

Green, Nancy L. "Expatriation, Expatriates, and Expats: The American Transformation of a Concept." *American Historical Review* 114, no. 2 (April 2009): 307–328, esp. 307.

Greiman, Jennifer. *Democracy's Spectacle: Sovereignty and Public Life in Antebellum American Writing*. New York: Fordham University Press, 2010.

Grobel, Kendrick. "Charles Thomson, First American N. T. Translator: An Appraisal." *Journal of Bible and Religion* 11, no. 3 (1943): 145–151.

Gronniosaw, James Albert Ukawsaw. *A Narrative of the Most Remarkable Particulars in the Life of James Albert Ukawsaw Gronniosaw, an African Prince, as Related by Himself*. In *Pioneers of the Black Atlantic,* ed. Henry Louis Gates Jr. and William L. Andrews, 31–60. Washington, DC: Civitas, 1998.

Grossman, Allen. "The Poetics of Union in Whitman and Lincoln: An Inquiry toward the Relationship of Art and Policy." In *The American Renaissance Reconsidered: Selected Papers from the English Institute, 1982–83,* New series, no. 9, ed. Walter Benn Michaels and Donald E. Pease, 183–208. Baltimore: Johns Hopkins University Press, 1985.

Grossman, Jay. *Reconstituting the American Renaissance: Emerson, Whitman, and the Politics of Representation.* Durham, NC: Duke University Press, 2003.

Gura, Philip F. *American Transcendentalism: A History.* New York: Hill & Wang, 2007.

Gustafson, Sandra. *Eloquence Is Power: Oratory and Performance in Early America.* Chapel Hill: University of North Carolina Press, 2000.

Gutjahr, Paul. *An American Bible: A History of the Good Book in the United States, 1777–1880.* Stanford, CA: Stanford University Press, 1999.

Habermas, Jürgen. *The Structural Transformation of the Public Sphere.* Translated by Thomas Burger and Frederick Lawrence. Cambridge, MA: MIT Press, 1991.

Hale, Edward Everett. [Annotations]. In *The New Testament . . . Conformed to Griesbach's Standard Greek Text.* Boston: William L. Lewis, 1828.

———. *The Bible and Its Revision: Three Addresses.* Boston: A. Williams, 1879.

———. "Democracy and Liberal Education." In *Addresses and Essays on Subjects of History, Education, and Government,* The Works of Edward Everett Hale Library, 43–64. Boston: Little, Brown, 1900.

———. "From the Ingham Papers." In *The Man Without a Country, and Other Tales,* 3. Boston: Roberts Brothers, 1886.

———. "The Man Without a Country." *Atlantic Monthly,* December 1863, 665–679.

———. *The Man Without a Country and Its History.* Boston: J. Stilman Smith, 1897.

———. *Philip Nolan and His Friends: A Story of the Change of Western Empire.* New York: Scribner, Armstrong, 1877.

———. "Preface." In *The Man Without a Country,* iii–viii. Boston: J. Stilman Smith, 1888.

———. "Preface." In *The Man Without a Country,* iii–xx. New York: H. M. Caldwell, 1897.

———. "Preface." In *The Man Without a Country,* ed. Thomas Tapper. Boston: Page Company Publishers, 1917.

———. Review of *Leaves of Grass* (1855), by Walt Whitman. *North American Review* 82 (January 1856): 275–277. http://www.whitmanarchive.org /criticism/reviews/leaves1855/anc.00018.html.

Hamilton, Cynthia S. "'Dred': Intemperate Slavery." *Journal of American Studies* 34, no. 2 (2000): 257–277.

———. "Models of Agency: Frederick Douglass and 'The Heroic Slave.'" *Proceedings of the American Antiquarian Society: A Journal of American History and Culture through 1876* 114, no. 1 (2004): 87–136.

Hanley, Mark Y. *Beyond a Christian Commonwealth: The Protestant Quarrel with the American Republic, 1830–1860.* Chapel Hill: University of North Carolina Press, 1994.

Hartman, Saidiya V. *Scenes of Subjection: Terror, Slavery, and Self-Making in Nineteenth-Century America.* New York: Oxford University Press, 1997.

Hatch, Nathan O. *The Democratization of American Christianity.* New Haven, CT: Yale University Press, 1989.

Hawthorne, Nathaniel. *The American Claimant Manuscripts.* Centenary Edition of the Works of Nathaniel Hawthorne. Vol. 12. Columbus: Ohio State University Press, 1977.

———. *The Blithedale Romance.* Edited by Richard H. Millington. New York: Norton, 2010.

———. "Chiefly about War-Matters. By a Peaceable Man." *Atlantic Monthly,* July 1862.

———. *The Consular Letters, 1853–1855.* Centenary Edition of the Works of Nathaniel Hawthorne. Vol. 19. Columbus: Ohio State University Press, 1988.

———. *The Custom House and Main Street.* Riverside Literature Series. Vol. 138. New York: Houghton, Mifflin, 1899.

———. "The Hall of Fantasy." *Pioneer,* February 1843, 49–55.

———. *The House of the Seven Gables.* Centenary Edition of the Works of Nathaniel Hawthorne. Vol. 2. Columbus: Ohio State University Press, 1971.

———. *The Letters, 1853–1856.* Centenary Edition of the Works of Nathaniel Hawthorne. Vol. 17. Columbus: Ohio State University Press, 1987.

———. *The Marble Faun; or, The Romance of Monte Beni.* Centenary Edition of the Works of Nathaniel Hawthorne. Vol. 4. Columbus: Ohio State University Press, 1968.

———. "The New Adam and the New Eve." In *Mosses from an Old Manse,* 247–267. Centenary Edition of the Works of Nathaniel Hawthorne. Vol. 10. Columbus: Ohio State University Press, 1974.

———. *The Scarlet Letter.* Centenary Edition of the Works of Nathaniel Hawthorne. Vol. 1. Columbus: Ohio State University Press, 1968.

———. *The Scarlet Letter.* Edited by John Stephen Martin. New York: Broadview, 2004.

———. "A Select Party." *United States Magazine and Democratic Review,* July 1844, 33.

Hawthorne Manuscripts. Clifton Waller Barrett Library, University of Virginia, Charlottesville.

Hay, George. *A Treatise on Expatriation.* Washington, DC: A. & G. Way, 1814.

"The Hero-Mutineers." *New York Evangelist,* December 25, 1841, 206.

Hickman, Jared. *Black Prometheus: Race and Radicalism in the Age of Atlantic Slavery.* New York: Oxford University Press, 2016.

———. "Political Theology." In *The Routledge Companion to Literature and Religion,* ed. Mark Knight, 124–134. New York: Routledge, 2016.

Hoffer, Johannes. "Medical Dissertation on Nostalgia or Homesickness." Translated by Carolyn Kiser Anspach. *Bulletin of the Institute of the History of Medicine* 2 (1934): 376–391.

Holloway, Karla F. C. *Legal Fictions: Constituting Race, Composing Literature.* Durham, NC: Duke University Press, 2014.

Hovet, Theodore R. *The Master Narrative: Harriet Beecher Stowe's Subversive Story of Master and Slave in Uncle Tom's Cabin and Dred.* Lanham, MD: University Press of America, 1989.

Hsu, Hsuan L. "Contexts for Reading 'The Man Without a Country.' " In *Two Texts by Edward Everett Hale: "The Man Without a Country" and "Philip Nolan's Friends,"* ed. Hsuan Hsu and Susan Kalter, 1–16. Lanham, MD: Lexington Press, 2010.

Hurley, Allison. "Peculiar Christians, Circumstantial Courtiers, and the Making of Conversation in Seventeenth-Century England." *Representations* 111, no. 1 (2011): 33–59.

Hutner, Gordon. "Whose Hawthorne?" In *The Cambridge Companion to Nathaniel Hawthorne,* ed. Richard H. Millington, 251–265. New York: Cambridge University Press, 2004.

Hyde, Carrie. "The Climates of Liberty: Natural Rights in the *Creole* Case and 'The Heroic Slave.' " *American Literature* 85, no. 3 (September 2013): 475–504.

———. "Novelistic Evidence: Denmark Vesey and Possibilistic History." *American Literary History* 27, no. 1 (Spring 2015): 26–55.

———. "Outcast Patriotism: The Dilemma of Negative Instruction in 'The Man Without a Country.' " *ELH* 77, no. 4 (2010): 915–939.

"Hyperspectral Imaging by Library of Congress Reveals Change Made by Thomas Jefferson in Original Declaration of Independence Draft." July 2, 2010. http://www.loc.gov/today/pr/2010/10-161.html.

"Introduction." In *The New Testament, in an Improved Version, upon the Basis of Archbishop Newcome's New Translation: With a Corrected Text and Notes Critical and Explanatory.* London: Richard Taylor, 1808.

"An Investigation of the Principal Causes which Have Led to the Condemnation of Novels." *Port Folio,* September 1820, 221.

Irving, Washington. "Rip Van Winkle." In *The Sketch Book of Geoffrey Crayon. Gent,* vol. 1, 53–90. London: John Murray, 1822.

Isenberg, Nancy. *The Fallen Founder: The Life of Aaron Burr.* New York: Penguin, 2007.

———. "The 'Little Emperor': Aaron Burr, Dandyism, and the Sexual Politics of Treason." In *Beyond the Founders: New Approaches to the Political History of the Early American Republic,* ed. Jeffrey L. Pasley, Andrew W. Robertson, and David Waldstreicher, 129–158. Chapel Hill: University of North Carolina Press, 2004.

———. *Sex and Citizenship in Antebellum America.* Chapel Hill: University of North Carolina Press, 1998.

"James Baldwin Breaks His Silence." *Atlas* 13 (March 1967): 47–49. Reprinted in *Conversations with James Baldwin,* ed. Fred L. Standley and Louis H. Pratt, 59–63. Jackson: University Press of Mississippi, 1989.

James, Henry. *The American.* New York: Charles Scribner's Sons, 1907.

Jameson, Fredric. "Magical Narratives: Romance as Genre." *New Literary History* 7, no. 1 (Autumn 1975): 135–163.

———. *The Political Unconscious: Narrative as a Socially Symbolic Act.* Ithaca, NY: Cornell University Press, 1981.

Jay, John. John Jay to George Washington, July 25, 1787. In *Correspondence and Public Papers of John Jay, 1782–1793*, vol. 3, ed. Henry Johnston, 250. New York: G. P. Putnam's Sons, 1891.

——. "Number II: Concerning Dangers from Foreign Force and Influence." In *The Federalist Papers*, by James Madison, Alexander Hamilton, and John Jay, 91. 1788. Reprint, New York: Penguin, 1987.

Jay, William. *The Creole Case, and Mr. Webster's Despatch; With the Comments of the N.Y. American*. New York: New York American, 1842.

Jefferson, Thomas. "A Bill Declaring Who Shall Be Deemed Citizens of the Commonwealth." In *Thomas Jefferson: Writings*, 274–275. New York: Library of America, 1984.

——. "To Charles Thomson." January 11, 1808. In *The Writings of Thomas Jefferson*, vol. 9, 1807–1815, ed. Paul Leicester Ford, 6–7. New York: G. P. Putnam's Sons, 1898.

——. "Jefferson's Letter to the Dansbury Baptists. Jan. 1, 1802." Library of Congress. http://www.loc.gov/loc/lcib/9806/danpre.html.

——. "To Nathaniel Burwell, March 22, 1818." In *Thomas Jefferson: Writings*, 1411. New York: Library of America, 1984.

——. "Special Message to Congress, Jan. 22, 1807." In *The Works of Thomas Jefferson*, ed. Paul Leicester Ford, vol. 9, 14–20. New York: J. P. Putnam's Sons, 1905. http://oll.libertyfund.org/titles/806.

Jehlen, Myra. *American Incarnation: The Individual, the Nation, and the Continent*. Cambridge, MA: Harvard University Press, 1986.

Johnson, Michael P. "Denmark Vesey and His Co-Conspirators." *William and Mary Quarterly* 58, no. 4 (2001): 915–976.

Jones, Douglas A. "Douglass' Impersonal." *ESQ* 61, no. 1 (2015): 1–35.

Jones, Howard. "The Peculiar Institution and National Honor: The Case of the *Creole* Slave Revolt." *Civil War History* 21, no. 1 (1975): 28–50.

Jones, Paul Christian. "Copying What the Master Had Written: Frederick Douglass's 'The Heroic Slave' and the Southern Historical Romance." *Southern Quarterly: A Journal of the Arts in the South* 38, no. 4 (2000): 78–92.

*Journal of the Convention, Called by the Freemen of North-Carolina, to Amend the Constitution of the State*. Raleigh, NC: Gales and Sons, 1835.

Jurvey, Edward D., and C. Harold Hubbard. "The Creole Affair." *Journal of Negro History* 65, no. 3 (Summer 1980): 196–211.

Kant, Immanuel. *Critique of Judgment*. Translated by James Creed Meredith. New York: Oxford World Classics, 2008.

Kaplan, Amy. *Anarchy of Empire in the Making of U.S. Culture*. Cambridge, MA: Harvard University Press, 2002.

Kareem, Sarah. *Eighteenth-Century Fiction and the Reinvention of Wonder*. Oxford: Oxford University Press, 2014.

Kateb, George. "Democratic Individuality and the Claims of Politics." *Political Theory* 12, no. 3 (August 1984): 331–360.

Kazanjian, David. *The Colonizing Trick: National Culture and Imperial Citizenship in Early America*. Critical American Studies Series. Minneapolis: University of Minnesota Press, 2003.

Kemp, Mark A. R. "*The Marble Faun* and American Postcolonial Ambivalence." *Modern Fiction Studies* 43, no. 1 (1997): 209–236.

*Kentucky Opinions: Containing the Unreported Opinions of the Court of Appeals.* Compiled by Hon. J. Morgan Chinn. Vol. 1. 1864–1866. Lexington, KY: Central Law Book Company, 1906.

Kerber, Linda K. "'May All Our Citizens Be Soldiers, and All Our Soldiers Citizens': The Ambiguities of Female Citizenship in the New Nation." In *Arms at Rest: Peacemaking and Peacekeeping in American History,* ed. J. R. Challinor and R. L. Beisner, 1–22. New York: Greenwood Press, 1987.

———. "The Meanings of Citizenship." *Journal of American History* 84, no. 3 (1997): 833–854.

———. *No Constitutional Right to Be Ladies: Women and Obligations of Citizenship.* New York: Hill & Wang, 1998.

———. "Toward a History of Statelessness in America." *American Quarterly* 57 (2005): 727–749.

Kettner, James H. *The Development of American Citizenship, 1608–1870.* Chapel Hill: University of North Carolina Press, 1978.

Klinghoffer, Judith Apter, and Lois Elkis. "'The Petticoat Electors': Women's Suffrage in New Jersey, 1776–1807." *Journal of the Early Republic* 12, no. 2 (Summer 1992): 159–193.

Koenigs, Thomas. "'Nothing but Fiction': *Modern Chivalry,* Fictionality, and the Political Public Sphere in the Early Republic." *Early American Literature* 50, no. 2 (2015): 301–330.

Koessler, Maximilian. "'Subject,' 'Citizen,' 'National,' and 'Permanent Allegiance.'" *Law Journal Company* 56, no. 1 (November 1946): 58–76.

Korobkin, Laura H. "Appropriating Law in Harriet Beecher Stowe's *Dred.*" *Nineteenth-Century Literature* 62, no. 3 (2007): 380–406.

Kramnick, Isaac, and Laurence Moore. *The Godless Constitution: A Moral Defense of the Secular State.* Updated ed. New York: W. W. Norton, 2005.

[Lafayette]. *Stories about Arnold, the Traitor, Andre, the Spy, and Champe, the Patriot: For the Children of the United States.* 2nd ed. New Haven, CT: A. H. Maltby, 1831.

Lash, Kurt T. *The Fourteenth Amendment and the Privileges and Immunities of American Citizenship.* New York: Cambridge University Press, 2014.

Lee, Maurice. *Slavery, Philosophy, and American Literature, 1830–1860.* New York: Cambridge University Press, 2005.

Le Row, Caroline B., comp. *Werner's Readings and Recitations: America's Recitation Book.* No. 10. New York: Edgar S. Werner, 1893.

Levine, Robert S. *Dislocating Race and Nation: Episodes in Nineteenth-Century American Literary Nationalism.* Chapel Hill: University of North Carolina Press, 2008.

———. "Edward Everett Hale's and Sutton Griggs's Men Without a Country." In *Jim Crow, Literature, and the Legacy of Sutton E. Griggs,* ed. Tess Chakkalakal and Kenneth W. Warren, 69–87. Athens: University of Georgia Press, 2013.

———. "Heap of Witness: The African American Presence in Stowe's *Dred*." In *Martin Delany, Frederick Douglass, and the Politics of Representative Identity*, 144–176. Chapel Hill: University of North Carolina Press, 1997.

———, ed. *Martin R. Delany: A Documentary Reader*. Chapel Hill: University of North Carolina Press, 2003.

———. *Martin Delany, Frederick Douglass, and the Politics of Representative Identity*. Chapel Hill: University of North Carolina Press, 1997.

———. "Uncle Tom's Cabin in Frederick Douglass' Paper: An Analysis of Reception." *American Literature* 64, no. 1 (March 1992): 71–93.

———, John Stauffer, and John R. McKivigan, eds. "Introduction." In *The Heroic Slave*, by Frederick Douglass, xi–xxxvi. New Haven, CT: Yale University Press, 2015.

Lewis, Jan Ellen. "The Republican Wife: Virtue and Seduction in the Early Republic." *William and Mary Quarterly* 44 (1987): 689–721.

———. "Rethinking Women's Suffrage in New Jersey, 1776–1807." *Rutgers Law Review* 63, no. 3 (August 2011): 1017–1035.

Lincoln, Abraham. "Second Inaugural Address." In *Lincoln's Selected Writings*, ed. David S. Reynolds, 364–368. New York: Norton, 2015.

Lippard, George. *Washington and His Generals; or, Legends of the American Revolution*. Philadelphia: T. B. Peterson, 1847.

"Literary." *New York Observer and Chronicle*, October 22, 1868, 341.

Locke, John. *Second Treatise of Government*. Edited by C. B. Macpherson. Indianapolis: Hackett, 1980.

———. *The Works of John Locke in Nine Volumes [1824]*. Online Library of Liberty: A Collection of Scholarly Works. http://oll.libertyfund.org/people/john -locke.

Lofft, Capel, ed. "Somerset *against* Stewart." In *Reports of Cases Adjudged in the Court of King's Bench*, 20. Dublin: James Moore, 1772.

Looby, Christopher. *Voicing America: Language, Literary Form, and the Origins of the United States*. Chicago: University of Chicago Press, 1996.

Loughran, Trish. *The Republic in Print: Print Culture in the Age of U.S. Nation Building, 1770–1870*. New York: Columbia University Press, 2007.

Lowance, Mason I., ed. "Biblical Typology and the Allegorical Mode: The Prophetic Strain." In *The Stowe Debate: Rhetorical Strategies in Uncle Tom's Cabin*, 159–184. Amherst: University of Massachusetts, 1994.

———. *A House Divided: The Antebellum Slavery Debates in America, 1776–1865*. Princeton, NJ: Princeton University Press, 2003.

Luciano, Dana, and Ivy Wilson, eds. *Unsettled States: Nineteenth Century American Literary Studies*. New York: New York University Press, 2014.

Lukács, Georg. "Realism in the Balance." In *Aesthetics and Politics*, trans. Rodney Livingstone, 28–59. New York: Verso, 2007.

Madison, James. *The Writings of James Madison, 1787–1790*. Edited by Gaillard Hunt. New York: J. P. Putnam and Sons, 1904.

Maier, Pauline. *American Scripture: Making the Declaration of Independence*. New York: Vintage, 1998.

————, ed. "Introduction." In *The Declaration of Independence and the Constitution of the United States*. New York: Bantam, 1998.

Malone, Dumas. *Jefferson and the Ordeal of Liberty*. Vol. 3. Boston: Little, Brown, 1962.

Mamdani, Mahmood. "Settler Colonialism: Then and Now." *Critical Inquiry* 41, no. 3 (Spring 2015): 596–614.

Marback, Richard, and Marc W. Kruman, eds. "Introduction." In *The Meaning of Citizenship*, 1–11. Detroit: Wayne State University Press, 2015.

Margolis, Stacey. *Fictions of Mass Democracy in Nineteenth-Century America*. New York: Cambridge University Press, 2015.

Mason, John. "Politics and Religion." In *A Compendium of American Literature*, ed. Charles Dexter Cleveland, 167–168. Philadelphia: J. A. Bancroft, 1859.

————. *The Voice of Warning, to Christians, on the Ensuing Election of a President of the United States*. New York: G. F. Hopkins, 1800.

Matthiessen, F. O. *The American Renaissance: Art and Expression in the Age of Emerson and Whitman*. New York: Oxford University Press, 1968.

McCall, Dan. *Citizens of Somewhere Else: Nathaniel Hawthorne and Henry James*. Ithaca, NY: Cornell University Press, 1999.

McGill, Meredith. *American Literature and the Culture of Reprinting, 1834–1853*. Philadelphia: University of Pennsylvania Press, 2003.

McPherson, James M. "'As Commander-in-Chief I Have a Right to Take Any Measure Which May Best Subdue the Enemy.'" In *This Mighty Scourge: Perspectives on the Civil War*, 215–216. New York: Oxford University Press, 2007.

Melancthon. "No External World." *Millennial Harbinger*, September 1853, 509–510.

Melville, Herman. *The Confidence-Man*. New York: Norton, 1971.

Meyers, Peter C. *Frederick Douglass: Race and the Rebirth of American Liberalism*. Lawrence: University Press of Kansas, 2007.

Michaels, Walter Benn. "Romance and Real Estate." In *The American Renaissance Reconsidered*, ed. Walter Benn Michaels and Donald E. Pease, 156–182. Baltimore: Johns Hopkins University Press, 1985.

Modern, John Lardas. *Secularism in Antebellum America*. Chicago: University of Chicago Press, 2011.

"More British Outrage." *Louisiana American*, December 3, 1841. American Antiquarian Society.

Morgan, Edmund S. *American Slavery, American Freedom*. New York: W. W. Norton, 1975.

Morrow, Rising Lake. "The Early American Attitude toward the Doctrine of Expatriation." *American Journal of International Law* 26, no. 3 (1932): 552–564.

"Mrs. Stowe's New Novel." *New Englander*, November 1856, 515.

Murison, Justine. "Feeling out of Place: Affective History, Nathaniel Hawthorne, and the Civil War." *ESQ* 59, no. 4 (2013): 519–551.

————. *The Politics of Anxiety in Nineteenth-Century American Literature*. New York: Cambridge University Press, 2011.

————, and Jordan Alexander Stein, eds. "Methods for the Study of Religion in Early American Literature." *Early American Literature* 45, no. 1 (2010): 1–29.

Murphy, Theresa Anne. *Citizenship and the Origins of Women's History in the United States*. Philadelphia: University of Pennsylvania Press, 2013.

Murray, Gail S. "Reviewed Work: *The Consent of the Governed: The Lockean Legacy in Early American Culture* by Gillian Brown." *Journal of the Early Republic* 21, no. 4 (Winter 2001): 700–703.

Nabers, Deak. "The Problem of Revolution in the Age of Slavery: 'Clotel,' Fiction, and the Government of Man." *Representations,* no. 91 (2005): 84–108.

———. *Victory of Law: The Fourteenth Amendment, the Civil War, and American Literature, 1852–1865*. Baltimore: Johns Hopkins University Press, 2006.

"Nathaniel Hawthorne." *New Englander,* January 1847, 56.

Nelson, Dana. *Commons Democracy: Reading the Politics of Participation in the United States*. New York: Fordham University Press, 2015.

———. *National Manhood: Capitalist Citizenship and the Imagined Fraternity of White Men*. Durham, NC: Duke University Press, 1998.

Nelson, William E. *The Fourteenth Amendment: From Political Principle to Judicial Doctrine*. Cambridge, MA: Harvard University Press, 1988.

Nevin, John. "Man's True Destiny." *Mercersburg Quarterly Review,* October 1853, 492–521.

Newberry, Frederick. *Hawthorne's Divided Loyalties: England and America in His Works*. Toronto: Fairleigh University Press, 1987.

Newcome, William, trans. *An Attempt toward Revising Our English Translation of the Greek Scriptures, or the New Covenant of Jesus Christ*. Dublin: John Exshaw, 1796.

*The New Covenant Formerly Called the New Testament . . . Newly Edited by the American Revision Committee*. New York: Thomas Nelson and Sons, 1901.

Newman, Judie, and Karen L. Kilcup. "Was Tom White? Stowe's *Dred* and Twain's *Pudd'nhead Wilson*." In *Soft Canons: American Women Writers and Masculine Tradition,* ed. Karen L. Kilcup, 67–81. Iowa City: University of Iowa Press, 1999.

Newman, Lance. "Free Soil and the Abolitionist Forests of Frederick Douglass's 'The Heroic Slave.'" *American Literature* 81 (March 2009): 127–152.

*The New Testament: The Version Set Forth A.D. 1611, Revised A.D. 1881*. Oxford, UK: Oxford University Press, 1881.

*The New Testament, in an Improved Version, upon the Basis of Archbishop Newcome's New Translation: With a Corrected Text and Notes Critical and Explanatory*. London: Richard Taylor, 1808.

Nissenbaum, Stephen. "The Firing of Nathaniel Hawthorne." *Essex Institute Historical Collections* 114, no. 2 (1978): 57–86.

Noble, Marianne. "Sympathetic Listening in Frederick Douglass's 'The Heroic Slave' and *My Bondage and My Freedom*." *Studies in American Fiction* 34, no. 1 (2006): 53–68.

Noll, Mark A. *America's God: From Jonathan Edwards to Abraham Lincoln*. New York: Oxford University Press, 2002.

———. "The Bible and Slavery." In *Religion and the American Civil War,* ed. Randall M. Miller, Harry S. Stout, and Charles Reagan Wilson, 43–73. New York: Oxford University Press, 1998.

———. *The Civil War as a Theological Crisis.* Steven and Janice Brose Lectures in the Civil War Era. Chapel Hill: University of North Carolina Press, 2006.

Nussbaum, Martha C. *Cultivating Humanity: A Classical Defense of Reform in Liberal Education.* Cambridge, MA: Harvard University Press, 1997.

Nwankwo, Ifeoma C. K. "Douglass's Black Atlantic: The Caribbean." In *The Cambridge Companion to Frederick Douglass,* ed. Maurice Lee, 146–159. New York: Cambridge University Press, 2009.

Onuf, Peter S. "Introduction: State and Citizen in British America and the Early United States." In *State and Citizen: British America and the Early United States,* ed. Peter Thompson and Peter S. Onuf, 1–23. Charlottesville: University of Virginia Press, 2013.

Otter, Samuel. "Stowe and Race." In *The Cambridge Companion to Harriet Beecher Stowe,* ed. Cindy Weinstein, 15–38. New York: Cambridge University Press, 2004.

Oxley, Beatrice. "The Man Who Wasn't There." *English Journal* 38 (1949): 396–397.

Packer, Barbara. *The Transcendentalists.* 1995. Reprint, Athens: University of Georgia Press, 2007.

Paine, Thomas. *Rights of Man.* In *Rights of Man, Common Sense and Other Political Writings,* ed. Mark Philp, 83–197. New York: Oxford University Press, 1995.

Parfait, Claire. *The Publishing History of Uncle Tom's Cabin, 1852–2002.* Burlington, VT: Ashgate, 2007.

Parrington, Vernon Louis. "Harriet Beecher Stowe: Daughter of Puritanism." In *The Romantic Revolution in America, 1800–1860,* 371–378. Vol. 2 of *Main Currents in American Thought,* ed. Bruce Brown. New Brunswick, NJ: Transaction Publishers, 2012.

Parton, James. *The Life and Times of Aaron Burr.* New York: Mason Brothers, 1858.

Patterson, Orlando. *Slavery and Social Death: A Comparative Study.* Cambridge, MA: Harvard University Press, 1982.

Peabody, Andrew P. *Our Conversation in Heaven, Jan. 23, 1859; Being the Sunday after the Death of Mary Lyman Lothrop, Wife of the Pastor of the Church . . . Printed for Private Distribution.* Boston: John Wilson and Son, 1859.

Pearce, Colin. "The Wisdom of Exile: Edward Everett Hale's 'The Man Without a Country.'" *Interpretation* 22, no. 1 (1994): 91–109.

Pemberton, Ebenezer. *Heaven the Residence of Saints: A Sermon Occasioned by the Sudden and Much Lamented Death of the Rev. George Whitefield . . . To Which Is Added, an Elegiac Poem on His Death, by Phillis, a Negro Girl.* Boston: C. Dilly, 1771.

Peters, Richard, ed. *The Case of the Cherokee Nation against the State of Georgia.* University of Michigan Library facsimile reprint. Philadelphia: John Grigg, 1831.

Phan, Hoang Gia. *Bonds of Citizenship: Law and the Labors of Emancipation.* New York: New York University Press, 2013.

———. "Imagined Territories: Comparative Racialization and the Accident of History." *Genre* 39 (Fall 2006): 21–38.

Phelps, Elizabeth Stuart. *The Gates Ajar.* Boston: Fields, Osgood, 1868.

———. "The Man Without a Country." *Independent,* May 6, 1880, 1.

Phillimore, Robert. *The Case of the Creole Considered in a Second Letter to the Right Hon. Lord Ashburton.* London: J. Hatchard and Son, 1842.

Phillips, Wendell. "Meeting of the American Anti-Slavery Society at Cooper Institute: Wendell Phillips on Negro Suffrage." *National Anti-Slavery Standard,* June 3, 1865.

Pocock, J. G. A. *The Machiavellian Moment.* Princeton, NJ: Princeton University Press, 1975.

Poirer, Richard. *A World Elsewhere: The Place of Style in American Literature.* New York: Oxford University Press, 1966.

"A Political Romance." *Observer,* January 3, 1864, 6.

Porterfield, Amanda. *Conceived in Doubt: Religion and Politics in the New Nation.* Chicago: University of Chicago Press, 2012.

Posner, Richard A. "Law and Literature: A Relation Reargued." *Virginia Law Review* 72, no. 8 (1986): 1351–1392.

Pratt, Lloyd. *The Strangers Book: The Human of African American Literature.* Philadelphia: University of Pennsylvania Press, 2016.

Price, Polly. "Natural Law and Birthright Citizenship in Calvin's Case (1608)." *Yale Journal of Law and the Humanities* 9, no. 1 (2013): 73–145.

"Probability of War—the Whigs." [New Orleans] *Jeffersonian,* March 20, 1842.

Pryor, Jill. "The Natural-Born Citizen Clause and Presidential Eligibility: An Approach for Resolving Two Hundred Years of Uncertainty." *Yale Law Journal* 97, no. 5 (April 1998): 881–899.

Ramsay, David. *A Dissertation of the Manners of Acquiring the Character and Privileges of a Citizen of the United States.* N.p., 1789.

Rancière, Jacques. "Who Is the Subject of the Rights of Man?" *South Atlantic Quarterly* 103 (Spring/Summer 2004): 297–310.

Read, Hollis. *The Hand of God in History; or, Divine Providence Historically Illustrated in the Extension and Establishment of Christianity.* Vol. 2. Hartford, CT: H. E. Robins, 1856.

*Report of Decisions of the Commission of Claims under the Convention of February 8, 1853, between the United States and Great Britain Transmitted to the Senate by the President of the United States, August 11, 1856,* ex. doc. no. 103, 53. Washington, DC: A. G. P. Nicholson, 1856.

*Reports of the Trials of Colonel Aaron Burr (Late Vice President of the United States) for Treason, and for a Misdemeanor . . . Taken in Shorthand by David Robertson, Counsellor at Law, in Two Volumes.* Philadelphia: Hopkins and Earle, Fry and Kammerer, 1808.

Review of *Dred,* by Harriet Beecher Stowe. *Methodist Quarterly Review,* January 1857, 156.

Review of *Les Rues de Paris*. Edited by Louis Lurine. *Edinburgh Review*, January 1847, 74.

Review of *The Scarlet Letter*. *Salem Register*, March 21, 1850. Reprinted in Benjamin Lease, "Salem vs. Hawthorne: An Early Review of the Scarlet Letter." *New England Quarterly* 44, no. 1 (March 1971): 110–117.

Reynolds, David S. *Walt Whitman's America: A Cultural Biography*. New York: Vintage, 2011.

Rezek, Joseph. *London and the Making of Provincial Literature: Aesthetics and the Transatlantic Book Trade, 1800–1850*. Philadelphia: University of Pennsylvania Press, 2015.

Richards, Jeffrey H., ed. "André." In *Early American Drama*, 58–108. New York: Penguin, 1997.

Rifkin, Mark. *Settler Common Sense: Queerness and Everyday Colonialism in the American Renaissance*. Minneapolis: University of Minnesota Press 2014.

Robinson, Gustavus H. *Handbook of Admiralty Law in the United States*. St. Paul: West, 1939.

Roche, John P. "Loss of American Nationality: The Years of Confusion." *Western Political Quarterly* 4, no. 2 (June 1951): 268–294.

Roosevelt, Eleanor. "Good Citizenship: The Purpose of Education." *Pictorial Review* 31 (April 1930): 4, 94, 97.

Rosaldo, Renato. "Imperialist Nostalgia." *Representations* 26 (1989): 108–109.

Rosenfield, Sophia. *Common Sense: A Political History*. Cambridge, MA: Harvard University Press, 2011.

Rousseau, Jean-Jacques. *On the Social Contract*. In *Basic Political Writings*, ed. and trans. Donald A. Cress and Peter Gay, 141–227. Indianapolis, IN: Hackett, 1987.

Rowe, John Carlos. *At Emerson's Tomb: The Politics of Classic American Literature*. New York: Columbia University Press, 1997.

———. "Nathaniel Hawthorne and Transnationality." In *Hawthorne and the Real: Bicentennial Essays*, ed. Millicent Bell, 88–106. Columbus: Ohio State University Press, 2005.

———. "Stowe's Rainbow Sign: Violence and Community in *Dred: A Tale of the Great Dismal Swamp* (1856)." *Arizona Quarterly* 58, no. 1 (2002): 37–55.

Ryan, Susan. "Charity Begins at Home: Stowe's Antislavery Novels and the Forms of Benevolent Citizenship." *American Literature* 72, no. 4 (December 2000): 751–782.

Sadler, Lynn Veach. "The Samson Figure in Milton's *Samson Agonistes* and Stowe's *Dred*." *New England Quarterly* 56, no. 3 (1983): 440–448.

Sale, Maggie. *The Slumbering Volcano: American Slave Ship Revolts and the Production of Rebellious Masculinity*. Durham, NC: Duke University Press, 1997.

———. "To Make the Past Useful: Frederick Douglass' Politics of Solidarity." *Arizona Quarterly: A Journal of American Literature, Culture, and Theory* 51, no. 3 (1995): 25–60.

Salyer, Lucy E. "Wong Kim Ark: The Contest over Birthright Citizenship." In *Immigration Stories*, ed. David A. Martin and Peter H. Schuck, 51–85. New York: Foundation Press, 2005.

Sanborn, E. D. "Article V. Moral and Literary Influence of Novels." *American Biblical Repository* (April 1843): 362.

Sanchez-Eppler, Karen. "Bodily Bonds: The Intersecting Rhetorics of Feminism and Abolition." *Representations* 24 (1988): 28–59.

Sansay, Leonora. *Secret History; or, The Horrors of St. Domingo; and, Laura.* Edited by Michael Drexler. Peterborough, ON: Broadview, 2007.

"*The Scarlet Letter:* A Romance." *Holden's Dollar Magazine,* June 1850, 337.

Schaffer, Arthur. *To Be an American: David Ramsay and the Making of the American Consciousness.* Columbia: University of South Carolina Press, 1991.

Schmitt, Carl. *The* Nomos *of the Earth in the International Law of the* Jus Publicum Europaeum. Translated by G. L. Ulmen. New York: Telos Press, 2006.

Schoolman, Martha. *Abolitionist Geographies.* Minneapolis: University of Minnesota Press, 2014.

———. "White Flight: Maroon Communities and the Geography of Antislavery in Higginson and Stowe." In *American Literary Geographies: Spatial Practice and Cultural Production, 1500–1900,* ed. Martin Brückner and Hsuan Hsu, 259–278. Newark: University of Delaware Press, 2007.

Scott, Walter. "Dedicatory Epistle." In *Ivanhoe,* ed. Graham Tulloch, 5–14. 1819. Reprint, New York: Penguin, 2000.

———. "Essay on Romance." In *Essays on Chivalry, Romance, and Drama,* 65–108. 1824; Reprint, London: Frederick Warne, 1887.

———. *The Lay of the Last Minstrel.* 1805. Reprint, New York: Woodstock Books, 1992.

Seaman, Ezra. *Commentaries on the Constitutions and Laws, Peoples and History, of the United States: And upon the Great Rebellion and Its Causes.* Ann Arbor, MI: Printed for the Author, at the Journal Office, 1863.

Shklar, Judith. *American Citizenship: The Questions for Inclusion.* Cambridge, MA: Harvard University Press, 1991.

Simms, William Gilmore. *Views and Reviews in American Literature, History and Fiction.* New York: Wiley and Putnam, 1845.

Simpson, Audra. *Mohawk Interruptus: Political Life across the Borders of Settler States.* Durham, NC: Duke University Press, 2014.

Slauter, Eric. *The State as a Work of Art: The Cultural Origins of the Constitution.* Chicago: University of Chicago Press, 2009.

———, Alison Games, Bryan Waterman, Eliga Gould, and Elizabeth Maddox Dillon. "The 'Trade Gap' in Atlantic Studies: A Forum on Literary and Historical Scholarship." *William and Mary Quarterly* 65, no. 1 (January 2008): 135–186.

Smith, Caleb. "From the Critique of Power to the Poetics of Justice." *J19: The Journal of Nineteenth-Century Americanists* 1, no. 1 (Spring 2013): 160–166.

———. *The Oracle and the Curse: A Poetics of Justice from the Revolution to the Civil War.* Cambridge, MA: Harvard University Press, 2013.

Smith, Douglas G. "Citizenship and the Fourteenth Amendment." *San Diego Law Review* 34, no. 681 (1997): 681–808.

Smith, Grace E. "'Chiefly about War Matters': Hawthorne's Swift Judgment of Lincoln." *American Transcendental Quarterly* 15, no. 2 (2001): 150–161.

Smith, James McCune. "Citizenship." *Anglo-African Magazine* 1, no. 5 (May 1859): 144–150.

Smith, Rogers M. *Civic Ideals: Conflicting Visions of Citizenship in U.S. History.* New Haven, CT: Yale University Press, 1997.

Snay, Mitchell. *Gospel of Disunion: Religion and Separatism in the Antebellum South.* New York: Cambridge University Press, 1993.

Spires, Derrick R. "Imagining a Nation of Fellow Citizens: Early African American Politics of Publicity." In *Early African American Print Culture*, ed. Lara L. Cohen and Jordan A. Stein, 274–289. Philadelphia: University of Pennsylvania Press, 2012.

"The Spy and the Traitor." *Atheneum; or, Spirit of English Magazines*, January 1833, 353.

Stauffer, John. "Interracial Friendship and the Aesthetics of Freedom." In *Frederick Douglass and Herman Melville: Essays in Relation,* ed. Robert S. Levine and Samuel Otter, 134–158. Chapel Hill: University of North Carolina Press, 2008.

Stepto, Robert. "Storytelling in Early Afro-American Fiction: Frederick Douglass' 'The Heroic Slave.'" *Georgia Review* 36, no. 2 (1982): 355–368.

Stout, Harry S. *Upon the Altar of the Nation: A Moral History of the American Civil War.* New York: Viking, 2006.

Stowe, Harriet Beecher. "Dred: A Tale of the Great Dismal Swamp." *Christian Examiner and Religious Miscellany,* November 1856, 474–475. *American Periodical Series Online.*

———. *Dred: A Tale of the Great Dismal Swamp.* Edited by Robert S. Levine. Chapel Hill: University of North Carolina Press, 2000.

———. *A Key to Uncle Tom's Cabin: Presenting the Original Facts and Documents upon Which the Story Is Founded. Together with Corroborative Statements Verifying the Truth of the Work.* Cleveland: John P. Jewett, 1853.

———. *The Minister's Wooing.* New York: Penguin, 1999.

———. *Uncle Tom's Cabin; or, Life among the Lowly.* Edited by Elizabeth Ammons. Norton Critical Editions. New York: W. W. Norton, 1994.

Stratman, Jacob. "Harriet Beecher Stowe's Preachers of the Swamp: Dred and the Jeremiad." *Christianity and Literature* 57, no. 3 (2008): 379–400.

Sundquist, Eric J. *To Wake the Nations: Race in the Making of American Literature.* Cambridge, MA: Harvard University Press, 1993.

Supreme Court. *E. Lockett versus the Merchants' Insurance Company. Brief of Slidell, Benjamin, and Conrad for Defendants.* New Orleans: n.p., 1842, 35.

Swann, Charles. "Hawthorne: History versus Romance." *Journal of American Studies* 7, no. 2 (August 1973): 153–170.

Tamarkin, Elisa. *Anglophilia: Deference, Devotion, and Antebellum America.* Chicago: University of Chicago Press, 2008.

———. "Black Anglophilia; or, The Sociability of Antislavery." *American Literary History* 14, no. 3 (2002): 444–478.

Tarr, Alan. "Religion under State Constitutions." *Annals of the American Academy of Political and Social Science* 946 (March 1988): 65–75.

Thomas, Brook. *Civic Myths: A Law-and-Literature Approach to Citizenship.* Chapel Hill: University of North Carolina Press, 2007.

———. *Cross-Examinations of Law and Literature: Cooper, Hawthorne, Stowe, and Melville*. New York: Cambridge University Press, 1987.

Thompson, G. R., and Eric Carl Link. *Neutral Ground: New Traditionalism and the American Romance Controversy*. Baton Rouge: Louisiana State University Press, 1999.

Thompson, Joseph Parrish. *The Duties of the Christian Citizen: A Discourse, by Joseph P. Thompson, Pastor of the Broadway Tabernacle Church*. New York: S. W. Benedict, 1848.

Thompson, Peter, and Peter S. Onuf, eds. *State and Citizen: British America and the Early United States*. Charlottesville: University of Virginia Press, 2013.

Thomson, Charles, trans. *The Holy Bible, Containing the Old and New Covenant, Commonly Called the Old and New Testament: Translated from the Greek*. Philadelphia: Jane Aitken, 1808.

———. Original manuscript of Thomson's translation from the Greek of *The New Covenant Commonly Called the New Testament*. Historical Society of Pennsylvania, Philadelphia.

Thoreau, Henry David. *Collected Essays and Poems*. New York: Library of America, 2001.

———. "Resistance to Civil Government." In *Aesthetic Papers*, 189–211. New York: G. P. Putnam, 1849.

"The Thorn that Bears Haws." *Liberator* 32 (1862): 102.

Tocqueville, Alexis de. *Democracy in America and Two Essays on America*. Translated by Gerald Bevin. Edited by Isaac Kramnick. New York: Penguin, 2003.

Tomlins, Christopher. *Freedom Bound: Law, Labor, and Civic Identity in Colonizing English America, 1580–1865*. New York: Cambridge University Press, 2010.

Tompkins, Jane. *Sensational Designs: The Cultural Work of American Fiction, 1790–1860*. New York: Oxford University Press, 1985.

"To the Editor." *Republic*, September 1, 1820, 18.

Traister, Bryce. "The Bureaucratic Origins of *The Scarlet Letter*." *Studies in American Fiction* 29, no. 1 (Spring 2001): 77–92.

*The Trial of Hon. Clement L. Vallandigham, by a Military Commission.* . . . Cincinnati: Rickey and Carroll, 1863.

Trilling, Lionel. *The Liberal Imagination: Essays on Literature and Society*. New York: Viking Press, 1950.

Troutman, Phillip. "Grapevine in the Slave Market: African American Geopolitical Literacy and the 1841 *Creole* Revolt." In *The Chattel Principle: Internal Slave Trades in the Americas*, ed. Walter Johnson, 203–233. New Haven, CT: Yale University Press, 2004.

Tsiang, I-Mien. *The Question of Expatriation in America Prior to 1907*. Baltimore: Johns Hopkins University Press, 1942.

Turner, Bryan. "Citizen." In *New Keywords: A Revised Vocabulary of Culture and Society*, ed. Tony Bennett, Lawrence Grossberg, and Meaghan Morris, 29–32. Malden, MA: Blackwell, 2005.

Twain, Mark. *Life on the Mississippi*. 1883. Reprint, New York: Harper and Brothers, 1901.

Tyler, Royall. *The Algerine Captive; or, The Life and Adventures of Doctor Updike Underhill*. New York: Modern Library Classics, 2002.

U.S. Library of Congress. "Hyperspectral Imaging by Library of Congress Reveals Change Made by Thomas Jefferson in Original Declaration of Independence Draft." July 2, 2010. http://www.loc.gov/today/pr/2010/10–161.html.

Wakefield, Gilbert, trans. *A Translation of the New Testament*. London: London Philanthropic Press, 1791.

———. "Wakefield to Rev. Mr. Gregory, Feb. 27, 1781." In *Memoirs of the Life of Gilbert Wakefield*, 2 vols., 1:432–433. London: J. Johnson, 1804.

Wakefield, Robert, trans. *A Translation of the New Testament*. Cambridge, MA: University Press, 1820.

Wald, Priscilla. *Constituting Americans: Cultural Anxiety and Narrative Form*. Durham, NC: Duke University Press, 1995.

Waldstreicher, David. *Slavery's Constitution: From Revolution to Ratification*. New York: Hill & Wang, 2009.

Walker, David. *Appeal, in Four Articles, Together with a Preamble to the Coloured Citizens of the World, but in Particular and Very Expressly Addressed to Those of the United States*. Boston: Printed for the Author, 1829.

———. *Appeal to the Coloured Citizens of the World*. Edited by Peter Hinks. University Park: Pennsylvania State University Press, 2003.

Walter, Krista. "Trappings of Nationalism in Frederick Douglass's *The Heroic Slave*." *African American Review* 34, no. 2 (2000): 233–247.

Warde, Ernest C. *The Man Without a Country*, DVD. Directed by Ernest C. Warde. 1917. Televista DVD, 2008.

Warner, Michael. *The Letters of the Republic: Publication and the Public Sphere in Eighteenth-Century America*. Cambridge, MA: Harvard University Press, 1990.

———. *Publics and Counterpublics*. New York: Zone Books, 2002.

———, Jonathan VanAntwerpen, and Craig Calhoun, eds. *Varieties of Secularism in a Secular Age*. Cambridge, MA: Varieties of Secularism, 2010.

Webster, Noah. "Literature." In *American Dictionary of the English Language,* ed. Noah Webster. http://1828.mshaffer.com.

———. "Romance." In *American Dictionary of the English Language,* ed. Noah Webster. webstersdictionary1828.com.

Weikle-Mills, Courtney. *Imaginary Citizens: Child Readers and the Limits of American Independence, 1640–1868*. Baltimore: Johns Hopkins University Press, 2012.

Weinstein, Cindy. "Heaven's Tense: Narration in *The Gates Ajar*." *Novel* 45, no. 1 (Spring 2012): 56–70.

———, and Christopher Looby, eds. *American Literature's Aesthetic Dimensions*. New York: Columbia University Press, 2012.

Wellek, René. "Style in Literature, Closing Statement." In *Style in Language,* ed. Thomas A. Sebeok, 408–418. Cambridge, MA: Technology Press and John Wiley, 1960.

Wesp, Edward. "Beyond the Romance: The Aesthetics of 'Chiefly about War Matters.' " *Texas Studies in Literature and Language* 52, no. 4 (Winter 2010): 408–432.

Wheatley, Phillis. "On Being Brought from Africa to America." In *Complete Writings,* ed. Vincent Carretta, 13. New York: Penguin, 2001.

Whitman, Walt. *Democratic Vistas: The Original Edition in Facsimile.* Edited by Ed Folsom. Iowa City: University of Iowa Press, 2010.

———. *Leaves of Grass and Other Writings.* Edited by Michael Moon. New York: Norton, 2002.

———. "Preface to Democratic Vistas." Edited by William White. *Walt Whitman Review* 9 (September 1963): 71–72.

Whitney, Lisa. "In the Shadow of Uncle Tom's Cabin: Stowe's Vision of Slavery from the Great Dismal Swamp." *New England Quarterly* 66, no. 4 (1993): 552–569.

Wiecek, William M. "Somerset: Lord Mansfield and the Legitimacy of Slavery in the Anglo-American World." *University of Chicago Law Review* 42 (Autumn 1974): 86–146.

———. *The Sources of Antislavery Constitutionalism in America, 1760–1848.* Ithaca, NY: Cornell University Press, 1977.

Wilf, Steven. *Law's Imagined Republic: Popular Politics and Criminal Justice in Revolutionary America.* New York: Cambridge University Press, 2010.

Williams, Raymond. *Marxism and Ideology.* New York: Oxford University Press, 1977.

Wilson, Ivy G. "On Native Ground: Transnationalism, Frederick Douglass, and 'The Heroic Slave.' " *PMLA* 121, no. 2 (2006): 453–468.

———. *Specters of Democracy: Blackness and the Aesthetics of Nationalism.* New York: New York University Press, 2011.

Wilson, James. "Pennsylvania Ratifying Convention, Nov. 28 & Dec. 4 1787." In *The Debates in the Several State Conventions on the Adoption of the Federal Constitution,* ed. Jonathan Elliott, 5 vols., 2:434–437, 453–454. http://press-pubs.uchicago.edu/founders/documents/v1ch14s27.html.

Wilson, Woodrow. "University Training and Citizenship." *Forum,* September 1894, 107–116.

Wise, Steven M. *Though the Heavens May Fall: The Landmark Trial That Led to the End of Human Slavery.* Cambridge, MA: Da Capo Press, 2005.

Wong, Edlie. *Neither Fugitive nor Free: Atlantic Slavery, Freedom Suits, and the Legal Culture of Travel.* New York: New York University Press, 2009.

———. *Racial Reconstruction: Black Inclusion, Chinese Exclusion, and the Fictions of Citizenship.* New York: New York University Press, 2015.

"The Works of Maria Edgeworth." *North American Review,* October 1823, 383–389.

Wright, Frances. "Novel Reading Unchristian." *Christian Advocate and Journal,* January 3, 1834, 73.

Yarborough, Richard. "Race, Violence, and Manhood: The Masculine Ideal in Frederick Douglass's 'The Heroic Slave.' " In *Frederick Douglass: New Literary and Historical Essays,* ed. Eric J. Sundquist, 166–188. New York: Cambridge University Press, 1991.

Yellen, Jean Fagan. "Hawthorne and the American National Sin." In *The Green American Tradition: Essays and Poems,* ed. H. Daniel Peck. Baton Rouge: Louisiana State University Press, 1980.

Zuckert, Michael P. "Completing the Constitution: The Fourteenth Amendment and Constitutional Rights." *Publius* 22 (Spring 1992): 69–91.

# Acknowledgments

It is a pleasure to publicly thank the many people and institutions that have supported the imaginative life, research, and writing of this book.

My work on the history of citizenship began to take formal shape in the English Department at Rutgers University in the early months of Barack Obama's first presidential campaign. As I reflect on the evolution of this project from the vantage of another, less sanguine moment of political change, I am doubly appreciative of the opportunities for archival research, humanistic inquiry, and scholarly exchange that made this book possible. For crucial funding support at key stages in the development of this project, I would like to thank Rutgers University, the McNeil Center for Early American Studies at the University of Pennsylvania, the American Antiquarian Society, the Mellon Foundation, the American Council of Learned Societies, the United States Studies Centre at the University of Sydney, the New England Regional Fellowship Consortium, UCLA, and the Hellman Foundation.

I would like to thank *American Literature* for their permission to reprint portions of an earlier article on the legal and literary narratives surrounding the 1841 slave revolt aboard the *Creole* ship. Chapter 3 is an expanded version of "The Climates of Liberty: Natural Rights in the *Creole* Case and 'The Heroic Slave,'" *American Literature* 85, no. 3 (September 2013): 475–504. © 2013 by Duke University Press. I would also like to thank *English Literary History* for providing a forum for me to develop and test an early discussion of themes and readings that provided the foundation for Chapter 5.

For their role in shaping and enriching the early development of this project, I would like to thank Nancy Bentley, David Kazanjian, and Meredith McGill, as well as Sean Barry, Matthew Brown, Brent Edwards, Myra Jehlen, Sarah Kennedy, Jonathan

Kramnick, John Kucich, Michael McKeon, Ezra Nielson, Colleen Rosenfeld, and Ann Laura Stoler. I would also like to thank Cheryl Wall, who valorously ran (and likely still runs) so much of the behind-the-scenes life of the Rutgers English Department. I owe a profound debt to Michael Warner, an ideal mentor, who left me with a deep-seated methodological appreciation of the things left unsaid and the clarifying power of the negative. I was fortunate to find another incomparable mentor and friend in Edlie Wong, who has offered crucial advice and feedback at every stage of my career. I also owe an enduring debt of gratitude to Jonathan Foltz, who shaped the formation of this project and my own intellectual history in more ways than I can readily enumerate.

I first conceived and subsequently wrote this study in two dynamic English departments—Rutgers and UCLA—but this book also owes a profound intellectual debt to the consecutive years I spent in residence in between at two unique interdisciplinary centers. As a fellow at the McNeil Center for Early American Studies, I benefited from being one of a handful of literary critics in a historian stronghold. At MCEAS, I learned through trial by fire the kinds of phrases and paradigms that tend to shut down and obstruct dialogue across English and History. I also gained a deep investment in developing ways of talking across disciplines that self-consciously embrace disciplinary difference as an opportunity for enriching scholarship on topics that span multiple disciplines. I am ever grateful to Daniel Richter for making MCEAS such an incredible intellectual home and for allowing me to stay on at MCEAS for a second year when I received a Mellon/ACLS fellowship. I benefited directly and indirectly from more scholars in the sprawling MCEAS community than I can name here, but I would especially like to thank Wayne Bodle, Max Cavitch, Irene Cheng, Brian Connolly, Paul Conrad, Dawn Peterson, Alyssa Mt. Pleasant, Wendy Roberts, and Elena Schneider. To Joseph Rezek, whom I first befriended in the halls of MCEAS, I owe my warmest thanks for being a true friend of this book, and a precise reader of so many of its pages.

As a postdoctoral fellow at the United States Studies Centre at the University of Sydney, I was fortunate to once again be in the position of a disciplinary "outsider." It was both strange and freeing to reconceive my work on citizenship from the perspective of an international American studies center in a very different former British colony. As the only literary critic in a cohort of fellows that included several historians of twentieth- and twenty-first-century politics as well as a statistically oriented political scientist, I had the opportunity to broaden my work on citizenship to address scholars who were both disciplinarily and historically far afield from my home discipline. I would like to thank Paul Giles for his engaged feedback, as well as Frances Clark, Sarah Gleeson-White, Malcolm Jorgensen, Margaret Levi, Brendon O'Connor, Marc Palen, Craig Purcell, Rob Rakove, Rodney Taveira, and Shawn Treier. I would like to warmly thank Nicole Hemmer, a fellow traveler, dear friend, and generous reader, who offered invaluable tips as I began to reimagine and write this book with multiple disciplinary audiences in mind.

At UCLA, I have been fortunate to find many generous readers, colleagues, and friends. My warm thanks to Michael Cohen, Joseph Dimuro, and Christopher Looby for their feedback, friendship, and many leisurely music and movie outings on the Eastside. I would like to thank Chris Chism, Helen Deutch, Sarah Kareem, and Arvind Thomas for being insightful readers of multiple sections of this book. I would also like to thank Ali Behdad, Allison Carruth, Michael Colacurcio, Joshua Dienstag, Nina Eidsheim, Lowell Gallagher, Anne Gilliland, Yogita Goyal, Jonathan Grossman, Ursula Heise, Rachel Lee, Marissa Lopez, Michael Meranze, Rafael Pérez-Torres, Richard Yarborough, and Steve Yeazell for conversations and advice that actively shaped the book in a number of ways. Louise Hornby was a friendly and rigorous reader of multiple drafts of almost every chapter, and I find myself already missing our luncheon book outings on the Eastside. I would like to thank UCLA's Friends of English for their generous book subvention. I am also grateful for the many things I've learned teaching an array of classes on citizenship to UCLA's wonderful and diverse undergraduates and PhD students. In quiet ways, the twenty-first-century personal narratives of citizenship and immigration that unfolded in lectures, seminars, and office hours inspired and also haunted the writing of this book. At UCLA, I also was fortunate to find wonderful graduate research assistants—Will Clark, Jené Pledger, Samantha Sommers, and Jordan Wingate—who facilitated discrete research queries related to this book.

As a participant in the second inaugural First Book Institute at the Center for Literary Studies at Penn State, I was fortunate to receive timely and detailed feedback on earlier versions of my introduction and Chapter 2. For their feedback and intellectual fellowship at what proved to be a key moment in the reconceptualization of this project, I would like to thank Hester Blum, Christopher Castiglia, Natalia Cecire, Joy Howard, Molly Pulda, Jillian Sayre, and Grant Wythoff. I am especially thankful to the institute's co-organizers, Sean Goudie and Priscilla Wald, for their insights and support. Priscilla ultimately ended up reading more material and more versions of this book than almost anyone else, so I owe her a tremendous debt of gratitude for her help in making this book what it is.

This book has benefited greatly from feedback, leads, and exchanges in a range of other professional forums. I would like to thank J. K. Barret, Lenny Cassuto, Russ Castronovo, Jeffory Clymer, Matt Cohen, Jeannine DeLombard, Wai Chee Dimock, Paul Erickson, Brad Evans, Duncan Faherty, Eric Foner, Dean Grodzins, Jeffrey Insko, Ashleigh Ismus, Virginia Jackson, Benjamin Kahn, Rodrigo Lazo, Maurice Lee, Mike LeMahieu, Justine Murison, Jordan Stein, and Matthew Stratton for their varied engagement with the ideas of this book. I am indebted to Gordon Hutner and Anne Savarese for their generous readings and engagement with the frame of this project. I also would like to thank Bert Emerson, Chris Hunter, and Michele Navakas and other members of SCAG for their engaging feedback on Chapter 2, and Amanda Claybaugh, Hunt Howell, Elizabeth Maddock Dillon, and others for their engaging dialogue and insights when I presented a version of my introduction at the Mahindra Humanities Center at Harvard. When I presented an earlier draft of my introduction to a law and literature group at the University of California, Irvine, Brook Thomas provided extensive written feedback and leads, for which I am deeply grateful. I also am grateful to Caleb Smith for crucial feedback in response to (a different) earlier version of the introduction and for further invaluable feedback when I later completed a full draft of this book. My warm thanks to Bob Levine for feedback on my introduction and Chapters 3, 4, and 5 and for countless e-mails of good cheer. I would like to thank my editor, John Kulka, for his attentive readings of multiple drafts of this book and his attention to questions of audience and disciplinary reach. This book also has benefited greatly from the insightful readers secured by Harvard University Press. I would also like to thank Brian Ostrander, Mihaela-Andreea Pacurar, Stephanie Vyce, Michael Higgins, and the dedicated general staff at Harvard University Press.

Tom Koenigs, Greta LaFleur, and Sal Nicolazzo offered invaluable feedback and camaraderie in the form of several intensive one-on-one exchanges over coffee and cocktails. This book has benefited from a few other key interlocutors, who were timely readers of snippets of this book as I was drafting it and revising it (and revising it). My thanks to Anna Krakus and Anna Rosensweig for a wonderful writing group; your feedback, friendship, and camaraderie have meant so much. My unending thanks to my husband, Daniel Yoder, who was my live audience for so many, many paragraphs. Your rare enthusiasm, yogurt pancakes, and inventive meals sustain and energize my writing every day. Our cat, Dane, has been this book's everyday companion, sitting across from me even now as I type the final words of this book.

I would like to dedicate this book to my parents, David and Gerry Hyde, for their inspiring work ethic and their unwavering investment in my education and career; to my brother and sister-in-law, David and Dara Hyde, for making the reading of literature into a family profession and social pastime; and to my nephew, Jackson, for his enchanted imagination.

# Index

Abolition, 24, 49, 51–52; Bible, slavery, and, 47, 51–52, 60–61, 76–77, 79–81, 84; Christian theology, Walker, and political subjunctive, 61–66; Delany and, 84, 227n160; Gronniosaw and, 52, 84; Hale and, 178; neo-Somerset doctrine and, 90–91, 94; Stowe and, 47, 66–78, 220n100, 220–221n104, 224nn126,127; Wheatley and, 47, 84, 212n20. *See also Creole* slave revolt; Douglass, Frederick; Higher law

Abrams, M. H., 118, 122, 242n20

Adams, John, 163

Aesthetic autonomy, 118, 128, 258n17. *See also* "Art-as-such" theory; Fictionality; Literary autonomy, and fabrication of allegiance

Aesthetic dimension of citizenship, 15–17, 199n39

Aesthetic dissent, 121, 199n38, 241n11

Affiliation: citizenship and, 44; heavenly versus political, 49–56, 140, 143. *See also* Allegiance; Civic longing; Disaffiliation

*Ainslee vs. Martin* (1813), 135. *See also* Expatriation

Alien and Sedition Acts (1798), 28, 157–158

Aliens, naturalization law and citizenship, 28

Allegiance, 5, 18–19, 175–176, 179, 184–185, 198n34, 204n25; defeasible (artificial and dissolvable), 26, 120, 122, 135, 151, 169; early debates about citizenship and, 30, 33–35; indefeasible, 25–26; Locke and, 21; *Man Without a Country* and, 156, 157–159, 162; political, 133–138; reciprocal obligation of protection and, 24, 28, 56, 94–95, 204n26; right to refuse, 25–27, 46, 52–54, 169. *See also* Expatriation; Literary autonomy, and fabrication of allegiance

Amar, Akhil Reed, 206–207n50

*American Claimant, The,* 149

*American Democrat, The* (Cooper), 11–12, 250–251n92

American Revolution, 3–4, 50, 200n45; "citizen" and "subject" and, 22, 203n15, 203n17; *Creole* slave revolt and freedom, 95–97, 99–100, 110–111; Hawthornian romance and, 120, 128, 134–135; meaning of independence and, 59

*American, The* (James), 137–138

*American Woman's Home; or, The Principles of Domestic Science, The* (Stowe and Beecher), 78–79, 225n138

Anderson, George, 89

*André* (Dunlap), 158

Andrews, William, 99, 236n67
Apess, William, 33–34, 209n67
*Appeal to the Coloured Citizens of the World* (Walker), 62–66, 218–219n81
Arac, Jonathan, 121
Arendt, Hannah, 55, 197n30, 246n46
Ark, Wong Kim, 14, 183–184
Arnold, Benedict, 158, 258n20. *See also* Negative instruction, and nationalization of citizenship; Treason
"Art-as-such" theory, 122. *See also* Aesthetic autonomy
Ashburton, Lord, 91, 229n13, 231n29
*Atlantic Monthly, The*, 143, 145–146, 156, 159
Augustine, and skepticism toward worldly enjoyments, 49, 50, 61, 214n34. *See also* Christian estrangement
*Autobiography* (Franklin), 157, 159

Bacon, John, 89
Bahamas, slavery abolished in, 88, 91. See also *Creole* slave revolt
Bailyn, Bernard, 201n9
Baldwin, James, 139, 150; *Uncle Tom's Cabin* and, 67–68, 69, 222n113
Ballard, Edward, 136
Bates, Edward, 19, 33, 35, 38; definitional ambiguities of citizenship and, 22–24, 28, 204n25
Baym, Nina, 166, 245n41, 262n47
Beecher, Catherine, 78–79
Beecher, Henry Ward, 77
Beecher, Lyman, 67, 214–215n39
Bell, Michael Davitt, 243n25, 248n67
Bennett, William J., 158
Bense, James, 146, 253nn120,123
Bentley, Nancy, 206n39, 254n130
Bercovitch, Sacvan, 213n31, 241n14, 247–248nn60,67, 255n138
Berlant, Lauren, 175, 193n14, 198n33, 245n39, 249n77, 250n78, 259n24
*Better Land; or, The Christian Emigrant's Guide to Heaven, The* (1853), 54, 215n49
*Beyond a Christian Commonwealth* (Hanley), 214n36
Bible: American Standard Version Bible, 56; "book of nature" and, 228–229n10; cultural impact of new translations of, 59–60, 218nn74,75; English Revised Version (1881), 56, 82; Galatians, 57, 217n66, 218n78; King James Version, 45, 55, 59, 218n75; major translations before

King James Version, 55; as textual touchstone for meaning of citizenship, 44, 47–50, 54–55, 213n22; used to justify slavery, 57, 60, 83–84, 217n66. *See also* Philippians 3:20
Birthright citizenship, 155, 205–206n38, 211n7; Bates and pre–Civil War question of, 22–23; U.S. Constitution and, 4–5, 86, 155, 182–183, 185; modern concept of, 4
"Black Atlantic," 51–52, 76, 88, 229n11
Black print counterpublics, 64–65, 219n89
Blacks, freeborn: Bates and pre–Civil War question of citizenship, 22–24; suffrage and, 31–32, 208n60. *See also* Chattel slavery
*Blake; or, The Huts of America* (Delany), 84
Blennerhassett, Harmon, 165
Bliss, Philemon, 36–37, 203n16
Bradburn, Douglas, 207n51
Breen, T. H., 201n9
Bridge, Horatio, 253–254n127
British common law, doctrine of indefeasible (natural and perpetual) allegiance, 25–26
Bromwich, David, 210n75
Brooks, Joanna, 64, 219n89
Brown, John, 149–150, 254n132
Brownson, Orestes, 53
Brown, William Hill, 168
Budick, Emily, 244n35
Buell, Lawrence, 130, 223n119, 242n20
Burke, Edmund, 127
Burr, Aaron, 158, 261n42; as character in *Man Without a Country*, 159–160, 162–165; Texas and, 174, 265n78; trial of, 165
Bushnell, Horace, 49–50

Cahill, Edward, 128
Calvin's Case, 26, 205n33, 205–206n38
Campbell, Lord, 90
Castiglia, Christopher, 198n34
Castronovo, Russ, 199n39, 212n21, 246n45, 265n88
Catholic Douay–Rheims Bible (1582), 55
Channing, William Ellery, 108, 238n83
"Charity Begins at Home" (Ryan), 67, 220n102
*Charlotte Temple* (Rowson), 163–164, 262n46, 263n59
Chase, Richard, 125, 244n35
Chase, Salmon, 22–23
Chattel slavery: Bible translations and defense of, 57, 60, 83–84, 217n66;

Galatians and, 57, 217n66; gendered transmission of, 26–27; as local, not federal, issue, 109–110; slaves as neither aliens nor citizens, 86–87; statelessness in *Man Without a Country* and, 176–178; statutory law and, 87–88; Taney and, 37–38; women's rights to hold property and, 31

*Cherokee Nation vs. Georgia,* 35, 209n69, 228n7

"Chiefly about War-Matters" (Hawthorne), 143–150, 255n136

Child, Lydia Maria, 167–168, 243n29

Chinese Exclusion Act (1882), 183

Christian estrangement, 45, 46–54, 157, 211n13; Paul's letter to Philippians and, 45–46; reimagined in *Dred,* 74–76, 80–81; romantic conception of literature and, 123. *See also* Augustine, and skepticism towards worldly enjoyments

*Christian Examiner, The,* 71

Christian nationalism, 67, 156; appeal of, 60–61; *Dred* and, 80; and political citizenship as precursor to higher theological membership, 47, 48, 50–51, 214n36

Christian theology, 43–84; abolition and, 49, 51–52, 61–66; Bible and theological uses of "citizenship," 43–47, 54–59; Christian estrangement, 45, 46–54, 211n13; Hawthorne and, 140; pro-slavery Biblical interpretation, 57, 60, 83–84, 217n66; Stowe, *Dred,* and abolition, 63–73, 220n100, 220–221n104, 224nn126,127; Stowe, *Dred,* and Christian domesticity, 78–83; Stowe, *Dred,* and idealization of suffering as redemptive, 73–78; theological common sense, and abolition, 61–66, 218–219n81; translation of Phil. 3:20, "conversation" versus "citizenship," 54–61, 216n52,58

Church and state, separation of, 43, 45–46, 49, 75–76, 213nn26,28

Citizenship: different meanings before and after the Fourteenth Amendment, 24–25; legal and literary status of, generally, 3–10; modern Constitutional definition of, 4–5, 86, 155, 182, 185,191n5; negative conceptualization of, 8–10, 28, 57, 107–108, 150–151, 157, 181–182; referring to spiritual membership in kingdom of God, 44–45; use of term in book, 24

Citizenship Clause, of U.S. Constitution's Fourteenth Amendment, 4–5, 14, 24–25, 35, 183, 184

Citizenship, retroactive invention of, 18–39; "citizenship" as term and concept, 22–27; exegetical history of "citizenship," 44–45, 54–59; naturalization law and citizenship, 27–32; sovereignty and, 32–35; Taney, *Dred Scott* decision and, 35–39; terminological origins of subject/citizen distinction, 20–22, 200–201n3, 203nn15,16

*City of God* (Augustine), 61, 214n34, 218n78

Civic longing, definition of, 9. *See also* Negative instruction; Nostalgia; Tragedy, citizenship and political subjunctive

Civil Rights Act (1866), 4, 206n48

Civil War: Hawthorne, confederate secession, treason, and defeasible allegiance, 143–152, 252n113, 253–254nn123,125,127,129,131; sacralization of nation during, 157

Clark, Laurel, 31

Cockburn, Francis, 89

Coke, Edmund, 26

Compromise Act (1850), 113

*Confidence Man, The* (Melville), 141–142

Constitution, of U.S.: Article III and treason, 164; Citizenship Clause, 4–5, 14, 24–25, 35, 183, 184; Comity Clause, 28–29, 34, 206n48; Fifteenth Amendment, 206n48, 208–209n63; as "Godless," 43, 210n2; Natural-Born Citizen Clause, 86–87, 113, 228n5, 267n12; Nineteenth Amendment, 185; reticence about citizenship in, 32. *See also* Fourteenth Amendment (1868), to U.S. Constitution

"Conversation," Biblical translations and, 54–61, 216nn52,58

Cooper, James Fenimore, 11–12, 139, 250–251n92

Cotugno, Clare, 222n110

Coverture, legal doctrine of, 27, 30–31

Coviello, Peter, 28

Cowper, William, 90–91

*Creole* slave revolt, 87–88; described, 88–89, 230n15; England and, 238n83; portrayed in "The Heroic Slave," 95–100, 103–109

*Cultivating Humanity: A Classical Defense of Reform in Liberal Education* (Nussbaum), 118

Curtis, Benjamin, 37
"Custom House, The" (Hawthorne), 123, 130–131, 133, 145; political allegiance and, 133–138

Davidson, Cathy, 200–201n3, 262n46
Declaration of Independence: Jefferson and, 58; Locke's influence, 21, 201n9; overreliance on, 25; Taney and, 36; Walker and, 62–63
Declaration of the Rights of Man and of the Citizen, in France (1789), 22, 56, 203n15, 216n59
Defeasible (artificial and dissolvable) allegiance, 26, 120, 122, 135, 151, 169
Delany, Martin, 84, 227n160
DeLombard, Jeannine, 74, 107–108, 195n18, 208n62, 237n75, 265n85
Democracy, 59, 208n61, 246n45; Bushnell and, 50; Douglass and, 109; Hale and, 168, 170, 179; Hawthorne and, 133; Whitman and, 17, 171–172
"Democracy and a Liberal Education" (Hale), 170
*Democracy in America* (Tocqueville), 143
*Democratic Vistas* (Whitman), 17, 171–172, 200n46
Denationalization, 153–154, 156
Deutch, Helen, 249n77
Dewey, John, 12, 127, 246–247n47
Didactic literature. *See* Education, civic; Hale, Edward Everett; Patriotism
Dillon, Elizabeth Maddock, 198n34, 199n41
Dimock, Wai Chee, 218n80, 267n7
Disability, 7
Disaffiliation, 138, 169; Hawthorne and aesthetic, 137, 140–145; Hawthorne and political, 150–151, 247n51, 249n73; political power of, 13, 46; presented as political good, 53, 76
Disenfranchisement, 10, 57, 158, 181–182
Disinterestedness, 104, 132–133, 198n34, 248n70, 249n73
Dissent: abolitionists criticized for promoting, 62, 75; aesthetic dissent, 121, 241n11; Hale and, 166; imagination and, 15; Protestant tradition of, 34, 53; rights and, 34, 107
*Dissertation on the Manner of Acquiring the Character and Privileges of a Citizen of the United States* (Ramsay), 20–22, 202n14

Divine law, 13, 87, 102, 112, 117, 152, 216n56. *See also* Christian theology; Higher Law; Natural law
Domesticity, Stowe and, 68, 78–83, 225–226n138
Douglas, Ann, 78, 216n58, 225n134
Douglass, Frederick, 24, 71, 112, 127, 204n26; citizenship and territoriality, 228n8; *Creole* case and climatological tropes, 88; "Freedom's Battle at Christiana," 94–95; Goodell on, 87; *Narrative*, 99; natural world as model for liberty and reform, 93–101; on *Uncle Tom's Cabin*, 84. *See also* "Heroic Slave, The" (Douglass)
*Dred Scott vs. Sandford*, 8, 19–20, 23, 35–39, 182; Stowe and, 69–70, 222nn111,112
*Dred* (Stowe), 68–73, 102, 221nn104,105, 222nn110,111, 225n133; abolition and, 63–73, 220n100, 220–221n104; Christian domesticity and, 78–83; idealization of suffering as redemptive, 73–78, 224nn126,127; interpretive problems of theological expectation, 70–73, 223nn117,119; original title of, 69; play version, 80
Dryden, Edgar, 245n38
Dunlap, William, 158
Duyckinck, Evert, 133–134
Dwight, Timothy, 242–243n23

Eagleton, Terry, 240–241n8
*Edinburgh Review, The*, 137
Education, civic, 7, 13, 14, 118–119, 123, 143, 154–157. *See also* Hale, Edward Everett; Imitative instruction; Liberal arts education, citizenship and; Negative instruction, and nationalization of citizenship; Patriotism
Egalitarianism, political versus Christian, 47, 63–64, 76
Eliot, George, 73, 84
Elk, John, 183–184
*Elk vs. Wilkins*, 183–184
Ellison, Ralph, 118
Elsewhere of citizenship. *See* Literary autonomy, and fabrication of allegiance
Emerson, Ralph Waldo, 102, 103, 122, 128, 133, 140, 235n59, 241–242n16, 251–252n96
England: abolition of slavery in British empire, 88, 91, 94–95, 233n43; *Creole*

slave revolt, 88–93, 110–111, 231n29, 238n83

*English Journal,* 179

English Revised Version, of Bible (1881), 82

Eschatology, in early United States, 50, 56, 67, 83, 212–213n21

"Essay on Romance" (Scott), 125

Everett, Edward, 131–132

"Everybody's Protest Novel" (Baldwin), 67–68, 69

Expatriation: Hawthorne as "citizen of somewhere else," 122, 133–138; right to, 53–54, 151; used as synonym for "exile," 138

Expatriation Act (1868), 24, 25, 26–27, 53, 122, 185

Extradition, *Creole* case and, 89

Fantasy, Hawthorne and reorientation toward worldly, 138–143

*Federalist Paper* No. 2, 85

Ferguson, Robert, 159, 201n9, 210n80

Fictionality, 117–119, 240n7. *See also* Romantic fictionality

Fiedler, Leslie, 82–83

Fields, James T., 145–146

Fifteenth Amendment, to U.S. Constitution, 206n48, 208–209n63

"Fighting Rebels with Only One Hand" (Douglass), 107

Florida, 31

Force majeure concept, natural law and, 92–93, 231nn32,34

Fourteenth Amendment (1868), to U.S. Constitution, 86, 113; Ark and territorial scope of, 183–184; Citizenship Clause, 4–5, 14, 24–25, 35, 183, 184; Privileges and Immunities Clause, 25; ratification of, 4

Franklin, Benjamin, 157, 159

Fredrickson, George, 225n128

*Freedom Bound* (Tomlin), 37, 210n78

"Freedom's Battle at Christiana" (Douglass), 94–95

French Revolution, 21–22

Fugitive Slave Act (1850), 94–95, 96, 110, 233n43

Gallagher, Catherine, 240n7

Garrison, William Lloyd, 71, 95, 232n40

*Gates Ajar, The* (Phelps), 81–82

Gender. *See* Coverture, legal doctrine of; Women

*Genius of Universal Emancipation* (Lundy, ed.), 66

Gifford (Creole shipmaster), 88–89

Gilroy, Paul, 229n111

Glazner, Nancy, 244n36

*Glory of the Columbia—Her Yeomanry, The* (Dunlap), 158

Goodell, William, 87, 108–109

Gould, Philip, 266–267n2

Graves, Robert, 77

Green, Nancy, 138

Gronniosaw, James Albert Ukawsaw, 52, 84

Grossman, Allen, 264n71

Grossman, Jay, 242n22

Gustafson, Sandra, 192n11

Gutjahr, Paul, 59, 60, 218n75

Habermas, Jürgen, 198n34

Hale, Edward Everett, 54–55, 82, 120, 260n26; *Washington Post* on, 170; Whitman and, 170–172. See also *Man Without a Country* (Hale)

Hale, Nathan, 260n26

"Hall of Fantasy, The" (Hawthorne), 140–141

Hamilton, Alexander, 159

Hamilton, Cynthia, 97, 222n13, 233–234n49

Hanley, Mark, 214n36

Hargrave, Francis, 90, 94, 96

Harper's Ferry raid, 149–150

Hatch, Nathan, 58, 217n70

Hawthorne, Nathaniel: Civil War, and defeasible allegiance, 143–152, 252n113, 253–254nn123,125,127,131; expatriation, and "citizen of somewhere else," 122, 133–138, 251n93; fantasy and reorientation toward worldly, 138–143; Henry James' biography of, 153–154; literary citizenship and, 18–19, 121, 176; political "neutrality" and, 129–133; rights of romance and, 122–128, 145–146, 169, 243nn30,32, 245n38

"Heavenly Elements of Earthly Occupations, The" (Graves), 77

"Heroic Slave, The" (Douglass), 233n47, 233–234n49; "citizen of nature" and judgment against slavery, 101–109, 235–236nn63,64,68; natural world as model for liberty and reform, 95–101; retrospective narration of, 236n68

Hewell, John, 89

Hickman, Jared, 212n16; 239n2

Higher law, 13–14, 35–36; Taney and
   Supreme Court, 36–37, 38; theological
   model of, 61–62, 83–84. *See also* Divine
   law; Natural law
Hillard, George, 131
*Holden's Dollar Magazine*, 131
*Holy Bible, Containing the Old and New
   Covenant, The* (Thomson, translator),
   58–59
"Home as Heaven, Home as Hell: *Uncle
   Tom's Canon*" (Fiedler), 82–83
*House of the Seven Gables, The*
   (Hawthorne), 124–125, 126, 169,
   243n32
Hovet, Theodore, 221n107
Hurley, Allison, 211n9
Hutner, Gordon, 243n30, 247n52
Hyde, Carrie, 199n42, 219–220n91,
   235n62, 257n11, 265n85

Idealism, in literature, 119, 123, 149–150
Imitative instruction, 157–159, 167–169
Immigration, 4, 109, 183–185, 192n12.
   *See also* Naturalization law, early
   juridical uses of "citizenship"
Indefeasible (natural and perpetual)
   allegiance, 25–26
Indigenous rights. *See* Native Americans,
   citizenship and sovereignty
Indian Citizenship Act (1924), 35, 185
*Indian Nullification of the Unconstitutional
   Laws of Massachusetts Relative of the
   Mashpee Tribe; or, The Pretended Riot
   Explained* (Apess), 33–34, 209n67
Irving, Washington, 82, 139, 174
Isenberg, Nancy, 165, 207n54, 260n29

James, Henry, 137–138, 153–154, 156
Jameson, Fredric, 84, 119, 239–240n6
Jay, John, 85–86, 112, 113
Jefferson, Thomas, 59, 117; Burr and, 159;
   Declaration of Independence and, 58, 63;
   literature's civic utility and, 256n9; on
   novels, 123, 155; separation of church
   and state and, 48–49, 213nn26,28
Jehlen, Myra, 241n14, 245n39
Jones, Douglas, 235n62
*Jus sanguinis* (right of the blood), 5, 86, 113,
   185; Fourteenth Amendment and, 24–27
*Jus soli* (right of the soil), 5, 86, 113, 121,
   136; Fourteenth Amendment and, 24–25;
   native allegiance and, 26–27; Native
   Americans and, 34–35

Kant, Immanuel, 259n23
Kaplan, Amy, 264n74
Kareem, Sarah, 242n22
Kateb, George, 255n137
Kazanjian, David, 246n45, 259n24, 266n1
Kentucky, right to expatriate and, 25, 135
Kerber, Linda, 10, 192n9, 207n54, 266n91
Kettner, James, 10, 86, 195n20, 205n33,
   206n48
*Key to Uncle Tom's Cabin, A* (Stowe),
   224n126
Koenigs, Thomas, 240n7
Koessler, Maximilian, 203n15
Kramnick, Isaac, 43

Law and Literature: historical connection
   between, 239n2; as movement, 196n25
*Leaves of Grass* (Whitman), 170, 264n71
Levine, Robert, 219n91, 221nn105,107,
   223n117, 227n160
Lewis, Jan, 163
Liberal arts education, citizenship and, 118,
   154–157, 170–172. *See also* Education,
   civic
Liberal individualism, 12–13, 46, 53, 108, 129
*Liberator, The,* 145
*Liberty of the Imagination* (Cahill), 128
*Life and Treason of Benedict Arnold, The*
   (Parks), 158
Lincoln, Abraham, 49, 67, 170; Valland-
   ingham and, 160, 166
Lippard, George, 158
Literary autonomy, and fabrication of
   allegiance, 117–152, 239n2, 241n9;
   Hawthorne and political "neutrality,"
   129–133; Hawthorne and rights of
   romance, 122–128; Hawthorne, expatriation, and "citizen of somewhere else," 122,
   133–138; Hawthorne, fantasy, and
   reorientation toward worldly, 138–143;
   Hawthorne, treason, Civil War, and
   defeasible allegiance, 143–152, 252n113,
   253–254nn123,125,127,131; realism in
   literature and, 118–119; romance in
   literature and, 119–122, 240–241n8
Literary nationalism, 155–156; defined,
   154; Hale and, 169–176; Hawthornian
   romance and, 126, 169, 245n39
*Lives of the Chief Justice of England* (Lord
   Campbell), 90
Locke, John, 21, 167, 201n9, 202nn11,12,
   243–244n32. *See also* Lockean liberalism;
   Liberal individualism

Lockean liberalism, early citizenship distinguished from, 21, 25–26, 68, 107–108, 202nn11,12, 263n57. *See also* Liberal individualism

Loftt, Capel, 90

Longfellow, Henry Wadsworth, 129–130, 251n93

Looby, Christopher, 192n11, 199n39

*Love and Death in the American Novel* (Fiedler), 82–83

Lowance, Mason, 217n66, 223n119

Loyalism, 182, 266–267n2

Luciano, Dana, 191n1, 199n39

Lukács, Georg, 119

Lundy, Benjamin, 66

Madison, James, 5–6, 191n7

Mahmood, Mamdani, 195n19

Mansfield, Lord, 88–89, 91

*Man Without a Country* (Hale), 153–154, 167–176; allegory of secession and, 133, 153, 155–156, 159–160, 175, 178, 182–183; Ark and, 184; changing interpretations of, 162, 178–180; nation as key to understanding of, 267n7; negative instruction in, 159–162, 258n15, 259n23; political inspiration of, 159–162, 261n39; publication history of, 257n12, 258n14, 266n91; seduction and negative instruction in, 162–166, 262n51; slave narrative and statelessness in, 176–178; used in educational settings, 156, 179–180, 184, 258n14; Vallandigham's story and, 160–162, 166

*Marble Faun, The* (Hawthorne), 125, 149, 244n36

Marx, Karl, 215n49. *See also* Jameson, Fredric; Lukács, Georg

Mashpee Revolt, 33–34, 209n67

Mason, John, 48–49, 213n26

Massachusetts, and doctrine of natural and perpetual allegiance, 135

"May Christians Be Politicians?" (British editorial), 53

McCall, Dan, 134

McCargo, Thomas, 88–89

McLean, John, 37

Melville, Herman, 82, 83, 102, 139, 141–142

*Methodist Quarterly Review, The*, 80

Meyers, Peter, 101, 234–235n57

Michaels, Walter Benn, 246n42

*Millennial Harbinger, The*, 50–51, 214n38

*Minister's Wooing, The* (Stowe), 163

Modern, John Lardas, 218–219n81

Moon, Michael, 200–201n3

Moore, Laurence, 43

*Moral Compass, The* (Bennett), 158

More, Thomas, 255–256n139

Morgan, Edmund, 111

Morris, Elijah, 88–89

*Mosses from an Old Manse* (Hawthorne), 140

*Mother's Book, The* (Child), 167–168

Murison, Justine, 212n16, 221n107, 252–253n114

Nabers, Deak, 111, 223n122

*Narrative* (Douglass), 84, 99

Nast, Thomas, 160, 162

Native Americans, citizenship and sovereignty, 33–34, 35, 209n69, 228n7. *See also* Settler colonialism

Natural-Born Citizen Clause, of U.S. Constitution, 86–87, 113, 228n5, 267n12

Naturalization Act (1790), 27, 28

Naturalization Act (1795), 28

Naturalization Act (1870), 183

Naturalization law, early juridical uses of "citizenship," 27–32

Naturalized citizenship, 4, 25, 57–58, 86, 183–184, 267n5

Natural law, 85–113; *Creole* revolt, Douglass, and judgment against slavery, 101–109; *Creole* revolt, Douglass, and natural world as model for liberty, 93–101; *Creole* revolt, Webster, and geography of agency, 88–93; early territorial formulations of citizenship and, 85–88; force majeure concept and, 92–93, 231nn32,34; political significance for human law, 109–113; trope of "book of nature" and, 87, 228–229n10. *See also* Divine law; Higher law

*Nature* (Emerson), 102

Negative civic exemplars, 10. *See also* Negative instruction, and nationalization of citizenship

Negative instruction, and nationalization of citizenship: civic education and, 156–159, 258n15, 259n23; exile and, 167–176; seduction in tradition of, 162–166, 262n51; slavery, exile, and statelessness, 72, 176–178; Vallandigham and, 160–162, 166

Nelson, Dana, 208n61, 246n45

Neo-Somerset doctrine, 90–91, 94

Neutrality, as political concept, 129–133, 145

Nevin, John, 50, 214n37

"New Adam and Eve, The" (Hawthorne), 139–140

New Jersey, Constitution of, 30, 43, 44, 207–208n55

Newman, Lance, 236n70

New York, 31

*New York Evangelist,* 100, 110

*New York Observer,* 168–169

Nissenbaum, Stephen, 131

Noll, Mark, 59, 60, 218n74

*North American Reader: Containing a Great Variety of Pieces in Prose and Poetry from Highly Esteemed American and English Readers* (1835), 10–11

*North American Review,* 170

Nostalgia, 12, 17, 95, 127, 140–143, 149–151, 157, 164, 174, 180, 182, 262n48. *See also* Civic longing; Negative instruction, and nationalization of citizenship; Tragedy, citizenship and political subjunctive

North Carolina, Constitution of, 30, 43–44

Nullification, as doctrine of sovereignty, 33–34, 120, 135, 147–148, 247n51

Nullification Crisis (1832), 34, 158

Nussbaum, Martha, 118

*Observer* (London), 168

Ocean: imagined as space of natural liberty, 87–88, 96, 105–109, 111–112, 236n70, 237n77; *Man Without a Country* and exile, 154, 160, 165, 176, 179

Onuf, Peter, 203n15

*Opinion on Citizenship* (Bates), 19, 22–24, 204n25

Originalism: founders and, 5–6; original intent, 6, 23, 39, 182; original meaning and, 39

Otis, Harrison Gray, 65

Otter, Samuel, 222n13

*Our Old Home* (Hawthorne), 148–149, 255n136

Oxley, Beatrice, 179

Packer, Barbara, 263n57

Paine, Thomas, 112, 127–128, 246n46

Parks, Jared, 158

Parrington, Vernon, 220–221n104

Patriotism: Hawthorne and, 251n93, 256n2; higher law discourse and, 112; *Man Without a Country* and, 72,

156–162, 164, 166–170, 173–180, 258n15

Paul, Saint. *See* Philippians 3:20

Pearce, Colin, 175, 264n73

Pennsylvania, 30

Phelps, Elizabeth Stuart, 81–82, 153–154, 156

Philippians 3:20, 60, 82; citizens of heaven concept and, 44–46, 53, 211nn9,10; "conversation" versus "citizenship" translation and, 54–61, 216nn52,58; cultural reception of, 65; *Dred* and, 68, 76–77; Wakefield's translation of, 56–57, 58

Phillimore, Robert, 91

*Philothea: A Romance* (Child), 243n29

*Pioneer, The,* 140

*Plea for the West* (Beecher), 214–215n39

"Political subjunctive," 16–17, 61–62, 100, 112, 117–118, 200n45

Positive law, authority of, 14, 38, 61–62, 65–66, 89–91, 106–107, 111–112

*Power of Sympathy, The* (Brown), 168

Pratt, Lloyd, 226n147

Price, Polly, 205–206n38

Property rights, 236n70, 246n42; citizenship requirements and, 30–31; Locke and, 21, 68; slaves and, 108–109, 111; women and, 27, 31

Pryor, Jill, 228n4

*Public and Its Problems, The* (Dewey), 12

Public sphere and theories of citizenship, 198nn33,34, 219n89. *See also* Arendt, Hannah; Dewey, John

Race: *Dred Scott* and the racialization of citizenship, 36–38; race, suffrage, and citizenship, 31–32; racial transmission of citizenship through father, 26–27; white men and presumptive claim to citizenship, 31, 182

Ramsay, David, 20–22, 25, 202n14

Ranciere, Jacques, 192n11

Read, Hollis, 51

Realism, in literature, 118–120, 241n11

Rezek, Joseph, 249–250n77, 256–257n10

Rifkin, Mark, 209n66, 243n32

*Rights of Man, The* (Paine), 127–128, 246n46

Romance: definition of term, 124, 126; differential use of novel and, 124–126, 244n35, 245–246n41; Hawthorne and rights of, 122–128, 143–146, 169,

243nn30,32, 245n38; illocality of, 126–127, 247n51

Romantic fictionality, 121, 138, 150–151, 240n7; definition of term, 119, 240n7; political allegiance and, 119–122, 240–241n8

Rousseau, Jean-Jacques, 21

Rowe, John Carlos, 224n127, 241n11, 245n39

Rowson, Susanna, 163–164, 262n46

Ryan, Susan, 67, 220n102

Sadler, Lynn, 221n107

Sale, Maggie, 233n46, 234n53

*Salem Register*, 131

Salyer, Lucy, 267n5

Sansay, Leonora, 261n42

*Scarlet Letter, The* (Hawthorne), 18–19, 133–134. *See also* "Custom House, The" (Hawthorne)

Schmitt, Carl, 255–256n139

Schoolman, Martha, 224–225n127, 238n83

Scott, Walter, 132; "Essay on Romance," 125; poem read in *Man Without a Country*, 173–174

Sea. *See* Ocean

Secession, 120, 135, 143, 145, 147–148, 166, 178, 212n17, 247n51; Hale and *Man Without a Country*, 133, 153, 155–156, 159–160, 175, 178, 182–183; Hawthorne's comparison of romance to, 145–146

Second Confiscation Act (1862), 143

*Second Treatise on Government* (Locke), 21, 201n9

*Secret History; or, The Horrors of St. Domingo* (Sansay), 261n42

Secularism, 50, 112; Christianity and, 14, 49, 67, 156, 172; Modern's definition of, 218–219n81; political history and, 118, 212nn16,21

Seduction, in tradition of negative instruction, 162–166, 262n51

"Self Reliance" (Emerson), 103

Seneca Falls Convention (1848), 79, 225n138

Settler colonialism, 8, 33, 195n19, 209n66

Seward, William Henry, 13

Shklar, Judith, 10, 181, 266n1

Simms, William Gilmore, 126, 158

Slavery. *See* Abolition; Chattel slavery

Smith, Caleb, 198n34, 199n39, 221n106, 239n2, 240–241n8, 257n11

Smith, Douglas, 268n13

Smith, Rogers, 10, 193n15

Smith, William, 202–203n14

*Social Contract* (Rousseau), 21

Sojourner Truth, 221n107

Somerset case, 89–91, 94, 111

South Carolina, 34

Sovereignty, citizenship and, 32–35, 209n69

Speculation: as defining trait of fiction, 14; relationship to political subjunctive, 16–17; role in shaping history of citizenship, 7–8

Spires, Derrick, 208n60

Statelessness. *See* Negative instruction, and nationalization of citizenship; Tragedy, citizenship and political subjunctive

Stauffer, John, 102

Stein, Jordan, 212n16

Stepto, Robert, 233–234nn49,50

Stowe, Harriet Beecher: *A Key to Uncle Tom's Cabin*, 244n126; *The Minister's Wooing*, 163. *See also Dred* (Stowe); *Uncle Tom's Cabin* (Stowe)

*Subjects and Citizens* (Davis and Moon), 200–201n3

Subject/citizen distinction, terminological origins of, 20–22, 203nn15,16

Sublime, and negative idealization of citizenship, 102, 259n23

Suffrage, citizenship and, 30, 207–208n55, 208–209n63; racial limits of, 31–33, 208n60, 209n63; women and, 38, 185

Supreme Court of the United States: *Cherokee Nation vs. Georgia*, 35; *Elk vs. Wilkins*, 183–184; right to expatriate and, 25–26, 204n30, 205nn34,36; *United States vs. Wong Kim Ark*, 183–184; women's property rights and, 27, 31. *See also Dred Scott vs. Sandford*

Swann, Charles, 244n36

Talbot, William, 135–136

Taney, Roger B., and *Dred Scott vs. Sandford*, 19–20, 23, 35–39, 182, 210n75

Tarr, Alan, 210n2

Tennessee, and racialization of suffrage, 31

Texas, Burr and, 174, 265n78

Theological common sense, 61–66, 218–219n81; defined, 62

Thomas, Brook, 137, 160, 177, 196n25, 200–201n3, 223–224n123, 239n2, 257n11, 265n77

Thompson, Joseph, 213n22, 216n56

Thompson, Peter, 203n15

Thomson, Charles, 58–59

Thoreau, Henry David, 135, 150, 254n132
Ticknor, William D., 135–136, 145–146
Tocqueville, Alexis de, 143
Tomlin, Christopher, 37, 210n78
Tompkins, Jane, 67, 199–200n43
Tragedy, citizenship and political subjunctive, 7, 10, 72, 148, 150–151, 169, 181–182. *See also* Civic longing; Disenfranchisement; Negative instruction, and nationalization of citizenship; Nostalgia
Traister, Bryce, 249n73
Transcendentalism, 53, 83, 102, 169, 243n29, 244n35, 263n57; Emerson and, 122, 235nn59,62, 241–242n16; Hawthorne and, 131, 133, 140, 249n73
Treason: Aaron Burr and, 157, 159–160, 165, 231n33, 265n78; Benedict Arnold and, 158, 258n20; Hawthorne and "a kind of," 121–122, 126, 143–147, 150, 154, 249–250n77; Lincoln's redefinition of, 262n50; *Man Without a Country* and, 154, 157–165, 178, 180, 260n33, 262n50; William Talbott and, 135–136
Trilling, Lionel, 125, 134, 244n35
Tsiang, I-Mien, 205n36
Turner, Nat, 65, 69, 72, 221nn106,107
Twin legal reformations of 1868, 24, 26, 185. *See also* Expatriation Act (1868); Fourteenth Amendment (1868), to U.S. Constitution
Tyler, John, 231n29
Tyler, Royall, 158
Tyndale Bible (1534), 55

*Uncle Tom's Cabin* (Stowe), 47, 67–68, 72, 76, 212n19, 236–237n71; Baldwin on, 67–68, 69; Christian domesticity and, 83–84; death and, 78, 225n134; Philippians 3:20, 76; Stowe on, 72
Undocumented residents, 185. *See also* Immigration
Unitarianism, 242n20
"United States," use of term before Civil War, 5
*United States Democratic Magazine and Review,* 139
*United States vs. Wong Kim Ark,* 183–184
*Utopia* (More), 255–256n139

Vallandigham, Clement, 160–162, 166
Vermont, and religious requirements for holding office, 44

Vesey, Denmark, and conspiracy of, 64, 65, 68–69, 70–73, 199n42, 219nn87,91
Vietnam War, *Man Without a Country* and curricula during, 179–180, 258n14
*Views and Reviews in American Literature, History and Fiction* (Simms), 158
Virginia, right to expatriate and, 25, 135, 136
*Voice of Warning, to Christians, The* (Mason), 48–49, 213n26

Wakefield, Gilbert, 56–57, 58
Walker, David, 62–66, 84, 218–219n81
Walter, Krista, 235n63
Warner, Michael, 132, 219n89, 246n44, 248n70, 259n24
*Washington and His Generals; or, Legends of the American Revolution* (Lippard), 158
Washington, George, 85–86
Washington, Madison: *Creole* slave revolt and, 88–89; portrayed in Douglass' writing, 95–102, 104–106, 108–109, 233n46
Webster-Ashburton Treaty (1842), 91, 231n31
Webster, Daniel, 132; *Creole* case, rhetoric of natural disaster, and agency, 88, 91–93, 103, 108–112, 229n13, 231n33; Douglass's response to, 95; Hawthorne and, 131
Webster, Noah, 244n35
Weikle-Mills, Courtney, 228–229n10
Wellek, René, 240n7
Wheatley, Phillis, 47, 84, 212n20
Whitman, Walt, 17, 118, 133, 170–172, 200n46, 251–252n96, 264n71
Whitney, Lisa, 221n107
Wiecek, William, 90
Williams, Raymond, 22
Wilson, Ivy, 191n1, 199n39, 233n46
Wilson, James, 29, 32–33
Wilson, Woodrow, 154–155, 171
Wirt, William, 165
Wise, Steven, 90
Women: gendered transmission of slavery, 26–27; pre-Fourteenth Amendment rights of, 30–31, 32, 207–208n55; property rights and, 27, 31; Stowe and domestic influence of, 78–79; suffrage, citizenship, and, 38
Wong, Edlie, 219n87, 233n43
Wycliffe's Bible (1382), 55

Yarborough, Richard, 233n46, 236n67